STUDIES IN CHRISTIAN HISTORY

Blood and Fire, Tsar and Commissar

The Salvation Army in Russia, 1907–1923

STUDIES IN CHRISTIAN HISTORY AND THOUGHT

A complete listing of titles in this series
appears at the end of this book

STUDIES IN CHRISTIAN HISTORY AND THOUGHT

Blood and Fire, Tsar and Commissar

The Salvation Army in Russia, 1907–1923

Tom Aitken

Foreword by General John Larsson

Paternoster:
thinking faith

MILTON KEYNES · COLORADO SPRINGS · HYDERABAD

First published 2007 by Paternoster

Paternoster is an imprint of Authentic Media
9 Holdom Avenue, Bletchley, Milton Keynes, Bucks, MK1 1QR
1820 Jet Stream Drive, Colorado Springs, CO 80921, USA
OM Authentic Media, Medchal Road, Jeedimetla Village,
Secunderabad 500 055, A.P., India
www.authenticmedia.co.uk
Authentic Media is a division of IBS-STL UK, a company limited by guarantee
(registered charity no. 270162)

13 12 11 10 09 08 07 7 6 5 4 3 2 1

British Library Cataloguing in Publication Data
A catalogue record for this book is available from the British Library

ISBN   978-1-84227-511-5

Typeset by the Author
Printed and bound in Great Britain
for Paternoster
by Nottingham Alpha Graphics

STUDIES IN CHRISTIAN HISTORY AND THOUGHT

Series Preface

This series complements the specialist series of *Studies in Evangelical History and Thought* and *Studies in Baptist History and Thought* for which Paternoster is becoming increasingly well known by offering works that cover the wider field of Christian history and thought. It encompasses accounts of Christian witness at various periods, studies of individual Christians and movements, and works which concern the relations of church and society through history, and the history of Christian thought.

The series includes monographs, revised dissertations and theses, and collections of papers by individuals and groups. As well as 'free standing' volumes, works on particular running themes are being commissioned; authors will be engaged for these from around the world and from a variety of Christian traditions.

A high academic standard combined with lively writing will commend the volumes in this series both to scholars and to a wider readership.

Series Editors

Alan P.F. Sell, Visiting Professor at Acadia University Divinity College, Nova Scotia, Canada

David Bebbington, Professor of History, University of Stirling, Stirling, Scotland, UK

Clyde Binfield, Professor Associate in History, University of Sheffield, UK

Gerald Bray, Anglican Professor of Divinity, Beeson Divinity School, Samford University, Birmingham, Alabama, USA

Grayson Carter, Associate Professor of Church History, Fuller Theological Seminary SW, Phoenix, Arizona, USA

For Ros
and my friends in the Salvation Army
and in Russia

Contents

Chapter 3

Chapter 4

Chapter 5

Chapter 6

Foreword

Blood and Fire, Tsar and Commissar is a remarkable account of a remarkable saga of Christian History—the establishment of The Salvation Army's work in pre-revolutionary Russia. It is a story that begins as early as 1907 and that ends only in 1923.

What makes the account so significant is the way that Tom Aitken sets the story in its wider historical context. The Salvationist pioneers in Russia did not work in a vacuum. They entered into a society with centuries of history—and a society then in turmoil. And it is the author's detailed description of the political, social and religious backdrop against which the pioneers had to minister that makes the account of their experiences so valuable to all who are interested in Christian history.

In the first chapter the author also sets the story in the context of The Salvation Army's development at that time. Recent historians have brought a welcome breath of fresh air to the study of early Salvation Army history by their openness to examine and evaluate all relevant material—even the negative. At times these historians have also interpreted their findings in new and sometimes controversial ways. These trends are reflected in Tom Aitken's text. But interpretations that suggest that overseas expansion was motivated by anything other than a desire to fulfil Christ's commission to take his message to the whole world are unlikely to resonate with most Salvationists.

In telling the story of The Salvation Army's early days in Russia, the author has drawn his material from impressively diverse sources. As far as Salvation Army sources are concerned, this is the first time that so much material relative to Russia has been brought together and marshalled into a comprehensive account. A great deal of this material is not available in the English language, which makes the feat even more noteworthy. In addition to a gift for incisive analysis, the author also has an eye for the telling detail and the arresting anecdote, and they sparkle like diamonds in his account of events and descriptions of people. In fact, the footnotes are often as fascinating as the main narrative.

I have a personal connection with this Russia story. Among the many personalities mentioned, the figure of Karl Larsson stands out. He was my grandfather. This Swedish Viking warrior dominates the scene primarily because he was a man of action. He made things happen. But he was also a man of the pen. He was a prolific writer who described in great detail the events of the times and the people he met. And so meticulous was his recording that, when The Salvation Army was seeking to re-establish itself in Russia in the 1990s, some exact reference details he had included in his writings helped to locate documents that persuaded the authorities that the Army had indeed worked in Russia previously.

My father, Sture Larsson, was a boy of 12 when the family moved to St Petersburg in 1918—a stay that came to an abrupt end some months later when the Larssons were forced to flee the country. Occasionally, when he was in an expansive frame of mind, my father would recall those days of his youth when as a family they lived in the middle of a revolution and when hunger was a permanent part of their lives. And, as Tom Aitken reminds us, Sture never forgot the pale faces of the Russian Salvationists and the tears that flowed when they had to say goodbye to them at the railway station that fateful December evening.

I am glad therefore to be able to contribute this foreword not only as a former international leader of The Salvation Army, but also as a grandson of one of the many heroes that took part in this epic venture. I only wish that more of these heroes could have lived to see The Salvation Army return to Russia—and to what now is Ukraine, Georgia, Moldova, Estonia, Latvia and Lithuania— following the fall of the Berlin wall. They were the pioneers who paved the way. We are greatly indebted to them—as we are to Tom Aitken for bringing their story to life.

John Larsson
General (Retd.)
International Leader of The Salvation Army 2002-06
Beckenham, Kent,
January 2007

Acknowledgements

This book owes much to The Salvation Army Heritage Centre in London, in particular to Jenty Fairbank, Gordon Taylor and the late Miriam Blackwell, all of whom gave painstaking and unstinting assistance. The idiosyncratic collections of the London Library yielded some unexpected treasures and, as always, the staff responded quickly and willingly to even quite unreasonable requests. At St Deiniol's Library (The Gladstone Memorial Library) in Hawarden, Peter Francis, Patsy Williams and many others maintain with encompassing friendliness and unobtrusive expertise an institution which is treasured by all who go there. Another source of unexpected but indispensable material, swiftly and efficiently dispatched by its Director and Archivist Bill Summers, was the Southern Baptist Historical Library and Archives in Nashville, Tennessee. The British Library Newspaper Reading Room and the British Library itself have also been consistently helpful.

Another essential resource, over many years, has been my colleagues, the historians and analysts of The Salvation Army. As a student in New Zealand in the 1960s I trod nervously in the footsteps of Cyril Bradwell and Charles Waite when I wrote on the history of the Army in that country. At that time also I met Harold Hill, whose groundbreaking study of Leadership in The Salvation Army was published last year. It was through him that I got in touch with Norman Murdoch, an American who more than most has demonstrated that the writing of Salvation Army History requires toughness as well as breadth of mind and largeness of heart. In this country I have had many useful conversations with John Coutts, Salvationist, Russophile and son of one of the most distinguished official historians of The Salvation Army. I have particularly to thank Norman, Harold and John for their part in the eventual publication of this book.

Other Salvationists who have contributed in valuable ways to its writing and publication include John Larsson, grandson of one of the principal figures in my story and his sister Miriam Fredricksen, both of whom have been prompt and generous in giving help. The same is true of Paul du Plessis, Laurence and Margaret Hay and Joan Williams, whose Bookworm Alley website is invaluable to students of Salvation Army history. Gunnar Nilsson, sometime Chief Secretary of The Salvation Army in Sweden, provided me with a copy of the video *Frälsingsarmén I Ryssland*.

Another helpful Swede whom I have never met, like myself a child of Salvationist parents, is Gunilla Allstig Lamos, of Stockholm University, who has made useful and encouraging comments and suggestions.

In Moscow my friend Anatoly Kurchatkin undertook much helpful research. In The Hague, Father Raymond Rafferty enabled me to obtain Heier's book on the Radstockites. Theo Richmond gave me advice on matters concerning the Jews of Eastern Europe. Kate Pool and Lisa Dowdeswell of The Society of Authors have given excellent guidance on technical matters. David Bebbington, Ruth Clayton Windscheffel and Simon Dixon read the book in typescript (not without difficulty in

Simon's case: his computer collapsed under the strain of receiving it as a series of attachments) and I thank them with affection and respect for their professionally astute opinions. Mr Jeremy Mudditt and Dr Anthony R. Cross of Paternoster Press have been consistently helpful and courteous in preparing the book for publication, as has Lyn Sneddon, Potion 9 Design, in drawing the maps.

Without the optimism and bubbly commonsense of my wife Ros I doubt whether I would have finished the book. She and my friend and editorial guru, Alan Sanders, have taken pains and exercised patience in proofreading the typescript.

My posthumous thanks to Alan Moorehead, whose book *The Russian Revolution* alerted me 47 years ago to the The Salvation Army's presence in Petrograd in 1917. Finally, had it not been for a suggestion made by Terry Hilton and Eileen Shaw, formerly of English National Opera, I might never have visited Russia—in which case this book would not have been written.

Every effort has been made to contact copyright holders; in the event of inadvertent omission or error, Paternoster should be notified and acknowledgement will be made in future printings. The following publishers and holders of copyrights have kindly given permission to quote copyright material (full details of all books listed are given in the Bibliography):

University of California Press, for *Mushik and Muscovite,* by Joseph Bradley;
Carcanet, for *The Paperbark Tree,* by Les Murray;
University of Chicago Press, for Subversive Piety, by Gregory L. Freeze, in the *Journal of Modern History;*
Columbia University Press, for *Church and State in Russia,* by John Shelton Curtiss;
Constable & Robinson, for *Daughter of Revolution,* by Vera Broido, *Theatre Street* by Tamara Karsavina and *The Guns of August,* by Barbara W. Tuchman;
Darton, Longman and Todd, for *The Russian Religious Renaissance of the Twentieth Century,* by Nicolas Zernov;
Gillon Aitken, on behalf of the estate of E.M. Almedingen, for *Tomorrow Will Come,* by E.M. Almedingen;
Greenwood Press, for *Land and Freedom,* by Deborah Hardy;
Harvard University Press for *Nikolai Leskov,* by Hugh MacLean;
Roy Hattersley, for *Blood and Fire: William and Catherine Booth and their Salvation Army,* by Roy Hattersley;
Hodder Education, for *A Social History of Twentieth-Century Russia,* by Vladimir Andrle;
Indiana University Press, for *Petersburg,* by Andrei Bely;
Little, Brown, for *Chaliapin, an Autobiography,* by Fyodor Chaliapin (as told to Maxim Gorky);
McGill-Queen's University Press, for *Popular Music in England 1840-1914,* by Dave Russell;
Mayflower Christian Books and Mrs Francis Fountain, for *Lord Radstock and the Russian Awakening,* by David Fountain;

University of Minnesota Press, for *Russian Orthodoxy under the Old Regime* by Robert L. Nichols and Theofanis George Stavrou;
University of Nebraska Press, for *Crusader in Babylon: W.T. Stead and the Pall Mall Gazette*, by Raymond L. Schultz;
Orion Publishing group, for *A Lifelong passion: Nicholas and Alexandra, Their Own Story*, by Andrei Maylunas and Sergei Mironenko;
Palgrave Macmillan, for *Literary Russia*, by Anna Benn and Rosamund Bartlett, *Civilizations*, by Felipe Fernández-Armesto, *Religion, Revolution and the Russian Intelligentsia*, 1900-1912, by Christopher Read and *The Proud Tower*, by Barbara W. Tuchman;
Pearson Education, for *Russia*, by Edward Acton and *The Russian Peasantry 1600-1930*, by David Moon;
Penguin Group, for *Letters from Russia*, by Marquis de Custine, trs. Robin Buss, *Anna Karenina*, by Leo Tolstoy, trs. Rosemary Edmonds and *The Church in an Age of Revolution*, by Alec. R. Vidler;
Penguin USA, for *A People's Tragedy*, by Orlando Figes;
PFD on behalf of the estate of Edward Crankshaw, for *The Shadow of the Winter Palace* and *Russia and Britain*, by Edward Crankshaw;
Princeton University Press, for *Thou Shalt Kill*, by Anna Geifman, *Time of Troubles*, by Iurii Vladimirovich Got'e and *The Women's Liberation Movement in Russia*, by Richard Stites;
Prion Books, for *The First Casualty*, by Phillip Knightley;
Quartet Books for *A Writer's Diary*, by Fyodor Dostoyevsky;
Random House Group, for *Reformation*, by Felipe Fernández-Armesto and Derek Wilson and *A People's Tragedy*, by Orlando Figes;
Random House, Inc., New York, for *Echoes of a Native Land*, by Serge Schmemann;
Routledge, for *History of Western Philosophy*, by Bertrand Russell;
St Vladimir's Seminary Press, for *A Vanquished Hope*, by James W. Cunningham;
Salvation Army International Headquarters, for Heritage Centre files relating to Russia and individual officers who worked there; and for the following Salvation Army publications: *All the World*, *The Officer's Review*, *The Salvation Army Yearbook*, *Vestnik Spaseniya*, *War Cry* and *Salvation Army Songs*; *The History of The Salvation Army*, vols. 4, 5, 6, 7 and 8; *Viking Warrior* and *All My Best Men Are Women*, by Flora Larsson, *A Funny Thing Happened on the Way*, by Will Pratt, *The Romance of the War Cry*, by William Nicholson, *Translator Extraordinary*, by Gladys Taylor, *Companion to the Songbook*, by Gordon Taylor, and *Soldier Saint*, by Bernard Watson;
The Salvation Army's Territorial Commander in Sweden, Commissioner Hasse Kjellgren, for *Tio År i Ryssland*, by Karl Larsson;
The Society of Authors, for *God's Soldier*, by St John Ervine and the Preface to *Major Barbara*, by George Bernard Shaw;
Springer Science and Business Media, for *Religious Schism in the Russian Aristocracy 1860-1900: Radstockism and Pashkovism*, by Edmund Heier;

Stanford University Press, for *A History of Russian Thought*, by Andrzej Walicki; Yale University Press, for *Russia's Rulers under the old Regime*, by Dominic Lieven and *A History of Russian Literature*, by Victor Terras.

A Note on Spelling, Dates and Other Matters

The spelling in English of transliterated Russian names of people and places is, as Sir Winston Churchill might have said, a mystery wrapped inside an enigma. I have chosen to be arbitrary, using by and large the spelling favoured by my sources, with occasional amendments.

The trust deed that established The Salvation Army insists that the definite article is part of its name and must be capitalized. I observe this convention out of politeness, although, like Roy Hattersley (who acts upon his preference), I would prefer ordinary usage.

Russia used the Julian Calendar until February 1918, when it switched to the Gregorian version in use elsewhere. This only affects my narrative in 1917 when much happened in a very short time. I have accordingly reminded readers of the disparity between Russian and western dates during that period. The maps in this book are not intended to provide comprehensive accounts of the topography of Russia and its two principal cities; rather, they locate places mentioned in the text.

When quoting the Bible I have used the Authorized Version because in several of the references subsequent translations have changed the wording in ways that would render the quotation less pointed or even seemingly irrelevant. This is, however, a complicated issue, given that the Bibles used by many of the people in this book would have been in either Swedish or Russian.

Maps

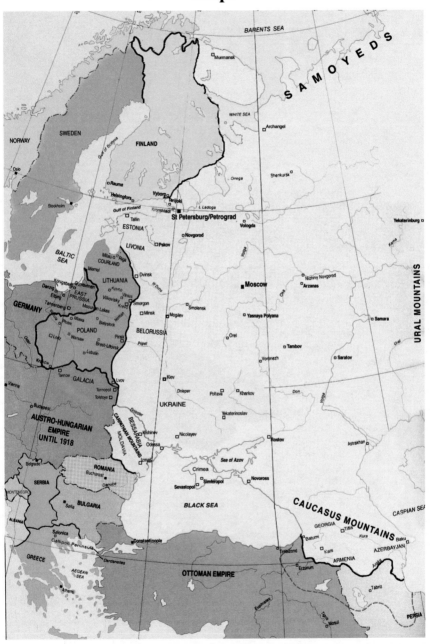

EUROPEAN RUSSIA 1907-1923

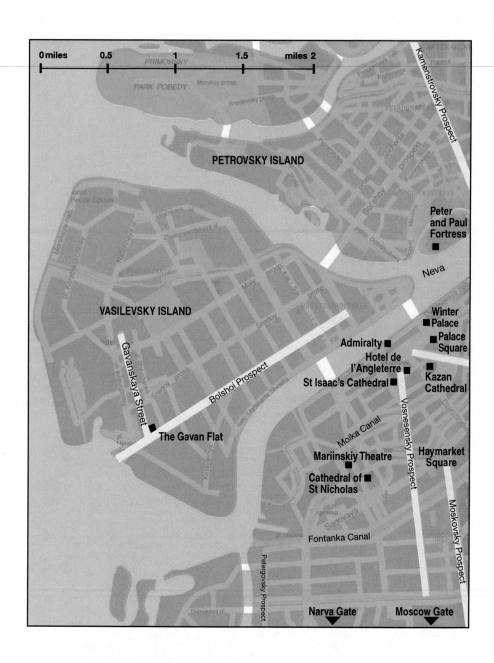

ST. PETERSBURG/PETROGRAD
1913-1923

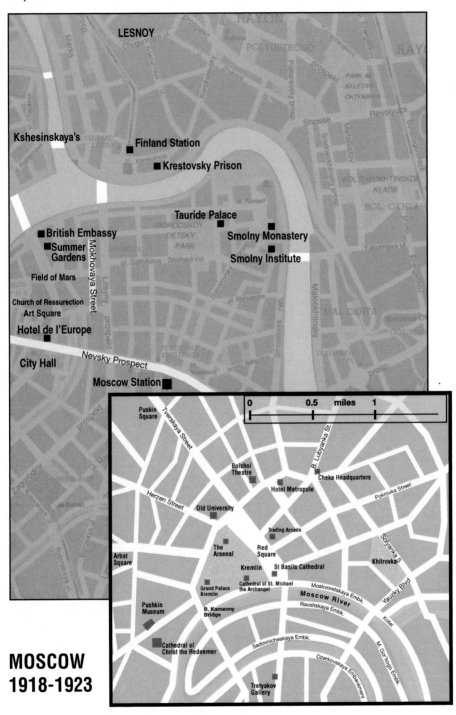

LESNOY

Kshesinskaya's

■ Finland Station

■ Krestovsky Prison

Tauride Palace
■ British Embassy   Smolny Monastery
■ Summer
Gardens   Smolny Institute

Field of Mars

Church of Ressurection
Art Square

Hotel de l'Europe
■

City Hall

Moscow Station ■

Mokhovaya Street

Nevsky Prospect

0   0.5   miles   1

Puskin
Square

Tverskaya Street

B. Lubyanka St.

Bolshoi
Theatre

Cheka Headquarters

Hotel Metropole

Pokrovka Street

Herzen Street

Old University

Trading Arcade

The
Arsenal

Red
Square

Solyanka

Arbat
Square

Kremlin   St Basils Cathedral

Khitrovka

Grand Palace
Kremlin

Cathedral of St. Michael
the Archangel

Moskvoretskaya Embk.

Yauzky Blvd

Pushkin
Museum

B. Kamenny
Bridge

Moscow River

Raushskaya Embk.

Kotel

Cathedral of
Christ the Redeemer

Sadovnicheskaya Embk.

Ozerkovskaya Embankment

M. Gor'kogo Embk.

**MOSCOW
1918-1923**

Tretyakov
Gallery

Introduction

In 1894 T.C. Booth, editor of *Timber and Woodworking Machinery*, set out to visit Russia, intending to write about its export timber trade.[1] As his train crept across the monotonous plains of East Prussia, passing rivers and pine-woods, grey towns, huge towering castles and occasional red-roofed villages, he was doubtless doing his homework: comparing statistics of board feet, types of timber, and cost.

At the Russian frontier the gauge of the railway track changed. Booth dismounted from the German train and queued to satisfy the immigration authorities before joining the Russian one. At the desk he received an unanticipated rebuff.

The trouble lay in his surname. 'Booth,' repeated an official, grimly pursing his lips as he consulted a list pulled from a drawer. 'Nyet.'

Booth protested as vigorously as he dared. He was a *bona fide* journalist, whose mission could only benefit Russia. It possessed great wealth in timber; he could describe new western machinery that would improve the Russians' ability to work it. His articles would surely attract new buyers in the west.

The answer remained the same: 'Nyet.'

Swallowing his irritation, Booth was put on the train back to Königsberg (now Kaliningrad). There he discovered that the frontier guards had suspected him of being an agent of William Booth, General of The Salvation Army.

He protested his innocence, but the ban on his entry remained in force. The Russian Government regretted any inconvenience he had been caused.

It would be interesting to know what T.C. Booth, making his disappointed way back to England, thought of The Salvation Army. Personal irritation aside, he may have somewhat approved the Russian Government's attitude. General Booth was widely regarded as a pious clown, a mountebank who had degraded religion to the status of a music hall performance. The Seventh Earl of Shaftesbury was only the most prominent of public figures and writers in the press who had said something of the kind.

Then again, T.C. Booth may have been one of an increasing number that had begun to admire Booth and his followers. Press muckraking had produced very little dirt that actually stuck. It was obvious that many of the Army's critics were grinding axes that had to do with profit and private interest, from the brewers and owners of West End brothels to those complacent clerics who assumed that the only way to God was through doors to which they held the keys.

What neither group in England would have understood was the complexity of the hopes and fears aroused in such a distant, foreign place as Russia by this originally English movement. The military language and uniforms, a joke to some commonsensical Englishmen but to Salvationists emblems of their total commitment and loyalty, were to those in Russia who administered Tsarist religious

---

1 Arch Wiggins, *The History of The Salvation Army*, Volume IV, London, Thomas Nelson & Sons, 1964, pp. 76-77.

policy neither a joke nor a metaphor. The Salvation Army was not merely foreign and Protestant—either consideration sufficient to render it seriously threatening—but it was a uniformed body that spoke of itself as having 'invaded' many countries all over the world. The Russians would not countenance any such 'invasion' of their own soil.

Earlier that year, on 9 January, the *Glasgow Herald* had reported from St Petersburg that

> The Salvation Army in Russia is doomed. I hear upon best authority that the Imperial Government views with extreme disfavour the continued propagation of General Booth's ideas which have of late taken deep root in various parts of Russia, principally in Finland, but also in St Petersburg itself. It is only a few days since a painful sensation was caused in aristocratic circles here by the action of the Princess Gargarine, who, it will be remembered, wished to have the religious service at the funeral of her late husband performed in accordance with Salvation Army notions and ordered the minister of the Greek Orthodox out of the house. In consequence of this and other cases which have been brought to the notice of the authorities, they have determined to take energetic measures to check the further extension of Salvationism.

Insofar as The Salvation Army was not officially at work in Russia at this date, the *Herald*'s report may seem odd, but in the early decades of its expansion it was not uncommon for enthusiasts acquainted with the Army's work to set up missions that imitated its methods, subsequently asking General Booth to take them into his world-wide organization. This, for example, was what had happened in neighbouring Finland.

For all the Imperial Government's hostility, however, the Army had some features that might, in the difficult times Russia was about to encounter, make it seem at least potentially useful, if only it could be made to function 'in harmony' with Russia's existing laws and customs. During the decade that followed T.C. Booth's aborted visit and the *Glasgow Herald*'s report, nothing further happened, but from shortly after the revolution of 1905 until 1923, a strange undercover melodrama unfolded itself against the background of much larger, far better known events, moving from the drawing-rooms of St Petersburg palaces, via a hygiene exhibition, to the slums of the capital and of Moscow, and to large houses in or near smaller cities, with the occasional country estate, jail and overcrowded hospital thrown in. It is a tale of bureaucratic inconsistency and ham-fistedness, of strings pulled in high places, of devotion unto death and what proved to be temporary, if lengthy, disappointment. The Salvation Army was trying, at first from outside Russia, later from within it, to win permission to work there. The Tsarist regime was determined to keep it within narrow bounds: it might save the bodies and improve the domestic conditions of the outcasts of Russian society but their souls must be left to the Established, Orthodox Church. Later, after the revolution and a brief interval of toleration, the Bolsheviks took over and even the saving of Russian bodies was no longer permitted.

That strange undercover melodrama, a story of disappointment but not of failure, is the subject of this book.

CHAPTER 1

The Salvation Army Looks East

An International Congress

In *The War Cry* for 26 March, 1904, General William Booth, Founder and leader of The Salvation Army, issued a Manifesto. Between 24 June and 8 July his organization would conduct an International Congress in London, the city where, 39 years earlier, it had begun its work. The opening and closing gatherings would be staged in Kensington's vast rotunda, the Royal Albert Hall. A Thanksgiving Day and a series of musical events would take place in Joseph Paxton's enormous Crystal Palace, on a hill in Sydenham, one of the south London suburbs.[1] Other meetings would be conducted in two buildings centrally situated on the Strand: the YMCA's Exeter Hall, which incorporated two auditoriums (the larger seating 3,000), and a temporary International Congress Hall to be built on a site previously given over to 'rookeries and dens of iniquity', to seat over 5,000 more.[2] The congregations required to fill these halls would be drawn from 49 countries and colonies, and, in the event, no opportunity to emphasize the real or aspirational racial and cultural inclusiveness of the worldwide Salvation Army was missed. A Gaucho accompanied the South American contingent; the Japanese attending included Captain Washima, 'one of only three or four Japanese women to have spoken in public outside her own country'. The Canadians brought a coloured Bermudan band and two pioneers from the Klondyke gold field. The 350 Americans (whose National Staff Band performed in cowboy costume) chartered a new Cunard liner, the R.M.S. Carpathia, at an individual cost (the statistic was quoted to illustrate the frugality of Salvationists' personal expenditure) of less than a halfpenny per mile. (During the Congress, all 350 marched from Exeter Hall to the American Embassy, where they were received in the drawing-room by the Ambassador, Joseph Hodges Choate, himself a worker for various charitable causes and for international peace.) The Australians included in

---

1 This giant prefabricated iron and glass conservatory was originally erected in Hyde Park for the Great Exhibition of 1851, then dismantled and re-erected (1852-54) on Sydenham Hill in the south London suburb of Upper Norwood, an area which, incidentally, has retained a strong Salvation Army presence to this day. The building (destroyed by fire in 1936) had a floor area of about 23 acres.

2 This structure was erected on the spot where Bush House now stands. 'Rookeries' here means densely populated tenements, the equivalent of 'Vasja's Village' in Petrograd (see 178-79, below).

their number Joseph Perry (English by birth), 'the foremost cinematographist in the Southern Hemisphere'.[3]

The meetings for which these 49 delegations had assembled attracted much favourable attention. The Bishop of Hereford mentioned the work of the Army in Westminster Abbey. The London press, which had often enough in the previous 39 years found The Salvation Army and 'General' Booth (as they liked to refer to him) fit and obvious subjects for mirth or hostile criticism, was greatly impressed. *The Times*, commenting on the opening meeting in the Royal Albert Hall, noted the remarkable spectacle of 'intense devotion to a cause and loyalty to a Leader'. *The Daily Telegraph* praised 'a model of skilful and dignified management' and 'admirable discipline... what was to all intents and purposes an indoor military review passed off with a distinction and picturesqueness which would scarcely have disgraced the Horse Guards Parade'. On 22 June, King Edward VII had granted an audience to William Booth at Buckingham Palace: the *St James's Gazette* remarked that 'General Booth wears no inverted commas around his title now'. The *Morning Leader* described him as 'this Caesar of evangelism, this Napoleon of the penitent form', while the *Daily News* thought him 'a theologian, argumentative in style, symmetrical and sermonic in the arrangement of his matter, and in delivery calm and decisive'. On the Thanksgiving Day, The Salvation Army's actual thirty-ninth birthday, 70,000 people visited the Crystal Palace. Twenty thousand Salvationists took an hour and a half to pass the General's saluting base.[4]

The delegates and leadership who took part in this Congress may be forgiven their triumphalism. As they saw it, God had not only raised the lowly of the earth so that they consorted with kings, He had raised a worldwide army to do battle with the forces of evil. Booth's enthusiasm for increasing the size and reach of his organization might nowadays be dismissed as 'empire building', but at the time this would have seemed a perverse accusation. That he was an imperialist of religion ('this Caesar of evangelism, this Napoleon of the penitent form') was obvious. Few thought worse of him for it. Moreover, as we shall see,[5] by 1904 the Army's growth, at home and abroad, had reached a plateau. Something had to be done.

A Mission Becomes an Army

Thirty-nine years before the International Congress of 1904, Booth's Christian Mission had set out to evangelize the tempestuous working class folk in and around the Mile End Road in East London. During those 39 years (after 1878 with a new, grander title) its banners, bonnets and bands had spread through a large part of the inhabited world. From Reykjavik to Invercargill, all over northern and western Europe, in Japan, India, Indonesia, the Philippines and Hawaii, throughout North America, in parts of Central and South America, and in Southern Africa, the yellow,

---

3 Perry's pre-eminence is confirmed by Bill Routt, in Geoffrey Nowell-Smith, (ed.) *The Oxford History of World Cinema*, Oxford, Oxford University Press, 1996, p. 422.

4 Wiggins, *The History of The Salvation Army*, vol. IV, pp. 253-60.

5 See pp. 18-19, below.

red and blue banner proclaimed its message: Blood and Fire! Begun as a purely
religious, revivalist body, the Army had acquired along the way a network of
agencies for social aid, reclamation, training and emigration. Uniformed officers and
soldiers toiled as evangelists and social workers, bringing salvation, godly conduct
and a chance to make a second, better, start in life, to, as they believed, the
unchurched masses of the earth. As the 1904 Congress made manifest, its
international impact was substantial. Never since the days of the Apostles, 19
centuries before (most Salvationists and a good few of their supporters liked to
think) had there been an organization so perfectly adapted to what Oscar Wilde's
Miss Prism had in 1895 disapprovingly called 'this modern mania of turning bad
people into good people at a moment's notice'.[6] In the British Isles 'great battles'
(in Salvationist terminology) were still being fought and 'amazing victories' won.
At Exeter Hall, London, in February 1907 (shortly before it was demolished to make
way for the Strand Palace Hotel), 1,041 recruits would be sworn in. A further 300
were unable to be present. This was exceptional, but, according to closely printed
weekly reports in the Army's newspaper, *The War Cry*, a steady flow of souls was
surrendering to Christ in corps all over the country.

General Booth, in his seventies looking every day more like everybody's
imagined Old Testament prophet, expended astonishing emotional and physical
energy in worldwide campaigns. His book, *In Darkest England and the Way Out*,
published in 1890, had shocked and stirred people with religious and social
consciences throughout the world—including Russia, where an official of the
Department of Finances in St Petersburg was prompted by it to write to local
authorities throughout the world, requesting their opinion of the organization.[7]

To liken Booth to an Old Testament prophet is to notice rather more than merely
his increasingly Hebraic appearance.[8] As thinker and speaker he had the single-
minded intensity and ferocity of some of the more judgmental and apocalyptic Old
Testament writers. He would despise the humane, gentle, politically correct
assumptions of modern liberal evangelicals, and be puzzled and angered by the view
of two modern Christian historians that 'the desire for a leaner, fitter Christianity is
itself unchristian...'.[9] Like Lenin he believed that an elite, centralized, totally
dedicated movement could transform the world. To accept the lukewarm as soldiers
would destroy his army's impact. He liked his religion as he liked his tea, 'hot and
strong'. Here he is, in 1885, urging readers of *The War Cry* to be good haters:

6 In Oscar Wilde, *The Importance of Being Earnest*, Harmondsworth, Penguin Books,
1979, p. 275. Miss Prism later remarks, somewhat unforgivingly, of the same miscreant,
'As a man sows, so let him reap' (p. 280).

7 Wiggins, *The History of The Salvation Army*, vol. 4, p. 76.

8 There are unproven but fairly convincing claims that Booth had Jewish ancestry.
See St John Ervine, *God's Soldier*, London and Toronto, Heinemann,1934, p. 8.

9 Felipe Fernández-Armesto, and Derek Wilson, *Reformation*, London, Bantam Press,
1996, p. 212.

I think sometimes that if some people had the privilege of making the Bible over again, they would take all the hatred and cursing and hell out of it. To them there is nothing more mysterious and distasteful than the full-handed penalties connected with the law of Israel, the tremendous curses so freely scattered about by Moses and David and the Prophets, the straightforward denunciations of the Lord Jesus Christ, and the red-hot damnation of the Book of Revelation.

These burning hatreds... are too strong for many. Their favourite notion is that no sin is very diabolical, and that no transgressor is very wrong, even the devil himself being an object of pity. They would explain away the rigid laws and anathemas and penalties of the Bible, and introduce in their place a goody-goody kind of article, which, though it would not make anyone extraordinarily happy, would not make anyone very miserable, but would be calculated to reach their ideal of perfection—that of making things agreeable all round....

Go on hating, night and day, in every place, under all circumstances. Bring this side of your nature well into play. Practise yourself in habits of scorn and contempt and loathing and detestation and revenge...[10]

Sin and all its works were to be the object of these powerful emotions.[11] Consciousness of salvation from sin was the source of the Salvationists' confidence, the getting of it for all mankind the Army's *raison d'être*. And the chief weapon in their armoury was the compelling knowledge that the consequence of unrepented sin was hellfire. This 'terrific' subject, Booth once wrote to his wife-to-be, was absolutely necessary to the revivalist preacher: 'They must have hellfire flashed before their faces or they will not *move.*' The thought of Christ weeping over lost souls did not work so well. 'We must have the kind of truth which will move sinners.'[12]

Booth, religious innovator though he arguably was, was a creature of his time and circumstances. The 11 *Doctrines of The Salvation Army* evolved out of the creeds of the American Revivalists James Caughey, Charles G. Finney and Phoebe Palmer, alongside the Wesleyan Arminianism ('free salvation for all men and full salvation from all sin') that had influenced him as a young man.[13] The Eleven Points of Doctrine required belief in: Scripture ('given by inspiration of God... the Divine rule of Christian faith and practice'); one God ('Creator preserver and Governor'); the Trinity ('undivided in essence and coequal in power and glory'); Jesus Christ ('truly and properly God and truly and properly man'); the fall ('all men have become

---

10 William Booth, *The General's Letters*, London, Salvation Army International Headquarters, 1886, p.191.

11 'Sin' included the practices of at least some other faiths. On 15July, 1913, *The War Cry* ran the headline, Horrible Hinduism is India's Chief Religion.

12 F. De L. Booth-Tucker, *The Life of Catherine Booth, Mother of The Salvation Army*, London, Salvation Army International Headquarters, 1892, vol. 1, p. 116.

13 See Norman H. Murdoch, *Origins of The Salvation Army*, Knoxville, University of Tennessee Press, 1994, pp. 1-20.

sinners totally depraved and as such are justly exposed to the wrath of God'); Christ's atonement by his suffering and death; repentance and regeneration; justification by Grace; the privilege of all believers to be 'wholly sanctified'; and in the immortality of the soul; in the resurrection of the body; in the general judgement at the end of the world; in the eternal happiness of the righteous; and in the endless punishment of the wicked.

Booth had a narrowly focussed view of what was essential to the faith. The Salvation Army did not celebrate even those sacraments that other Protestant denominations allowed. Booth and his wife considered such observations divisive, a view that indicates a certain pragmatic good sense,[14] if not much sensitivity to Christian history. As far as the Eucharist with its bread and wine was concerned, it was not altogether irrelevant that Booth, under pressure from his wife (whose formerly Wesleyan father had become in later life an alcoholic, precipitating in the teenage Catherine a religious crisis followed by conversion), had decreed that his Army would be compulsorily teetotal.

Nurtured on such uncompromising tenets and disciplines, many of Booth's original colleagues were still going strong in 1904. Some members of his family had quarrelled with him and departed, usually to found organizations more or less similar to his own, but his eldest son Bramwell and daughter Evangeline remained faithful (albeit, in Evangeline's case, resistant to disciplines imposed on all other Salvationist officers). The Salvation Army and the Booths remained synonymous. Although the Army's unity had several times been strained almost to breaking point, the irreconcilables had departed, and Bramwell Booth, Chief of the Staff and principal executive administrator, had put his regulatory, institutional mind to the problem of persuading those who remained to see themselves as members of a single movement, going in the strength of the Lord wherever He sent them, marching to the music of bands, tambourines and concertinas and following the flag to the beat of the Army drum.

Revivalist Dishes from the Music Hall's Table

Music, borrowed or original, popular, brash or sentimental in mood and style, had provided one of the most immediately identifiable characteristics of The Salvation Army. Booth and his song writers asked, with the Reverend Rowland Hill,[15] 'Why should the devil have all the best tunes?' They plundered the Music Hall, so much enjoyed by Booth's original target audience, setting its rousing or lugubrious

---

14 Because mainstream Christians regard the Eucharist and Baptism as central to the faith, their differences tend to be centred upon those acts. The Booths supposed that they could outflank all this disagreement. See Felipe Fernández-Armesto and Derek Wilson, *Reformation*, pp. 71-81, for a discussion of Reformation and post-Reformation debates over the meaning of the sacraments.

15 Not the later Sir Rowland Hill, inventor of the penny post, who is often wrongly credited with this aphoristic enquiry.

melodies as anthems in march time or devotional summonses to righteousness.[16] Champagne Charlie was born again, singing 'Bless His Name, He Sets Me Free!' The Daring Young Man on the Flying Trapeze proclaimed that 'I'm Washed in the Blood of the Lamb, Yes, I Am'. 'Pretty Little Polly Perkins of Paddington Green' became 'a salvation soldier' and learnt (rather coyly) that

> If you're properly converted and your heart is quite clean
> You can snap your fingers at Beelzebub—You know who I mean!

Booth took more from the Halls than their tunes. The Army's 'sing-songs' and 'free-and-easies' were direct copies of Music Hall institutions. The leader of a Salvation Army meeting was much like a Master of Ceremonies, presiding over a succession of items that, apart from the absence of dancing, tobacco, drink, blue jokes and prostitutes (those actually plying their trade, that is), and the inclusion of a sermon, bore a marked resemblance to those featured in the Halls: community singing, sentimental monologues, vocal and instrumental solos (cornet and xylophone especially popular), together with sundry forms of audience participation, such as personal testimonies, scripture readings and the like. Laughter (albeit of a sanctified sort) was encouraged. Sobriquets like those used in the Halls were also common. It was not too far a cry from The Lancashire Loon (one of the *personae* of George Formby senior) to The Hallelujah Dutchman (the nickname of Gerrit J. Govaars, who in 1909-10 would be abortively selected to begin Salvation Army work in Russia).[17] There was an architectural influence as well. Many of the buildings Booth rented before the Christian Mission began to own its own property were music halls. The nascent Army took them over quite often, and when it began to design its own citadels the arrangement of stage (rebaptised as 'platform') and seating areas and the placement of the band and chorus (now 'songsters') would have been familiar to devotees of Wilton's, the Alhambra, the Empire and the Hippodrome.

It would be absurd to push such parallels too far, but we may note that Charles Morton, later known as the 'Father of the Halls', opened his first hall in the East

---

16 It is a teasing thought that present day laws of copyright would have stopped Salvation Army musical development in its tracks. In using popular tunes as it did, The Salvation Army was following the example of Lutherans and Calvinists at the time of the Reformation, while in terms of its contemporaries it was only doing more systematically and publicly what many people did in private as a matter of course. Les Murray remarks, of Nineteenth-Century Australia, that 'it was almost a mark of a tune's genuine popularity that people kept putting new sets of words to it.' See Peter Burke, *Popular Culture in Early Modern Europe*, Aldershot, Scolar Press, 1994, pp. 226-27, and Les Murray, *The Paperbark Tree, Selected Prose*, London, Minerva, 1993, p. 233. Another long-term effect of the Music Hall on The Salvation Army was that its fondness for selections from operas and other classical music was eventually to influence the repertoire of Salvation Army bands. See Dave Russell, *Popular Music in England 1840-1914*, Kingston and Montreal, McGill-Queen's University Press, 1987, p. 87.

17 See below, p. 131.

End of London in 1852,[18] while the Music Hall 'business', like Booth's Christian Mission, crystallized during the 1860s. Like the Army, the Halls were approved of by some middle class people and by the police, because they limited the excesses of working class drinking (many of those who attended came in family parties) and diverted people from politics and rebellion. Both the Halls and the Army were essentially conservative and imperialist at heart. (In the world portrayed by Music Hall songs the gulf between rich and poor was assumed to be inevitable, and offences against conventional morality were always punished.) Both the Halls and The Salvation Army appealed principally to the upper working class and the lower middle class, and from 1880 onwards became more 'respectable' and expanded into middle class areas in London and the provinces. By 1914 both had become accepted national institutions.[19]

Whether or not we find these comparisons suggestive, it is safe to say that Music Hall tunes and their brash theatrical presentation helped carry the Army round the world, while its mottoes, 'Blood and Fire!' and 'The World For God!' were reminiscent of Music Hall catch-phrases. The name 'The Salvation Army' was adopted in 1878 during a meeting in Booth's bedroom (recovering from 'flu, he was pacing the floor in a long yellow dressing gown). The question of whether the Christian Mission was an independent body or merely an appendage to the churches could no longer be avoided, and some of Booth's subordinates (by no means all) were anxious for him to establish autocratic rule. According to conflicting accounts, either George Scott Railton or Bramwell Booth questioned the phrase 'volunteer army' in the Mission's annual report, saying 'I'm a regular or nothing', whereupon, after a pause, Booth abruptly struck out the word 'volunteer' and substituted 'Salvation'. His son and Railton leapt from their chairs shouting 'Thank God for that'.[20] The idea of the Mission as an 'army' had already been around for some time. In 1877 one of

---

18 Russell, *Popular Music*, pp. 73-75. Russell disputes Morton's role as 'Father of the Halls', since his achievements 'appear to have been preceded elsewhere in London or in the provinces'. For the purposes of this comparison, however, we may observe that neither did Booth spring fully formed from the Mile End Road in 1865. Both borrowed freely from the methods of others (without necessarily going out of their way to admit the fact), both advertised their ventures in dramatic ways, and both enjoyed the benefits of longevity and hagiographic biographers.

19 Russell, *Popular Music*, pp. 73, 76, 80, 85, 86, 87-111, and 114. Harold Begbie in *The Life of William Booth, the Founder of The Salvation Army*, London, Macmillan, 1920, vol. ii. p. 23, describes William Booth as 'a monarchist, a constitutionalist, a conservative, and certainly not a lover of radicals and socialists; he kept his eyes averted from the political problem, he never once was tempted to make himself the leader of a revolution, the captain of an angry, avenging democracy; his whole emphasis was on religion, and the only war he understood, the only war for which he had the smallest inclination, was the war against sin'.

20 See Catherine Bramwell Booth, *Bramwell Booth*, London, Rich & Cowan, 1933, p. 97, Begbie, *The Life of William Booth*,, vol. I, pp. 438-39 and Ervine, *God's Soldier*, p. 428. Railton himself does not include the story in his account of events in *General Booth*, London, Hodder & Stoughton, 1913.

its preachers, Elijah Cadman, had 'declared war' on Whitby and called himself 'Captain'. The title, once chosen, struck a chord with the public. It had, as G. Kitson Clark noted,[21] associations with the heroic and romantic pictures of military action put into circulation by vivid press reporting of the Crimean War (1854-56) and the Indian Mutiny (1857-58). In time, Booth's lyricists would lift a good many tunes from an even more recent conflict, the American Civil War (1860-65). However, although the connection between the idea of a religious army and the mid-Victorian zeitgeist was more than fortuitous, The Salvation Army was also an embodiment of a metaphor, the *Miles Christi*, or 'Soldier of Christ', which dated back to St Paul, who instructed the Ephesians to 'Put on the whole armour of God', including 'the breastplate of righteousness,' 'the shield of faith,' 'the helmet of Salvation' and 'the sword of the spirit, which is the word of God'.[22]

Thus, after a long and turbulent apprenticeship Booth had found his way, sometimes by happy accidents that he took some time to accept,[23] to a form of evangelism that conformed to the prerequisites of successful revivalism as defined by Fernández-Armesto and Wilson, who, writing about George Whitfield, early Methodist and 'the first international Protestant evangelist', remark that

> Successful revival depends heavily upon novelties. If men and women are to be jolted from the complaisant rut of religious or irreligious conformity something must first make them 'sit up and take notice'. It may be the personality of a charismatic preacher, the evidence of signs and wonders, clever publicity or the testimony of those prepared to suffer or die for their faith.[24]

The World Resists Salvation

The Salvation Army offered all these things, and was much admired for doing so. There was always opposition, however. Gangs of roughs calling themselves 'the Skeleton Army', cheered on by publicans, attacked Army open-air meetings and magistrates often blamed The Salvation Army for these breaches of the peace. When, in 1890, Booth published *In Darkest England and the Way Out*, a scheme to solve the problem of unemployment by moving surplus labour from English cities to

---

21 G. Kitson Clark, *The Making of Victorian England,* London, Methuen, 1962, p. 189.

22 See *The Epistle to the Ephesians,* 6, 11-17 (A.V.), and John D. Cox's discussion of *Miles Christi,* in David Lyle Jeffrey (ed.), *A Dictionary of Biblical Tradition in English Literature,* Grand Rapids, Eerdmans, 1992, pp. 506-09.

23 Salvation Army bands, for example, came into being in imitation of the band established by the Fry family in Salisbury. Booth waited to see how this 'pleasing novelty' worked before giving bands his official sanction. See Brindley Boon, *Play the Music, Play!* Second Edition, London, Salvationist Publishing and Supplies,1968, pp. 1-3. and the same author's *ISB: The Story of the International Staff Band,* Bristol, Record Greetings, 1985, pp. 1-10.

24 Fernández-Armesto and Wilson, *Reformation,* pp. 187-89.

farm colonies overseas (a book for which the journalist, W.T. Stead, and Commissioner Frank Smith—later to become an MP and leading member of the Independent Labour Party—did most of the research and writing), it was widely hailed as a practical, pragmatic scheme, but it was also vigorously attacked by a number of writers, including T.H. Huxley, under such titles as *The Wrong Way to Do the Wrong Thing*. These attacks sometimes included malicious personal criticisms, with the writers professing particular amusement at Booth's assumption of military rank. They also poured scorn upon the self-publicizing and boundlessly self-confident Stead. Nonetheless, Booth's scheme, as a recent critical account concludes, had at least 'limited success'.[25] The scheme was also one of the most obvious signals that the Army was moving away from purely evangelical work, which upset a number of serving Salvationists, including Commissioner George Scott Railton, one of Booth's earliest and until this time most unquestioningly loyal right-hand men. Booth's military-style administration, with himself as sole general and commander-in-chief, also attracted much criticism, often from former Salvationist officers who thought it dictatorial.

Other objections tended to focus on the point where the Army's religious enthusiasm crossed the accepted boundaries of socially acceptable behaviour, good taste and aesthetics. The Seventh Earl of Shaftesbury (that 'gloomily handsome philanthropist with the sad, humourless eyes and ungenial jowl', as Booth's biographer, St John Ervine, describes him), was impressed by Mrs Booth, but disapproved majestically of William. There had been, briefly, a chance that they might work together, but at a conference to consider how overlapping religious organizations might be united Booth had upset delegates by his scepticism regarding—ironically—choirs as instruments of evangelism. They were, he thought, infested with three devils: the quarrelling devil, the dressing devil, and the courting devil. Mrs Booth tried subsequently to reconcile Shaftesbury to Salvationist methods, but in vain. The more closely he became acquainted with what the angry Professor Huxley called 'corybantic Christianity',[26] the more hostile he grew. He assured guests at a garden party in Blackheath that The Salvation Army was 'clearly anti-Christ', and one of his followers asserted that—if certain arcane calculations were applied—the letters in the name William Booth made up 666, the mark of the beast.[27]

In 1881, invited by Admiral Fishbourne to support the Army, Shaftesbury replied at length. There was no authority in scripture, he wrote, for the Army's system and discipline, its employment of extravagant actions and offensive expressions. He quoted the late Bishop McIlvaine:

...the time of revival... is especially the time for watchfulness... beware of all attempts to kindle excitement. Be animated, be diligent, be filled with the spirit of prayer, but be sober-minded. Let all noise, and all endeavours to promote mere

---

25 Murdoch, *Origins of The Salvation Army*, p. 146, and pp. 217-18.
26 Begbie, *William Booth*, vol. ii, p.124.
27 Ervine, *God's Soldier*, pp. 339-40.

animal feeling, be shunned. You can no more advance the growth of religion in the soul by excitement than you can promote health in the body by throwing it into a fever.

There were, he thought, enough missions in London already to render Booth's not merely offensive but superfluous. Even Mrs Booth had begun to attract his contumely: her

> plain and unhesitating assertion, that... stimulating appliances are necessary to render the Gospel acceptable to the masses, is simply to declare that the Gospel, in itself, is weak and spiritless, unless presented to them with the grotesque and heathenish accompaniments of man's invention—an assertion in direct contravention of Scripture itself...[28]

Shaftesbury's view of The Salvation Army could be summarized by Marshall McLuhan's famous remark about television, made in 1964: 'The medium is the message'. Crudeness in presentation must imply crudeness in what was presented. William and Catherine Booth, however, had they not been concerned to defend themselves against attack by a leading public figure, might well have asserted their own more positive version of the same motto. They were dealing with people to whom reverence, solemnity and holy hush, necessary to the respectable classes, were alien. A song and a cup of tea might indeed gain their attention, and the message that followed was one that the song and the cup of tea would help confirm. A recent biographer of Shaftesbury comments that his opposition 'may have owed something to that resentment of newcomers in the field which he was apt to betray in his old age' and that he 'underestimated' the potential longevity of the Army's work.[29] Lord Shaftesbury thought that the Army's methods, and therefore such success as it enjoyed, debased scripture; the Booths thought their success proved that they had correctly understood scripture's appeal to Everyman.

Needful MONEY, Necessary Officers: The Trials of Autocracy

Shaftesbury's criticisms had some impact during his lifetime, but, as we have seen, the organization that so pained him had, by 1904, won national approval. In 1905, George Bernard Shaw wrote, in his Preface to *Major Barbara*, of the Salvationist

> ...repudiating gaiety and courting effort and sacrifice, yet always in the wildest spirits, laughing, joking, singing, rejoicing, drumming and tambourining: his life flying by in a flash of excitement, and his death arriving as a climax of triumph... in the poorest corner of this soul-destroying Christendom vitality suddenly begins to germinate again. Joyousness, a sacred gift long dethroned by the hellish laughter

---

28 See Edwin Hodder, *The Life and Work of the Seventh Earl of Shaftesbury K.G.,* London, Cassell, 1886, vol. iii, pp. 433-40.

29 Geoffrey B.A.M. Finlayson, *The Seventh Earl of Shaftesbury, 1801-1885,* London, Eyre Methuen, 1981, pp. 582 and 607.

of derision and obscenity, rises like a flood miraculously out of the fetid dust and mud of the slums; rousing marches and impetuous dithyrambs rise to the heavens from people among whom the depressing noise called 'sacred music' is a standing joke; a flag with Blood and Fire on it is unfurled, not in murderous rancour, but because fire is beautiful and blood a vital and splendid red; Fear, which we flatter by calling Self, vanishes; and transfigured men and women carry their gospel through a transfigured world, calling their leader general, themselves captains and brigadiers, and their whole body an Army: praying, but praying only for refreshment, for strength to fight, and for needful MONEY (a notable sign, that); preaching, but not preaching submission; daring ill-usage and abuse, but not putting up with more of it than is inevitable; and practising what the world will let them practise, including soap and water, colour and music. There is danger in such activity; and where there is danger there is hope...

Presciently, Shaw followed his own 'impetuous dithyramb' with a sober warning:

For the present, however, it is not my business to flatter The Salvation Army. Rather I must point out to it that it has almost as many weaknesses as the Church of England itself. It is building up a business organization which will compel it eventually to see that its present staff of enthusiast commanders shall be succeeded by a bureaucracy of men of business, who will be no better than bishops...[30]

In 1906 these points, especially the question of 'needful MONEY' were made the focus of *The Salvation Army and the Public: A Religious, Social, and Financial Study*. This hostile analysis of The Salvation Army was by John Manson, the latest in a line of writers, often ex-Salvationists who, beginning in the 1880s, had adversely criticized the Booths, their financial and disciplinary methods, and their claims to evangelical success.[31]

From its inception, the Christian Mission had been financed by subsidy and donations. Relations between Booth and the donors were seldom easy, particularly when he developed a preference for working inside throughout the year, rather than moving back into tents or the open air during the summer. He tended to go over budget, failing to conform to the 'notions of evangelism and frugality' of his philanthropic and evangelical backers. Later he appointed a committee to advise him on finance and property—but ignored its advice. After 1867, thanks in considerable part to the efforts of Catherine, who recruited wealthy subscribers by her preaching in St John's Wood, the West End and other well-off parts of London, the Mission became a little more self-sufficient. In 1870 it acquired another advisory committee whose membership provided prestige as well as advice. Again Booth's ideas differed from theirs. In 1870, amid accusations of mismanagement and extravagance, and

---

30 G.B. Shaw, *The Complete Prefaces of Bernard Shaw*, London, Paul Hamlyn, 1965, p. 126.

31 See Murdoch, *Origins of The Salvation Army*, p. 219 for a list. Murdoch states that Manson was, as many supposed when his book was published, a former Salvationist, but Manson denied this firmly in the preface (p. viii) to his second augmented edition (1908).

suggestions that he should live in a smaller house and keep his wife and daughters at home to do the housework, he became a property owner for the first time. The permanent occupation of a particular site that this implied was a milestone on Booth's journey from the life of a travelling evangelist to that of settled head of an established religious denomination. Later, as social work became increasingly important, so the need to raise funds also grew. A distinction also came into being between Headquarters officers, who were salaried (albeit at no very munificent level) and those in the field, who were guaranteed nothing and had to raise what they could. Sales of *The War Cry* and other publications became an essential component of the Army's income, as were collections taken from the public during regular indoor or outdoor meetings and, at longer intervals, in special appeals such as 'Self-Denial Week'. From a very early stage it was apparent that The Salvation Army could not survive on the money contributed by its own members.[32]

Manson contended that Booth's high-handed methods of dealing with these matters had led to the Army's spiritual work being pushed into second place by its need to raise money. His book was a severe critique, only partly vitiated by repetitiveness, reliance upon anecdotal evidence (some of it shocking enough), and fondness for airy and tendentious exaggeration: he writes, for instance, of the Army's 'expenditure of public money running into millions' and the 'almost unlimited funds' it collected from the British public.[33] These collections depended upon the givers supposing that most of their money would be spent on social work, whereas much was siphoned off to cover the expenses of a top-heavy bureaucracy (which Manson thought absurdly unnecessary) at National and International Headquarters, officer training, publications, struggling corps, and so on. This practice might have been acceptable had two things been indisputably the case: that the British public wanted to pay for the conversion to Salvationism of those not reached by other churches, and, secondly, that the Army could claim especial success as a 'converting machine'. Neither proposition, he argued, was true. The Army's figures for attendance in London, according to a census published in 1904 by the *Daily News* under the title The Religious Life of London, proved beyond doubt that it was less successful in attracting members than the other churches and missions operating there. The Army, wishing to conceal this embarrassing fact, published neither attendance figures nor an adequate balance sheet.[34] According to its own soul-saving expectations (Manson quoted extensively from the *Orders and Regulations for Field Officers* to show what these were) it was a failure. The failure, furthermore, was the consequence of William Booth's overweening confidence that his methods were God-given and successful. Manson did not wish to suggest that any junior officers were

---

32 Murdoch, *Origins*, pp. 41, 51-53, 55-61, and *passim*.

33 John Manson, *The Salvation Army and the Public: A Religious, Social, and Financial Study*, London and New York, Routledge, 1906; Second edition, Augmented, London and New York, 1908, pp. 151 and 154.

34 A balance sheet certified by a reputable firm of accountants was in fact obtainable on request from International Headquarters, but Manson thought this did not amount to 'publication', and that it was in any case insufficiently detailed.

guilty of laziness or deceit. On the contrary, they, of all the victims of Booth's system, were the most unfortunate. They were not permitted to know how the organization they served was run. They were required to swear never to criticize it publicly, not merely while they continued as officers but, should they be so ill-advised as to resign, ever afterwards. They were ill-paid (when they were paid at all) and ill-supported. Booth's financial and administrative system forced them to spend the bulk of their time raising money, and this had become the sole measure of their effectiveness as officers. When, through unwillingness to work under these conditions, or collapsing health brought on by deprivation, they were no longer of any use, they were thrown onto the scrap heap. Comparison of the number of officers in service with the numbers who had undergone training proved that there was a very high wastage. Worse, the Army exhibited less interest in former officers fallen on hard times than it did in alcoholics or, significantly, middle class people able to support it financially. Its social institutions, because they were, whatever Booth claimed, intended principally as places where the unfortunate could be exposed to religious propaganda, were grossly overstaffed. Claims that they were effectively reforming thousands of drunkards and making good citizens from the dregs of society were patently exaggerated, wishful thinking at best. The Army's ventures into banking, insurance and other commercial activities probably contravened the provisions of the Foundation Deeds of 1878 under which Booth was supposed to operate.[35]

From the reaction in the press it might appear that Manson, single-handed, had undone the propaganda success achieved by the International Congress of 1904—which he described as 'a magnificently engineered advertisement rendered necessary by the Army's numerical and spiritual weakness, which is largely the result of its system of government and largely the cause of its absolute dependence everywhere on sensationalism'.[36] The Catholic weekly *The Tablet* (then as now generally fair-minded and intelligent) remarked waggishly that '...the step from all this to the dogma of the infallibility of the General would not seem to be a very long one!' The *Methodist Recorder* felt 'very unhappy about General Booth and his Army'. *Christian Endeavourer* found the chapter on High Finance 'startling'. Two papers that had often supported the Army, the *Daily News* and the *Pall Mall Gazette*, saluted Manson's seriousness and calmness of attack. The *Glasgow Herald* noted the book's 'combination of ruthless logic with intimate and detailed knowledge'. The *Church Times* summed up the views of all 31 papers (ranging from the *Spectator* and the *Manchester Guardian* to the *World's Carriers and Contractors' Review* and *Japan Chronicle*) whose reviews were printed in the second, augmented edition of

---

35 It should be said, however, that after more than 300 pages of (very repetitive) argument Manson concludes that it is not the Booths' honesty he wishes to question, but their wisdom. The Salvation Army should be reorganized on non-autocratic lines so that there could be no possibility of financial malpractice, which had not occurred in the past, occurring in the future.

36 Manson, *The Salvation Army and the Public*, p. 213.

1908, when it wrote: 'There may be a good answer forthcoming; we shall hope to see it'.

As Manson had anticipated, The Salvation Army did not respond directly to his book, although it caused two articles on related matters, dating from 1892 and 1905, to be reprinted. In 1892, in response to allegations by T.H. Huxley and others, Booth had invited a Committee of Enquiry to report on the use of moneys contributed to the In Darkest England and the Way Out appeal.[37] The Committee exonerated the Army—without, however, according to George Scott Railton, silencing its critics.[38] Manson had considered both these items while writing his book. He thought the Committee's remit had been too narrow. Furthermore, it had made various recommendations that Booth had not as yet implemented.

Manson claimed, in the preface to his second augmented edition, that a spokesman at Salvation Army Headquarters had 'airily' admitted that his book contained 'a good deal of truth', and that a series of special articles in the *Japan Chronicle* analyzing his book created difficulty during Booth's visit to Japan in 1907: the Army's press officers played this down and concealed the fact that Booth had cancelled an interview with a journalist from that paper. Manson also claimed that the Self-Denial collection for 1907 registered a fall for the first time in 14 years, a decline from which it did not recover in 1908. Despite these undeniable facts, he complained, the press, which in his view had mistakenly created the Army's popularity in the first place, soon reverted to deluded praise of the organization.[39]

Booth, whose sole response was a reference to attacks 'too silly to need refutation', had in fact been considering criticisms of his autocratic rule for some years. In 1896 W.E. Gladstone had suggested that provision should be made both for the election of future generals and for the removal of any who might be found unfit to hold office.[40] In 1904 Booth finally took heed of the second head of this argument, and the constitution of the Army was amended to allow the removal of a General from office, a provision that was to have sad results for his son Bramwell in 1929.

Manson's claim that the Army failed to achieve evangelical success on anything like the scale to which it aspired is much the same as that contained in Murdoch's academic study published almost 90 years later, and there seems little reason to question it. His argument that the social work gained nothing from the work in the corps is less sound, since the officers who did the social work would have been recruited from the soldiers in the corps. To his underlying argument, fuelled by his disapproval of William and Bramwell Booth, that the Army was, by 1906, obsolete in its theology, sensationalist in its evangelism ('a species of religious terrorism')[41]

---

37 Ervine, *God's Soldier*, pp. 729-34.
38 George S. Railton, *General Booth*, London, Hodder & Stoughton, 1913, p. 215.
39 Manson, *Preface to The Salvation Army and the Public, second edition*, London and New York, 1908.
40 William Booth, *A Talk with Mr Gladstone at His Own Fireside*, London, Salvation Army International Headquarters, 1897, pp. 31-33.
41 Manson, *The Salvation Army and the Public*, p. 153.

and tyrannical in government, it might be said that enough people were energized by these outdated methods to help Booth to build the world-wide Christian army that had evolved in his imagination over some 40 years, even if in any single place they were, and would remain, a tiny minority. These few apparently deluded souls also contrived, by no means incidentally, to impress a variety of governments, as well as of general publics, with their utility.

Nonetheless, we will find that the Army's systems of government and finance were on occasion seriously to sabotage its work in Russia, and that there, as elsewhere, it attracted only small numbers of enrolled members. We will notice too that the Army's conviction that no other body was trying to reach, let alone actually reaching, the people they claimed for their own, was based on the assumption that all other varieties of Christian experience were inferior and could therefore be discounted.[42]

International Standstill

Meanwhile, the Army did not need Manson to tell it that, for all the success of the International Congress, there had been in the world at large as well as in the British territory—not for the first time—a worrying hiatus in its expansion. In 1958, after his retirement, the Army's sixth General, Albert Orsborn, wrote, of this period:

> The second phase of Army development had been reached. We were not turning away from our original militancy. By the grace of God we can, I think, rightly claim that we remain to this day a fighting, marching, Army of the Living God. Yet, maintaining militancy, we had to face the fact that revival conditions are not perpetual... the turn of the century saw The Salvation Army in Great Britain fighting a defensive if not precisely a rearguard action. Dissidents and critics were both numerous and vocal. Meetings were not so well attended, save for the special occasion, and many corps were unable to pay their way. At the same time,

---

42 Few, if any, people believe that The Salvation Army is or ever was a gigantic fraud upon a gullible public and, since much of the money the Army draws from 'the public' nowadays comes via government agencies and local authorities, its use has to be accounted for in detail. Manson's arguments about the governance of the movement received a kind of confirmation in 1929, when Bramwell Booth was deposed by officers who (whatever the arguments advanced about his fitness or otherwise to continue holding office) wanted the Army's future leaders to be elected. Manson's attack (p. 175) on the notion that 'in the doctrines and activities of Salvationism alone reside all the elements and incentives necessary for the full development of all the religious, social and civic virtues desirable in the members of a civilized community' was better founded, as was his sceptical comparison (pp. 177-82) of the large numbers of conversions claimed week by week in *The War Cry* with the relatively small numbers of people listed on Army rolls.

discipline was tightening, and was resented by those who had scant patience with organization.[43]

Internationally, the expansion that between 1880, when The Salvation Army 'opened fire' in the United States, and 1898 when work was begun in Alaska and Barbados, had taken it into 37 countries, including most of western and northern Europe, North America and parts of South America, much of Southern Africa and India, Japan and Indonesia. It had made a substantial start on the conquest of the English-speaking world, the British Empire and many other, broadly speaking, Protestant countries. But, since many of the rest were Catholic, Orthodox, or Islamic, it is not surprising that after two hectic decades of expansion there was a hiatus. Between 1898 and the Third International Congress in 1904 work was commenced in a number of areas in the Caribbean and Central America but there was no major new start until 1907, when the Army arrived in Korea. Austria, Manchuria and Palestine would follow before the decade ended and, all told, between 1900 and the outbreak of war in August 1914 The Salvation Army made 'pioneering assaults' on 23 countries in which it would eventually establish itself.

The Gravitational Pull of the Great Bear

Under the circumstances prevailing in 1904, with most countries which might be expected to welcome The Salvation Army having already done so, few in Protestant England would have thought worse of him for turning his imperial eye upon Russia, which was seen in the pre-First World War years as an 'immense and discordant Empire... thinly peopled by innumerable races speaking as many different dialects and professing sharply differing faiths'.[44] The reference to races and faiths is significant. Russia lay at the extreme edge of Europe and Christendom. Orthodox Christianity was strange, even alien, and, to most evangelicals, scarcely Christian at all. Further, of the many non-Russian races in the Russian Empire, most were Asiatic, which in England still carried overtones of barbarism and heathendom. In November 1862, *Missionary Magazine*, in considering 'Russia as a Field for Evangelistic Labours' had written:

> The position and influence of Russia make it one of the most important countries for Christian effort. The Russians are Asiatic in their origin, manners, instincts. Their desire for conquest is very much in the direction of Asiatic countries, or Asiatic people, rather than the countries of Western Europe. And if the Russians possessed as much knowledge of the true gospel as the English, they could and would do great things for the salvation of the entire Asiatic continent.[45]

---

43 Albert Orsborn, *The House of My Pilgrimage*, London, Salvationist Publishing and Supplies, 1958, p. 43.
44 Edward Crankshaw, *Russia and Britain*, London, Collins, n.d., (c.1944), p. 15.
45 *Missionary Magazine*, vol. 42, no. 11, November, 1982, p. 424.

In 1937, 75 years later, in his account of the Army's attempt to conquer this 'Asiatic' place, Commissioner Karl Larsson, in regretting that Russia had not been more influenced by the Swedes, of whom he was himself one, remarked that 'perhaps Russia's fate would have lain elsewhere, had not the Asiatic Tartars... taken the land under their rule and brought about... a less wholesome mixture of races'.[46]

Such assumptions about race were commonplace at the time, but to evangelicals in particular the prospect of a huge empire that considered itself Christian but, so *Missionary Magazine* went on to remark, enjoyed 'but little true apprehension of the glorious gospel of our Lord' was irresistible. So was Russia's sheer size. An army bent on conquering the world could not ignore so vast a slice of it.

William Booth felt that the Army's 'delay' in going to Russia could 'only be excused because of the gigantic difficulties that have barred the way'.[47] Salvationists had been visiting the country, overland, on their way to the Far East, or via the relatively accessible Black Sea port of Odessa, for several decades. They had a low opinion of the Orthodox Church. On 15 February, 1882, W.T. Stead, editor of *The Pall Mall Gazette* had felt impelled to write reproving George Scott Railton, one of Booth's right-hand men, for his unsympathetic views:

> I have read your account of your visit to the Russian Church with much interest not unmixed with some regret. I have so often had to defend The Salvation Army from precisely the charges you bring against the Russian Church, and that to Russians themselves, that I confess I had hoped you would have been more sympathetic, not to say charitable. My dear Mr Railton, do you remember that you do not understand Slavonic, that what to you is mummery is to a hundred millions of men, women, and children rich with all the associations of a faith cradled at Bethlehem and glorified at Calvary, and that an intelligent foreigner witnessing the excited services of The Salvation Army—say at an All-Night—might retort upon you with effect if he were unable to understand what was said...[48]

Stead puts his finger on a failure of Salvationist perception which few officers at that time made any sustained attempt to overcome. The Salvation Army was and largely remained, prejudicially ill-informed about and arrogantly dismissive of the Russian Church. They could not even get its name right, although they were not the only ones to fall into this error: as James Muckle remarks, the mistranslation of the Russian *pravoslvnyy* as Greek Orthodox, 'once very common, has always been

---

46 Karl Larsson, *Tio År I Ryssland*, Stockholm, FA-Press Bokförlag, 1967, p. 7.
47 *The War Cry*, 30 January, 1909.
48 Begbie, *William Booth*, pp. 5-6. I have not been able to find Railton's offending article. Stead's interest in Russia, like Railton's, persisted until his death. In 1888 he would write a book, *The Truth about Russia*, and he argued the Army's case for working in Russia to Stolypin, the Russian prime minister, in August, 1908. Railton's relations with Booth worsened after 1894, but he was to visit Russia on two further occasions after that, and he is an important figure in our story. See pp. 99-100 and 109-16 below.

incorrect'.[49] (The national churches of the Orthodox communion have been independent of each other [with Russian Orthodox the largest and most influential] since the fall of Constantinople to the Turks in 1453, although they continue to acknowledge the primacy of the Patriarch of that city.) Salvationists, given to rhapsodizing over the deeply spiritual nature of the Russians, steadfastly believed that this spirituality had nothing to do with the Orthodox Church and its mystical style of worship. Railton's complaint about 'mummery' touches a chord that reverberates through most of the attitudes evinced by the Salvationists who feature in this book. Repeatedly surprised that some members of the Orthodox Church very nearly conform to their idea of what constitutes a 'true Christian', they nonetheless assume that any of their converts who continue to show affection for the Church have not yet fully seen the light.

To recognize that the Army's attitude to Orthodoxy was blinkered is not necessarily, as we shall see, to concede that its criticisms lacked any foundation. But what, meanwhile, was the situation of this Army that so confidently presumed itself called to deliver, to 106,000,000 Russians, a life-transforming message previously unheard by the benighted Orthodox?

In the late 1870s Booth had not been in favour of expansion, fearing that if the Army became an international body he would not be able to retain control. When this proved not to be the case, his attitude changed radically. His enthusiasm for starting work in new countries was, of course, driven by his vision of Salvation for all mankind and between the Third International Congress and his death in 1912 he toured the world virtually continuously, preaching to the people and negotiating with governments.

Because of the hiatus in growth described in Section 6, above, Booth's evangelical enthusiasm for the salvation of souls was tinged with a necessary practical awareness that in order to attract the financial support and loyalty of its soldiers (without either of which it could not survive) The Salvation Army had to be seen to be growing. That there was a problem in this respect has occurred to most historians of The Salvation Army: because of the class snobbery typified by the Earl of Shaftesbury and the demands it made upon its members it was unlikely ever to attract more than a small minority of any given population.[50] Geographical expansion, therefore, was an essential precondition of its continued growth.

---

49 James Muckle, Introduction to Leskov's *Schism in High Society: Lord Radstock and his Followers*, Nottingham, Bramcote Press, 1995, p. 5.

50 A rough assessment of Salvation Army membership as a percentage of total national population in some of the 120 countries where the Army works, based on statistics of officers, soldiers, adherents, junior soldiers and personnel working elsewhere, published in *The Salvation Army Yearbook 2001*, gives the following results: Australia, 0.15%; Canada, 0.32%; India, 0.28%; Indonesia, 0.4%; Japan, 0.3%; Mexico, 0.34%; Sweden and Latvia, 0.15%; United Kingdom with Republic of Ireland, 0.97%; United States of America, 0.16%; Zambia and Malawi, 0.68%; Zimbabwe, 0.7%. The worldwide figure is 0.32%. These figures are approximate but they indicate that The Salvation Army is very much a minority organization.

Booth never made it to China, another vast, mysterious Eastern Empire, untouched in his mind by the true gospel and having the significant advantage of a very large population, constituting almost infinite numbers of souls to be saved, 'fields', in the Biblical phrase, 'white unto harvest', but he seized with enthusiasm the first opportunity that presented itself to visit Russia.

That Russia was high on the list of proposed fields was made clear in 1906. In the first issue of *The Salvation Army Year Book*, under the heading Where We Hope To Be, was printed (and reprinted in subsequent annual editions) the following description of that huge country:

> An empire of vast extent, embracing more than one-half the European Continent, and considerably more than a third of Asia—the largest of all the continents. Bounded on the North by the Arctic Ocean; on the west by the Baltic Sea, Germany and Austria-Hungary; on the south by Roumania, the Black Sea, the Caucasus and the Caspian; on the east by Siberia and Russian Central Asia. Area, 2000,000 square miles. Population, over 106,000,000. No representative Government, no free speech or free Press until last year. State religion, the Greek Church. Nine-tenths of the people are engaged in agriculture. Wheat principal export; England buys largely its bread-stuff here. Salvation Army not yet represented.

It may seem odd that a summary so stuffed with facts and figures mentions the 1905 Revolution only by implication ('...no free speech or free press until last year') and does not mention the Russo-Japanese War of 1904-5. Both events had shocked Europe. Japan's victory showed the world that an apparently powerful western nation could be humiliated by Orientals and reminded the Russians that the autocracy under which they lived was prone to mismanage wars. Subsequent domestic upheavals, beginning with the massacre of 200 demonstrators in St Petersburg on Bloody Sunday in January 1905, provided further evidence that the autocracy was not securely in charge. When, in October, a general strike paralyzed St Petersburg, the Government was at last persuaded to act other than repressively. An Imperial Manifesto was issued, which first stated that autocracy was inviolable, then, apparently, abolished it. There was to be a legislative Duma elected by popular franchise. Although the Tsar could continue to legislate by decree, the Duma's consent was required for all new laws. Full civil liberties were granted to all.

The revolution had upset Booth greatly, and a popular newspaper had published his declaration of what he would do if he were Tsar: abolish martial law; confer with the most benevolent, wisest, most practical and intelligent men of all parties; act for the honour of God and the highest well-being of the nation. Apropos the war, Bramwell Booth had written to his father of the Japanese ruse which led to victory at Port Arthur that 'One is almost inclined to wonder whether the use of these secret methods is not opposed to the principle of real fighting. The 800 people on that ship had no chance of striking a blow for themselves or their cause.' William, replying, demonstrated that his fondness for military imagery did not indicate any approval at all of bloodshed. War, he wrote, was 'the silliest and most devilish system of settling disputes'. The defeat was 'an awful humiliation for Russia. She won't get over it in my time—whatever she may do in yours.'[51]

Among the civil liberties granted in October 1905 was religious freedom, proclaimed by ukase in April. This concession may well have led, the following year, to the Army's announcement that it wished to go to work in Russia. If so, it was doomed to disappointment. Like many other elements in the Imperial Manifesto of 1905, religious freedom was never fully implemented. The concessions had been intended to detach liberals and moderates from more extreme revolutionaries, but when it became apparent that liberals and moderates were themselves demandingly reformist, the concessions were withdrawn. When the Duma met in April 1906, the Tsar allowed it very limited powers, and its call in May for a genuinely constitutional regime provoked him to dissolve it in July. The three further Dumas which sat before 1916 achieved only small reforms and were constantly in conflict with those who believed that autocracy should not have been abandoned, and could and should be, revived.

Political matters were underplayed in the *Year Book* entry probably because from its earliest years (despite Booth's essential conservatism) The Salvation Army had adopted an apolitical stance. It comprised the front-line troops of a Kingdom that was not of this world. It rendered unto Caesar that which was Caesar's, but most of what seemed to it essential had nothing to do with Caesar. The political complexion of governments was of secondary importance—although the tendency of socialists to lean towards freethinking and atheism was not approved. The Army's belief in its own non-political nature demonstrated a certain naiveté—since any action or attitude that has or implies social or political repercussions is *ipso facto* necessarily political—but also some degree of reactionary common sense. Salvationist leaders were of the school that believed, approvingly, that John and Charles Wesley, by diverting men's minds from politics to God, had helped save England from political revolution in the late Eighteenth Century. This they would have regarded as both non-political and useful. Therefore, although the Army has usually contrived to avoid publicly taking sides in political situations in countries where it has worked,[52] its stance has been in effect politically conservative. Its work, when successful, ameliorated the harsher realities of social and economic life in part by persuading people to think about the 'land of pure delight where saints immortal reign'—the very factor that provoked Marx's dictum that religion was the opium of the people.[53] Hence, as we shall see, some part of the Army's appeal to the world's established but fearful ruling classes. To many of them the Army represented much-needed moral revival; to others it was, with its social work and slum posts, its bands and banners, a modern equivalent of the bread and circuses so ably deployed by the more

---

51 Begbie, *William Booth,* vol. ii, pp. 318-19, and 335-56.

52 There is evidence, however, to suggest that one important Salvationist leader failed, with unfortunate consequences, to maintain this policy following the Bolshevik seizure of power in Russia: see pp. 233-36 below.

53 In his Introduction to The Critique of Hegel's Philosophy of Right, in *Deutsch-Französche Jahrbücher,* Paris, 1844.

successful of the later Roman emperors and so very obviously necessary once more in the turbulently dawning Twentieth Century.

Anarchy, Salvation and Order

It was not so much Marx's 'spectre of Communism' which haunted the well-to-do of early Twentieth-Century Europe as that of Anarchism. During the 20 years before 1914 Anarchists, in pursuit of a world without states, governments, laws, or ownership of property, in which corrupt institutions had been obliterated and man was be free to be good as God intended, assassinated five heads of state (presidents of France and the United States, two Spanish premiers and King Humbert of Italy) and the Empress Elizabeth of Austria. These terrorist acts were 'propaganda of the deed' intended to precipitate the revolution, which the perpetrators believed was merely awaiting its signal to begin. In Russia the tradition of the bomb-throwing Anarchist was already well established. In March of 1881 Tsar Alexander II was killed by a bomb in a Petersburg Street. Five years later there was an attempt on the life of his successor, Alexander III.

Anarchism had more far-reaching effects than the often rather arbitrary deaths of its immediate victims. One of those who had plotted the death of Alexander III, subsequently executed, was Alexander Ulyanov, older brother of Vladimir Ilyich Ulyanov, who changed his name to Lenin and devoted himself to revolutionary activity as a result. As the new century dawned and discontent and instances of 'propaganda of the deed' increased, Russian statesmen fell back on their standard method for diverting their countrymen's attention from the causes of their discontents, which was, as one of them put it, to 'drown the revolution in Jewish blood,' a policy whose implementation, in the form of a pogrom in Kishinev during the Passover of 1903, shocked the civilized world.

It might seem that The Salvation Army, an evolving but carefully designed hierarchy centred upon one man, its Founder and General, had in common with the Anarchists a passionate, self-sacrificial longing for the betterment of mankind, if little else. But, despite the fact that many people regarded it as almost · equally dangerous, if less to life and limb than to decorum and true doctrine, it was inclined to see itself as an instrument to cure the disease of Anarchism. It was very much in favour of legitimate authority, properly used to produce an ordered society in which it could get on with its own proper business of saving individual souls. Therefore it was happy to present itself (and be presented by its friends) as willing to cooperate with governments, including that of Russia, while retaining, in the party doctrinal sense, a non-political stance.

Nonetheless, the Army was to make some contact with Anarchists and ex-Anarchists during its time in Russia and Salvationists and Anarchists proved to have a surprising amount in common. Many Anarchists had once been enthusiastic Christians, taking up the bomb and the pistol when they grew disillusioned with established religion, partly because society seemed to them to need more radical and rapid amelioration than the church could provide. In part, of course, they were driven by a taste for self-sacrificing danger. W. Weidlé comments: 'Scratch the terrorist and you discover the philanthropist; continue to scratch and you will end by discovering the Christian gone astray'.[54] Some of these idealistic converts in due course reconverted, bringing a passion with which they had made bombs to bear on the saving of souls. Some, disillusioned all over again, revised their loyalties a third time and became Bolsheviks.

Were there 'Fields White Unto Harvest'?

Although political considerations cannot have been absent from the minds of the Army's leaders as they prayed and manoeuvred to be allowed into Russia, they were not uppermost. For Salvationists it was an article of faith that in any country of the world, no matter what its established religion or lack of it, there are always thousands, or millions, languishing disconsolate outside the pale of organized churches, lost to God and to themselves. Whatever Manson might say as he picked over his statistics and discreditable instances, they passionately believed that God had raised up the Army to seek and save the lost, not to poach existing believers from other religious organizations.

Booth himself had emerged from the Methodist New Connection and many of his most committed colleagues and a high proportion of the soldiery had similarly religious backgrounds. Indeed, as Norman H. Murdoch demonstrates, more dispassionately than Manson, with statistics, graphs and close argument, only a minority of Salvationists came in out of the absolute cold: most joined the Army because they liked its way of doing things better than that of their own church, or were returning to belief in the manner of prodigal sons. And—something which Booth never quite admitted—few of his converts were slum-dwellers. The 'respectable working class' was much more receptive to evangelism.[55]

Nonetheless, at the time under discussion, it had not yet been admitted by the Army that the teeming masses whom William Booth identified to Bramwell as 'our people' were statistically amongst the least likely to join up. The theory continued to be that in Russia, as elsewhere, Salvationists would seek out those who never went to church and knew nothing of Christ. In the nature of things, these people would tend to be poor and uneducated, living hard, often brutalized and drunken lives in the slums of St Petersburg and Moscow, the two largest, rapidly growing, ill-governed cities.[56] Because of this focus, the Army knew from experience that it would probably attract the favourable attention of concerned members of the educated and governing classes, and, in consequence, receive substantial donations to finance

---

54 Quoted in Edmund Heier, *Religious Schism in the Russian Aristocracy 1860-1900: Radstockism and Pashkovism,* The Hague, Martinus Nijhoff, 1970, p. 12.

55 Murdoch, *Origins*, p. 117, and *passim.*

56 'In both cities the city Dumas were dominated by men with an interest in real estate who were answerable to electorates limited by property qualifications to about two per cent of the male populations.' Vladimir Andrle, *A Social History of Twentieth-Century Russia,* London, Hodder Education, 1994, p. 91.

its work. The Army's socially rehabilitative activities would attract the conservatively minded, some of whom would have heard of Johannes Miquel, an ardent socialist, who once famously stopped a friend giving money to a beggar, saying 'Don't delay the Revolution!'[57] Some segments of society welcomed the Salvationists for these reasons, but later, after the Bolsheviks had seized power, Salvationist thinking was bound to be in collision with state ideology.

There was, however, no need for the Army to wait until the Communist take-over in 1917 to find itself in conflict with the Russian state. It is difficult to be sure how much William Booth and his International Headquarters knew about the religious and national attitudes that were embedded in the constitution and the fabric of the Russian state, but not at all difficult to be certain that their probable relative ignorance was a source of courage and strength. In Booth's mind, God could and would confound all rational expectation. When millions were dying unsaved it was not the Salvation Army's task to distract itself with consideration of constitutional niceties and rational expectations: God, the supreme commander, had issued unconditional orders to seek out and destroy unbelief and ungodly living, in Russia as elsewhere.

In any case, although Booth himself did not think in this way, if the Army was not to begin a long, slow death by contraction, it must continue to expand.

---

57 *Andrle, Social History*, p. 382.

CHAPTER 2

The Third Rome[1]

A Gulf Fixed

If The Salvation Army was to persuade Russians to accept its brand of evangelical Christianity it would need to build bridges between systems of Christian belief which could scarcely have stood further apart. People whose idea of religion had been formed by Orthodoxy would, if they chose to become Salvationists, have to make numerous large cultural, spiritual and intellectual adjustments.

The Salvation Army's theology and practices were derived from its immediate antecedents, the American evangelists of the Nineteenth Century, and beyond them from the Methodist revival of the Eighteenth. From the Salvationist point of view, these were heroes who, the Reformation having cleansed the faith from the corruptions of Catholicism—the popes, the cult of the Virgin, the indulgences, the immoral living, the worldly splendours and all the rest—had begun the work of carrying the true Gospel to the newly industrialised masses of Great Britain and North America. Now it was time for the soldiers of Christ to rescue those who had fallen through the nets of Catholic and Orthodox Europe and, in due time, the pagan remainder of the world.

Catholics and pagans, however, were in some ways more accessible targets than was Russian Orthodoxy, which, since the Eleventh Century, had developed in almost complete isolation from the rest of Christendom. It was untouched by the intellectual and political structures of the classical world in which Christianity was born and upon which its historical and theological cast of mind and administrative habits were based. It followed that Orthodoxy approached questions of faith and order from directions quite other than those followed in the West, which they regarded as heartless and rationalistic. It was the absence from Russian history of any legacy from ancient Rome that gave Orthodoxy its supposed monopoly of the true faith. Slavophiles (a group who resisted westernization in favour of the primacy of traditional Russian culture) approved heartily of the fact that Russians had never lived under Roman law, regarding the civilization of that city as 'the triumph of naked and pure reason relying on itself alone and recognizing nothing outside itself'.[2] Rome's dominance, they thought, depended upon jurisprudence, a science that, far

---

1 This chapter will examine theological and liturgical differences and similarities between The Salvation Army and Russian Orthodoxy; their respective approaches to social work will be compared in Chapter 4.

2 I.V. Kireevsky, *Polnoe sobranie sochineii*, (1911) quoted in Andrzej Walicki, *A History of Russian Thought*, Stanford, Stanford University Press, 1979, p. 94.

from binding society together, had destroyed it by rationalizing and formalizing what ought to be organic social bonds. Catholicism, far from inhabiting what St Augustine called 'The City of God', had been corrupted by this evil, while 'Russia... spared this fatal heritage... was therefore established on purely Christian principles' and was 'held together by what was primarily a moral bond—a bond of convictions—that united the entire land of Rus' into one great *mir*,[3] a nationwide community of faith, land, and custom'.[4] (During the period covered by this book, however, the idea of a 'nationwide community' was increasingly exposed as an ideal which was falling apart.) This anti-rationalism made Orthodoxy comparatively uninterested in the history of Christian origins: that Jesus lived within the Roman Empire and Christianity was partly shaped by interreaction with the civil power was seen as almost wholly irrelevant. In consequence, Orthodoxy was in effect an ahistorical form of Christianity, its beliefs divorced from their original contexts in space and time. Hence its mystical character and its dislike of doctrines rationally apprehended and stated. Insofar as Orthodoxy sought the irruption of eternity into the temporal order, it was supposed to override time and history.

The western tradition of theological debate had little place in Russia, and many Russians would have regarded it as rationalist in spirit and therefore antithetical to the purpose of worship, which was to achieve communion with God. It followed that they did not regard the sermon as the principal source of teaching in religious life. In August 1839 the French writer and traveller, the Marquis de Custine, noted in a letter from Russia: 'The Russian people certainly has a reputation for great piety; but what is a religion about which it is forbidden to teach? There is no sermon ever given in a Russian Church: the Gospel would discover freedom to the Slavs.'[5] De Custine exaggerates: sermons were sometimes preached, but they had to be submitted for censorship in advance, a sufficient discouragement for all but the keenest preachers. He was right about freedom, however. In his novel, *Cathedral Folk* (1872), Nikolai Leskov has a character (admittedly a cynical and self-serving one) say:

> ...does Christianity make all men equal, or does it not? You know that the famous statesmen, so to speak, discerned mischief in the translation of the Bible into the vernacular tongue. Yes, sir, Christianity may easily be interpreted, you know, in a dangerous sense. And every priest may be such an interpreter[6]

---

3 *mir* can mean 'village community', ' world' and 'universe'.

4 Walicki, *Russian Thought*, pp. 94 and 96. As Walicki goes on to remark (pp. 105-08), Slavophile thinkers were aware that there was a wide gap between their idealized vision of the Orthodox Church, itself a form of conservative utopianism, and the reality. This, however, would never have convinced them that Western evangelists could perform any useful function in Russia.

5 Marquis de Custine, *Letters from Russia*, translated and edited by Robin Buss, London, Penguin Books, 1991, p. 153.

6 Leskov, *The Cathedral Folk*, trs. Isabel F. Hapgood), London, John Lane, The Bodley Head, 1924, pp. 225-26. I shall refer frequently to novels as evidence because in

The plot of the novel turns on a sermon preached by Archpriest Savély Tuberózov in which he proclaims that most of the worshippers listening to him are:

> ...crafty and lazy servants, and that their prayer is not a prayer but rather a commercial transaction, a traffic in the temple, beholding which our Lord Jesus Christ not only was troubled in His divine spirit, but taking a scourge of small cords, He drove them out of the temple.

> Following His Divine example, I reprimand and condemn this traffic in conscience, which I see before me in the temple. This mercenary prayer is repulsive to the church.[7]

Savély resists requests from higher authorities for an apology, but gives way when he is commanded to do so. Shortly thereafter he dies.

This distrust of free, rational interpretation underpinned two qualities of which political and religious conservatives would certainly have approved: incuriosity and passive acceptance of fate. The novelist and satirist M.E. Saltykov-Schedrin wrote of his fictional town of Glupov (a symbol of Russia at large) that:

> Travellers of the time all declared how astonished they were at the integrated character of life in Glupov, and they justly attributed this to the fortunate absence

---

Russia during the Nineteenth Century (and later) autocracy had the unlooked for effect of making fiction the only form of printed discourse which provided a platform for relatively free discussion of social, political, philosophical and religious questions. These could be related to the 'experience of the individual through the medium of narrative' and such narratives, read aloud *en famille*, stimulated intense debate, particularly about the movements in the souls of the characters. Novels were part of a continuous dialogue about social and religious matters, and Russian writers were conceived of as having a moral duty to guide and instruct society. Many novelists and poets conducted, in effect, a continuous exchange of ideas with the Gospels. Frequently, also, novels were a substitute for scientific writings on psychology. Neither readers nor writers ever lost sight of the fact that the oppressive state was a third, silent element in their dialogue. See Jones and Miller (eds.) *The Cambridge Companion to the Classic Russian Novel*, Cambridge, Cambridge University Press, 1998 pp. 2, 5-6, 88-9,139, 195 and *passim*. A related point is that, according to Nicolas Zernov, *The Russian Religious Renaissance of the Twentieth Century*, London, Darton, Longman & Todd, 1963, pp. 284-85, 'the vigorous search for truth zealously pursued by many Russians was carefully concealed behind the official facade of immobility and immutability. The books and magazines published under the auspices of Eastern Christendom's ecclesiastical authorities seldom reflected this side of Christian life. Men trained in seminaries and academies were discouraged from discussing contemporary problems. It was inevitable therefore that the genuine spokesmen of Russian Orthodoxy in the Nineteenth Century were lay writers who had no theological degrees and who were therefore less bound by the secular and ecclesiastical censorship so heavily imposed upon all formal orthodox pronouncements'.

7 Leskov, *The Cathedral Folk*, p. 309.

there of any spirit of enquiry. If the Glupovites could suffer the most appalling disasters with fortitude and go on living afterwards, this was solely due to the fact that they saw every disaster as something quite outside their control, and so inevitable.[8]

Orthodox Clergy

Good preaching, had it been wanted, would have required a better-educated priesthood than was reliably available. There was a widespread view, which The Salvation Army shared, that Russian parish priests were of low standing and calibre. This, however, is disputed. The journalist Harold Williams suggested that the general level was at least acceptable:

> The average priest is neither conspicuously devout nor conspicuously negligent; he is a hearty fellow with a broad accent, rather overburdened with the cares of his office and with family responsibilities.... sincere in his religious beliefs... There are not a few priests who delight in their office, who are full of a warm, simple faith, and who toil in poor parishes all their lives without any other object than that of doing good. The wonder, considering all the conditions of their service, is not that there are so few good priests, but that there are so many of them.[9]

But, as the final sentence implies, many were less good. The clerical salaries paid by the government were miserly, and in any case some priests were not salaried. All, therefore, had to supplement their income with whatever they could derive from cultivating a small holding of glebe land, together with what they could persuade their parishioners to pay for baptisms, weddings and funerals.[10] This necessity undermined their authority by making them appear to be money-grubbers rather than pastors. Another factor in their frequent lack of zeal was that the priesthood was effectively a caste; priests were commonly married to daughters of priests, and their children attended provincial seminaries to become clergymen or parish schoolteachers.[11] Vocation was less important than family tradition, and the priesthood was drawn from a narrow, generally undistinguished social stratum. Members of the nobility were discouraged by the state from becoming clergy, being more urgently needed elsewhere, while sons of peasants and artisans who felt a call to the priesthood were handicapped by the educational requirements, undemanding

---

8 M.E. Saltykov-Schedrin, (trs. I.P. Foote), *The History of a Town*, Oxford, Willem A. Meeuws, 1980, pp. 140-41.

9 Harold Whitmore Williams, *Russia of the Russians*, London, Pitman and Sons, 1914, p. 147.

10 Edward Acton, *Russia: the Tsarist and Soviet Legacy*, 2nd Edition, London and New York, Longman, 1995, p. 104.

11 Many common Russian surnames derive from clerical clans—Popov, Diakonov, Ponomaryon, Voznesensky, Arkhangelsky, Rozhdestvensky: Serge Schmemann, *Echoes of a Native Land*, London, Little, Brown, 1997, p. 118.

though these might be.[12] Consequently some village priests were indeed of poor calibre and could be accused of behaviour unsuited to their calling: drunkenness, venality and sexual irregularities.

Both the character of such priests and their failure to preach the word were of concern to Salvationists, who like other Protestants, were emphatically 'people of the book'. (This, in practice, meant the Bible in the King James translation, since few Salvationists had studied either Greek or Hebrew. The first of the Army's 11 points of doctrine stated that 'the Scriptures of the Old and New Testaments were given by inspiration of God and that they only constitute the Divine rule of Christian faith and practice'. Although this wording does not necessarily imply that every word in the Bible is inerrant and of equal standing with every other, it does make it clear that for the Army the Bible overruled the supposed authority of the Pope or any other church leader or council, and precluded the belief that adherence to church tradition was a guarantee of doctrinal purity.[13] This was taken to reduce virtually to vanishing point the necessity of those sacraments that had been instituted, as they saw it, by the church, not Jesus himself. As already noted, the Army went two steps further than most evangelical groups by dispensing with baptism and the Eucharist as well, on the grounds that these ceremonials caused division rather than unity amongst Christians.

The importance attached to the Bible was the root of the emphasis placed on preaching. The pulpit had always dominated Protestant churches, as did the lectern on the platform of a Salvation Army hall. Verbal communication was important in other ways as well. Apart from the necessity of preaching the word of God, other less formal forms of discourse helped promote the growth of Christian fellowship and allowed testimony to the active presence of the Holy Spirit within. Russian Orthodox services, for all their majesty, seemed to Salvationists to allow for none of these things, which to them were essential.

Important as they were, these differences regarding the way in which faith and doctrine were best communicated were trivial compared with the differences between Orthodox and Western understanding of what Christianity was and how it ought to affect the lives of believers. The Russian theologian Alexis Khomiakov had expressed this difference in a letter written to an English friend in 1846: 'All Protestants are Crypto-Papists... all the West knows but one datum a; whether it be preceded by the positive sign +, as with the Romanists, or with the negative -, as

---

12 Edmund Heier, *Religious Schism in the Russian Aristocracy, 1860-1900*, and Zernov, *Russian Religious Renaissance*, p. 45.

13 It is a moot point whether Salvationists at the time realized that, like the religious groupings whose idea of tradition they objected to, they also read and understood and preached the word of God according to a tradition—that outlined in the second paragraph of this chapter. Nor did they have any answer to the traditionalists' complaint that personal interpretations exposed churches to the risk of propagating error, or to the consequential objection that the principle of individual responsibility and freedom of conscience could lead to sectarianism and other disorders.

with the Protestants, the a remains the same.' [14] The shaping crises of western
Christianity had no parallels in Russian history. There had been neither Middle Ages
nor Renaissance, neither Reformation nor Counter-Reformation. The cultural
upheavals and religious conflicts, which overturned western Society during the
Sixteenth and Seventeenth Centuries, had touched Russia only distantly. Even Peter
the Great's attempt, in the Eighteenth Century, to open up his country to western
influence by building St Petersburg, his capital and seaport on the Baltic, had little
effect, so far as religion was concerned, outside a small circle of his fellow
westernizers.

It was fundamental to Orthodoxy that it was a national church of which all true
Russians were by definition members. Contrariwise, it was fundamental to
Salvationism that no-one could simply be born and baptised into the Faith and grow
within it as a matter of course. The Salvationist idea was more strenuous. Personal
conversion from the state of sin to the state of grace was *de rigueur* and must take
place at a specific, identifiable moment, the moment when, in Army argot, a person
'got saved'. The Army followed mainstream Protestantism in its reaction against the
doctrine that sacramental grace was conferred automatically by baptism, emphasising
instead the formula of 'justification by faith', to which Martin Luther had added the
word 'alone'.[15] Unless people accepted for themselves the forgiveness of God, the
sacrament was useless. It followed from the individual, personal nature of
Justification by Faith—or, as Salvation Army had it, 'by grace through faith in our
Lord Jesus Christ'—that 'he who believeth hath the witness in himself'. No-one
who had 'the witness in himself' needed formal ordination to preach the gospel to
others. All were ordained into the priesthood of all believers.

If Salvationism was built on the twin pillars of the Bible and personal salvation,
for Orthodoxy church tradition was the fount from which everything flowed.
Tradition included the Bible, but also the creed, decrees of ecumenical councils,
patristic writings, canons, service books and holy icons. Orthodoxy regarded itself as
strongly scriptural, but thought that the Bible derived its authority from the Church
rather than the reverse. Without each other, scripture and tradition were devoid of
meaning. It was through the life of the Church, rather than through the Bible or
personal experience, that Christ revealed himself to mankind, and the Church lived in
its rituals and observances, not in preaching, or Bible study. 'Fellowship', as
understood by evangelicals, might have struck Orthodox as a sentimental travesty of
their own central notion of unity, or *sobornost*, according to which the Church
'called all its members to loving cooperation and loving participation in its life, and
is opposed to every form of sectarianism, exclusiveness and submission to the rule

---

14 Timothy Ware, *The Orthodox Church*, Harmondsworth, Penguin Books, 1981, p.
9.

15 My analysis of the relationship between Protestantism and Orthodoxy owes much
to Muckle, *Nikolai Leskov and the 'Spirit of Protestantism'*, Birmingham, Department of
Russian Language and Literature, University of Birmingham, 1978, pp. 7-20.

of one person'.[16] In sum, while aware that tradition could become supine archaism, and despite the difficulty westerners had with the traditionalists' apparent unwillingness to distinguish what was obviously vital from that which was apparently trivial, Orthodox believed that tradition had to be accepted or rejected as a whole. When Old Believers clung passionately to the use of two fingers only when making the sign of the cross, they were not, as they saw it, being obsessive about a small detail. The gesture did not merely, in some outward way, embody the belief: Orthodoxy made so little distinction between the material and spiritual worlds that the two were inseparable. Russian worship was a matter of concentrated mystical searching, assisted by music, bells and icons. The practice of prayer embraced, in an essentially non-rational, almost non-verbal way, the true apprehension of correct doctrine.

The idea that individuals could decide for themselves what the Bible or church doctrine 'meant', or how the church ought to conduct itself, was obnoxious to Orthodoxy. Schisms and sects within Orthodoxy were impossible (those who differed were held by definition to have removed themselves from the fold), as was the notion that the Church could ever require reform. The Church was infallible when it expressed itself in ecumenical council on doctrine. The authority of the bishops who composed such councils derived from Christ through Apostolic succession. Although it was possible for the people to decide that a bishop's doctrine was incorrect, in which case they were absolved from their duty of obedience, such a procedure could never derive from the operation of an individual conscience, or an individual conviction of inner leadings or light. The people must be as conciliar as was the Church as a whole. The right of a parish to dismiss its priest was rigorously circumscribed.[17]

Common Ground?

Despite these very significant differences there were a number of points on which Orthodox and Salvationists might possibly understand each other, at least partially. The doctrine of Justification by Faith was not absolutely remote from Orthodoxy, which believed that man must strive to become God-like through the action of faith. That endeavour, however, should find expression in good works—an idea which Salvationists also embraced. However, the Protestant doctrine that man had no part in his own salvation was considered erroneously one-sided, justifiable only as a reaction against what Orthodox and Protestant alike regarded as the 'Catholic arithmetic of merit'.

Another potential point of sympathetic contact between Russians and Salvationists lay in the metaphor of 'fire' which both employed. What drove

---

16 Zernov, *Russian Religious Renaissance*, p. 71. As has been noted, the 'nationwide community of faith' implied by *sobornost* was increasingly revealed during this period as an ideal, not something achieved.

17 James W. Cunningham, *A Vanquished Hope: the Movement for Church Renewal in Russia, 1905-1906*, New York, St Vladimir's Seminary Press, 1981, p. 193.

Salvationists (whose motto, it will be recalled, was 'Blood and Fire') was the love of God the Father, the Salvation obtained for them by the blood of God the Son, and the fire of the Third Person of the Trinity, God the Holy Spirit. For Russians also, the Holy Spirit had come in the form of tongues of fire, to which the characteristic onion domes of Moscow churches were often compared. An essential traditional metaphor for the fusion of God and man in Christ was that of the infusion of fire into iron: heated by fire, iron itself acquired the ability to set aflame anything it touched. Fire had other connotations as well, which inspired both fear and fascination. For forest dwelling medieval Russians, and as far into modern times as 1812, in the wooden city of Moscow, fire had all too often signified catastrophic destruction. It was, at the same time, the source of warmth and light in a country which was frequently very cold and very dark. The lighting and extinguishing of fires for cooking and domestic heating traditionally required reverent silence. Salvationist preachers would have found this body of imagery instantly serviceable had they been aware of it—and may often have discovered, when eventually they came to address Russian congregations, that they had achieved a greater impact than they expected simply because they had unwittingly invoked it.[18]

There was also common ground on the subject of class-consciousness within the Church. Konstantin Pobedonostsev, the austere, professorial Procurator of the Holy Synod, the civil servant who ran the Church on behalf of the state, had seen Anglicanism *in situ* and contrasted it with Orthodoxy in terms some of which Booth himself might have used:

> In our churches all social distinctions are laid aside, we surrender our positions in the world and mingle completely in the congregation before the face of God. Our churches for the most part have been built with the money of the people... in all cases our churches are the work... of the whole people. The poorest beggar feels, with the greatest noble, that the church, at least, is his... the only place (how happy are we to have one such place!) where the poorest man in rags will not be asked, 'Why art thou here, and who art thou?'. It is the only place where the rich may not say to the poor, 'Your place is not beside me, but behind'.[19]

Salvationists working in Russia would later have been able to testify that Pobedonostsev was not being over-idealistic: they noticed the same easy mixing of classes in their own meetings. (They tended, however, as with other Russian characteristics of which they approved, to attribute it to an innate Russian spirituality, a quality which they thought had little to do with the Orthodox Church. Indeed, some remarks by Pobedonostsev about the mysteries of peasant religious faith almost seem to confirm their assumption.[20])

---

18 For a discussion of fire imagery see James H. Billington, *The Icon and the Axe*, London, Weidenfeld & Nicolson, 1966, pp. 23-26.

19 Konstantin Pobedonostsev, (trs. Robert Crozier Long), *Reflections of a Russian Statesman*, London, Grant Richards and Co., 1898, p.190.

20 See pp. 37-38 below.

But, although parallels (admittedly over-simplified) between Orthodoxy and Salvationism may be drawn at a distance by a detached observer, at the time they would have seemed (to Orthodox Russians at least) overstretched and absurd. The Salvation Army and the Russian Orthodox Church were so different in their understanding and practice of Christianity that neither could have recognised each other as fully Christian. The music hall familiarities of the Army would have seemed blasphemous, undignified and trivial to most Orthodox, while the mystical detachment and the social passivity of Orthodoxy, which accepted grinding poverty and insanitary living conditions as part of the natural order, would have seemed to the Salvationist a dereliction of duty. Russians might have agreed that it was the privilege of believers to be 'wholly sanctified' but would have been so far apart from Salvationists on the implications of that belief as to be completely out of touch. Salvationists would have been bewildered by the apophatic strand in Orthodoxy, which revived somewhat during the late Nineteenth Century, according to which God could not be known, described or understood in rational terms; that in its approach to God, as described by Dionysius the Pseudo-Areopagite, the soul enters a 'darkness beyond understanding' where it is 'wholly united with the ineffable'.[21]

Many of the issues dividing Orthodoxy from Protestantism were irreconcilable. A church cannot be both free and authoritarian; the clergy either have a special position or they do not; and correct performance of ritual is either essential or not. Orthodox rejected what they considered the rationalistic nature of Protestantism: the powers of reason could not attain the truth of God. Equally, its individualism suggested to them that it must regard truth as merely a matter of personal opinion. Yury Samarin, a leading Slavophile, wrote that Protestantism was 'reason, trying to find out a self-made truth for itself and sacrificing unity to subjective sincerity'.[22]

In 1963, Nicolas Zernov wrote about Russian and Western interpretations of man and of his place in the universe as follows:

> The West treats man primarily as the citizen of an organized society. A Russian Christian sees himself rather as a son of mother earth. He is the summit of the animal and plant world and represents the most advanced expression of cosmic life. For an Orthodox the Church is not a society or an institution but the fullness of creation, the completion in Christ through the Holy Spirit of the Divine plan for the universe. The church is Divine Wisdom, the plenitude, the pledge of the transfiguration of all beings and a source of victory over disunity, disease and death.[23]

Salvationists would have found the references to the Divine plan for the universe and to victory over disunity, disease and death almost common ground but the emphasis and priorities implicit in the rest would have seemed very strange.

---

21 F.L. Cross and E.A. Livingstone (eds.) *The Oxford Dictionary of the Christian Church*, (3rd edn.), Oxford, Oxford University Press, 1997, p. 88.
22 Quoted in Muckle, *Nikolai Leskov*, p. 22.
23 Zernov, *Russian Religious Renaissance*, p. 281.

Ironically perhaps, such matters as music, processions and a love of colour and spiritual excitement, which the two sides might be thought to have in common, marked the point of their widest separation. The Salvation Army was once described by an aesthetically-minded wit as an organization for Christians who dislike music, and although they would have disputed this indignantly, leading Salvationists felt conscientiously obliged to keep music and other aesthetic matters under rigorous control. These must never be allowed to distract the minds of the congregation from the preaching of the word. Elaborate liturgical use of music and the visual arts could only be regarded as unnecessary decoration of what ought to be unvarnished truths. Icons were regarded as equally unnecessary, if not positively idolatrous: the Army, although it was aware of the degree of illiteracy in Russia, did not readily connect it with the use of icons as a necessary means of teaching the faith to those who could not read.

Orthodox might likewise have described the Army as an organization for Christians who dislike religion. Father Bulgakov wrote, in 1925, that:

> Orthodoxy is first of all the love of beauty. Our entire life must be inspired by the vision of heavenly glory, and this contemplation is the essence of Orthodoxy... Russian asceticism aims at manifesting God's Kingdom on earth...[24]

Liturgical and visual beauty, words, music, painting and architecture were essential to Orthodox services. These 'prepare the soul for... encounter with God' and are intended as 'a vision of the spiritual world'.[25] Towards the end of the Nineteenth Century, the Synod provided funds to encourage the revival or establishment of good choirs in parish churches.[26] Icons, an essential feature of the visual beauty of the Church, were not regarded by Orthodox as infringements of the commandment forbidding the making of and bowing down to graven images,[27] since God, having become flesh as Jesus and therefore himself the creator of his own image for mankind to see, could be depicted without offence in an icon, which was not the image of God, but the image of the image.[28] It was the subject of the icon who was worshipped, not the picture itself nor the materials of which it was made. Icons were

---

24 Quoted by Zernov, *Russian Religious Renaissance*, 230-31.
25 Zernov, *Russian Religious Renaissance*, p. 275.
26 Cunningham, *A Vanquished Hope*, p. 44.
27 Exod. 20, 4-5.
28 See Jaroslav Pelikan, *The Illustrated Jesus through the Centuries*, New Haven and London, Yale University Press, 1997, 87-101 and Cross and Livingstone, *The Oxford Dictionary of the Christian Church*, pp. 815-16, for brief accounts of the iconoclastic controversy which resulted in this formulation. The Eastern Church led the way in the representation of biblical and divine figures in icons, which in its turn allowed the creation of some of the greatest works of western art. The Salvation Army does not use such pictures in worship or decoration of its halls, but may do so in material designed for Sunday school children. It did however, countenance the use of icons for a time in Russia: see pp. 189-91 below.

'books for the illiterate'.[29] They also, of course, illustrate the nature of the Orthodox faith: 'whereas the quintessential religious image of eastern Christianity was the icon of Christ the glorious God-man, that of the West was the crucifix, the symbol of Jesus, the Son of God, who had suffered and died like any other man'.[30]

The Peasantry: The Great Hope, the Great Unknown

These beauties of Orthodoxy were inescapably present, as Nineteenth Century visitors testify. Russia was filled with the sights and sounds of religious observance: tall churches with wooden, multi-coloured or golden domes; icons, displayed not only in churches, but also in houses, shops, restaurants, government offices, and railway stations; processions; the boom and clang of bells; the dark, intense harmonies of Russian liturgical music. What this meant in terms of popular belief has been much debated. Some argue that peasants were deeply religious, others that they were merely superstitiously afraid of what might happen after death, others still that Christianity and ancient paganism were inextricably mingled in their spiritual make-up.[31] Stories are told of peasants who lit candles to both St George and the dragon, and to the Devil as well as to God.[32] Pobedonostsev was as puzzled as anybody else:

> What a mystery is the religious life of a people such as ours, uncultivated and left to itself! We ask, whence does it come? and strive to reach the source, yet find nothing. Our clergy teach little, and seldom; they celebrate the service in the churches, and direct the administration of the parishes. To the illiterate the Scriptures are unknown; there remain the church service and a few prayers, which, transmitted from parents to children, serve as the only link between the Church and its flock. It is known that in remote districts the congregation understands nothing of the words of the service, or even of the Lord's Prayer, which is often repeated with omissions and additions that deprive it of meaning.[33]

---

29 The Russian attitude to icons was, however, strongly influenced by 'an intense awareness of God's presence *in matter*, which finds its special expression in the love and veneration of sacred objects'. (Zernov, *Russian Religious Renaissance*, p. 230.)

30 Charlotte Allen, *The Human Christ: the Search for the Historical Jesus*, Oxford, Lion Publishing, 1998, pp. 69-70.

31 Nicolas Zernov, *Eastern Christendom*, London, Weidenfeld and Nicolson, 1961, p. 24-27.

32 W. Bruce Lincoln, *In War's Dark Shadow*, New York and Oxford, Oxford University Press, 1994, pp. 61-62.

33 Orthodox services were conducted in Church Slavonic, which had been the literary language of Russia until displaced by Peter the Great. The celebrated opera singer Feodor Chaliapin, who began his career as a freelance church singer, remarks, of his first encounter with opera: 'As a choir singer I wasn't surprised by the fact that... sometimes words did not seem to make sense. For instance, I understood little of the actual words of the marriage service.' Maxim Gorky (as told to), trs. and ed. Nina Froud and James

Nevertheless, in all those untutored minds has been raised, one knows not by whom, an altar to the Unknown God; to all, the intervention of Providence in human affairs is a fact so indisputable, so firmly rooted in conscience, that when death arrives these men, to whom none ever spoke of God, open their doors to Him as a well-known and long-awaited guest. Thus, in the literal sense, they give their souls to God.[34]

The Salvation Army's conviction that it was needed by the Russian peasantry seems almost to be confirmed by the words of one of the most reactionary men in the country. In his comprehensive survey of Russia in the 1880s, *The Empire of the Tsars and the Russians*, Leroy-Beaulieu credits the peasants with a more specifically Christian faith; one that, again, would almost have made them likely recruits for The Salvation Army:

> The Russian peasant is almost the only one in Europe who still seeks for the pearl of the Gospel parable... He loves the cross, and this is the essence of Christianity. He not only wears it in brass or wood on his chest, but also rejoices in carrying it in his heart.[35]

It has to be said, however, that this idealized view took many severe knocks during the late Nineteenth Century. Dostoyevsky might argue that the peasants' yearning for the sacred outweighed 'their frequent acts of bestiality' but was nevertheless shocked by the sadistic violence with which they beat their wives.[36] In 1897, Chekhov shattered the myth of the gentle, spiritual *moujik* in *Peasants*, a story that was denounced as 'a sin before the people' by Tolstoy. (Tolstoy, as often, was blinded by his own strongly held, idealistic views: Chekhov based *Peasants* and his later, even grimmer, account of peasant fecklessness, dishonesty, rapacity and cruelty, *In the Gully*, on what he saw at and around his own country estate, Melikhovo, just south of Moscow, where he was recognized as a good and sympathetic master and, in his capacity as a doctor, gave his peasants free medical treatment.) While admitting that the circumstances of their lives—killing work, harsh winters, poor harvests, overcrowding—allowed plenty of room for excuses, Chekhov, using the idyllic scenery surrounding his fictional village of Zhukovo as an ironic backdrop, showed its inhabitants as shiftless, dishonest, filthy, drunken, coarse, superstitious folk who lived in mutual fear and suspicion and were their own worst enemies insofar as those who exploited them most were other peasants. (These

---

Hanley, *Chaliapin, an Autobiography*, London, Macdonald, 1968, p. 57.) During the 1890s liturgies in non-Russian languages were developed for use in non-Russian-speaking parts of the Empire (Cunningham, *A Vanquished Hope*, p. 45), although the Russians themselves had to remain content with Church Slavonic.

34 Pobedonostsev, *Reflections*, p. 138.

35 Anatole Leroy-Beaulieu (trs. Zénaïde A. Ragozin), *The Empire of the Tsars and the Russians*, Vol. III, New York and London, G.P. Putnam, 1896-1903, pp. 44-45.

36 Orlando Figes, *Natasha's Dance: A Cultural History of Russia*, London, Allen Lane, 2002, pp. 251-53.

predatory peasants—Chekhov's best known portrait of such a man is Lopakhin in *The Cherry Orchard*—were sometimes known as *kulaks*, a term never precisely defined but which, during the late Nineteenth and early Twentieth centuries, indicated a man whose energy and personality enabled him to dominate village assemblies and courts and accumulate wealth (they were often money-lenders) and—by buying the land of bankrupt nobles—property. To the surprise of many, most peasants did not greatly resent such men; rather, they aspired to emulate them. A.N. Engelgardt, an eminent agriculturalist, wrote that, 'the ideals of the *kulak* reign among the peasantry; every peasant is proud to be the pike who gobbles up the carp. Every peasant, if circumstances permit, will, in the most exemplary fashion, exploit every other'.

Chekhov's story reflected the advancement of a process, which westernizers thought inevitable and in the long run useful—the rise of commercial, industrialized cities and a corresponding decline into isolation and poverty in the villages—whereas for Slavophiles and Populists the idealized peasantry was at the heart of their vision of Russia. But although The Salvation Army's idealized notion of the peasantry was shared and endorsed by many Russians, it would need to find and face the darker realities, which lay behind the ideal, and exercise all of its forbearance if it was to make any impact upon them.[37]

Schismatics, Sceptics and Sects: Orthodoxy Divided

Sophisticated Orthodox believers lived worlds away from the peasants with their superficial Christianization and crude superstitions, and they embraced a range of conservative or liberal attitudes. During the Nineteenth Century, many educated or aristocratic Russians, although remaining nominally Orthodox, were sceptics, while others practised an intense inward piety. For some of the visionary thinkers of the early Twentieth Century,

> the Church was neither a refuge from the frustrations and conflicts of earthly life nor primarily a pledge of eternal salvation. They saw Christianity as the most dynamic and challenging force in the history of mankind, the main hope of men's liberation from enslavement to the blind forces of nature and the despotism of their deified rulers... a religion of salvation from their nihility, from the tragic impotence of earthly existence.[38]

---

37 See Anton Chekhov, (trs. Ronald Wilkes), *The Kiss and Other Stories*, London, Penguin Books, 1982, pp. 12-15, 49-81, 165-204; Figes, *Natasha's Dance*, pp. 255-57; Victor Terras, *A History of Russian Literature*, New Haven and London, Yale University Press, 1991, pp. 467-68; Richard Pipes, *Russia Under the Old Regime*, London, Weidenfeld & Nicolson, 1974, pp. 159-60, and *The Russian Revolution 1899-1919*, London, Fontana Press, 1992, pp. 729-30.

38 Zernov, *Russian Religious Renaissance*, pp. 298-99. Some of these ideas, as Zernov notes, were reiterated by Pasternak in *Dr Zhivago*.

There were, however, dissenters who, dissatisfied with Orthodoxy, had formed a number of schismatic sects. These, unlike the aristocratic dissenters in St Petersburg, whom we shall examine in chapter 3, owed nothing to western thought, and practised rituals which were often heretical, and in the more outlandish cases, wild, neurotic or Dionysian.

The Old Believers (also known as the *Raskolniki*) were amongst the most passionate of those who embraced the idea of 'Holy Russia', which had reached its zenith in Muscovy around 1650. They crossed themselves with two fingers rather than three and sang 'Alleluia' twice rather than thrice, on the grounds that these were the ancient Russian practices, as opposed to the newer Greek ones, which had been introduced by Patriarch Nikon in the Seventeenth Century.[39] They retained their beards and old-fashioned caftans, eschewed tobacco and orgiastic drinking. They encouraged frequent preaching. Although persecuted and subject to legal discrimination, they continued to attract converts from Orthodoxy. Some had to function without priests since proper ordination of Old Believer priests had not been possible since the schism. Others made do with renegade Orthodox priests, or, after the 1860s, those ordained by a cooperative Bosnian prelate.

The *Dukhobors* ('spirit-fighters') practised agriculture on Communist lines, refused to cooperate with civic authorities, interpreted the Bible and all Christian dogmas in a merely allegorical sense, and were inclined to remove their clothes in public. In conflict with the government since their beginnings in about 1740, they finally migrated *en masse* to Canada in 1899, assisted financially by Tolstoy (who donated the profits from his novel *Resurrection*) and the Quakers.

The *Khlysty* believed that to sin was to take the first step towards salvation, and practised flagellation and ecstatic dancing, which often erupted into orgiastic group sex. (It was alleged that Rasputin, the *soi-disant* holy man who would exercise so unhealthy an effect on the Imperial Family, had been a member of this group. Even if this is not the case, he could easily have come into contact with them, and some of his own activities suggest that he found their ideas attractive, particularly the notion that women were purified when they had sex with their religious leader.)

The Eunuchs, by contrast, practised castration, while *Molokans* drank milk (*moloko*) during fasts.

These dissenters were, of course, a blemish on the greatly prized *sobornost*, the religious unity of Russia, and their existence indicated that the reality of the Russian Church did not match its theory. Nonetheless, when we take into account the eccentricities of some sectarian beliefs and practices and the large numbers of Orthodox who were lukewarm about or ignorant of their purported religion, we can understand how it came about that while the Russians regarded themselves as the most purely Christian people on earth, William Booth and his Salvationists thought they were in desperate need of the gospel and proposed to 'invade' the imperial

---

39 Nikon attempted to establish, or, as he saw it, restore the primacy of the church over the state: this led to his fall from imperial favour in 1858, which cleared the way for the westernizing reforms of Peter the Great.

domains in order to bring it to them. But in addition to the theological differences between the would-be invaders and the invaded there were historical and constitutional barriers.

Orthodoxy, Nationality and 'Religious Freedom'

The Russian Orthodox Church, by far the largest of the four ancient patriarchates and 11 other autonomous churches which made up Orthodoxy (which had no centralized organization or leader but were in full agreement with each other on doctrinal questions) was a defining element of the ideological formula of 'Official Nationality', first enunciated in 1832 in response to the challenge of liberal ideas and nationalist aspirations within the Empire. The formula 'exalted the principles of Orthodoxy, Autocracy and Nationality'. 'Orthodoxy' was to be preferred to both 'the Voltairean scepticism of the Eighteenth-Century court and... the experiments with biblical fundamentalism conducted by Alexander I'. 'Autocracy' reinforced 'the notion of personal rule sanctioned by divine right', necessarily incompatible with either enlightened absolutism or radical reform. 'Nationality' stressed the unique character of the Russians—'trusting, faithful and pure of heart'—and therefore 'the inappropriateness of foreign political and social institutions for Russia'.[40] This romantically conceived cultural cement, it was hoped, would hold together the 80 million Great Russians, Ukrainians and Belorussians who comprised the members of the Orthodox Church, the majority of whom observed its rituals. It should be noted, however, that the census of 1897 recorded that only 43 per cent of the population of the Empire were Great Russians. The rest, the so-called 'minority nationalities' were alienated by the regime's identification with that 43 per cent and with the Orthodox Church.[41]

Leroy-Beaulieu, writing in 1896, sums up the constitutional position:

> Everybody is free to remain true to the religion of their fathers but not to make new proselytes. That privilege is reserved for the Orthodox Church alone; it is explicitly so stated in the text of the law. Everybody may enter that Church; nobody may leave it. Russian Orthodoxy has doors which open only one way... One article of the Code forbids Orthodox Russians to change their religion; another states the penalties incurred for such offences... The apostate forfeits all civic rights; he cannot legally own or inherit anything. His kindred may seize his property or step into his inheritance... It is a crime to advise anybody to abandon the Orthodox religion; it is a crime to advise anybody against entering it.[42]

---

40 See David L. Ransel, *Pre-Reform Russia*, in Gregory L. Freeze (ed.), *Russia, a History*, Oxford, Oxford University Press, 1997, p. 159.

41 Acton, *Russia*, p. 106.

42 Leroy-Beaulieu, *Empire of the Tsars*, pp. 512-13. Many of these provisions were restated vigorously in 1891 at a conference of Orthodox ecclesiastics from all 41 Russian episcopates, called by Pobedonostsev to consider how to prevent the spread of sectarianism, with which 28 dioceses were said to be badly infected. (See Robert Sloan

These provisions were relaxed in 1905, when it ceased, for instance, to be an offence to convert to another religion, but they remained part of the mental furniture of the Russian administration. Marc Szeftel remarks:

...in practice the legal condition of the church was not much changed after [1906]. On several occasions the government stated in the Duma that no change of any sort had occurred. If the relationship between church and state had been legally unclear before the October Manifesto, this and the 1906 constitution merely obscured things further.[43]

Proselytizing organizations such as The Salvation Army would, clearly, continue to face official and perhaps public hostility. Although, as we shall see, the Army found ways around these difficulties, it was only during the months between the February and October Revolutions of 1917 that Salvationists were able to operate in Russia as they operated in most of the rest of the world, that is to say, with public processions and openly advertised evangelical meetings. During the rest of the difficult decade, 1913-23, when it was at work in Russia, the Army functioned clandestinely, forced often to deny its own existence, fearful that a knock at the door at three a.m. would announce not a soul in spiritual or bodily need but a policeman.

There would have been no difficulty had The Salvation Army wished to establish a corps in St Petersburg for the benefit of Salvationists of foreign nationality who happened to live there. Observances by non-orthodox faiths were neither proscribed nor regulated, but all such faiths were classified by the Imperial Government as 'foreign confessions', and, as such, irrelevant to Russians. Foreignness was not much approved of by the conservative elements in Russian society. Tsar Nicholas II disliked his own capital, St Petersburg, because it was un-Russian and had come into being as part of the westernizing reforms of Peter the Great. His wife, a fanatical convert to Orthodoxy, brought emotional pressure to bear on him whenever she thought the Church was in danger. The Tsar, therefore, was unlikely to welcome The Salvation Army, even though members of the Imperial Family were among its patrons and friends.

The Third Rome

For many Russians, Orthodoxy was inextricably bound up with their assumption that, as A.J.P. Taylor crisply expresses it, 'Russia was the greatest, or even the only, Power in the world'.[44] Much of the reason for this derived from the belief that

---

Latimer, *Dr Baedeker and His Apostolic Work in Russia*, London, Morgan and Scott, 1907, pp. 189-91.)

43 Marc Szeftel, Church and State in Imperial Russia, in L. Nichols and Theofanis, George Stavrou (eds.), *Russian Orthodoxy under the Old Regime*, Minneapolis, University of Minnesota Press, 1978, p. 137.

44 A.J.P. Taylor, *The Struggle For Mastery in Europe 1848-1918*, Oxford, Oxford University Press, 1954, p. 445.

Russia's former capital, Moscow, was the 'Third Rome', divinely chosen to be the centre and bastion of the true faith. This idea, current since the Fifteenth Century, was vividly expressed in 1511 by Philotheus, a monk from the Eleazar Monastery in Pskov, in a letter to Tsar Vasily III:

> The Church of ancient Rome fell because of the Apollinarian heresy, as to the second Rome—the Church of Constantinople—it has been hewn down by the axes of the Hagarenes [the Turks]. But this third, new Rome, the Universal Apostolic Church under thy mighty rule radiates forth the Orthodox Christian faith to the ends of the earth more brightly than the sun... In all the universe thou art the only Tsar of Christians... Hear me, pious Tsar, all Christian kingdoms have converged in thine alone. Two Romes have fallen, a third stands, a fourth there shall not be..[45]

Although Philotheus may have been flattering the Tsar in order to retain his support, the notion he expressed was clearly an idea whose time had come and it remains, in various permutations, embedded in the thinking of many Russians to this day, especially those who constitute the hierarchy of the Orthodox Church. It reflected the fact that of the two forces which had brought the Russian state into existence—the fear of invading hordes from the east felt by the disparate tribes and peoples inhabiting the Russian plain, and the spiritual energy derived from the growth of monastic Christianity—Orthodoxy had survived longest. Blurring civil and spiritual power, Orthodoxy became, as Billington remarks, 'an uncritical and unreflective collective memory'.[46]

The notion of Moscow as the 'Third Rome' nourished a set of related convictions: that all other religious beliefs were inferior, that the fate of Russia and its government had universal significance, and that Russian Imperial expansion was morally justifiable. The same idea lies at the root of Russian xenophobia and, in particular, Russian anti-Semitism. Billington argues that the 'newly proclaimed chosen people felt hostility toward an older pretender to this title'.[47] Other factors involved were 'the eastward migration of a Western attitude and... peasant antipathy to the intellectual and commercial activities of the city'. Although Orthodoxy habitually used Old Testament imagery in thinking about itself, it rendered it anti-Semitic in the process. Ivan the Terrible, who was fond of reading the *Book of Kings*, thought of himself as Moses, sole leader of the chosen people, locked in battle with the Hagarenes and Ishmaelites (i.e., for his purposes, the Jews).[48] These attitudes survived the eventual fall of the Romanovs and would result in increasing purges of Jews, from the Russian population at large, from the Third International, and even from the Communist Party itself.[49]

---

45 Quoted in Billington, *The Icon and the Axe*, p. 58.
46 Billington, *The Icon and the Axe*, p. 62.
47 Billington, *The Icon and the Axe*, p. 72.
48 Billington, *The Icon and the Axe*, p. 75.
49 Perhaps it would not overstate the case to suggest that this Old Testament-fuelled anti-Semitism helped put a pickaxe in Trotsky's head in Mexico in 1940.

Although church and Tsarist government supported each other, the Tsar derived most advantage from the arrangement. Recognition of the Tsar as the champion and protector of Orthodoxy in succession to the Roman and Byzantine Emperors bolstered his standing, giving him quasi-divine authority. In return he defended the Church and gave it some practical and moral support, including, for example, payment of some clerical salaries. But (and this was a caveat uttered within as well as outside the church), the reverse side of the strength of Orthodoxy, its strong sense of community, was that it identified church and nation 'to such an extent that religious concerns become subordinate to national interests and ambitions; the Orthodox belief in the gradual transformation of society encourages submission to the dictates of the state and promises little encouragement to an individual stand in the defence of moral principles and social justice'.[50]

The relationship between Tsar and church is crucial to a question on which historians divide: the extent and plausibility of the movement for the revival of Orthodoxy during the decades before the First World War. In 1981, James W. Cunningham, writing under the imprint of St Vladimir's Seminary, New York, complained that:

> One of the common assumptions made by historians of pre-Bolshevik Russia is that the Russian Orthodox Church was a moribund relic of the cultural past, content to serve as a quaint but sometimes oppressive instrument of the Tsarist government. This traditional view of the church was fostered by anti-church intellectuals... [but] ...even the most cursory investigation [makes it] clear that the church was neither withdrawn, intolerant, quaint, nor as moribund as secular historians, Russian and western, Marxist and non-Marxist would lead one to believe. [51]

Early in the Twentieth Century a small but significant number of Russian intellectuals, influenced by the late works of Dostoyevsky and the philosophical writings of Vladimir Solovyev (1853-1900) demonstrated—against the tide of fashion and despite the anti-intellectualism of the Church—renewed interest in Orthodoxy. Solovyev was the leading figure in a disparate group known as the metaphysical idealists. He urged reintegration of fields of belief, knowledge and experience that had increasingly been seen as mutually contradictory: Orthodoxy and Catholicism, faith and science, body and spirit. He was especially opposed to the later thought of Tolstoy, which sought to repress human sensuality and creativity and, in a literary work written in the year of his death, he gave many Tolstoyan characteristics to the figure of Antichrist. Taken in conjunction with the Church's burgeoning desire to be more in charge of its own fate, this revival of intellectual interest might in time have stimulated Orthodoxy into becoming more active and outward-looking.

---

50 N. Arseniev, *Russian Piety*, London 1964, p. 89, quoted in Muckle, *Nikolai Leskov*, p. 19.

51 Cunningham, *A Vanquished Hope*, p. 9.

The Tsar and St Serafim

Meanwhile, towards the end of the previous century, the Church itself, spurred by Slavophile ideas and fearful of the growth of heresy and foreign influence, and, in the case of the younger, more energetic clergy, driven by a sense of what its own spiritual stature ought to be, began to resent the fact that although it propped up the state by proclaiming the virtues of Tsarist autocracy, it was allowed little in the way of initiative, let alone autonomy, in return. The Tsar and other members of the Imperial Family were wont to say that this or that could not be done because the Church would not allow it, but he consistently refused to allow it to develop its own self-governing *sobor* (council), a body that was proposed with increasing urgency after 1905. There is both a certain poetic justice and a certain arbitrary unfairness in the fact that while Nicholas's refusal to undertake reforms which might offend the Church was a factor in his downfall, the Church, unable to distance itself from his increasingly disastrous rule, was very nearly destroyed when he fell.

But in the first years of the century an important change of emphasis had begun in the relationship between the Tsar and the Orthodox Church.

As a modern scholar, Gregory L. Freeze, remarks, historians have traditionally thought of the Church, with its 'phalanx of reactionary clergy' and the 'opiate of pious submissiveness which it enjoined', as a conservative, stabilizing influence, and, as already noted, one of the four pillars upon which autocracy rested.[52] At the turn of the century it became at once more crucial in this respect, but was less willing to play the role expected of it. The other three, secular, pillars of Tsarist power—'the persona of the ruler, the prosperity of his subjects, and Russia's power in international affairs'—were visibly crumbling. Following defeat in the Crimea and the loss of gains made during the Turkish War of 1877-78 forced upon the Russians at the Congress of Berlin in July of the latter year, it had appeared to Alexander II by the time of his assassination in 1881 that 'unvarnished autocracy was no longer sustainable'.[53] His successors, Alexander III and Nicholas II, thought otherwise, but the famine of 1891-92 (during which, it was reported, peasants stripped thatch from barns and houses to feed starving livestock),[54] the industrial depression of 1901-03 and the country's defeat in the Russo-Japanese War of 1904-05, made autocracy seem ineffectual once more. Nicholas, although from time to time he asserted his autocratic rights (usually not very effectually), was withdrawn and domestic by temperament. Intellectually he was ill-endowed and poorly educated. He had received no training for the role of Tsar, since his father, Alexander III, thought him a 'dunce' and had decided to delay the ungrateful task until his son was 30.[55] As it happened, Alexander died unexpectedly when Nicholas was only 26,

52 Gregory L. Freeze, 'Subversive Piety: Religion and the Political Crisis in Late Imperial Russia', in *The Journal of Modern History,* June 1996, pp. 308-50.

53 Acton, *Russia*, p. 88-89.

54 Acton, *Russia*, p. 102.

55 Orlando Figes, *A People's Tragedy: The Russian Revolution 1891-1924*, London, Jonathan Cape, 1996, p. 17.

plunging him into a role for which he was comprehensively unfitted. By comparison with, say, Peter the Great and his father, he inspired no awe, and was derided as 'a pathetic provincial actor cast in the role of emperor, which did not become him'. His aunt's husband, the Prince of Wales, thought him 'as weak as water', with 'no character'. Kaiser Wilhelm II, his cousin, thought him 'only fit to live in a country house and grow turnips'. His appearance of imperturbability 'was in reality apathy—the indifference of a mind so shallow as to be all surface'.[56]

He tried, intermittently, to find a role for himself. In 1899, driven by economic stringency and the rising costs of defence, he astonished the world by issuing an invitation to the powers to join in a conference on arms limitation. The result, the first Hague Congress, was less of an impasse than had been expected, because the initially contemptuous delegates found themselves a little caught up by the peaceable aspirations of their various populations, but within months Britain was at war in South Africa, and other armed conflicts would follow, albeit all outside Europe. Nicholas had gained little moral credit and no strategic breathing space. In 1904-05 defeat by the Japanese (the first time an Asiatic country had been victorious over a European power) humiliated the Russians, still instinctively and passionately convinced that their country was 'the greatest, or even the only, Power in the world'. Meanwhile, agricultural and industrial crises made the Tsar's subjects feel poor when they thought they ought to be getting richer.

These secular disasters made the religious foundation of the monarchy all the more important, and it is clear that someone with influence over the Tsar realized as much, since there was, at this period, a deliberate attempt to revitalize it. This took many forms, but the most visible one was the canonization of new saints, a process which both Tsar and Church were capable of exploiting for their own ends. During the previous two centuries there had been only four canonizations; during the 20 years preceding the revolution there were six, with more in the pipeline when the monarchy fell in 1917. Some of these canonizations, given the low level of literacy in Russian villages, and the significance of saints in popular Orthodoxy, were intended to reunite the Russian people at large (as opposed to intellectual, aristocratic and establishment circles in St Petersburg and Moscow) in the conviction that the Tsar was a sacred figure. Others were intended by the Church to boost its own standing. Freeze argues that these ornately designed exercises in religious politics actually eroded the Tsar's authority, 'most overtly in clerical circles, but also (if less stridently) among the laity. As the Church 'espoused an alternative political culture, the Emperor embraced an alternative Orthodoxy'. Canonization itself was 'debased by scandalous intrigue and elevation of dubious candidates to sainthood'.

Freeze points out that 'despite stereotypical representations of the Church as the "handmaiden" of the state', Church/state relations had always been fraught with tensions. From the mid-Nineteenth Century onwards these tensions increased.[57]

---

56 Barbara W. Tuchman, *The Proud Tower*, London, The Folio Society, 1995, p. 230, and *The Guns of August*, London, The Folio Society, 1995, pp. 7, 56, and Chapter Five, *passim*.

57 Freeze, *Subversive Piety*, pp. 308-50.

Pobedonostsev played a reactionary role in these events, his attitude summed up in the literally chilling aphorism of K. Leontiev: 'We must freeze Russia to save her from rotting'.[58] He wrote:

> Faith is interwoven and interconnected with the roots and psychological characteristics of each different society. Union beyond this tribal realm, with some other church, would be impossible or totally false.[59]

This dry, legalistic, bureaucratic, disciplinarian civil servant seemed to senior clergymen to be violating, by extending his control over, the Church's traditional prerogatives and powers. These violations coincided, as the century approached its end, with concessions to Russian dissenters and foreign confessions. After 1900 the Church's fears intensified when government affirmed the principle of freedom of conscience and considered liberalizing the divorce laws, reducing the numerous religious holidays, adopting the Gregorian calendar and secularizing education. These ominous departures, however, were balanced by official reaffirmation of the importance of the links between Orthodoxy and autocracy: the rituals of the coronation, the liturgies on behalf of the Imperial family and the teaching that the Tsar was 'God's anointed'. Financial subsidy of parish schools and clerical salaries was increased. Nicholas himself expressed concern about these matters, as well as about dissolute monks, radical seminarians and the growth of factory production of cheap icons. The three-way link between autocracy, Orthodoxy and the people was additionally affirmed when, in 1903, 42 years after the event, a special liturgy was established, to be used each year on 18 February, in commemoration of the emancipation of the serfs.

This innovation was quite clearly political in its purpose, as was, in part, the canonization, also in 1903, of Serafim, a monk who had lived in Tambov province, some 250 miles south-east of Moscow, from 1760 to 1833. Empress Alexandra had been persuaded that if she placed herself under the protection of St Serafim of Sarov, and bathed in a spring which he had blessed, she would (having already given birth to four daughters) at last have a son—who would ensure the Romanov succession.[60] When it was discovered that no such saint was listed in the Orthodox calendar, but that there had been a monk of that name—a virtuous man at whose grave miracles had taken place—Nicholas instructed the Holy Synod to canonize him at once. Pobedonostsev told him that saints could not be created by Imperial order, but was informed in his turn by the Empress that 'The Emperor can do anything'.[61] Nicholas

---

58 Walicki, *Russian Thought*, p. 302.

59 Quoted by John D. Basil, in Geoffrey A. Hosking, (ed.): *Church, Nation and State in Russia and Ukraine*, London and Basingstoke, Macmillan, 1991, p. 136.

60 Tsar Paul, who disliked his mother, Catherine the Great, had ruled that the succession should be through the male line only.

61 See Andrei Maylunas and Sergei Mironenko: *A Lifelong Passion, Nicholas and Alexandra, Their Own Story*, London, Weidenfeld & Nicolson, 1996, pp. 228-30, from

was involved in every stage of the planning and execution of this exercise in 'high politico-religious theatre',[62] and considered it a brilliant success, which, along with the mood of the crowd, gave him an 'enormous lift'. He wrote in his diary:

> God is miraculous through his saints. Great is his mercy towards dear Russia; there is inexpressible comfort in the evidence of this new manifestation of the Lord's grace towards us all; let us put our hope in the Lord for ever and ever. Amen!

His description of the event is uncharacteristically emotional, although even in these inspiring circumstances he is not immune to bathos:

> During the procession, when the relics were brought out of the church of Sts Zosima and Savvaty, we carried the coffin [of Serafim] on a litter. It was an incredible spectacle, to see how the crowd and especially the invalids, cripples and unfortunates reacted to the holy procession. It was a very solemn moment when the glorification began and then the kissing of the casket. We left the church at this time, having stood for three hours.

At one point, having unexpectedly taken a short cut when walking to the monastery, Nicholas was mobbed by the peasants. People pressed around him, longing to touch his uniform, and two of his entourage had to lift him (somewhat against his will) onto their shoulders, where he was able to enjoy 'a veritable thunder of hurrahs' in comparative safety.[63]

Meanwhile, a paralyzed child, dipped by her mother into the stream where Serafim had bathed, had been instantly cured. Ever hopeful, at ten o'clock on the night of 19 July, the Tsar and Tsarina, under the eye of Cavalry Captain Garardi, bathed in the spring which was the source of the stream, as the captain reported in a coded telegram to the Director of the Department of Police. One year and 11 days later Alexei Nikolaevich, the long-awaited male heir to the throne, was born.

Despite this happy event, it is questionable whether the short-term hidden agenda, that of associating Nicholas with Serafim's aura of spirituality, was achieved. The synod, troubled by the degree to which Serafim differed, socially and spiritually, from the traditional archetype of a Russian saint, had been debating the case for his canonization since 1892, and resented the pressure placed on it by the Tsar and, still more, his failure to wait for their formal decision before pressing ahead with preparations for the event.

Meanwhile, the common people, shocked to discover that Serafim's body and mantle had decomposed, which seemed to them to disqualify him, were as unhappy

---

which the quotations from Nicholas's diary for 18 and 19 July, 1903, and the telegram from Captain Garardi, are taken.

62 Freeze, *Subversive Piety*, p. 314.

63 A.A. Mossolov, *At the Court of the Last Tsar*, London, Methuen, 1935, pp. 134-35. Mossolov uses the story as evidence that Bolsheviks were wrong to claim that 'the people never manifested any other sentiments towards the dynasty than those of envy and hatred'.

as the hierarchy, a situation that sparked off damaging controversy within the church and gave ammunition to its enemies. There were threats that Serafim's coffin would be opened for inspection of the contents: his skeleton, hair and beard, and his monastic clothing. The students of St Petersburg University opposed the celebrations, and revolutionary groups, fearful that the canonization would endorse the Tsar's authority and legitimacy, distributed scabrous leaflets to pilgrims on their way to the monastery at Sarov.

Staging the event entailed controversial expense. Why, the educated public wished to know, should the government spend an alleged 1,600,000 roubles on mounting the celebrations when basic necessities such as schools were neglected?

But although the Sarov Monastery was remote—60 kilometres from the railway station at Arzamaz, south of Nizhniy Novgorod, where the royal train arrived, something between 300,000 and half a million people attended the event,[64] causing the press to hail a spiritual union of Tsar and people and giving Nicholas and Alexandra 'probably the most uplifting religious experience of the whole reign'.[65] There was a price to be paid: the extremes of the Russian class system, instead of renewing their sacred sense of 'nationwide community', found themselves staring at each other in fascinated, uncomfortable close-up. A conservative newspaper wrote of the 'sadness and horror' of the crowd, the enormous number of sick and ailing, the blind, the deaf, the mentally retarded, 'holy fools', the infirm, epileptics, and the insane. Some crawled on all fours, others pulled themselves along on their stomachs. One was carried in a sack, another had an outsized head, and on every side were severe wounds, dirty bandages and the murmurings, cries and prayers of the masses as they were passed on the road by the gilded carriages of the fashionable. At the monastery itself, those who were used to starving continued to do so, since insufficient provision had been made. They also found themselves shut out of the ceremonies. Even after the elite had departed the police, who evidently had not consulted Pobedonostsev on the classlessness of Orthodoxy, kept them out of the churches. Their role was to line the streets and cheer, then go home.

Despite all this, however, Freeze's contention that the event was a failure, and that Sarov did not become a national shrine because the Russian sense of the sacred was essentially local, is unconvincing. Even if few bishops mentioned the event in their reports for 1903, there is plenty of evidence that Serafim was considered an important saint by Russians who went on pilgrimage and by historians of Orthodoxy. He is also widely recognized outside Russia. Indeed, ironically enough, the only interested party who failed to derive much advantage from the canonization

---

64 Robert L. Nichols, 'The Friends of God: Nicholas and Alexandra at the Cononization of Serafim of Sarov, July 1903' in Charles E., Timberlake (ed.), *Religious and Secular Forces in Late Tsarist Russia: Essays in Honor of Donald W. Treadgold*, Seattle and London, University of Washington Press, 1992.

65 Dominic Lieven, *Nicholas II, Emperor of All the Russias*, London, John Murray, 1993, p. 163.

was Nicholas himself, although he no doubt believed that there was a causal connection between the event and the birth of his son Alexis the following year.[66]

Father Gapon and 1905

However that may be, other advantages the Tsar may have hoped to gain from the event—improved relationships with the Church and the people—were dissipated by the events of 1904-06. The humiliating surrender of Port Arthur to the Japanese took place on 22 December, 1904. Ten days earlier, fearful that continued repression of religious minorities would lead to an increase in civil violence as the scale of the humiliation became apparent, the Tsar had issued a ukase promising religious toleration to such minorities as soon as the necessary legislation could be drawn up.[67] For churchmen of the more reactionary sort this was an ominous development, and the year which followed was dominated by a figure whose career embodied tendencies which concerned reactionaries and reformers alike.

Georgy Gapon was born in the Ukraine in 1870, to peasant parents who had been liberated in the emancipation of 1861. He grew up resenting the double dealing and tyranny to which peasants remained subject. (They might still, for instance, be flogged naked in public.) In 1885 he entered the Poltava Seminary on a government scholarship. His reading of the late works of Tolstoy and his dissertation, which compared the virility of Slavonic parochial life with the torpor of the Russian equivalent, provoked a warning that he might lose his scholarship; he pre-emptively renounced it. Later he was prevented from switching from the priesthood to medicine by an unfavourable reference from the seminary. He became a *zemstvo* (local government) clerk, read revolutionary literature and fell in love. Urged by his wife, he returned to the Church and was sent to a cemetery church without a defined parish, which he was soon packing with his sermons and his Eucharistic devotion. His wife's death after four years left him with two children to support and led to a recurrence of the depression, which affected him at various points during his life. He withdrew from priestly functions, but in 1898 Pobedonostsev and Sabler pulled strings and obtained him a post in the Petersburg Theological Academy, where he joined the Society for the Spread of Religious and Moral Enlightenment in the Spirit of the Orthodox Church. During a Crimean convalescence following a further bout of ill-health and depression he thought of retiring to a monastery, but his friends the writer Chekhov and the painter Vereschagin persuaded him that this would be escapist. In 1900 he returned to St Petersburg to devote himself to working with the

---

66 Approving accounts of Seraphim appear in *The Oxford Dictionary of the Christian Church* and *The Oxford Dictionary of Saints*.

67 Cunningham, *A Vanquished Hope*, p. 81. The account of Father Gapon which follows is drawn from Cunningham, pp. 83-94 and Dixon, The Church's Social Role in St Petersburg, in Hosking (ed.) *Church, Nation and State in Russia and Ukraine, pp.* 185-6, Figes, *A People's Tragedy*, pp. 174-9, Felix Patrikeef, in Harold Shukman (ed.), *The Blackwell Encyclopedia of the Russian Revolution*, Oxford, Blackwell, 1994, pp. 322-23, and Pipes, *The Russian Revolution*, pp. 22-25.

proletariat and Sabler secured him a dockside parish on Vasilevsky Island, where most of the parishioners were peasants recently arrived from remote villages in search of work.

From this time onwards his pastoral work became increasingly embroiled with workers' organizations on the one hand and the secret police on the other. Initially, although he was supposed to pass on any rumblings of political dissent which he heard in the confessional he did not do so. Convinced that there was more to be done for the workmen in his parish than preach temperance and sexual abstinence to those whose wives and fiancés were hundreds of miles away, he (apparently with Sabler's assent) turned the Society into a workmen's compensation organization. He was denounced to the Okrana, but nevertheless urged the Church to withdraw from cooperation with government-sponsored labour organizations. The government's response was to invite him to cooperate with the Ministry of the Interior. (They regarded him as a lesser evil than the Marxist revolutionaries.) This placed him in a dilemma. He had striven to avoid becoming a police agent, but to reject the government's overture might lose him the support of influential supporters such as Witte and Sabler.

He arrived at an arm's length *modus vivendi*, and in 1903 established the Assembly of Russian Workers, which, functioning under police protection, had within the year 11 branches comprising 9,000 members and perhaps ten times as many sympathizers. It had also been infiltrated by Social Democratic agitators, and its objectives tended to be expressed in an uneasy mix of militant demands and peaceable suggestions for economic reform.

In December 1904 the major Petersburg factories, led by the Putilov Works, determined to destroy the Association. Sackings provoked strikes, which, by 2 January, had paralyzed the capital. A proposed meeting between Gapon and the Tsar was evaded by the latter. Instead, in a series of victory or death mass rallies, Gapon organized a demonstration which, at any rate in appearance, was supposed to be of a traditionally Orthodox kind: processions of the cross bearing a petition to the Tsar (150,000 signatures were collected) would converge upon the Winter Palace from the Association's various headquarters around the city. Gapon appears to have believed that the Tsar would not refuse the legitimate demands of the people and that his soldiers would not attack a peaceful demonstration, especially since he ensured that women and children were placed at the head of each procession precisely to deter such attacks. He was mistaken.

On 'Bloody Sunday', in January, 1905, the cavalry charged the marchers and the infantry opened fire. At least 200 were killed and 800 wounded. Gapon said as people died around him, 'There is no God any longer. There is no Tsar'. The Revolution of 1905 had begun with an attack by the soldiers of the Tsar upon an organization funded and manipulated by the Tsar's government and led by a priest of the Orthodox Church.[68]

---

68 Estimates of Gapon's character and abilities vary widely—almost as widely as accounts of his death a year later. Having survived the attack on his group of marchers at

Reform Frustrated: Autocracy on the Slide

For the Church, one result of the months of upheaval, which followed, was that the Tsar, anxious to placate his potentially most loyal supporters, agreed in principal to summon a *sobor*, or council of the Church, to consider and implement reforms. However, when in March 1906 a pre-*sobor* commission was convened to prepare the ground, its debates demonstrated that reform-minded churchmen who thought state domination harmful to the Church were likely to make demands far exceeding anything the Tsar could conceivably be persuaded to concede. Their complaints were legion. The ruling, already noted, that sermons (unless entirely non-controversial) must be submitted for censorship before delivery, crippled the Church as spiritual teacher. Further, the state required priests to be supernumerary policemen and civil administrators, helping control vagrants and reporting political dissent; to act as registrars and statisticians; and to assist tax collectors, assistance which frequently led to the arrest or imprisonment of parishioners. If they failed to report any offence they might go to jail themselves. They had to promulgate imperial decrees, support the government's social, economic and foreign policies, and teach Russian children loyalty, deference and obedience to the Tsar and the great host of their betters.[69] Many clergy resented these provisions, and felt that when injustice was done their duty was to support their parishioners, not the civil authorities. Standardized policies handed down by the Procurator in St Petersburg often did not suit local conditions or needs and could not be implemented. In some areas they merely provoked further anti-Orthodox missionary activity by the sectarians.[70] Much Orthodox missionary work during the Nineteenth Century had been tainted by association with Russian imperialism: one missionary, the monk Spiridon, said that Christianity was made to seem 'a religion of horse-thieves'.[71] (After 1917, this identification with Tsarist imperialism was one of the Bolsheviks' justifications for their attacks on the Church.)

As well as imposing unwanted tasks, which diminished its spiritual impact, the state reinforced Orthodoxy's traditional conservatism and timidity in certain areas. It discouraged public statements on moral and ethical issues and attempts by

---

the Narva Gate, he went abroad, where he became a celebrity, wrote his autobiography and may have engaged in gun-running on behalf of the revolutionaries. Disillusionment radicalized him, and he was suspected of wishing to become leader of the revolutionary movement. On his return to Russia in December, however, he resumed his covert relationship with the secret police. In March 1906 he was killed when, according to Anna Geifman (*Thou Shalt Kill: Revolutionary Terrorism in Russia 1894-1917*, Princeton, Princeton University Press, 1993, pp. 65-66), a group of workers, former fervent admirers of Gapon, overheard him negotiating with his police contact, P.I. Rachovskii, at his summer cottage, and, convinced of his treachery, used a clothes line to hang him from the hallstand. Cunningham, Patrikeef and Pipes identify the killers as 'socialist revolutionaries', but Figes says they were 'agents of the secret police'.

69 Figes, *A People's Tragedy*, p. 63.
70 Cunningham, *A Vanquished Hope*, pp. 146-47.
71 Fernández-Armesto and Wilson, *Reformation*, p. 197.

churchmen to ameliorate social conditions. It opposed Bible reading by lay people. The Church, apparently so powerful, and believing itself the purest and most perfect in the world, guardian of a Russia unpolluted by false faiths, had neither independence nor any scope for initiative.

It followed that the pre-*sobor* commission had first to address the question of church administration. Some had little faith that reforms would be implemented. 'The Orthodox', wrote one of the more radical bishops, Antonin of Narva, 'wait in fear and anxiety to see whether the Apostle Paul will come forth once again, chained to the arm of the Roman centurion.'[72] The proposed administrative reforms were complex and potentially expensive. Should the Moscow Patriarchate (abolished by Peter the Great in 1721, when he humiliated the Church by imposing upon it alien, and, as many thought, virtually Protestant reforms) be revived, replacing the lay procurator with someone who would speak and act in the interests of the Church? Which bishops should have seats, permanent or revolving, on the *sobor*, when, as was expected, it began to meet at regular intervals? How, in the presumed absence of state support, would such meetings be financed? Should the church be governed by its bishops, as those who adhered to ancient Byzantine canons insisted, or, as some Slavophiles argued, be made more democratic, even Presbyterian?[73] Those who opposed lay participation in church government pointed to the example of the newly constituted Russian parliament, the Duma, which seemed to be divided against itself. It would be tragic if the *sobor* were to spread discord rather than unity.[74]

These debates, the regrouping within the Church which followed the resignation of Pobedonostsev,[75] and the turmoil in society at large following the events of 1905, put a brake on the movement towards reform to such an extent that the debaters were urged to resolve the issues quickly so that the *sobor* could meet soon. They did indeed 'resolve a staggering number of issues in a relatively short time in 1905 and 1906',[76] but they lacked the political foresight which might have given them a still greater sense of urgency. In 1907, when he could have summoned a *sobor*, Nicholas chose not to do so, fearing that the Church might become the voice of the people:

The state feared an open forum in the Church... as in all other spheres of political and social activity, and, above all... that the Church itself would become politically

---

72 Zernov, *Russian Religious Renaissance*, p. 66.

73 See the Opinion on Church Reform January 1906, by the Bishop of Saratov, in Gregory L. Freeze, *From Supplication to Revolution: A Documentary History of Imperial Russia*, Oxford and New York, Oxford University Press, 1988, *pp.* 229-31.

74 Cunningham, *A Vanquished Hope*, pp. 154, 214, 228, 249, 269 and 277-78.

75 Zernov, *Russian Religious Renaissance*, pp. 65-66. Pobedonostsev first upset Nicholas by being worsted in argument with the reformist Prime Minister, Witte, in 1903. Subsequently, in March 1905, he was too ill to attend a meeting of the Synod, and his deputy, V. K. Sabler, was unable to prevent the bishops from petitioning the Tsar to summon a *sobor*. This unexpected defeat led to Pobedonostsev's resignation. Sabler will appear in our story again in connection with William Booth's visit to St Petersburg.

76 For this and the following quotation see Cunningham, *A Vanquished Hope*, p. 328-29, also pp. 104-05, 206-07, 210-11, 214, and 216-18.

antagonistic. So the brief dawn of hope for Church emancipation was deliberately darkened.'

The *sobor* did not meet until 1917, after Nicholas had abdicated.

Meanwhile, some Orthodox clergy were pursuing related ends by overtly politically means. After 1905 priests elected to the Duma, moved by 'feelings of anxiety over religious disaffection, concern for the people's material welfare, and overt sympathy for the political liberation movement'[77] were often critical of the government. Even the hierarchy, which remained broadly conservative, with patches of fierce reaction (especially when lay people, such as Leo Tolstoy—whose international eminence did not protect him from excommunication—urged it to consider social problems as well as nice points of liturgical practice), was growing increasingly distressed by 'irreligious tendencies in lay society and by the state's wanton intrusion into ecclesiastical affairs'. In 1905 two archpriests, nine priests, five deacons and seven sacristans in the Yalta district signed Resolutions in which they announced, *inter alia*, that, in praying, as enjoined, for the governing authorities, they prayed for the Tsar but not the autocrat. They called for internal church reforms: some of the clergy did not live up to the demands of their office, thus arousing 'animosity toward the clergy and even the divine Church'.[78] In June 1906, clergy from the 1st Superintendency of Sarapul'sk District, Viatka Diocese, sent a telegram to the Duma, hoping that the Lord would help it bring about 'freedom of speech, conscience, assembly, association, press, petition and the inviolability of person and residence' and demanding 'a complete amnesty, abolition of capital punishment, and resolution of the agrarian question in accordance with the wishes of the people'.[79]

However, it was a peculiarly Russian feature of the ferment of the second half of the Nineteenth Century and the first decade of the Twentieth that for most people it did not promote secularization of consciousness. Of course some political rebels, like Lenin, believed that the only true position in all human affairs was a materialist one, that all worship of a divinity was necrophily, and that all modern religious organizations were 'instruments of bourgeois reaction that serve to defend exploitation and to befuddle the working class'. But even some Marxists thought otherwise. Lunacharsky, for example, who was to become the first Soviet People's Commissar for Popular Enlightenment—in effect Minister of Education and Culture—made a careful study of Christianity. It had reached its peak, he thought, under Augustine, and at that time had been the ideology of four conflicting classes: proletarians, traders, aristocracy and ecclesiastical hierarchy. Its aim, he concluded, was 'to give relief from the sorrows of earthly life to the worn out human heart'. It resolved the conflict between the laws of life and the laws of nature. Unlike Lenin,

---

77 For this and the following quotation, see Freeze, *From Supplication to Revolution*, p. 228.

78 Freeze, *Supplication*, pp. 234-35.

79 Freeze, *Supplication*, pp. 237-38.

he thought this no bad thing, and devoted much time and energy to an attempt to synthesize Marxism and religion.[80]

Many non-Marxists, such as the poet Zinaidia Gippius,[81] couched political criticism in explicitly religious terms. In 1901, with her husband Dmitri Merezhovsky, she established the Religious Philosophical Society, the aim of which was to reconcile the Orthodox Church and the Russian intelligentsia. Autocracy, she asserted, was a blasphemy, a perversion of those very religious conceptions from which it claimed its legitimacy. While she accepted that some of the Orthodox representatives who attended meetings 'believed blindly, in the old way, with true childlike holiness', she dismissed others as 'half-believing prelates and real bureaucrats' and 'totally uncultured', a defect which was 'impossible to repair'. Her scorn of them led her, mischievously, to attend meetings in a black dress whose many pink-lined pleats separated whenever she moved, giving the impression that beneath it she was naked, but nevertheless, for Gippius, as for many thoughtful Russians, the traditional 'cursed questions'–love, death, God and immortality, were still at the root of all others. She and her husband were 'Maximalists', who sought reconciliation between 'Christ and the world, church and society, God and man' and, in the situation in which they found themselves, reconciliation between the intelligentsia, Orthodoxy and the Russian people at large.[82] But they were only one of many groups within the intelligentsia, which was so argumentative and fissiparous as to be inherently incapable of producing a united front.

It is clear, then, that at the time when The Salvation Army was beginning to think seriously about working in Russia, relations between the Tsar and the principal surviving pillar of his regime, the Church, were in a state of agitated disorder, which, in the case of some clergy remained only a few degrees short of overt hostility. It might have seemed that Orthodox Russia was tottering, ripe for conquest by the uniformed front line troops (as they saw themselves) of the Protestant west. The religious situation in Russia, however, was more complex (and, in a somewhat stuck-in-the-mud fashion, more stable) than that.

Orthodoxy, whatever its failings as an institute of Christian teaching, however slack its apparent hold on many of its members, especially the intelligentsia, enjoyed a self-confident assurance of its own universal mission. It would not stand idly by while its adherents were proselytized. If pushed, it would assert that as the one true embodiment of Christianity it could not allow its adherents to profess Salvationism while continuing within its fold. The issue of its ability to absorb *quasi*-Protestant teaching, discussed by both Dostoyevsky and Leroy-Beaulieu, would be put to the test so far as The Salvation Army was concerned in 1915. Colonel Larsson, the Swede under whose aegis the Army was first (albeit unofficially) active in Russia, describes how Salvationist converts often maintained, for some months

---

80 See Christopher Read, *Religion, Revolution and the Russian Intelligentsia 1900-1912*, London and Basingstoke, Macmillan, 1979, pp. 80, 83, 90 and 93.

81 More properly 'Hippius' but I will use the most common spelling.

82 Paul R. Valliere, The Idea of a Council in Russian Orthodoxy in 1905, in Nichols and Stavrou (eds.), *Russian Orthodoxy under the Old Regime*, pp. 191-92.

and with his assent, Orthodox practices (including confession).[83] In the event, neither the Salvationists nor their Orthodox priests were eager for this situation to continue for long. The Salvationists realized that they were not welcome at confession in their Salvationist uniforms, while Orthodoxy's apparent willingness to absorb did not imply toleration, but at best a sense that, whatever the details of their beliefs, all must be Orthodox. Had the Army survived long enough to contest this issue with the Orthodox Church, the situation would have been one of great difficulty.

The Salvation Army, glorying as it did in its internationalism, was also set on a course of inevitable collision with the Tsarist state. Tsars naturally deplored the notion that there might be any organization of significant size within their Empire which owed allegiance elsewhere. This had always been one of their objections to Roman Catholicism.[84] As Leroy-Beaulieu remarked, 'Russia's system in regard to alien religions is to corner them and keep them down'. It sought to impose on all cults within the Empire a bureaucratic organization similar to that of the Orthodox Church, centralized, and under Russian control rather than that of any foreign organization or government. It was inconceivable that the state would ever willingly abdicate its authority over the clergy.[85] Clearly the same would apply, *mutatis mutandis*, to Salvation Army officers, should their numbers and influence ever become significant.

Equally, when it determined to begin work in Russia, The Salvation Army had objections to Orthodoxy, which were clear and fundamental. Orthodoxy did not demand personal conversion as a condition of salvation. It did not accept the priesthood of all believers. It lived by its traditions, rather than by the sole authority of the Bible. It did relatively little to discourage drunkenness, gambling and other social evils. It enjoined resignation to the miseries and abominations of earthly existence. The splendid visual and aural effects of its services were merely so much magnificent but unnecessary decoration of the liturgy—which few Orthodox could understand and in which, therefore, few could participate.[86] Although Salvationist officers were trained not to engage in polemics against other faiths, these attitudes were bound to become known and constitute a source of friction.

But it was not necessarily impossible for The Salvation Army to function in Russia. Many Russians were beginning to suspect that the ecclesiastical and liturgical preoccupations of the would-be reformers would not touch those Russians

---

83 See pp. 197-99 below.

84 Tsar Alexander I (1801-25) was to some extent an exception, and in any case the Eighteenth-Century Tsars were not nearly so enamoured of Orthodoxy as were Nicholas II and his wife. Freemasonry, although originating elsewhere, was only intermittently perceived as a threat to the state, since it was not particularly identified with either any other specific nation or with a desire for political power.

85 See Leroy-Beaulieu, *Empire of the Tsars*, pp. 516, 521 and 547.

86 Something Orthodoxy and the Army had rather curiously in common was that the former had earlier allowed women to become deaconesses, who fulfilled an important function until 'the pressure of Islam led to the disappearance of the order'. See Zernov, *Russian Religious Renaissance*, p. 80.

who felt that Orthodox spirituality was not for them. Something less formal and abstract, more closely related to the practicalities of everyday life, was needed.[87] The novelist and religious thinker Nikolai Leskov reported that the prayer book was considered 'rather out of date' and seemed to many 'not to express those feelings which they wish to express in prayer'.[88] Many who thought in this way regretted the fact that for Russians there was no legal alternative to Orthodoxy. Many aristocrats would have become Catholic had that been possible, while much of the peasantry, given the chance, would have defected to the Old Believers. The ideal of the 'nationwide community of faith' was visibly crumbling. Meanwhile, Liberal Orthodox were striving to develop a more active social ministry of social work among the poor and sick, charitable assistance and popular education.[89] They were likely to be interested in a movement which had earned respect in most of these fields.

Secondly, so far as the constitutional impasse was concerned, theory and practice did not altogether coincide. The Tsar's attempts to protect orthodoxy were ineffectual and seldom met with the Church's unqualified approval. In the fashionable salons of the capital, opposition to autocratic tradition in matters of politics, administration, society, culture and religion was a constant subject of gossip and debate. In any case the autocracy was to some extent theoretical rather than actual. The theory was that under an all-powerful Tsar, the Church, the military, the bureaucracy and the police ensured total compliance with a system which subordinated everyone, both as individuals and as members of classes within society, to clearly defined rules about how they should act and what they should believe. The reality was patchy. Given Russia's sheer size, and despite rising standards, the bureaucracy was too small, inadequately financed, and lacked a clear chain of influence and command. Overlapping jurisdictions and agencies—ad hoc, unsystematic outgrowths of the Tsar's personal power—competed perpetually and inefficiently with each other. As early as 1882, Pobedonostsev had complained to the Minister of the Interior that the civil censor had authorized publication of Bunyan's *The Pilgrim's Progress* and 'peculiar pamphlets' on religion without consulting the clerical censor. At any level within this warren of ministries, normal administrative rules might be ignored by those with friends at court. A later Minister of the Interior, A.A. Khvostov, complained that provincial governors could easily sabotage his department's work: 'One has an aunt who is friendly with the Empress, another a gentleman-in-waiting for a relative, and a third a cousin who is Imperial Master of the Horse'.[90]

It might appear, then, that the beginning of the new century was an ideal time for William Booth's soldiers to arrive in Russia. Here was a country reputedly

---

87 More frivolously, perhaps, some were reluctant to stand through services which might last for several hours.

88 Nikolay Leskov (trs. and ed. James Muckle, *Schism in High Society: Lord Radstrock and His Followers*, Nottingham, Bramcote Press, 1995, p. 36.

89 Valliere, Theological Liberalism and Church Reform, in Hosking (ed.) *Church Nation and State in Russia and Ukraine*, p. 118. See pp. 90-94, below.

90 Figes, *A People's Tragedy*, p. 45.

'naturally' religious, in which nevertheless a minority was significantly discontented with its traditional religion. Those within it who thought themselves progressive were inclined to look westward in search of a way forward. And, finally, thanks to the activities of an eccentric English nobleman, The Salvation Army would find a western-style evangelical group already in place, eagerly awaiting its arrival.

CHAPTER 3

Lord High Evangelist

Radstock on the Neva

Improbably, The Salvation Army was able to call upon enthusiastic and apparently influential support from prominent members of Petersburg society, including members of the Imperial Family and aristocrats. These were Radstockites (later Pashkovites), members of a group of Evangelical Christians, which had come into existence during the 1870s.[1] Radstockism had attracted considerable attention in its day, and three of Russia's major writers, Tolstoy, Dostoyevsky and Leskov, had written extensively about it. Its history not only explains why The Salvation Army was welcomed by Russians of some social standing, but also illustrates the obstacles confronting Western evangelical movements which wished to establish themselves permanently in Russia.

Granville Augustus William Waldegrave, Third Baron Radstock (1833-1913), was educated at Harrow and Balliol. While serving as Colonel Commandant of the West Middlesex Volunteers he visited the Crimea, was stricken with a fever and, following his recovery, became an evangelical Christian. In 1859 he visited the United States, where he was impressed by the advertising technique of repeating simple formulae 'addressed not to the mind but to the unconscious', and determined to apply it to Christian evangelism. His evangelical message was similar to that proclaimed by William Booth. Radstock 'preached a strong emphasis on faith over works... The core of his message was Salvation; God so loved the world that he gave his only begotten son to redeem it and God's love and Jesus's sacrifice provided for believers assurance double sure of redemption. Christians, therefore, should put aside their accumulated ecclesiastical differences, abandon vain efforts to reason too much about religion, and in their love for one another try to emulate God's love for them.[2]

---

1 The appellations derive from the names of Lord Radstock and his helper and successor, V.A. Pashkov.

2 Hugh MacLean, *Nikolai Leskov: The Man and His Art*, Cambridge (Mass.) & London, Harvard University Press, 1977, p. 332. For Radstock's life, see David Fountain, *Lord Radstock and the Russian Awakening*, Southampton, Mayflower Christian Books, 1988, Mrs Edward Trotter, *Lord Radstock, an Interpretation and a Record*, London, Hodder & Stoughton, n.d., and MacLean, *Nikolai Leskov*, pp. 300, & 331-50. Unlike Lord Shaftesbury, Radstock approved of The Salvation Army, and in 1897, when it began work in Itchen, near his estate and its members were pelted by the crowd, he 'stood by them and it was never repeated'. He opened the corps hall in North East Road in 1987. (Fountain, p. 58). The Radstock estate has now been taken over by the City of

Orthodox Russians found this simple theology mistakenly limited, and even those, such as the novelist and religious thinker Nikolai Leskov, who objected neither to Radstock's foreignness nor the fact that he was not ordained, subjected it to searching criticism.

In the winter of 1873-74, aged forty, Radstock made the first of three visits to Russia as a preacher, at the invitation of a great lady who had heard him in France.[3] For ten to 15 hours daily he moved from salon to salon, preaching (ramblingly, in imperfect French) to the upper classes.[4] His followers remained initially within the Orthodox Church,[5] although he regarded Orthodoxy as a transitional stage towards the true faith: Orthodox, in his view, had yet to find Christ.

Radstock's impact on Russian society, particularly Russian society women, is not altogether easy to explain, even given that in St Petersburg at the time society and the court were fascinated by religious novelties such as spiritualism, theosophy, the occult and the supernatural. Séances and ouija boards joined other rituals of social life. In *Anna Karenina*, Tolstoy indicates that noble ladies might be adherents of both spiritualism and Radstockism. Even Karenin, the heroine's sceptical husband, is assumed to be acting under the influence of a French spiritualist—'in his real or pretended trance' —when he decides not to grant Anna a divorce. Educated Russians felt at ease in embracing Orthodoxy, paganism and rationalism simultaneously.[6] As we shall see, some were happy to add Salvationism to the mix.

In this overheated atmosphere, generated by *ennui* and a sense of moral disequilibrium in high society, the factor that especially favoured Radstock's evangelicalism was the perceived shortcomings of the Orthodox Church, in particular its paucity of teaching and preaching. Leskov, in his substantial, by no means

---

Southampton. The former British Cabinet Minister, William Waldegrave, is a member of another branch of the family.

3 His exact date of arrival is not known. See James Muckle's Introduction to Leskov's *Schism in High Society*, p. 3. Leskov (p. 104), states that it was Yuliya Denisovna Zasetskaya who invited Radstock to Russia. Mrs Trotter opts for 'a certain Grand Duchess', while Heier, (*Religious Schism in the Russian Aristocracy*, p. 34) thinks it was probably Mme. Chertkova, as does William B. Edgerton (*Leskov, Pashkov, the Stundists, and a Newly Discovered Letter*, in Gerhardt, Weintraub, & Winkel (eds.), *Orbis Scriptus*, p. 188 n. 6). Princess Natalie Lieven has also been suggested.

4 During 1877-78, according to Heier, p. 51, he was conducting meetings in 'no less than 40 aristocratic homes'.

5 To many of them the new teaching was merely an intensification of their existing faith, a spiritual enrichment of what Orthodoxy offered. This dual adherence, however, did not last. Such traditions of Orthodoxy as the veneration of saints and the Virgin Mary were eventually neglected. See Heier, *Religious Schism in the Russian Aristocracy*, pp. 54-55. Larsson describes a similar process in Salvationist converts: see pp. 189-91.

6 Figes, *A People's Tragedy*, p. 29, Kochan, *The Last Days of Imperial Russia*, London, Weidenfeld & Nicolson, 1976, pp. 43-44, and Tolstoy, *Anna Karenina*, Part 7, chapters 21 and 22.

unsympathetic essay,[7] attributes initial interest in him to the fact that 'many active women found themselves bored with nothing to do'. Some people of high standing felt the need 'if not fully and seriously to repent, then to toy with repentance. Radstock's arrival at such a moment could not have been better timed: and he got going very quickly'.[8]

Leroy-Beaulieu develops, more waspishly than Leskov, the theme of boredom in Petersburg society:

> Simple, primitive natures are not alone tormented with the longing for religious renovation. In the higher classes, among the cultured and hyper-refined, there are found souls hungry for truth and disgusted with the staleness of the traditional viands served by the official clergy on its ponderous golden plate... [Towards the end of the Nineteenth Century] Petersburgh [sic] society, half detached from Orthodoxy, seems at times possessed with a craze for getting up some other creed... it is usually abroad that the epicures look for their spiritual nourishment..

> In the capital, the imperial residence, the stirrers of souls could not be plain Protestant ministers or common German colonists. A very different prophet was needed for so fastidious a public. And lo! the Word of God was brought to them by an English lord... He delivered his familiar homilies at evening receptions, at five-o'clock teas, just as the popular prophets held forth in taverns, around the steaming samovar... the evangelical seed sprouted vigorously, for all that it fell on carpeted floors.

> It would be unjust to look on... *Radstockism* merely as one of fashion's vagaries. Lord Radstock made his appearance in Petersburgh in 1878-79, at a most unquiet time, at the beginning of the nihilist crisis, when many were the souls which, having gone astray, were seeking comfort and guidance... Radstock... avoided all semblance of dogmatical controversy, merely commenting on the gospel... the success of this drawing-room revival was due principally to the fact that it answered a spiritual need too long neglected by the Orthodox clergy. Since the priests would not preach, laymen preached in their place...

> So long as *Radstockism* was confined to the privileged classes, the government did not pay much attention to it. If there is freedom anywhere in Russia, it is in the drawing room. It was different when the propaganda passed from the dress coat to the sheepskin.[9]

---

7 Leskov, *Schism in High Society,* although ostensibly a largely adverse criticism of Radstockism, is more especially a critical account of the inadequacies of the Orthodox Church, of which by 1875 he was no longer a 'convinced' adherent. Heier, (*Religious Schism*, p. 71), reports that Radstock himself was said to have liked Leskov's book 'immensely', although Edgerton, *Orbis Scriptus*, p. 192, wonders how 'Lord Radstock arrived at any opinion at all about a book written in a language he could not read'.

8 Leskov, *Schism in High Society*, pp. 74 and 104-05.

9 Leroy-Beaulieu, *The Empire of the Tsars and the Russians*, vol. iii, pp. 470-73. He is apparently referring to Radstock's third and final visit.

To a detached observer the Church's shortcomings were balanced by those of Radstock himself. He was not, superficially, an especially engaging personality, as Leskov makes clear:

...not only is he far from handsome and elegant, but he lacks what is termed 'presence'. Radstock is of medium height, stocky and muscular; his face may be described in the words of the Russian saying: 'badly styled, but firmly stitched'. His hair tends towards ginger and he has rather pleasant gentle grey-blue eyes... Radstock's gaze is direct, clear and calm. His face is for the most part reflective, but sometimes it becomes very gay and humorous, and then he laughs, sometimes quite loudly, with a sonorous and carefree child's laugh. His manners are lacking in any excessive refinement... his way of collapsing onto sofas and loafing around on them is not entirely proper and has a bad effect on some people...

His salutation when he meets a friend is contrived and always the same: 'How are you spiritually?' Afterwards the second question is: 'What news for the glory of the Lord's name?' Then he takes a Bible out of his pocket, opens it at random, and begins to read and expound it...[10]

When he knelt at a chair to pray, his short jacket rode revealingly up his back; his genteel lady acolytes bit their lips in order not to laugh. His preaching induced Leskov to muse wryly upon the apophthegm that 'it is possible to enjoy all forms of literature except the boring':

...it is impossible to listen to Lord Radstock with anything approaching pleasure, since he is completely lacking in talent and has a poor grasp of scripture... he has every characteristic of the most unattractive of preachers: sluggish pace and a tendency to dawdle which undermine any confidence one may have that he knows what he wants to say... total lack of any gift for language... very unpleasant diction. He never prepares what he is going to say and, it must be said, gains nothing in spontaneity from this omission: at first he will pray quietly for about five minutes, then for about three minutes he will leaf through the Bible and then in a desultory way begin...[11]

Leskov reports, moreover, that Radstock's own family thought him confused, vague and illogical,[12] and Mrs Edward Trotter, in her generally favourable 'interpretation and record', records that 'there was an element of incompleteness on the intellectual side... He did not know what other minds were receiving and treated with some suspicion new facets of light. In habits of thought he belonged to a past generation'.[13] Some of his female admirers got around the difficulty by saying that he was 'above intellect' and claimed that, although his preaching was colourless and tiresome 'at the beginning... as he goes on, he ever more powerfully touches the

---

10 Leskov, *Schism in High Society*, pp. 33-34.
11 Leskov, *Schism in High Society*, p. 46-47.
12 Leskov, *Schism in High Society*, p. 40.
13 Trotter, *Lord Radstock*, pp. 99-100.

hearts of the listeners, smoothing the way to salvation through faith in Christ and vividly portraying the inescapable sorrow which awaits those who do not choose the narrow way'. By expounding the boundless love of God he aroused 'noble feelings in the hearts of the listeners'.[14] Countess Tolstoya, in response to a request from her nephew Leo (researching for *Anna Karenina*), summed up his strengths and weaknesses with friendly acuity:

> I like him very much because of his extraordinary integrity and sincere love. He is fully devoted to a single cause and follows his path without turning to left or right. The words of Apostle Paul can almost be applied to him. 'I do not wish to know anything but the crucified Christ.' I say 'almost' because in wisdom and thoughtfulness he is not only below Apostle Paul but also below many other less significant teachers of the Church. He is a dear and kind sectarian who does not understand everything and who in his naiveté fails to see in how many respects he deviated [sic] from the Gospel. He is fully ignorant of human nature and pays no attention whatsoever to it because, according to his system, every human being can divest himself in no time at all of all his passion and evil inclinations provided he has the desire to follow his Saviour. But where are these sudden and total conversions? Are there many examples if we exclude Apostle Paul, the chosen working tool of God? He talks often of such cases... in which the conversion took place in about half an hour... This is his weak point. But then, what devotion to Christ, what warmth, what immeasurable sincerity! His message resounded here like a bell, and he awakened many who before never thought of Christ and their salvation. But out of others he made complete spiritual caricatures, which is incidentally not his fault...[15]

Tolstoy, a searchingly religious man who regarded obedience to the Sermon on the Mount as a Christian's central duty, deplored Radstock's idea of redemption and satirized it in two novels. In *Anna Karenina* (1877), Countess Lydia Ivanovna is described as 'touched by her own lofty sentiments, which had a flavour of that new, ecstatic, mystic exultation which had recently spread in Petersburg...' Having 'long given up being in love with her husband... she had never ceased being in love with someone or other', and the variegated list of those so favoured with her regard includes '...an English missionary'. Her friend Karenin, a leading bureaucrat who has always been 'a sincere believer, interested in religion primarily in its political aspect' has always found Ivanovna's expressions 'distasteful, if not excessive' and dislikes 'this new ecstatic fervour', but later, confronted with a spiritual crisis of his own when his wife leaves him, he takes comfort from these manifestations.

---

14 Leskov, *Schism in High Society*, p. 40.

15 Heier, *Religious Schism*, pp. 84-85. Countess Tolstoya does not explain in what sense it is not Radstock's fault that he made 'complete spiritual caricatures' out of some of his followers.

Significantly, however, Tolstoy writes of him clinging to 'this delusion of salvation as if it were the real thing'.[16]

Published much later, in 1899, Tolstoy's *Resurrection* featured Kiesewetter, an evangelist based on Radstock's associate, Dr Friedrich Baedeker. Again the devotee is a Countess, Katerina Ivanovna (clearly something about this patronymic put Tolstoy in mind of Evangelicals), 'a woman of 60, tall and stout, with a black moustache on her upper lip. She was jolly, robust, energetic and talkative'. She is amused by the novel's hero, her nephew, Nekhludov, whose beliefs, like Tolstoy's own, are centred on the Sermon on the Mount: '*Vous posez pour un Howard*, helping criminals, visiting prisons, putting things right.' While regarding these activities as 'a good thing', she is disgusted by fallen women and thinks Nekhludov 'a goose' for wanting to marry one. Tolstoy's analysis of the conflicts within her character—she believes in redemption but doubts its full efficacy when applied to prostitutes, and clings to old doctrines and practices while experimenting with new ones—throws light on the aristocratic ladies who formed Radstock's flock. She,

> however inconsistent it may appear with her temperament and character, was a devout adherent of the doctrine which teaches that redemption is the essence of Christianity; she went to all the meetings where this doctrine, fashionable at the time, was expounded, and she also held meetings at her own house. But although the doctrine excluded all ritual, icons, and even sacraments, the Countess had an icon in every room and even one above her bed, continued to observe all the ceremonial of the Church, and saw no inconsistency in it.[17]

With some coercion she persuades Nekhludov to listen to Kiesewetter, who, she says, 'speaks with such eloquence that the most hardened criminals fall on their knees and weep and repent'. Tolstoy's description of the gathering gives a clear, if uncharitable, idea of a Radstockite service, as well as prefiguring the meeting which took place in the Grand Duchess Constantine's Petersburg salon when William Booth visited the city in 1909. In the evening, after an elaborate dinner,

> rows of high-backed carved chairs were arranged as for a meeting, with an easy chair and a table carrying a tumbler and a decanter of water for the preacher, and the company assembled for a sermon by the distinguished Kiesewetter. Expensive carriages drove up before the entrance. Women, dressed in velvet and silk and lace, with false hair and padded busts, came in and sat down. There were men, too, both officers and civilians, as well as five or six of the common sort of people: house-porters, a shopkeeper, a footman and a coachman.

> Kiesewetter was a robust man with hair just turning grey. He spoke English and was readily and smoothly translated by a thin girl wearing *pince-nez*. So great were our

---

16 Leo Tolstoy, trs. Rosemary Edmonds, *Anna Karenina*, London, Penguin Books, 1975, Part Five, chapters 22 and 23.

17 Leo Tolstoy, trs. Vera Traill, *Resurrection*, Geneva, Heron Books, 1968, chapter 14.

sins, he said, so severe and unrelenting the punishment they deserved that no one could go on living under such a threat.

'If we pause, my dear brothers and sisters, to reflect on the sins we commit every day of our lives, on the way in which we offend our Heavenly Father and our dear Lord, His Son, then we may come to understand how vast is our sin, and that we are doomed to eternal damnation. Dreadful doom, everlasting torment await us!' he cried in a trembling voice, the tears about to fall. 'Oh, how can we be saved from this unquenchable fire? The house is already in flames and there is no escape.'

He paused, and tears were running down his cheeks. He had been giving the same address for eight years and, whenever he came to this passage (which he especially liked), he always felt a tickling in the nose, a choking in the throat, and the tears always began to flow.

These tears increased his emotion. Sobs were heard throughout the room. Countess Ekaterina Ivanovna was sitting beside an inlaid table, leaning her head on her folded arms while her broad shoulders heaved convulsively. The coachman gazed at the foreign gentleman with fear and trembling, looking as though he were about to run someone down who refused to get out of the way. Most of the company sat in attitudes not unlike that of the Countess. Wolf's daughter, a thin fashionably dressed girl... was kneeling with her face in her hands.

Suddenly the speaker raised his head and, assuming the smile that actors use to express joy, began in a sweet and gentle voice:

'But lo, salvation lies before us: so simple, so blissful! Our salvation is the blood of the only-begotten Son of God, who gave Himself up to be tortured for our sakes. His agonies, His martyrdom will be our salvation. Oh, my brothers and sisters!' he cried in his tearful voice, 'let us praise the Lord who gave His only Son for the redemption of mankind. His precious blood...'

Nekhludov felt so deeply disgusted that he rose, frowning, and keeping back a groan of shame, left on tiptoe...[18]

Tolstoy and Chertkov

Ironically, although these passages illustrate that the Radstockite idea of redemption as the essence of Christianity was inimical to Tolstoy, he was from 1883 onwards influenced by Vladimir Grigoryevich Chertkov, Radstockite son of the Radstockite Chertkova and her enormously wealthy husband, General Chertkov, ADC to Tsar Alexander II. Chertkova and her son will appear many times in this book. V.G. Chertkov was a gently good-looking man with a prominent nose and ears, a thick black beard and a penetrating gaze. As an officer of the Guard he had read the Gospel

---

18 Tolstoy, *Resurrection*, Book II, chapter 17.

to sick and wounded soldiers. At the age of 30 he decided that military service and its associated pleasures and debaucheries were incompatible with the doctrine of Christ.[19] He initially visited Tolstoy, unannounced, as an admirer. Tolstoy read him some of *What I Believe*, a work that asked whether the moral teaching of Jesus was really true, and if so, what impact must it have on how we behave. For him its impact led to extreme ideas about chastity, the universal brotherhood of man, and non-resistance to evil, along with an absolute ban on the taking of human life and the swearing of oaths. This and others of his works on religion were regarded as heretical by the Orthodox Church. He, in turn, denounced its ritual and sacraments as mumbo jumbo and useless sorcery.

Chertkov, initially disconcerted, became a passionate, dictatorial disciple. Aylmer Maude, Tolstoy's friend, translator and biographer, said of him, 'I never knew anyone with such a capacity for enforcing his will on others', while Sonya Tolstoy, who at first welcomed him because unlike many of her husband's followers he exhibited gentlemanly breeding and manners, discovered that:

> this new type of disciple was more intransigent than his master on questions of doctrine. Chertkov had a narrow, systematizing mind, and was so attached to Tolstoy's ideas that he would not suffer him to depart one iota from them himself. On any and every matter, however trifling, he would respectfully call the master to order in the name of Tolstoyism. Instinctively he sided with the thought against the thinker, with the work against the man. At first, the family was amused by his stern application of the rules. Then Sonya dimly began to sense that a rival had crept under her roof and, uneasy and uncertain, she put up her guard.[20]

Domestic conflict arising from his religious opinions played a part in Tolstoy's death. In 1910, he fled from Sonya and barricaded himself in a rural railway station. Nonetheless, the disapproval of Tolstoy's fervid idealism shared by Sonya and others in the family did not affect their hospitable reception of The Salvation Army when it came to Russia. Meanwhile, the systematizing, bureaucratic Chertkov, who lived abroad for some time following Tolstoy's death, helped transmit much of the sage's later thought to the West, greatly influencing the way in which European evangelicals, including Salvationists, thought about Russian spirituality, particularly that of the peasantry. After his return to Russia, although he no longer professed Radstockite opinions, Chertkov thought of himself as a non-

---

19 My account of Chertkov is drawn from: Heier, *Religious Schism,* and biographies of Tolstoy by Henri Troyat (see next note) and A.N. Wilson (London, 1988). Chertkov's influence over Tolstoy and the degree to which the novelist's spiritual crisis in middle age changed his thinking have sometimes been exaggerated. Many of the ideas that dominated Tolstoy's writings in his later years, can be found in a quite highly developed form in essays and novels, which he wrote much earlier, before he met Chertkov, in particular in the character of Pierre, in *War and Peace*. Levin, in *Anna Karenina*, which was written at the time when Tolstoy was passing through his crisis, is a spiritual descendant of Pierre.

20 Henri Troyat (trs. Nancy Amphoux), *Tolstoy*, London, W.H. Allen,1968, p. 436.

denominational Christian as Radstock had done, and as, in a very different way, Salvationists did. His bureaucratic expertise would several times be put at the service of the Army during the years immediately before and after the Revolution of 1917.

Radstock and Dostoyevsky

Russia's other leading novelist at the time, Fyodor Dostoyevsky, also had a Radstockite connection, and his criticisms of the aristocratic evangelist were equally severe. A complex and turbulent personality—passionately Orthodox, a compulsive gambler, xenophobe, anti-Catholic and anti-Semite—Dostoyevsky was bound to find Radstock's simplistic evangelical doctrines inadequate to the great issues of human existence, although he too valued simplicity. He 'believed that Western civilization was in decline but might yet be regenerated by Russian spirituality, if only the Russian elite would find a way back to the Christian faith of the simple Russian people'.[21] Radstock, with his rambling sermons, do-it-yourself prayers, crude manners, poor understanding of the human heart and tendency to perpetrate simple factual mistakes, did not please him.

Yuliya Denisovna Zasetskaya, the 'great lady' who according to Leskov invited Radstock to Russia and who helped found St Petersburg's first night-shelter for the homeless in 1873, met Dostoyevsky when she invited him to visit the institution in his capacity as editor of *The Citizen*, a conservative periodical. They became friends and she took him to hear Radstock preach. Their relationship was affectionate and respectful but often stormy. Much as he deplored it, Dostoyevsky admired her courage in proclaiming her Protestant faith, an act that was still a punishable offence, but, as Leskov records, they had frequent heated and bitter disputes, in which Dostoyevsky could neither outdebate Zasetskaya nor match her knowledge of the Bible.[22] When she asked repeatedly 'exactly what in Russia was supposed to be better than in other countries', his answer was that everything was better: her inability to understand the point showed her ignorance of the Orthodox faith. On one occasion he tried to terminate discussion by defining his yardstick for sound religious views: '...just ask your peasant in the kitchen. He'll teach you!'[23]

---

21 Terras, *A History of Russian Literature*, p. 346.

22 See Malcolm Jones, Dostoyevsky, Zasetskaya, and Radstockism, in *Oxford Slavonic Papers*, XXVII, Oxford, Oxford University Press, 1994, pp. 106-20 for details in this and the following paragraphs.

23 'The peasant in the kitchen' became a much-debated catch phrase in Petersburg society. Jones suggests that Dostoyevsky's last great novel, *The Brothers Karamazov* (1879-80), which urgently attempts to express and validate the truths of Orthodoxy, is as much an answer to Zasetskaya as it is (as is commonly supposed) to the nihilists and the socialists who had been his friends in youth and with whom he had faced a firing squad. Walicki (*Russian Thought*, p. 320) suggests that Dostoyevsky was also strongly influenced by his friendship with Pobedonostsev, the reactionary Chief Procurator of the Holy Synod, but notes that Pobedonostsev was alarmed by aspects of *The Brothers Karamazov*: '...there could be no guarantee that its readers would see the threat to freedom

In March 1874, an unsigned article (thought to be by Dostoyevsky) appeared in *The Citizen,* contending that Radstockites and followers of other foreign evangelical movements had abandoned Orthodoxy through ignorance. In making justification by faith alone the touchstone of his teaching, Radstock was *ipso facto* rejecting the dogmas and mysteries of Orthodoxy.[24] The result, if left unchecked, would be a generation of leading citizens who, by embracing Protestantism, had cut themselves off from the Russian people. This could only lead to hostility between classes.

The publisher of *The Citizen,* Prince V. P. Meshchersky, added an outraged postscript, deploring the manner in which Radstock conducted his services. After complaining that Radstock spoke in private homes as well as in regular places of worship, and that people attending had received *printed invitations* (Meshchersky's italics presumably indicate his especial outrage at this particular vulgarity), he went on:

> The Church was full of Russians, all from the aristocracy, women, men, and children. The noble... apostle ascended into the pulpit and called the congregation to silent prayer.
>
> He stood there in a theatrical pose, putting his hand to his brow and lowering his head into his hand. Then the whole congregation raised their hands to their brows, bowed their heads and stood like that for about three minutes. What a spectacle!
>
> Then he began to speak. When he had finished speaking he started to sing a psalm. Suddenly the whole church was filled with the sound of Russian ladies, gentlemen and their children, singing psalms in English.

Meshchersky's complaint, then, is fourfold. Radstock, a lay person, presumed to lead a congregation in prayer.[25] Worse, he allowed them to make up prayers of their own, in the uncensored privacy of their own heads. Thirdly, Radstockite worship was histrionic and undignified, a debased substitute for Orthodox ceremonial. Finally, perhaps worst of all, Radstock taught Russians to sing psalms in English. Meshchersky added, as hearsay, that in Switzerland Radstock had 'given Communion

---

and individuality as coming solely from Catholicism and socialism and not, for example, from the Orthodox autocracy in whose services the Director General of the Holy Synod laboured so faithfully'.

24 The traditional argument about the relative merits of faith and works was frequently rehearsed in connection with Radstock's doctrine of justification by faith alone: see Müller, *Russischer Geist und Evangelisches Chrisentum,* Witten/Ruhr, 1951, pp. 98-103. It is only fair to point out that Radstock regarded good works as both a measure of faith and its necessary concomitant: see Leskov, *Schism in High Society,* pp. 68-89.

25 Leskov, *Schism in High Society,* pp. 44-45, dismissed the complaint that Radstock was not ordained as canting hypocrisy based on scandalous ignorance, and listed ordained people who had done great harm as well as lay people who had done great good.

with his own hands to those whom he acknowledged to have *achieved perfection* of the soul'.[26]

Dostoyevsky parted company with Meshchersky after the latter published a novel, *A Noble Apostle in St Petersburg High Society*, which travestied Radstock as a hypocrite who used evangelism as a front for sexual licence. Dostoyevsky thought parts of it 'simply appalling'. But when Radstock returned to Russia in 1876, Dostoyevsky resumed his attack, denouncing English Protestantism as ugly, vulgar, narrow and stupid. In it '...the doors are left open to all sorts of opinions and conclusions... you must swim in the boundless sea and save yourself as you please'. It amounted to a deification of humanity, in which, however, Dostoyevsky detected 'a thirst for prayer and worship and a craving for God'. The yearning was sincere, but that sincerity seemed 'to border on despair'.[27] In attempting to assuage that yearning, Radstock preached as if he had 'Christ in his pocket', treating Him and his grace with 'extraordinary levity'. Nonetheless, Dostoyevsky somewhat reluctantly admitted, '...he produces remarkable conversions and arouses magnanimous feelings in the hearts of his followers'. That could not, however, be allowed to hide the fact that Lord Radstock 'has departed from the true church and thought up his own', which would end up like all the other sects, the 'Jumpers, the Shakers, the Convulsionaries, the Quakers awaiting the millennium, and, finally, the Flagellants...'[28]

Radstockism, Pashkovism and Orthodoxy

Dostoyevsky, like the Slavophiles, detested westernization of Russia in any form, but particularly in religion. Catholicism, he thought, was governed by materialistic rationalism, which replaced true Christian love with an arithmetical doctrine of salvation and blind submission to authority. To the Catholic ideal of the Church as state Dostoyevsky opposed the Orthodox ideal of the state as Church.[29] Protestantism, conversely, governed by *idealistic* rationalism, abolished all outward symbols of the religious bond so that its adherents became, necessarily, lonely individuals lost in a society which was itself fragmented. Protestants, consumed with subjective concern for the state of their own individual souls, were unwittingly marching down the road to atheism and nihilism.[30]

For Dostoyevsky Radstockism was merely one more example of the proliferation of small sects of fugitives from Orthodoxy. Despite its failure to attract the ignorant,

---

26 Meshchersky would later (having meanwhile become a member of the Tsar's reactionary kitchen cabinet) be known as '...the notorious newspaper editor, Prince Meshchersky, whose homosexual lovers were promoted to prominent positions at court': see Figes, *A People's Tragedy*, p. 21.

27 Fyodor Dostoyevsky, trs. Kenneth Lantz, *A Writer's Diary*, London, Quartet Books, 1995, Vol. I, p. 416-17.

28 Dostoyevsky, *A Writer's Diary*, Vol. I, p. 419.

29 Walicki, *Russian Thought*, p. 320.

30 Walicki, *Russian Thought*, p. 104.

Orthodoxy was the purest, most correct form of Christianity. To embrace any other could only be a grievous mistake. Dostoyevsky had found within himself the grassroots simplicity of 'the peasant in the kitchen' and in doing so gave words to feelings, which, however subliminally, were widespread in Russia.

It is clear, then, that Russians with reservations about western evangelicalism objected to its concentration on redemption or salvation to the exclusion of other elements in the Christian faith, its lack of theological rigour, and its undignified meetings and services. Radstock was a layman, unordained and ignorant. Dostoyevsky and Leskov supposed that Radstock had only a slight knowledge of the Bible, relying on a few, incessantly reiterated texts. Leskov later withdrew the charge of ignorance, but held fast to his opinion that Radstock was theologically unsophisticated by comparison with Wesley and did get 'stuck on' certain texts: he was not so much a sectarian as a textarian,[31] preaching an incomplete version of Christianity. Pobedonostsev, discussing Radstock's successor, Pashkov, developed the same complaint:

> In the popular mind, along with a deep sense of religion, there exists a mysterious sense of the letter of Holy Scripture—this is the reason why all Russian sects have for foundation of their faith some one text of Holy Scripture misunderstood or perverted. A man who believes in some peculiar interpretation of a passage in Holy Scripture becomes its obstinate defender, and a fanatical follower of the sect based upon it. The Church alone possesses the full, clear, catholic interpretation of the whole text... every one who separates himself from the Church, or sets himself up for a preacher, becomes a sectarian. Mr Pashkov is just such a self-called preacher...[32]

All of these objections could and would be made against The Salvation Army.

Meanwhile, although Pobedonostsev had (as ever) identified the situation clearly, he failed to recognize its cause. The Church's pre-revolutionary attempts to reform itself from within (which, as we have seen, he resolutely opposed) were confined to a minority and came too late. The promise of reform may have kept some people loyally Orthodox, but others who felt that Russia was in the grip of a chronic social, political and spiritual crisis continued to search elsewhere for a cure for their desolation. Of those who hoped to find it in religion, some looked towards western European evangelical Protestantism, repudiating traditional and formalistic doctrines and seeking to eliminate any intermediary between God and men.

In pursuit of these ideas during what Heier called a time of 'seething agitation and distressing anxieties' the sectarians followed emotional, mystical or rational lines of enquiry. Although they would not have found much that was mystical in either Radstock or The Salvation Army they could find emotionalism and, if only by comparison with the fiercely anti-intellectual tradition of Orthodoxy, a sort of rationalism. Although those who think of themselves as rationalists might find little

---

31 Leskov, *Schism in High Society*, p. 113.
32 Quoted in Heier, *Religious Schism*, p. 128.

of rationalism in evangelical Christianity, its doctrines of sin, redemption and salvation were, given the premises on which they depended, rational in structure. Other ideas to which sectarians were drawn followed from those doctrines, especially asceticism and reformist radicalism. As Heier remarks,

> It was only natural that some began to seek their answer or expected to find it in the radical social movements of the time, while others believed that it lay in a new religious ethical teaching. But no matter what nature the various currents assumed, whether it was that of Tolstoy, V. Solovyev, Dostoyevsky, or that of the Evangelical revival which advocated religious freedom with a personal relation with a personal God, at the base of their origin was the general disillusionment of the age, the lack of faith in the direction taken by the state and the official Orthodox Church of Russia.[33]

In 1878, Pobedonostsev ended Radstock's third visit to Russia by expelling him and condemning his beliefs as heresy. For two decades he laboured to suppress what remained of the movement, which he saw as a threat to the stability of the state. Pashkov was exiled, at first to the provinces, where he began work amongst the peasantry, and finally, in 1884, abroad. His wealth, however, enabled him to continue from a distance the work of propagandizing the peasantry on his several estates. Meanwhile, those of his followers who remained in Russia had, especially during the summers, when they visited their country estates, carried their evangelical and philanthropic work into almost all of the provinces of European Russia. It was this expansion outwards and downwards which alarmed Pobedonostsev: the aristocracy might indulge in religious and other intellectual fads, but it was essential that the people at large remain Orthodox. At a time when Nihilist terrorism (believed to have spread from the West) was increasing, western evangelicalism had no place in Holy Russia. Its proponents were repeatedly charged with the offences of distributing Bibles and tracts, holding prayer meetings, repudiating Holy Images, and inviting friends, neighbours or relatives to attend Bible readings. Many were deprived of their official positions and sent into internal exile. The consequent loss of leadership and the 'uncertainty caused by the lack of religious theories or dogma', drove many of its adherents to search for established beliefs and preachers. These they found in the Baptists and Stundists (a Protestant sect of German origin), with whom they eventually merged, leaving only a small group in St Petersburg, mainly of aristocratic ladies, as authentic Pashkovites. These, since no male leader emerged from their own ranks to continue the work of the exiled Pashkov, kept themselves going with visits from foreign preachers at meetings conducted in the homes of Princess Lieven, Princess Gargarina, Madame Chertkova, Miss Peuker, or the German book dealer, Grote.[34]

---

33 Heier, *Religious Schism,* p. 18.
34 Heier, *Religious Schism,* pp. 117-18, 122-23 and 142-46; Heier, *A Note on the Pashkovites,* Canadian Slavonic Papers, V, Edmonton, University of Alberta, 1962, p. 120; and MacLean *Nikolai Leskov,* p. 332.

Even sympathetic historians debate whether Radstockism/Pashkovism succeeded or failed. Heier, who regards the movement as essentially an attempt to establish non-denominational Christianity as a permanently going concern, argues that, following the exiling of Pashkov and police harassment of those who conducted secret Bible-reading assemblies, the movement, always characterized by dependence upon a strong personal leadership, was diluted beyond recognition. Even the great ladies, who organized prayer meetings and invited foreign Stundist and Baptist preachers, created

> a development which deviated even further from the ecumenical venture, which sought at the beginning to do away with denominational, differences... Pashkovites, like all Evangelicals evolved into just another sect with a distinct congregational theology and structure.[35]

William B. Edgerton, who regards the mergers not as dilutions but as strategies of survival, wrote in 1966, in a somewhat triumphalist, perhaps naive manner, that

> More than 80 years have now passed since Leskov proclaimed that the Radstockites had nothing in common with the Stundists and predicted that they would not long survive the absence of Pashkov and his money. During those 80 years history has played an ironical joke on Leskov's prediction. The Radstockites —later known as Pashkovites and still later as Evangelical Christians —have not only survived all forms of persecution and steadily grown in numbers instead of fulfilling Leskov's prediction and dying out; they have also joined that very group with which Leskov claimed they had nothing in common. In 1944 they formed a union with the descendants of the Russian Stundists, who by then had taken the name of Baptists. Today the All-Union Alliance of Evangelical Christians and Baptists, with about 55,000 baptized members and perhaps as many as three million 'fellow travellers', is the largest Christian group in the Soviet Union apart from the Orthodox and the Old Believers.[36]

Radstockism and The Salvation Army

It will be noticed that Edgerton's idea of 'survival' is identical with Heier's idea of absorption. It is also clear that when, in 1909, the rump of the Radstockites invited William Booth to St Petersburg, he went as the latest in a long line of foreign preachers from whom they hoped to derive the leadership and identity they had lost.

In any case, whether or not Radstockism 'failed', its initial impact and eventual fate had clear implications for The Salvation Army's Russian venture. When Commissioner Railton (in 1908) and General Booth (in 1909) arrived to make the

---

35 Heier, *Religious Schism,* pp. 146-47.
36 Edgerton, *Leskov, Pashkov, the Stundists, and a Newly Discovered Letter,* p. 199. Edgerton derives his figures from Walter Kolarz, *Religion in the Soviet Union,* London, Macmillan, 1961, p. 286.

first Salvationist reconnaissance in Russia, the times were once again, in Leroy-Beaulieu's word, 'unquiet', for the after-effects of the Revolution in 1905 were still being strongly felt. 'Souls' were once again seeking 'comfort and guidance'. Subsequently, the Army's sustained attempt to establish itself (1913-23) coincided with the First World War, the Revolutions of 1917, the Civil War and the establishment of Bolshevik Government. Like Radstock, the Salvationists were welcomed and lionized by some aristocrats and members of the Imperial family, proving perhaps, that spiritual messengers from abroad did not necessarily have to be noblemen. Like Radstock, Railton and Booth eschewed 'dogmatical controversy' and complex, closely worked out systems of dogma and liturgy. (Leskov noted with approval their instructions to their preachers to 'preach not about such matters as arouse discontent, but pass on to other matters'.)[37] Like him, they taught people to believe themselves to be assured of salvation, the evidence of which was their consciousness of intimate union with the Saviour.

But, also like Radstock and equally unhappily, they were to learn the truth of Leroy-Beaulieu's remarks about dress coats and sheepskins. What little religious freedom there was in Russia was confined to high society and was in any case liable to be withdrawn without notice. In its turn The Salvation Army would be regarded with suspicion by the bureaucrats, and just as Radstock was not saved by his aristocratic fan club, neither would the Army be. Its pleasure in the welcome given it by the aristocracy, on the assumption that these people were influential, even powerful, and in some sense leaders of the people, was based on a fallacy. Not only were some of these people not very influential,[38] but as a group they had proved on one significant occasion to be broken reeds. During Radstock's first visit to Russia in the winter of 1875-6, he was accused of begging and dishonesty. He was said to have refused to pay hotel bills on the grounds that 'the labourer is worthy of his hire'. His friends were outraged but their attempts to answer the charges were ineffectual or non-existent; his 'high society admirers refrained from protest on behalf of their leader certainly not out of doubt of his honesty, but out of the strangest indifference and ignorance of how to stand up for another person'.[39] This sort of indifference was not, it should be said, confined to evangelically minded aristocrats. Recounting a similar experience of his own, the opera singer Chaliapin remarks, 'In Russia we are not particular about slander, even though it may be directed against a friend'.[40]

Such specific cases aside, how influential were these people? Titles such as prince and princess and count and countess could be used by all members of the families

37 Quoted by James Muckle, *Nikolai Leskov and the 'Spirit of Protestantism'*, p. 78. Manson, *The Salvation Army and the Public*, pp. 159-60, regards the instruction as mere hypocrisy.

38 Leskov asserts that almost all the Radstockites who had ever been influential had toppled from that position before they met Radstock, although this has been disputed in a number of cases.

39 Leskov, *Schism in High Society*, p. 70.

40 Gorky, *Chaliapin*, p. 184.

upon which these ranks, generations before, had been conferred, so that possession of a title did not necessarily imply wealth or power—although it should be noted that between 1894 and 1914 90 per cent of the State Council were drawn from the hereditary nobility, which in 1914 numbered only about one per cent of the Russian population. The rulers of late-Tsarist Russia, by comparison with ruling classes elsewhere, were untrammelled by a parliament until the Duma came ineffectually into being in 1906—and the Duma itself was far more dominated by the gentry than were the representative institutions of, for example, contemporary Britain and Germany. But the Tsar—who was neither obliged to consult the State Council, nor to follow its advice—could easily marginalize individual aristocrats or aristocratic families. Significantly, the conversion of some members of the Lieven family to Radstockism was one of the factors, which 'radically reduced the influence of, and imperial goodwill towards, what had for three generations been a powerful court family very close to the Romanovs'.[41] Nicholas, in any case inclined to regard the Petersburg aristocracy as westernized heretics, was unlikely to be much impressed by their support for The Salvation Army, since he thought that his role was to reach out beyond the aristocracy and bureaucracy to the common people, with whom he was—or so he thought—at one, and to whom he was a benevolent 'little father'. Individual princes and counts were well advised to seek to influence the Tsar only upon issues and in directions, which they could be sure he would approve. Under Nicholas and Alexandra, increasingly, autocracy was to become wayward and petulant. Even members of the Imperial Family (up to and including the Tsar's mother) might find themselves put out in the cold for offering unwelcome advice. Although The Salvation Army in Russia was on a number of occasions able to call on help from its noble Radstockite friends, the results were only ever temporary and palliative. For all that, noble influence was to prove useful on occasion. If no one could overrule the Tsar, aristocrats and members of the Imperial Family could sometimes make difficulties for the police. On balance, the Army was probably right to ignore the English Prayer Book's injunction to 'put not your trust in Princes... for there is no help in them', since without the assistance of such people it might never have arrived in Russia at all.

Most of them in any case still had disposable wealth at their command, and were friends of others similarly placed. Given the ways in which The Salvation Army financed its work, and the policy of requiring all territories to become self-supporting as soon as possible, this was a factor of no small importance. In the event, the Radstockites who supported the Army usually made donations in kind, particularly by placing houses and other large buildings at its disposal, often for peppercorn rents or no rents at all. Although such gifts were never entirely disinterested (particularly after the Revolution, when the Army as sitting tenant provided property with some protection against requisitions and depredations by the authorities) they generally worked to the Army's advantage.

---

41 Dominic Lieven, *Russia's Rulers under the Old Regime*, New Haven and London, Yale University Press, 1989, p. 145.

Radstockism anticipated The Salvation Army's work in Russia in many respects. Both began with an Englishman preaching in the aristocratic drawing rooms of St Petersburg, and both claimed to be above denominational rivalry. Like The Salvation Army, Radstockism and Pashkovism were characterized by their philanthropic activities and regular social work among the lower classes.[42] They impressed upon the more reformist Orthodox the idea that sectarians got things done,[43] another one of the Army's attractions so far as those most fully conscious of Russian impracticality were concerned. Pashkov, especially, shared the Army's wish to speak to all sorts and conditions of men. When he became leader, every grade of Russian society was represented in his congregations: 'writers, civil servants, senators, princes, counts, military officers, merchants, students, tradesmen and.. servants.' This bridging of gaps between social classes in religious gatherings not organized by the Orthodox Church and therefore not open to easy official surveillance aroused official suspicion,[44] which deepened when he began to frequent 'the cabmen's lodgings and other similar meeting places of the working people.'[45] Pashkov also did what he could to ameliorate the hardships of the less well off classes. He established three restaurants in the workers' district north of the Neva called the Vyborg side and every day thousands of workers and students received free meals in them, accompanied by religious tracts and Bibles. (It seems probable that these restaurants were those which The Salvation Army was to take over in 1917 as halls for their corps in that district.)[46] These practices gave rise to the suggestion that Pashkov was using his considerable wealth to bribe the poor into accepting the gospel.[47] In time (allowing for the fact that the Army could not be described as wealthy), the Bolsheviks would take a very similar view of The Salvation Army.

---

42 Heier, *Religious Schism*, p. 20. Leskov conceded that for all Radstock's denial that men could buy salvation through their own works, and despite his own view that Radstock merely 'subjugates and turns to God those whose subjugation began long ago and who were ready to turn in some direction before they met Radstock', there was something miraculous in the influence he brought to bear upon 'the cold, self-interested nature of the smooth-skinned people', chasing them 'into poor quarters and slums...' They visited poor families, hospitals, prisons and common lodging houses, bearing philanthropy as well as preaching justification by faith. He added, however, that 'the material help brought to the poor by these women preachers is utterly negligible... Unfortunately this does not embarrass them in any way'. (Leskov, *Schism in High Society*, pp. 31, 43 and 93).

43 See Dixon, The Church's Social Role in St Petersburg, in Hosking (ed.), *Church, Nation and State in Russia and Ukraine*, pp. 173 and 175.

44 Heier, *Religious Schism*, pp. 110-11.

45 Heier, *Religious Schism*, p. 126.

46 See p. 224 below. Larsson does not mention any Pashkovite connection with these buildings but it seems probable that they are identical. He may have been unaware of their origins, or he may have wished, as he sometimes does, to emphasize the provision made by God at the expense of more mundane explanations.

47 Heier, *Religious Schism*, pp. 114-16 and 132.

It is clear then that many of those who welcomed The Salvation Army to Russia were Radstockites and that the two groups used similar methods.[48] But although Radstock had created a platform upon which The Salvation Army could in time achieve a foothold, he had also stimulated a backlash against evangelical creeds and English Protestant evangelism in general. Few Orthodox were inclined to accept Leskov's conclusion that those who left the Church to become Radstockites had 'preferred a rather imperfect movement to a fully perfect one in stagnation'.[49]

Those Radstockites who eventually supported The Salvation Army were drawn from those whom Leskov considered 'the best sort... the practitioners'. These were not so much apostles of Radstock as 'interlocutors and friends'. They did not necessarily part company with the Church.[50] Among the dozen most prominent supporters of Radstockism listed by Heier,[51] half would become friends of the Army: Mme. E.S. Chertkova, Princess N. Lieven and her sister, Princess Gargarina, Mme. Peuker and Baron Nicolay. Count von Pahlen, as Minister of Justice in 1887, had somewhat daringly likened the persecution of the Pashkovites to the Inquisition,[52] and would be among those who welcomed Booth to St Petersburg in 1909.

Baron Nicolay was also there, 'a slender man with deep, dark eyes who did not say much... but whose words... left a deep impression of spirituality and earnestness'. He had written in terms of high but precisely judged praise of Radstock after his death, and in 1899, following a meeting at the home of Princess Lieven, he left his career in government (five years in the Imperial Senate, 1885-89, and a further ten in the Privy Council) to found and lead the Russian Student Christian Movement, part of the World Student Christian Federation. He regarded evangelism and Bible study as the pillars of his work, and devoted much energy to producing textbooks designed to suit 'the Russian point of view'. He was an internationalist, which doubtless explains his willingness to welcome The Salvation Army.[53]

These people all play walk-on parts in the story of The Salvation Army in Russia. Mme. Chertkova, an intimate friend of the Empress Marie Feodorovna and sister-in-law of Colonel Pashkov, was considerably more central until she left for Finland during the upheavals of 1917.

Another Radstockite name which will stay with us until almost the close is that of Miss (Alexandra Ivanovna) Peuker, daughter of Maria Peuker, an early love of Leo

---

48 It is likely, of course, that Radstock and Pashkov had themselves been influenced by what they knew of The Salvation Army.

49 Leskov, *Schism in High Society*, p. 108.

50 Leskov, *Schism in High Society*, p. 95.

51 Heier, *Religious Schism*, p. 53.

52 Heier, *Religious Schism*, p. 144.

53 Heier, *A Note on the Pashkovites and L.N. Tolstoy*, p. 115, and *The Student World*, January 1920, pp. 23-28. Nicolay was an internationalist with a keen, if basic, sense of humour: at a 'Stunt Evening' during a conference in England in 1913, he led the European delegates in a performance of 'The Concert of Europe', which consisted of them all singing simultaneously, in their own language and at the top of their voices, their respective national anthems.

Tolstoy's, who, with Chertkova, was one of what Leskov called Radstock's two sturdy crutches in St Petersburg, and editor of a periodical *The Russian Worker* (modelled on *The British Worker*) intended to carry Radstock's message to the Russian peasant masses. Mme. Peuker, who seems to have enchanted everyone who knew her, retaining their regard and friendship even when they disagreed with her beliefs, died unexpectedly in 1881: Alexandra Ivanovna took over her editorship and would continue to be a valuable friend of The Salvation Army until her death in the early 1920s.[54]

Evangelicals and, as we shall see, Salvationists also, found what they thought of as the unrigorous sentimentality of Radstock's admirers unsatisfactory. Countess Tolstoya, whose cogently expressed judgement of Radstock was quoted earlier, was not immune, although, as we have seen, the point of view she expresses in the following quotation is that of the Orthodox tradition: Christ the glorious God-man, as opposed to Jesus, the Son of God who suffered and died. In conversation with the Baptist Pastor Fetler in 1925, she wanted

> some cure for nervous trouble or some *help for the soul.* 'Ah, yes! religion, let us talk about religion.' She told us that she longed for true peace, and one could see that she had real soul trouble... She assured us she could not but believe in Christ as God, though she did not understand about salvation by atonement. She longed to be assured of the divine forgiveness but did not like to hear of the Blood of Christ, 'Why do you speak of blood, of death? Speak of His beautiful life, His example.' But if there is one text which has proved more powerful than another in Mr Fetler's soul-winning ministry, it is 'The blood of Jesus Christ, His Son, cleanseth us from all sin'; and he had no other Gospel for the Countess than that which had been s o blessed to the common people.[55]

The princesses V. Gargarina and K. Galitzin[56] also became friends of The Salvation Army. Prince Nicholas Galitzin, son of the princess, was to become very closely involved with its work, albeit, for some reason, outside rather than within Russia.

---

54 See MacLean, *Nikolay Leskov,* p. 333, Leskov, *Schism in High Society,* pp. 64-65, Heier, pp. 53, 71-74 and 93. Leskov did not altogether approve of Mme. Peuker; his criticisms of *The Russian Workman* appeared in an article entitled 'Sentimental Piety' in the *Orthodox Review* in 1876. He was much exercised by how one should or should not write for 'the people'. 'The magazine's effectiveness, [he] maintained, was vitiated by its editor's ignorance of the mentality and way of life of the Russian peasants to whom it was addressed. Consisting of material adapted from English Protestant sources, it was full of undigested, un-Russian lumps of English life'. He also disliked its inept attempts to use the Old Testament for moral and religious teaching. Tolstoy also criticized the paper in some detail, feeling that Mme Peuker's religion 'smelled of Petersburg drawing rooms'. See MacLean, pp. 333, 539, and 712, and Muckle, p. 71.

55 A. McCaig, *Wonders of Grace in Russia,* Riga, The Revival Press, 1926, p. 79.

56 To an even greater extent than most Russian family names this one has been variously transliterated in English. I have adopted a pragmatic policy of using the spelling most often favoured by my sources. 'Galitzine' was the form preferred by the members of the family living in London in 1997.

Although, as has already been noted, the rank of prince was not so grand as English usage would imply, and did not necessarily suggest either wealth or high social standing, The Salvation Army was correct in supposing that Prince Nicholas was a member of one of one of Russia's oldest families. He may not have been particularly well off, although the apparent freedom with which he travelled suggests that he was.[57] In England and America he studied the evangelistic and social work of The Salvation Army, and later accompanied William Booth on a tour of Holland. In 1894 he was amongst those international dignitaries who sent telegrams congratulating General Booth on his 50 years of Christian warfare. That same year he returned to Russia determined to correct any misunderstanding there about the nature and work of the Army.

At that time his relationship with the Booths had taken a personal turn. He had the misfortune to fall besottedly in love with Booth's strikingly attractive and extrovert daughter Evangeline, who was, like all her siblings, a full-time officer in The Salvation Army. Unlike some of them, she continued as a Salvationist until her death. She could only have accepted Galitzin's proposal of marriage (supposing he was not prepared to undergo training as an officer himself) by resigning her commission, and this, after some consideration of the attractions of his offer ('wealth, jewels, a position near the Court, passionate adoration—all that a young heart could desire. He was a Christian too.')[58] she determined not to do. Galitzin wrote two pleading, tearful letters from Paris where he was doing his best 'in a private way' for The Salvation Army:

> Paris,
> April 2nd, 1894
>   My dearest!
> Commissioner Clibborn and everybody here are indeed very kind for me and they do their best—but it is not *my dearest*—and *I cry!* When I remember what you are for me and that you are so far away, *I cry!*..

and

> Tomorrow I have to go to a little water-place near Havre... and afterwards Paris—Berlin—Petersburg... and, I hope, *not* Siberia or Caucasus. It is hard, very hard, because it means Goodbye to you, my dear Dearest... Tell, please, the *Little Lamb* to send me a few lines—dear sweet Little Lamb, MY Little Lamb—is she? *is she not tired of me?*

---

57 In his generation there were no fewer than 168 princes and princesses Galitzin, and while some of them were amongst Russia's greatest landowners, others were relatively poor. One of them, a novelist, significantly puts into the mouth of one of his characters a complaint about the difficulty of maintaining the dignity of an ancient name and title on the bare salary of a state official. See Lieven *Russia's Rulers Under the Old Regime*, pp. 2 and 48.

58 For this and the letters quoted, see P. Whitwell Wilson, *General Evangeline Booth*, New York, Charles Scribner's Sons, 1948, pp. 46-48.

God bless you!
Yours in Jesus,
Galitzin

Ten years later the Prince attended the International Congress in London described in Chapter One. Thereafter, however, he disappears from Salvation Army history. When William Booth went to St Petersburg in 1909 he was at some pains to meet all those Russians who might be expected to assist the cause. Galitzin was apparently not among them.

Perhaps the persecution Galitzin feared actually occurred, and he was out of reach. Perhaps, since rumours of a forthcoming noble marriage had continued to plague Evangeline (who dealt with them with some panache) her father was anxious not to extend any apparent encouragement to the hapless suitor, or to reopen old wounds.

By the end of the century Pashkovism, Heier argues, was demonstrably incapable of the ethical and religious transformation of Russia.[59] Orthodoxy, on the other hand, in part in response to the challenge of Radstockism and the sects, seemed to be on the brink of revitalization. Some Orthodox priests became effective preachers. Specially trained missionaries were sent into the 21 (out of 41 Russian dioceses where Pashkovism was strong. But the fissures in Russian religious life were still enormous. Apart from their own internal divisions and the hostility of the state, intellectual and aristocratic Orthodox were not as much in touch with 'the peasant in the kitchen' as they hoped. (The peasants on Tolstoy's estate derived some amusement from his attempts to reform them, particularly their use or misuse of alcohol. They found ways of evading his displeasure.)

Social changes, which began during the last decades of the Nineteenth Century and accelerated as the Twentieth began, made these fissures increasingly important. Probably those peasants who remained in the country and whose lives had not therefore been disrupted by the growing industrialism of the cities, retained an instinctive, more or less unquestioning belief in Orthodoxy—or at least in the form of it, much interlarded with surviving pagan beliefs and customs, which they had traditionally embraced. But the growth of industry brought with it a large floating population of peasants who spent some part of the year in towns, separated from home, family and parish. Orthodoxy, with its emotional, liturgical and theological bent towards unchanging verities, endorsed and was endorsed by a purportedly stable society; as a result it needed persuasion to notice change as it occurred.

Was the time now ripe for William Booth and the aggressive ambition of his Salvation Army? It might have been. In the event, the issue debated by Heier and Edgerton, whether Radstockism could be said to have survived when it had merged with other groups and changed its character, was also to prove central to The Salvation Army's struggle to establish itself in Russia. Very willing to accept help from other Evangelicals and unwilling to engage in dogmatic controversy with any group, the Army nevertheless regarded its doctrines and its visible characteristics—uniforms, parades, music which was popular in style—as part of its

---

59 Heier, *Religious Schism*, pp. 148-49.

God-given heritage. They could not be sacrificed in the interests of mere survival. When the last officers left Russian in 1923, they urged the converts they left behind to link up with other suitable groups, but there is no evidence of any official attempt to arrange such mergers. The Salvation Army operated by itself, in accordance with its own customs. If defeated it would retreat and hope to fight again another day.

But that is to anticipate. Now we must examine in more detail the transformation of working and living patterns in late Nineteenth- and early Twentieth-Century Russia, and the pressures and agitations which they brought in their wake, seeming to create conditions which The Salvation Army believed it been called in to existence to cure.

CHAPTER 4

Khitrovka

Skid Row, Russian Style

The late Nineteenth Century saw the growth of skid row districts in Russian cities; areas, which combined overcrowded slums with prostitution and heavy drinking. One of the most notorious of these was Moscow's Khitrovka, a sloping, cobbled market square, surrounded by two-storeyed lodging houses and a Dickensian warren of variously foul alleys and courtyards. The houses filled every night with day labourers who could find nothing nearer the railway stations, freight yards and timber yards where they worked. These transients were crammed in with the dispossessed, the out-of-work and prostitutes with their children. Khitrovka was situated near the centre of town in the angle between Yausky Boulevard and Solyanka Street, not far from the Kremlin and a couple of blocks from the Bolshoi Theatre and the spot where, in 1899-1903, a British architect, Walcott, would build the *style moderne* Metropole Hotel. This juxtaposition of the elegant and the sordid embarrassed the city's administration, but their attempts to rid themselves of that embarrassment proved ineffectual. In 1879 they decided that epidemics of tuberculosis and other diseases which spread from Khitrovka and places like it demanded the provision of low-cost municipal housing and Morozov Municipal Lodging House, accommodating 510 lodgers, was opened in that year. Throughout the 1880s and 1890s investigations and reports followed one another. A certain amount was achieved and by the mid-1880s the Society to Encourage Industriousness had established ten cafeterias providing free or low cost meals. But in 1898 Khitrovka was still synonymous with iniquity, criminality and disease[1] and a byword for its pervasive smell, compounded of stagnant fog, cheap tobacco and sweat, greasy cooking and human and animal excretion; all steeped in the universal anaesthetic, alcohol.[2]

Rescue the Perishing, Duty Demands It

The existence of such places as Khitrovka lay behind the enthusiasm for The Salvation Army felt by some members of Russia's governing class. Little as William Booth would have relished the thought, they were less interested in the evangelism which was the Army's primary purpose than in its social work among

---

1 See Joseph Bradley, *Muzhik and Muscovite*, Berkeley, University of California Press, 1985, pp. 273-91.

2 See W. Bruce Lincoln, *In War's Dark Shadow*, New York and Oxford, Oxford University Press, 1983, pp. 123-24.

the urban poor—although the probability that religious conversion might well make people more law-abiding and malleable was a useful bonus. Primarily, however, they looked to Booth's Army to help Russia deal with its increasingly menacing underworlds.

The Army had conducted various forms of social work in England and elsewhere since 1883, when William Booth concluded that it was idle to try to interest sinners in their souls while poverty and other social evils acted as powerful distractions from spiritual considerations. The Army's social work, like most other things about it, was an improvised response to such pressures. Social conditions in East London were undoubtedly deplorable and Booth, pushed by Bramwell and others, sponsored rescue homes for fallen women, brigades to save drunkards and prisoners, and slum sisters who visited the poor women and children of London.

He had taken a step whose significance was only dimly perceived at the time. Recent historians of the Army, most notably Norman H. Murdoch, have argued that Booth's new tactics were in fact a recognition that he had failed in his initial aim of bringing mass revival to the East End of London. His London mission had ceased growing after less than a decade, stimulating him to achieve growth by extending his mission to other towns elsewhere in the British Isles and overseas, in territory already well worked over by previous evangelists, and often suburban in character. Once again, however, mass revival remained elusive. The numbers rallying to the Army banner remained small in comparison to the masses who remained indifferent. Social work was intended in part as a new approach to the problem of bringing Christ to the disaffected millions, but, at a time when corps were in debt and membership was not growing, it was also intended to attract new support by broadening the Army's scope.[3]

This interpretation of Salvation Army history seems to me generally accurate but must be treated with circumspection. It does not follow that Booth was merely an opportunist, casting about in desperation for any tactic that would promote statistical growth. His adaptability as to means in his relentless quest to evangelize the world was one of two important ways in which his personal character shaped the organization that he had called into being. The other was the fact that, having himself rebelled against what he considered excessive bureaucratic interference from his superiors in the Methodist New Connection and set up a mission of his own that was initially notable for its informality and reliance on the individual initiative of its officers (the more bizarre the better), he subsequently made of the Army a hierarchy with far more ranks than any other Church, subject to intensive, detailed regulation.[4] In part this may have been due to the influence of his son and Chief of Staff,

---

3 Murdoch, *Origins*, pp. 113-14.

4 The 1925 edition of *Orders and Regulations for Officers of The Salvation Army*, for example, a volume of 541 pages, covers, in addition to faith and order, such unexpected matters as where an officer may spend his holidays and how he should dress at such times, and includes a detailed exposition of the Water Treatment for various diseases. The fact that much of the book is eminently sensible cannot disguise the degree to which officers were assumed to need direction in every aspect of their lives.

Bramwell, who delighted in making 'the concern' run according to businesslike procedures. Neither he nor his father was a democrat (nor were most early Salvationists) but the control exercised by Headquarters in London over an increasingly international army was dictatorial in the most precise, unemotive sense of that word. William Booth, as General, gave orders, which others obeyed. If anyone objected, pressure was brought on them to recant. For most of his followers (there were exceptions, as we shall see) there were only two options: capitulation or departure.

Although most Salvationists in the mid 1880s would not have agreed with Murdoch's interpretation, which is disputed by many of their present-day successors, some perceived a conflict between what came to seem two almost separate wings of the Army's work. George Scott Railton, one of Booth's closest associates, was particularly outspoken in favour of a purely evangelical and spiritual Salvation Army. Social work, he thought, wasted time caring for bodies that should be devoted to saving souls. He was not alone. There was debate, even dissension. Booth rode out the storm and the Army changed character irreversibly. From the perspective of the third millennium it seems unlikely that without government and other subsidies and widespread public support for its social work it would have survived as an evangelical organization on its present scale, in England, America or anywhere else. But that thought was not in many Salvationists' minds in 1883.

The debate within The Salvation Army over social work has a parallel in the history of Russian Orthodoxy. The dispute over whether monasteries should own land (in the Fifteenth Century they held about one third of Russian land) related to the question of whether the Church should be entirely devoted to prayer or had social responsibilities which would be paid for by the income from landholdings. By the beginning of the Twentieth Century, although there had been some attempt to persuade the Church to engage in formal social work in addition to personal almsgiving, the conflict had been resolved predominantly in favour of a spirituality divorced from temporal concerns. It is no coincidence that Railton was sympathetically disposed towards Russian spirituality, although it is difficult to imagine this hyperactive man standing for hours repeating the Jesus Prayer—'Lord Jesus Christ, Son of God, have mercy on me'—much as he would have approved of its content.

The Industrial Empire

Some of Russia's social problems—disruption of family life, desperate shortage of accommodation and an increase in prostitution—were direct consequences of the industrial revolution which had brought about great changes in Russian life during the latter half of the Nineteenth Century. Those in authority managed to ignore these difficulties for several decades: as Edward Acton remarks, 'the illusion was preserved, among conservative ministers as well as by Alexander III and Nicholas II themselves, that in Russia industrialization need not upset the traditional social structure...'[5] Other problems, most notably drunkenness, had been part of the country's social landscape for very much longer.

In the last decades of Tsarist power the Russia economy was expanding, its structure changing. Urban growth was enormous and uncontrolled. During the 1890s, fuelled by enthusiastic investment from Western Europe, heavy industries—iron, steel, coal, oil, railroads, machine tools and chemicals—doubled their output. By 1905 they had doubled it again.[6]

St Petersburg and Moscow (two of the ten largest cities in the world at the time, with Moscow equalling New York in the speed of its growth) expanded rapidly and chaotically with the influx of a large, often transient, casually employed labour force, with the further consequences which had become familiar elsewhere in Europe and North America during the previous century: shortage of low-cost housing and inadequate welfare services, medical care, education and public transport. Most peasant immigrants were entirely unused to city life and even skilled blue-collar or office workers who established more or less permanent residence might well spend part of the year in their native villages as the seasonal fluctuations of the casual labour market dictated.

Some of the strains these conditions imposed were ameliorated by the networks of fellow villagers which became a feature of city life, but even so families were frequently divided, with the husband working in the city while the wife remained in the village with the children. Alternatively, husband and wife might be together, leaving their children with relatives in the country. The conjugal nuclear family became almost a rarity in Moscow. Nevertheless, some (very few) male workers did marry and have children (during the 1890s increasing numbers of peasant widows and spinsters came to the cities in search of work), and some factory owners provided accommodation for married couples plus children in their dormitories. These, however, were often neither lit nor heated, and were frequently used on the Cox and Box system, with men sleeping during the day, and women in the same spaces at night. Some women slept on the factory floor next to their sewing machines. There was little provision for child-care, and the presence of women and children in the factories was accompanied by all the abuses associated with female and child labour in industrial revolutions elsewhere in the world during the Nineteenth Century. There were primitive child labour laws, but they were habitually violated. In 1882 child labour was actually outlawed, but a year later a group of factory owners petitioned the Minister of Finance for permission to *lengthen* children's workdays, already 12 hours per day. Fearful that absence would cause them to lose their jobs, some mothers gave birth on the factory floor, and none took more than two or three days of maternity leave. They often worked an 18-hour day, from four in the morning to ten at night.

---

5 Acton, *Russia*, p. 96.

6 This and the following five paragraphs are drawn from Lincoln, *In War's Dark Shadow*, pp. 107-22.

Hunger and disease were commonplace. There were no safety guards on factory machinery and the accident rate was high. (Factories themselves kept no records of accidents: the figures had to be established by investigators sent in from outside.) Badly maintained and dirty machinery added to the danger, since cleaning was supposed to be done by the workers in their own time and in consequence was often neglected. Workers were given no protective clothing even when working with poisonous chemicals—including phosphorus in match factories, the deleterious effects of which ('phossy jaw') The Salvation Army had already campaigned against in Bethnal Green. Serious illness was frequent and, although factories were supposed to have infirmaries, the sick were often left to fend for themselves. Mortality, especially that of children, was very high.

Workers had no redress against absolutist employers, although during the 1890s strikes (which were illegal) become more frequent. The working day also became shorter, stabilizing at about 12 hours. Pay, however, remained low—little above subsistence level for men, considerably less for women and almost nothing for children. Payment was arbitrarily irregular. Workers were customarily forced to buy their food from the company store at prices up to twice those on open market. There were cases of employers who refused to pay wages on the grounds that they came to less than the value of food bought on credit. This grim picture changed little before 1905. Some workers formed cooperatives to buy and prepare food (necessarily of the worst quality) more cheaply. A worker's basic diet consisted of *such* (pickled cabbage soup) to which potatoes might be added as a treat to mark a holiday.

Workers' incomes were further reduced by the imposition of fines—for lateness, fighting, intoxication, meeting in groups, and breaking tools (even if this occurred through normal wear and tear). Since food and fines between them absorbed most of a family's income, their clothing was of poor quality, worn for years and exchanged, when it was falling to pieces, at rag merchants.

There were, nonetheless, people who were worse off than even the most exploited workers. Although many peasants found work and some even prospered, unstable conditions caused many others to fail. People left the cities as well as coming to them, their employment prospects worse than when they had arrived. Both the principal cities soon had populous skid rows, a disproportionately large number of the inhabitants of which were or had been craftsmen. Housing did not increase in either availability or quality to meet increased demand. Tenements were repeatedly subdivided. There were cases of families who had moved *en bloc* to the city having to sleep in different buildings. Illegal immigration (Russians were required to carry internal passports) added to the numbers and the problems. Dress, manners and informal, small scale methods of production and distribution marked off hawkers and street vendors from established city-dwellers, and this visibility fostered widespread notions that newcomers were idle and feckless and that the city was on the verge of moral collapse. During the Nineteenth Century the disorderly life of the city streets, even when accompanied by drunkenness and crime and compounded by crowds of beggars and vagrants, had been thought of as vibrant, exciting, and quintessentially Russian. With the advent of the Twentieth, both the growing merchant class conducting business amidst the medieval glories of Moscow and the Petersburg nobility in their elegant Eighteenth Century houses wanted to live in modern, Europeanized cities, not in overgrown peasant villages where primitive, disorderly behaviour disturbed them day and night. The streets of these cities swarmed, so it was said, with 'vagrants, paupers, idlers, parasites and hooligans'. Such people, 'who avoid a normal life and regular work' were a threat to the authorities, industrialists, the fabric of the cities themselves, and their respectable residents.[7]

Fear bred intensification of efforts by the concerned upper classes to deal with the problem. The comparatively well off had always given alms; it was important in Orthodoxy to help those less fortunate. The aged and infants could find shelter in almshouses, orphanages and the Imperial Foundling Home. For their part, the police had kept lodging houses under surveillance and routinely arrested vagrants and mendicants and sent them to the workhouse or back into the countryside. But increasingly these charitable and administrative activities were seen as mere palliatives. Ordinary citizens felt threatened. They had objective reasons for this, but doubtless fear and prejudice made the situation seem even worse than it was. 'Dark masses' of wild and criminal paupers were, it was believed, bringing up yet greater hordes of children in their own image. This image, it was widely held, was a compound of 'idleness, improvidence, indolence, intemperance, impulsiveness, thriftlessness, apathy, fatalism and weakness of will'.[8]

The sociological realities behind the social stereotypes were more complex and less susceptible to easy moralizing. In 1900 Russia's factory workers and the urban poor numbered about 13 million, most of whom (even apart from the denizens of Khitrovka and similar areas) lived on the edge of destitution in grievously overcrowded tenements. In one case 50 men, women and children, some with tuberculosis or syphilis, were found living in a single room barely 20 feet square. In St Petersburg, the damp and oozing cellars, never previously used as housing, had been pressed into service. Every fall of rain caused an incursion of liquid tainted by excrement. In 1881 every fourth person in the city lived in a cellar. Every sleeping space in the capital and its suburbs was competed for by between 2.4 and 2.8 workers.

Since many men had left their wives behind in faraway villages, prostitution was rampant and was conducted in sordid and unhealthy stews. Three out of ten randomly selected workers were infected with syphilis.[9] By 1905 something between two and three per cent of Petersburgers were prostitutes, and about 70 per cent of the city's men, some women—even husbands and wives together—used their services. Almost any prostitute could earn 40 roubles a month, nearly twice the average wage for all workers and almost three times what women could earn in mills. The most successful were said to earn 700 roubles per month. From time to time there were official announcements that prostitution was carefully regulated: frequent medical

---

7 Bradley, *Muzhik and Muscovite*, pp. 1-2.
8 Bradley, *Muzhik and Muscovite*, p. 352.
9 Lincoln, *In War's Dark Shadow*, pp. 105-07.

inspections supposedly protected prostitutes and their clients alike.[10] That this was not so was asserted in 1909 when *Yama (The Pit)*, a novel by Alexander Kuprin, 'a graphic but overly sentimental study of life in a brothel', caused a minor sensation.[11] Kuprin's principal character, the prostitute Zhenchka, asks, 'What am I anyway? Some sort of universal spittoon, a cesspit, a public shit-house!'.[12] The pit that Kuprin described could have been found in any city in Russia. St Petersburg's equivalent was the Haymarket, the setting for Dostoyevsky's *Crime and Punishment*, in which it is vividly evoked.

The Alcoholic Empire[13]

It was only in the misty haze of a drunken stupor that many of the dwellers in such districts could hope to enjoy visions of a better, less unjust world. But the Russian propensity to extreme drunkenness dated from centuries before the upheaval brought by industrial expansion, and the Tsarist state was in large measure to blame. In the 1850s an English traveller, Laurence Oliphant, noted that

> men, while in a state of intoxication, have, in this country, an especial claim upon the protection of the government, since the sums drawn from the monopoly of vodka form an important item of the revenue. That there was a due appreciation of the obligation conferred by either party, I learned from a Russian gentleman, who told me that the police had strict orders not to take up any person found drunk in the streets. The numbers of tipsy men who reeled unnoticed about the large towns seemed living testimonies to the accuracy of this statement.[14]

Drink was traditionally a vital ingredient in Russian life at all levels. In the early Nineteenth Century peasant assemblies (*skhod*) featured 'noise, screams, curses, threats and at times brawling'. Vodka was frequently used to bribe voters. It would have been inconceivable for the end of the harvest, a wedding or a religious feast day to pass without copious consumption of hard liquor. Peasants were well aware of the state monopoly and 'reviled tavern keepers as robbers'. David Moon sums up the situation as follows: 'It was the state's thirst for revenue as much as the peasants'

---

10 Lincoln, *In War's Dark Shadow*, pp. 377-78.

11 Terras, *A History of Russian Literature*, p. 474.

12 Quoted in Lincoln, *In War's Dark Shadow*, p. 123.

13 The title of this section is borrowed from Patricia Herlihy's invaluable book *The Alcoholic Empire: Vodka and Politics in Late Imperial Russia*, Oxford and New York, Oxford University Press, 2002.

14 Laurence Oliphant, *The Russian Shores of the Black Sea*, Köln, Könemann, 1998, pp. 85-86. The vodka monopoly lasted from the mid-Eighteenth Century until 1863 and contributed an average of 33 per cent of state revenue. It was revived in 1896. See also David Moon, *The Russian Peasantry 1600-1930: The World the Peasants Made*, London, Longman, 1999, pp. 84-85 and 114.

thirst for forgetfulness that made vodka so important at both the national and local levels of Russian life'.[15]

Amongst more genteel classes drunkenness was common not only during leisure hours but also at work. Junior officials were frequently drunk and disorderly in taverns, as the records of the St Petersburg Criminal Chamber for the first six months of 1788 indicate. In the same year the secretary of the St Petersburg district court was accused of being drunk while reading the evidence for a murder case. During the reign of Peter the Great, a visitor recorded priests lying drunk in the street, and his astonishment that it was so far from scandalous to be intoxicated that even women of distinction and fashion did not scruple to admit that they had been very drunk. Consumption of spirits increased greatly during the Eighteenth Century and another visitor noted that, while the nobility tended to live soberly, it was scarcely possible to drink with a merchant without becoming intoxicated.[16]

Even amongst the revolutionaries, some of whom were rather puritanical, there were many egregious drunkards. A Maximalist leader, G.A. Nestroev, described a scene in a prison in Iakutsk, where:

> a group of fifteen radicals drank all day, with one man dying, apparently of alcohol poisoning. When the doctor arrived, he found one person lying unconscious next to the corpse, with a third drunkard still trying to force his dead companion to drink another round, while the others continued with their orgy.[17]

The Orthodox Church gave an impression of detachment from such realities. It was mystical, one-sidedly dedicated to liturgical contemplation of eternal truths, and forgetful of the concrete needs of human society.[18] Despite the importance it placed on good works, it was seldom assertive on ethical or social matters. For instance, although Pobedonostsev, Procurator of the Holy Synod, had identified the problem of drunkenness and its deleterious effects upon religion in his report to the Tsar for 1888-89, and thereafter looked for ways of dealing with it, he had only limited success, and drunkenness, both clerical and lay, continued.[19] The Church's attitude was not one of indifference. Many regarded drunkenness as a sin which separated the drunkard from God but in general a fire and brimstone approach to this particular weakness was avoided; kindness, sympathy and patience, it was thought, would cure the unfortunate victim of what was not so much depravity (let alone illness) as an avoidable bad habit. Some priests formed temperance societies, often based on the

---

15 Moon, *The Russian Peasantry*, pp. 85 and 234.

16 Janet M Hartley *A Social History of the Russian Empire 1650-1825*, London, Longman, 1999, pp. 81,116, 120 and 188.

17 Geifman, *Thou Shalt Kill*, p. 165.

18 Dixon, The Church's Social Role in St Petersburg, 1880-1914, in Hosking (ed.), *Church, Nation and State in Russia and Ukraine*, p. 167. Dixon goes on to show that this widely held view is not altogether accurate.

19 Dixon, The Church's Social Role, in Hosking (ed.) *Church, Nation and State*, p. 180.

device of the renewable, short term (six months and upwards) vow of abstinence. It remained the case, however, that church festivals, as well as the harvest and other significant points in the working year, were all celebrated with heavy drinking. Furthermore, educated and upper class Russians tended to regard abstinence as something that was good for peasants, but unnecessary for themselves. There were many exceptions, however. Tolstoy, of course, and his associates V. G. Chertkov and Vladimir Bonch-Brevich, both of whom we will meet again in other contexts, were active temperance campaigners. Indeed it was because of them and others like them that temperance became associated with radical politics, giving rise to the presence of secret policemen, suspiciously prowling the aisles, at temperance meetings. Such suspicions were particularly prevalent in the turbulent years following the 1905 uprising, but conservative figureheads were sympathetic when it seemed safe to be so; by 1909 (the year William Booth visited St Petersburg) the president of the council of ministers, P. A. Stolypin, endorsed the conference of the All-Russian Congress for the Struggle against Drunkenness and gave its committee 10,000 roubles towards its expenses.

After 1894, the state's theoretical promotion of moderate drinking was compromised by its monopoly on the production and distribution of vodka, which was revived in that year after having been discontinued in 1863. Intended to ensure official supervision of the quality and quantity of liquor manufactured, it was nevertheless widely criticized, in the Duma, and even by members of the Royal Family, such as the Grand Duke Konstantine Konstantinovich, whose wife we will meet in connection with Booth's visit. The state also ran its own temperance movement, the quaintly named Guardianship of Public Sobriety, centred upon People's Houses, where social and cultural activities were provided in an alcohol-free milieu. These, however, tended to be too expensive for the workers and peasants who needed them most and in the long run did more for Russian music and drama than for the cause of temperance. The state never succeeded in achieving its preferred solution to the problem—the consumption of one glass per day by every Russian, as opposed to the periodic binge drinking most of them indulged in. And although, when it was renewed in 1894, the monopoly had explicitly not been intended as a source of state revenue, it became clear in 1914, when Nicholas II, eager to boost the Russian war effort, banned the sale of vodka throughout the Empire (first class restaurants and clubs excepted) that the state depended upon it for 25 per cent of its revenue.[20]

Just as Church and state were not as active as they might have been in the fight against alcoholism, they very seldom initiated or carried out social work of any kind, although private charity was an indispensable part of the Orthodox faith, and organized help for those in need was encouraged. During the Nineteenth Century, Orthodox, led by Slavophiles, had begun to give serious thought to the social

---

20 The politics of alcohol in late Tsarist Russia is a complex subject, well covered by Patricia Herlihy in *The Alcoholic Empire*. My discussion is based on the book at large, but see particularly pp. 6, 12, 14-35, 52, 65-68, 69-89 and 128. For the economic consequences of prohibition, see Richard Pipes, *The Russian Revolution 1899-1918*, pp. 234-35, and pp.173-75, below.

responsibilities of Christians. Theology must be lived, since, in the view of St Maximus, 'Theology without action... is the theology of demons'.[21] The Church, nonetheless, sought to transform social or national life not by moralistic proclamation but by working from within on the hearts of its members. Since 1867, diocesan convocations, previously confined to raising money and reviewing developments, had built orphanages, churches, schools and retirement homes for priests. They had supported widows and established insurance and burial societies. Priests, themselves better educated than formerly, began teaching peasants how to break out of the poverty cycle and, following epidemics of cholera, diphtheria and scarlet fever in the 1890s, how to avoid unsanitary conditions. More recently they had engaged in pastoral counselling, and agitation for the revival of the parish as a moral and social unit,[22] working to improve relations between priest and congregation, standardize fees for services and improve their own morals and level of education. (Some bishops, however, thought of these convocations as forums for anti-episcopal agitation and other dangerous practices, which had to be curbed.)[23] In the event, this attempt to revitalize the parishes failed.[24]

Therefore there were many who felt that there was ample reason for Russia to welcome The Salvation Army's down to earth approach to the problems of the urban masses.

Tolstoy, Khitrovka and the Sermon on the Mount

As we have seen, neither the civil administration nor the Church had the will to do anything effective about homelessness, poverty, disease and drunkenness. Some Russian citizens, however, refused to believe that these evils were inevitable and ineradicable. When, having passed most of his early life in the country, Count Leo Tolstoy moved to Moscow in 1881, he discovered the scale and sordidness of poverty in the city. Influenced to an extent by the Radstockite Vladimir Chertkov, he looked to the words of Jesus for a solution to the problem, re-examining the Sermon on the Mount as a practical basis for everyday life. Since his views were considered heretical, his books on religion had to be published abroad, where he underwent a transformation from respected novelist into a public figure with international standing as saint and prophet.

---

21 Ware, *The Orthodox Church*, p. 215.

22 Most bishops agreed that after 1905 the parish was dead, a mere caricature of itself, which explained the indifference or antagonism to religion that had become so widespread in Russia. Yet the parish was the natural basis for the durable community so necessary in rural Russia, and priests had to play a role in public life if the humble Russian masses were not to become a raging mob, as the year 1905 had all too vividly demonstrated. (Cunningham, *A Vanquished Hope*, 184 and 186.)

23 Cunningham, *A Vanquished Hope*, pp. 22-23, and178-79.

24 Paul Valliere, Theological Liberalism and Church Reform in Imperial Russia, in Hosking (ed.), *Church, Nation and State*, p. 118.

The first economic indicator he had noticed in Moscow was the difference between urban and rural begging. In the country, the saying went, beggars carried with them 'a bag and the name of Christ'. [25] In Moscow the police were trying to stamp out mendicancy, and often beat offenders, which encouraged a manner of begging which Tolstoy describes with characteristic clarity:

> The Moscow beggars neither carry a bag nor ask for alms. In most cases when they meet you, they try to catch your eye, and then act according to the expression of your face.

> I know of one such, a bankrupt gentleman. He is an old man who advances slowly, limping painfully with each leg. When he meets you, he limps and makes a bow. If you stop, he takes off his cap, ornamented with a cockade, bows again, and begs. If you do not stop, he pretends to be only lame, and continues limping along.

Begging, Tolstoy discovered, was illegal, but the law was inconsistently enforced: some offenders were arrested and jailed, some not. When he decided to investigate the cause of and possible solutions to the problem, Muscovites, who seemed almost to boast about the numbers of impoverished in their city, sent him to Khitrovka to see the situation in its rawest state.

He visited the Liapin Free Night Lodging House and sensed that those he was observing were in two minds about him. Was he 'a self-satisfied man of wealth, desiring to be gladdened by the sight of our need, to divert yourself in your idleness, and to mock at us? or are you that which does not and cannot exist—a man who pities us?'.

When he overcame their mistrust and got them talking he found that one man from Smolensk, whose (internal) passport had been stolen, actually hoped to be arrested when the regular Thursday police check was made: a spell in prison followed by a compulsory return (on foot) to Smolensk, seemed to him highly desirable. Tolstoy gave him a drink, whereupon a succession of other men, each more grotesquely dressed or deformed than the last, accosted him. Eventually requests for drink became demands for money. Tolstoy distributed the 20 or so roubles he had about him, almost causing a riot in doing so, and went home, ashamed, to a meal of five courses served by liveried footmen. He was seized by the conviction that by enjoying and accepting his own superfluous goods while there were people who had none, he was (as he had been when watching the guillotine in action in Paris) 'by my silence and my non-interference, an aider, an abettor, and participator in the sin'.

His reactions to what he had seen and the ferocity with which he expressed them caused his wife and friends, not for the last time, to suggest that he was being foolish. (They also wished to avoid having to donate money to his impractical

---

25 My account of Tolstoy's experiences and interpretation of them is taken from the early chapters of his book, written between 1882 and 1886, *What Shall We Do?*, London, Free Age Press, n.d. (c. 1903). The quotations come from pp. 1-2, 10, 13, 18, 19, 21 and 43. (The title varies slightly between translations of this work.)

schemes: he tells us that although money was promised, none was ever actually donated.) He proposed to establish a charitable society whose members would divide the needy areas of Moscow between them and, by ameliorating the conditions that had brought them into being, ensure that blots such as Khitrovka would disappear forever. (In recounting this, incidentally, he accuses himself of an egocentric desire to be noticed doing good.) He realized early on that nothing would come of this scheme, but, prevented by 'false shame' from withdrawing his hand from the plough, he persisted. Part of his scheme had required the cooperation of census officials. They refused to help him, so he became a volunteer census official himself and was appointed to 'make the census of the section of Khamovnitchesky police district, near the Smolensky Market in the Prototchni Lane between the Shore Drive and Nicolsky Lane... the lowest circle of poverty and vice'.

Once again his first visit made him search his conscience and adjust his notion of what had to be done:

> I now realized, for the first time, that all these poor unfortunates, whom I had been wishing to help, had, besides the time they spent suffering from cold and hunger in waiting to get a lodging...[had somehow to] fill up the rest of the 24 hours of every day—a whole life, of which I had never thought before... [They] must live through the rest of every day of their life as other people have to do, must get angry at times, and be dull, and try to appear light-hearted, and be sad or merry...the task which I was undertaking could not simply consist in feeding and clothing a thousand people (just as one might feed a thousand head of sheep, and drive them into a shelter).

William Booth and Leo Tolstoy would have found much to talk about.

For all that, Tolstoy had not penetrated the lowest circle of this Russian *Inferno*. That took longer. He perceived that three different classifications of needy subsisted in these warrens: those who had come down in the world (either a long or a very short way) and were hoping to regain their former position; women of the town; and children. He found in each case that his own position in society prevented him from helping these people. Mere charitable acts (such as taking a boy from the slums to live in the servants' quarters of his own house) could not of themselves rescue slum-dwellers from the only world they understood, and were in any case often misunderstood or resented. (The boy in question ran away after a week and hired himself out to appear in costume leading an elephant in a menagerie.)

Tolstoy's disillusionment came to a head one night when he and his helpers set out to complete the census returns on the inhabitants of one lodging house. They, hearing that an official visitation was imminent, had instinctively, 'like hunted animals' tried to escape: Tolstoy was obliged to order the gates locked to keep them in. Once he set about his work a worse horror presented itself. He had supposed he knew the house and the people in it—but he had only been there in the daytime. Now:

All the lodgings were filled, all the pallets occupied, and not only by one, but often by two persons. The sight was dreadful, because of the closeness with which these people were huddled together, and because of the indiscriminate commingling of men and women. Such of the latter as were not dead drunk were with men. Many women with children slept with strange men on narrow beds.

[There was] everywhere the same fearful stench, the same suffocating exhalation, the same confusion of the sexes, men and women, drunk, or in a state of insensibility; the same terror, submissiveness, and guilt stamped on all faces, so that I felt deeply ashamed and grieved... At last I understood that what I was about to do was disgusting, foolish, and therefore impossible; so I left off writing down their names and questioning them, knowing that nothing would come of it.

I felt deeply hurt.

...I was like a doctor who comes with his own medicines, uncovers his wound only to mangle it, and to confess to himself that all he has done has been done in vain, and that his remedy is ineffectual.

He retired to lick his wounds and write his book. The solution he arrived at has been described by Victor Terras as 'nihilist, anarchist, and pacifist' in its advocacy of 'the abolition of modern society and a return to communal subsistence farming. He sees the way to his utopia in passive resistance to draft boards, tax collectors, and all the blandishments of modern civilization'.[26]

Tolstoy and Booth: Two Who Never Met

It is clear that Booth, who cultivated kings and prime ministers as patrons of his work, would have found much of this both inappropriate and implausible, but he would have recognized and applauded Tolstoy's strength and sincerity of feeling. The principal difference between them was that Tolstoy's instincts led him to propose a solution that was as radical politically as it was spiritually. Booth would have drawn a firm distinction between saving a person's soul, which had eternal consequences, and saving their body, which did not. Tolstoy would have thought that distinction shallow and absurd. For him the actions of the body were an expression of the state of the soul; neither could be thought of separately.

While the municipality did too little too late, Tolstoy practised utopian levels of self-abnegation (whilst remaining conscious of his own aristocratic impotence) and Communists dreamed of five-year plans, Booth, a pragmatist where Tolstoy and Lenin embraced dogmatic systems, seemed to offer a fourth way. The Salvation Army was western, experienced, believed to be successful, and was not inhibited by involvement in the Russian class system and bureaucracy. Perhaps it could provide the kind of charitable action that Tolstoy had conceived but had had to abandon. Certainly it would seek to do so without at the same time trying to overthrow the

---

26 Terras, *A History of Russian Literature*, p. 451.

government. So far as the authorities were concerned, a municipal official had already investigated its claims,[27] while the surviving followers of Lord Radstock were also willing to make it welcome.

Thus, not for the first time, the Army was looked to for services that its Founder and many of its officers regarded as secondary to its primary evangelical purpose. Booth thought he could contain what some thought of as a conflict between the Army's Field and Social departments, maintaining the Army's evangelical thrust while using social work as a tool in the Lord's service. When in 1909 he came to visit St Petersburg, he spoke to aristocratic audiences about the transforming power of conversion to Christ in the lives of individual people. Charitable activity was only a means to an infinitely more important end. Nonetheless, a historian cannot ignore the fact that many of those who welcomed the Army were impressed by what they had heard of the means without necessarily sharing Booth's ambition to see that end accomplished.

Meanwhile, the first Salvation Army officer to visit Russia had been among the most outspoken in denouncing social work as a dilution of the Army's original mission. He was Commissioner George Scott Railton, who, in 1904 (characteristically failing to refer the matter to International Headquarters) made the first application for the Army to be admitted to Russia.

---

27 See p. 99 below.

CHAPTER 5

Diplomatic Prelude

Railton, Rodjestvensky and the Hull Fishing Fleet

Commissioner George Scott Railton was small and balding, with a straggly but copious white beard. He led a life spartan to the point of austerity, but his eyes twinkled and he was uninhibited and hyperactive. His personal history and his relationship with the Booths give the clue to his attempts, made without reference to International Headquarters, to initiate The Salvation Army's work in Russia. The son of a Methodist minister, he had been a born-again Christian since the age of ten and was single-minded in his yearning to lead the rest of mankind into the same experience. (He once told a brother officer who was using a train journey to read Dante's *Inferno* that he would find out more about hell by visiting the East End of London.)

In 1880 he led The Salvation Army's invasion of America. In New York, on being informed that Harry Hill's Variety Theatre, from which he proposed to attack the Kingdom of the Devil, was the most disreputable den in the country and to appear there would destroy the Army's reputation, he replied 'Then that's the place for us'. In St Louis, denied the use of a hall, he preached to the skaters on the frozen Mississippi.[1] In later years he was to be, simultaneously, a pillar of The Salvation Army[2] (in particular of its autocratic style of government), and a dangerous loose cannon who never supposed that discipline and the desirability of a united front should constrain his own behaviour.

General Albert Orsborn, recalling his time as an office boy at International Headquarters (101 Queen Victoria Street, London), described him thus:

...not a Headquarters man, he spent very little time in office work. He was a fighter, happiest on the battlefield. He hurried in or out of '101', usually alone, carrying his campaign requirements in one Gladstone bag. He said he 'travelled third-class because there was no fourth'. He appeared to be not too comfortable in a uniform fully trimmed to the rank of Commissioner. Only on 'State' occasions, at Exeter Hall, or one of the big centres, did I see him in 'full dress'. Usually he came bustling through the swing door of 'the building'—as we called I.H.Q.— clad in a modified edition of a Commissioner's uniform, open from collar to hem, displaying the

---

1 Herbert A. Wisbey, Jr., *Soldiers Without Swords*, New York, Macmillan, 1955, pp. 1-2, and 27-28.

2 Railton was the first person to hold the rank of commissioner (the only non-military title the Army employed), in functions and status roughly equivalent to a bishop.

garment he most loved, a red guernsey with an outsize fiery cross. Often he attended knee-drill [prayers] in our department. His advent was electrifying. His prayers were those of a friend of God. His short, pithy homilies swept away all unreality and made my young heart long for sincerity. The halls and corridors of our Headquarters had a cleaner and stronger air when Railton passed through... Officially he was often a beloved rebel, but he had that wideness of mind and depth of religion which Sir Walter Scott must have noted when he wrote 'noble adversaries ever love each other'. I wish I had seen more of Railton.[3]

During the 1890s it had became apparent that Railton was out of sympathy with many new developments (especially those masterminded by Bramwell Booth, the Chief of the Staff). These developments were all of a kind that, in his view, could only distract the Army from its essential evangelical purpose. He was not won over to the idea of social work. He disapproved of the Army's increasing commercial activities such as the sale of goods produced by the Army and advertised in *The War Cry*. He was dismayed by the offer to the public of shares in The Salvation Army Building Association. He was contemptuous of the Army's increasing exploitation of the patronage of royalty, the nobility and politicians (although, when he arrived in St Petersburg he proved not altogether immune to such 'snobbery').

These conflicts came spectacularly into the open at the International Congress of 1894, with the launching of The Salvation Army Insurance Society, in an incident which led eventually to Railton's employment as a kind of travelling scout for the Army in lands where it was totally or almost completely unknown, relieved of specific administrative responsibilities and to a large extent cut off from other officers of equivalent rank whom he might try to win round to his point of view. As it happened, Booth's venture into the cut-throat jungle of life assurance was a financial success which provided funds which the Army used for purposes which Railton would have approved. But for Railton part of the essential definition of a Salvationist was that they would 'take no thought for the morrow' and that any penny they had to spare would be ploughed straight back into the Army's soul-saving work.[4]

What happened that July afternoon in 1894 at the Queen's Hall, later home to the Promenade Concerts, later still destroyed by German bombers, is vividly described by Bernard Watson:

Railton entered at the last moment and took his place on the platform barefooted and dressed in sackcloth—just like a friar, just like Railton! With no hint of what was to follow Booth joined in the general applause. Everyone loved Railton's eccentric gestures; all knew that he was a holy man. Dear Railton! One never knew what he would be doing next!

---

3 Orsborn, *The House of My Pilgrimage*, pp. 31-32.
4 Railton's stand on this matter was perhaps somewhat undermined by the fact that his wife had a private income, left her by her father (a Free Church minister in Torquay), who had deliberately tied it up in a trust so that Railton could not use any of it for Salvationist purposes.

He waited his moment, which came when opportunity was given for personal testimony.

He held up the handbill which had been produced by Colonel Bremner, who was the first managing director of the Army's assurance society. The numerous stenographers present were so dumbfounded that not one of them recorded Railton's words... Railton's copy of his speech has survived...

'I was so glad to hear our General in the holiness meeting this morning lay down the principles of self-sacrifice which he deemed necessary for successful salvation warfare. Judge then of my surprise when I found lying at my feet a dirty piece of paper.'

He brandished the paper, telling his now transfixed audience that

'It is inviting our officers to pay twenty shillings of the Lord's money and offering to give them thirty-three farthings yearly in return—a farthing for each year of Christ's life on earth', [Some reported that he here made an unpleasant reference to Judas, but this is probably a mishearing.] 'Worst of all, this dirty piece of paper bore the signature of a staff officer bearing the commission of our General and professing to be issued with his authority. Therefore, when I heard the General, whose commission I am proud to bear, say this morning that he still believed in the necessity of a life of self-denial and sacrifice such as enabled The Salvation Army to win its victories in the past, I was glad.'

He then dropped the paper and trampled on it. Booth was embarrassed and headquarters officers were thrown into angry confusion.

It was an unprecedented action. Though some Salvationists agreed with Railton, official reaction was that he was 'mental,' a condition brought on by overwork and worry.[5]

There was an undignified scramble of staff officers eager to sign a round-robin dissociating themselves from the malcontent and, after much agitation, he was relieved of all duties and told to go on holiday for a few months to recover himself. Having rejected this gambit, he was sent (officially on sick furlough) to the Argentine. The Army there was small and poverty-stricken and officers had been imprisoned, threatened at gunpoint and innocently caught up in periodic revolutions.

---

5 Bernard Watson, *Soldier Saint: George Scott Railton, William Booth's first Lieutenant*, London, Hodder & Stoughton, 1970, pp. 128-29 (Watson's square brackets). Watson was a colonel in the Army's editorial department in London, and his biography of Railton was objective to a degree not previously found in Salvationist historical and biographical writing. The suggestion that Railton was 'mental' was the same explanation, as Watson goes on to report, as had been used two years before when Colonel John Lampard withdrew from his engagement to one of William Booth's daughters, 'an act' Watson tells us, 'of staggering courage'.

He did courageous, committed work there and in other distant, uncomfortable places, as the Booths' use of him as a travelling evangelist and intelligence agent evolved. He spent much of 1907 in the Far East. In 1908, the year with which we shall be most concerned, he visited Germany, Austria, the Baltic provinces, Russia, Bulgaria, Serbia, Romania, Greece, Turkey, Egypt and Italy, sometimes staying for weeks or months, sometimes quickly taking stock of the situation and passing on. He undeniably had a talent for this sort of work. He thought internationally and believed that the true Salvationist should feel at home anywhere. He could communicate with anybody, of whatever race or class. He had a smattering (sometimes much more than a smattering) of many languages, acquired in a typically bull-at-a-gate manner: he would fight his way through some suitable book in the language to be conquered, using a dictionary and working out the grammar as he went. Pronunciation had to wait until he was among native speakers of the language and in the early stages was idiosyncratic.

But for all it might be thought that God and the Army had placed Railton just where he was most needed, it is clearly the case that he was sent on his travels partly to keep him out of International Headquarters, where his nostalgia for the days of the Christian Mission (when converting sinners and fitting them to be evangelists was the sole aim) made his presence increasingly problematic. Although Railton could be unaffectedly charming, he was no diplomat. He once told Commissioner Lawley, with whom he disagreed about the direction the Army was taking, that he was a 'backslider'. This, indicating as it did that Lawley had gone back on his binding commitment to God and the Army, was as hurtful a statement as one Salvationist could have made about another. Railton was simply not interested in what has since become known as 'public relations'. Directness was all.

His virtually uninterrupted journeyings had unhappy repercussions for his private life. The very words 'private life' would probably have struck him as childish frivolity, but his wife Marianne almost certainly thought otherwise. She had joined the Army in order to share his life, sacrificing social respectability and family esteem in order to do so: in the event they were separated repeatedly for months on end. His sons and daughter saw little of him and resented the Army for what in their view it had done to their parents.[6] Whenever he was at home (in Margate) he was likely to be discontented. International Headquarters kept him at arm's length. He was never told what was going on. *The War Cry* rejected articles of his on the grounds that they were too outspokenly critical.

Railton was suffering a peculiarly painful form of rejection: that of the favourite son banished from his father's side, sent to the margins after being at the centre of events. For all that, the life that he led after the *contretemps* of 1894 was clearly congruent with some deep-seated element in his character. That he became a

---

6 After his death his wife joined the Church of England, in which their two sons later became priests. One of them, David, made the suggestion which in time resulted in the placing of the Tomb of the Unknown Warrior in Westminster Abbey. A granddaughter, Dame Ruth Railton, demonstrated her fighting inheritance by founding the National Youth Orchestra of Great Britain.

peripatetic loner, working himself into the grave for a conception of The Salvation Army which none of his equals in rank quite shared, was only partially the fault of the Booths.

In October, 1904, Railton was sent to Finland, where he averted a nationalist separatist coup and conducted the Congress Meetings with great success. He took the opportunity of travelling to Helsinki via St Petersburg, which he saw 'at its dreariest, on one of those drizzly days when its wide, ill-paved streets were at their very worst'. Russia was in a state of upheaval. In July, rioters outraged by their country's poor showing in the Russo-Japanese war (which had broken out in February when the Japanese, without warning, attacked and blockaded Port Arthur, Russia's only year-round ice-free port on the Pacific coast) had been fired on by troops in the Nevsky Prospect, with great loss of life. Visiting the spot, Railton imagined soldiers of The Salvation Army marching down that broad avenue claiming Russia for God.

He did more than dream: he made application to the Tsar for the Army to be admitted to Russia.

The application will have gone first to the Department of Foreign Faiths, a bureau within the Ministry of Internal Affairs, but the word 'Army' in the title would cause it to be sent also to the Minister for War.[7] The precise nature of The Salvation Army and its interest, if any, in politics, had aroused occasional official interest in Russia during the previous 16 years. In 1888 the censor had allowed admission to Salvation Army publications.[8] In 1892 Paul Nardin, a civil servant in St Petersburg, had written to local authorities throughout the civilized world requesting their opinion of the organization. He had read *In Darkest England and the Way Out*[9] and other Salvationist publications and been impressed, but he knew also the various accusations made against the Army. What, he asked, were the facts? Was it genuinely charitable, and to what extent had it affected the moral and material welfare of outcasts? Whatever may have been the tone of the replies Nardin received, official hostility to the Army was demonstrated only two years later when, as was mentioned in the Introduction, a timber merchant named Booth was prevented from entering Russia because of his presumed association with it. In that same year Prince Nicholas Galitzin (he who had in 1894 unsuccessfully proposed marriage to Evangeline Booth), having investigated the Army's evangelistic and social work in England and America and accompanied William Booth when he was campaigning in Holland, returned to Russia to defend its work and methods against misunderstandings which had evidently arisen there.

Russian officialdom may have linked the Army's military language and appearance with British imperialism at a time when relations between Russia and

---

7 Colonel Larsson was told this would almost certainly happen when he was considering making a further application in 1913.

8 This suggests that these papers would still be being examined by his department in 1904.

9 Written by W.T. Stead and Commissioner Frank Smith and published in 1890 under William Booth's name, this expounded his policies of social amelioration and reform.

England were barely beginning to improve after 50 years when an Anglo-Russian war had been widely expected; if not in the Near East then in central Asia or, after Britain became an ally of Japan in 1902, in the Far East.

Railton's application thus came at a politically inopportune time. Nothing is known about its reception by the Russian bureaucracy, but it may well have fallen foul of the backlash from an incident that occurred in the month when it was made. Russia, humiliated in the Far East, sent its Baltic Fleet to attack the Japanese. In the North Sea, in what became known as the Dogger Bank incident, officers of the watch identified Hull fishing trawlers as a squadron of Japanese torpedo boats and shelled them heavily for about 20 minutes, sinking the trawler *Crane* and decapitating its skipper and mate. About twenty other fishermen were wounded, some severely.[10] Many commentators ascribed the incident and Russia's subsequent humiliation by the Japanese to alcoholism amongst the armed services.[11] The British press trumpeted its outrage and *The War Cry* joined in with Booth's relatively restrained condemnation, which used such words as 'irresponsible' and 'serious violation of international law'.[12] If the paper was indeed still monitored by Russian officials, his comments may have suggested to them that the attitudes of The Salvation Army were indistinguishable from those of the British Empire.

Stead Meets Stolypin

The Salvation Army's second attempt to gain admission to Russia followed a serendipitous meeting in 1908. Bramwell Booth, on a train to Stockholm, encountered W.T. Stead, newspaper editor and 'flamboyant, eccentric egotist who humbly served a Puritan God'.[13] Once editor of the crusading tabloid, *The Pall Mall Gazette*, now in charge of the *Review of Reviews*, Stead was on his way to St Petersburg to interview the Russian Prime Minister, P.A. Stolypin. Bramwell, instant and constant for the Kingdom, asked him to raise the topic of the Army's admission to Russia, authorizing him to offer five assurances to Stolypin on the Army's behalf.

Bramwell Booth had known Stead since the 1880s when they had crusaded together against child prostitution, a trade that Stead headlined as 'The Maiden Tribute of Modern Babylon'. In 1885 they were charged with abduction when their scheme to show the world how the trade in young girls operated was turned against

---

10 The deceased had been near neighbours of The Salvation Army's Hull Corps V, and the Hull Icehouse Corps band was on parade for their funeral, playing *The Dead March in Saul*, with brief intervals, all the way from the house to the cemetery.

11 See Herlihy, *The Alcoholic Empire*, p. 52, for quotations from Ernest Gordon ('alcoholized visions of Japanese warships') and others, including 'a German correspondent', who wrote, '"Who defeated the Russians?" ask foreigners, and they answer, "The Japanese did not conquer, but alcohol triumphed, alcohol, alcohol."'.

12 29 October, 1904.

13 Raymond L. Schultz, *Crusader in Babylon: W.T. Stead and the Pall Mall Gazette*, Lincoln NE, University of Nebraska Press, 1972, p. 255.

them by the brothel owners. Bramwell was acquitted, but Stead, the moving spirit behind the affair, was sentenced to three months' imprisonment.

Bramwell admired Stead and they had remained on good terms, but were strikingly different in character. The one trait they shared was an overriding ambition to make the world a better place. Bramwell was careful, precise and shy, and—despite the fact that in the crisis of his last years he showed little ability to understand the minds of those who disagreed with him—less overtly egocentric than some other members of his family. Stead was, as Barbara W. Tuchman describes him,

> a human torrent of enthusiasm for good causes. His energy was limitless, his optimism unending, his egotism gigantic. As the self-estimated pope of journalism his registered telegraphic address was 'Vatican, London'... He was short in stature, with high colour, bright blue eyes and a reddish beard, and in defiance of black broadcloth wore rough tweeds and a soft felt hat. Strong in goodwill he was weak in judgement.[14]

William Booth would have endorsed that last sentence. He admired and was bewildered by Stead in equal measure.[15] They had been particularly at odds over the 'Maiden Tribute' campaign, Booth feeling that Stead had dragged the Army into a questionable position, then left it in the lurch, while Stead felt that General Booth had been unhelpful. Booth had, nonetheless, been prepared to put Stead's energy and abilities to use: Stead, with Frank Smith, had written *In Darkest England and the Way Out* for him, and the editorial conflicts which arose during the collaboration are readily imaginable, since Stead, for all his impetuosity, was a journalist who had some respect for precise language, nice distinctions and exact dates, all matters of indifference to Booth.[16]

Stead was a Russophile. In 1888, despite his own belief in liberty, he had spoken out for Tsarist Russia in a book, *The Truth about Russia*, and a series of dispatches from St Petersburg. Now, in 1908, he intended to elicit from Stolypin comforting assurances that the spirit of 1905 was dead and future reforms would take place under a stable government. Admiring The Salvation Army as he did, having been, at least according to his own lights, one of its staunchest supporters, and regarding it as undeniably a force for social amelioration (and therefore for social and political peace) he was happy to accept Bramwell's commission. Knowing Russia, he thought that The Salvation Army would be successful there: some years earlier the Russian painter Vasily Vereshchagin (1842-1904), a freethinker, who thought he knew what Russian peasants wanted from religion, had told him that if the 'bright, brotherly, social religion', such as he had seen in The Salvation Army in London were introduced to Russia, 'it would spread like a prairie fire'. At the Regent Hall, he told Stead, he had seen 'the kind of religious service that exactly suits the Russian

---

14 Barbara W. Tuchman, *The Proud Tower*, pp. 228-29. Tuchman's zestful account of Stead is both tolerantly sympathetic and perceptively critical.

15 See Begbie, *William Booth*, vol. 2, pp. 255-56.

16 Ervine, *God's Soldier*. p. 701-02.

peasant. It is simple, homely, friendly, sociable, plenty of music, no formality, everyone on [terms of] equality, each one free to sing and pray as he chooses, and the whole company together as jolly as if they were tea-drinking in a *traktir*.[17] I have never seen any other religion which so exactly suits our *moujiks*'.[18] (His paintings suggest that he had an accurate grasp of what ordinary Russians wanted, since the depth of emotion and patent sincerity of his war paintings drew large crowds, including peasants, and 'did more than the works of any other individual artist to develop the Russian people's interest in painting'.)[19] Armed with his own and Vereshchagin's confidence, Stead went to St Petersburg to interview the man thought by many, including William Booth, to be the most impressive Russian statesman of his time and Russia's hope for the future. Peter Stolypin (1862-1911) was a bear-like man of 46 who had attracted the Tsar's attention in 1905 by the ferocity with which, as Governor of Saratov Province, he suppressed peasant riots: he executed the ringleaders after summary trial by field courts martial. (The gallows became known as 'Stolypin's necktie' and trains that carried political prisoners to Siberia as 'Stolypin carriages'.) In July 1906 he was appointed Prime Minister and part of his task was to suppress terrorism. He did this with what Edward Crankshaw describes as uncanny calm and clinical detatchment,[20] qualities unaffected even by terrible injuries suffered by his own children when a terrorist group, the Maximalists, planted a bomb in his house in 1906.

He pursued moderate reforms with the objectives of modernizing Russia and removing the causes of discontent that lay behind the upheavals in 1905. He enjoyed

---

17 Tea drinking in The Salvation Army is a motif that will recur.

18 Quoted in *All the World*, July 1915.

19 Tamara Talbot Rice, *Russian Art*, West Drayton, Penguin Books, 1949, p. 246; Figes, *Natasha's Dance*, pp. 411-14. Vereshchagin, an impressive figure with a high forehead, long straight noise and voluminous dark beard threaded with white, was a member of the school of painters led by Ilya Repin who resolved to paint Russian subjects only, in a 'remorselessly realistic style'. The government recognized the popularity of that style by appointing Vereshchagin to serve as 'artistic chronicler of the Russo-Turkish War [1877]. But some of his paintings were awesomely realistic in portraying the horrors of war and inspired emotions other than the intended one of patriotic exultation.' (Billington, *The Icon and the Axe*, p. 406). (... 'both sides pray to the same God,' he wrote... 'this is the tragic meaning of my art.') One of his best known works, *Apotheosis of War* (1871), shows vultures flocking around a pile of skulls in an arid, defoliated landscape near a ruined town. His work was vehemently supported and equally vehemently denounced, as 'barbarous' and the work of someone who had ceased to be Russian and 'taken on the mind of one of his Asian savages'; he received death threats and fled to western Europe before the exhibition closed. He returned to Russia 20 years later, only to die during yet another war: he was on Admiral Makarov's flagship *Petropavlovsk* when it struck a Japanese mine off Port Arthur, Manchuria, in April 1904, and sank with all on board. Oddly, Stead would also perish at sea, going down with the *Titanic* in 1912.

20 Edward Crankshaw, *The Shadow of the Winter Palace*, London, Macmillan, 1976, pp. 366-67.

some success: his agricultural policy, by increasing freedom and prosperity in parts of the countryside, stimulated a surge of agricultural production that brought Russia's farm output in 1914 to a level that would not be reached again until the 1960s. His success made Lenin feel pessimistic.[21] He was at the zenith of his career when Stead interviewed him in 1908, but his two years in office had already provoked an informal coalition of groups opposed to modernization, and the Tsar's initial grudging support was veering towards indifference that would in turn be followed by hostility.

Amongst his proposed reforms was freedom of religion,[22] which made Booth and Stead hopeful. Pious himself, he believed that Russia should continue to be a religious country and that government should play a significant role in religious affairs and give preference to Orthodoxy, the majority religion, but he sought to ease existing restrictions on other religions (except Judaism) and to make the state less intrusive in religious matters. This 'represented a radically different view of relations between temporal and spiritual authorities from anything the Russian state had previously envisaged' and was 'almost guaranteed to produce a hostile reaction from the Orthodox Church',[23] even though he did not intend to grant official recognition to non-Orthodox groups, merely to turn a blind eye on their activities. Under his direction, ministers discussed the possibility of introducing civil procedures for registering births, deaths, and marriages, easing of the conditions imposed on partners in mixed marriages, elimination of religious instruction in schools and the possibility of recognizing atheism as a 'belief'. He also proposed that in future people should be able to become members of other Christian groups (which would themselves be permitted to proselytize) without having to seek government permission. This last provision gave particular hope to bodies such as The Salvation Army. Some of these proposals were in due course drafted as bills, but their fate epitomized that of all of Stolypin's religious reforms: Orthodoxy and its sympathizers paid lip service to the idea of religious freedom while simultaneously arguing that permission to embrace atheism, civil registration and the abolition of religious teaching in schools would produce a class of people belonging to no religion, which would be unacceptable to church and state alike.[24] At the time Stead

21 Lincoln, *Passage through Armageddon*, New York and Oxford, Oxford University Press, 1994, pp. 229-30.

22 My consideration of Stolypin's activities in the matter of religion is based on Abraham Ascher, *P.A. Stolypin: The Search for Stability in Late Imperial Russia*, Stanford, Stanford University Press, 2001, pp. 295-302, and Peter Waldron, Religious Reform after 1905: Old Believers and the Orthodox Church, in MacRobert, C.M., Smith, G.S. and Stone, G.C. (eds.) *Oxford Slavonic Papers*, vol. 20, 1987, pp. 110-39.

23 Waldron, *Religious Reform after 1905*, pp. 119-20.

24 The principal beneficiaries of Stolypin's proposed religious reforms would have been the Old Believers. For a time the Tsar supported this aspect of the proposed reforms; in January 1906 he received a deputation of Old Believers, who were anxious to declare their loyalty to Tsar and country. In the not very long run, however, after having their hopes greatly raised, they found themselves no better off. The Orthodox Church opposed

interviewed Stolypin, the Prime Minister was of necessity diluting his proposals on proselytizing by non-Orthodox groups and the right to change from Orthodoxy to other Christian faiths. The Church, becoming more actively defensive as it saw its position threatened, had rebuffed his concessions, objecting as they did to an assumption which they detected in them: 'the painful suggestion that there exists a gulf... between the Church and its own flock'.[25]

Stead's conversation with Stolypin, which took place on about 10 July and was reported in *The Times* on 3 August, must be understood in the light of these developments.

After they had discussed the current political situation, agricultural problems, and the fact that some cities were still under martial law following the revolution of 1905, Stead fulfilled his promise to Bramwell Booth, asking whether there was any possibility that The Salvation Army might be admitted to Russia. Stolypin enquired whether The Salvation Army really did good work, and was told that it did excellent work, *apart altogether from its distinctive religious teachings*,[26] and was one of the most useful philanthropic organizations in the world. It was absolutely apolitical. Even in England it abstained entirely from political action, and elsewhere there had never been any suggestion that it meddled in politics or attacked the creed, ritual or prejudices of any other Christian church.

Stolypin wondered whether the Army could be relied upon not to inflame popular sentiment against non-Christians; Stead told him it was too Christian to be hostile to anybody. In every country people of all religions and of none, freethinkers and Roman Catholics, recognized the solid philanthropic value of the work of the Army and supported it financially. Lord Rothschild was one such. In Russia, as, for example, in Germany and Japan, Salvationists would render valuable service to the state. Twelve years ago they had been under the surveillance of the German police. Now German cities including Hamburg and Elberfeld subsidized them. In Berlin they had about 40 halls and centres of activity. Other supporters included the Japanese Emperor, the King and Queen of England and the Presidents of France and the United States.

Three times during the conversation Stolypin remarked that he 'saw no political reason why there should be any obstacle placed in the way of the coming of the Army into Russia'. Stead does not record what degree of surprise he felt on hearing this surely amazing statement. He recapitulated the assurances authorized by Bramwell Booth: The Salvation Army would neither engage in politics nor

---

any change, on the grounds that 'whilst the Orthodox Church had no objections to the provision of the freedom specified in the edict of 17 April, 1905 and indeed "could only welcome the release of the Old Believers from restrictions on the exercise of their faith", this had to be balanced against the rights which the Orthodox Church possessed as the established church of the Russian Empire,' and the Chief procurator argued that the April 1905 edict had done nothing to alter the fundamental position of orthodoxy. (Waldron, *Religious Reform after 1905,* pp. 127-28.)

25 Waldron, *Religious Reform after 1905,* p. 133.
26 My italics.

antagonize any other religious organization; it would observe bans on open-air meetings and processions;[27] notice of all meetings would, if required, be given to the police; and Government representatives would always be welcome to attend them. He concluded by declaring that Salvationists were good people, who made bad citizens into good ones and did the state no harm. Stolypin requested a copy of The Salvation Army's statutes, and these were submitted when Stead sent an advance copy of his interview.

The interview was revised then endorsed by Stolypin's secretary, but this was the last The Salvation Army heard of Stolypin's apparent welcome.

The published interview was enthusiastically welcomed by leading Salvationists. William Booth wrote in his journal on 3 August:

> Yesterday Mr Stead's long letter *re* his recent visit to St Petersburg appeared in *The Times*... referring to his conversation with M. Stolypin *re* the permission for the S.A. to enter Russia. This is itself important, but to have the open approval of the strongest, some say the only real strong public man in the [Russian] Empire, and this chronicled in the leading newspapers of Europe, is something worthy of note.

He wrote to Stead, thanking him for the 'straight and courageous manner in which you expounded the truth about the S.A.'[28]

On 15 August Bramwell wrote to his father that in Berlin he had heard a great deal about Russia.[29] As far as he could gather, both the Russian police and Russian university authorities would support the Army. As for potential personnel, there were several officers in Germany who spoke Russian; one or two who had resided in the North of Russia. He thought there would be no difficulty in 'making up a party of very decent Officers who know the language to start with'. There was one *caveat*: the only Russian press comment he knew of was a comment in a St Petersburg

---

27 In England open-air meetings and processions were among the Army's principal means of attracting the curious (the Army was fond of saying that the open air was its cathedral), but most European countries banned them. Finland conceded the privilege in 1914, but only during the summer. Stolypin could have but did not mention that, since the revolution of 1905, merely to wear a uniform in the streets in Russia had become very dangerous. Some terrorist groups took the wearing of uniform to be evidence that the wearer was employed by the state and, in that sense at least, supported it, an offence which they regarded as punishable by death. He might equally have told Stead that some terrorist groups used military terminology (e.g. the Combat Organization), and some individual terrorists were overtly Christian, so that the Army's militant, uniformed Christianity might attract the unexpected support or hostility of various groups within Russian society. See Keifman, *Thou Shalt Kill*, pp. 40, 48-49, 70 and 128.

28 Quoted in Begbie, *William Booth*, Vol. 1, p. 407.

29 A copy of part of the letter is in the Russia files held by The Salvation Army Heritage centre.

newspaper: 'We do hope The Salvation Army is not going to send foreign agents here.'[30]

Nevertheless, The Salvation Army convinced itself that Stolypin had given it the green light. On the day that Bramwell wrote the letter quoted above, *The War Cry* proclaimed that at last the way was clear for the entrance of The Salvation Army into Russia. Optimism had blinded the Army's leaders to the fact that Stolypin's remark voiced a possibility not a policy. Perhaps, arrogantly (and Stolypin was certainly arrogant), he supposed that if he eventually decided that The Salvation Army 'might be useful' as a convenient agency to help deal with social problems, he could find a way of letting it in. That was something to be considered for the undiscernible future. Meanwhile, there was nothing to be gained by antagonizing Stead, who could give him favourable publicity in 'the leading newspapers of Europe'. His delaying action—the request to see the Army's statutes before reaching a decision—was not recognized for what it was.

The headlines on page nine of *The War Cry* for 15 August, 1908 read:

RUSSIA!
At Last the Way is Clear for the Entrance of the Army
THE RUSSIAN PRIME MINISTER SAYS, "I SEE NO REASON" TO THE CONTRARY.
An Appeal for immediate Financial Help

The long article under these headlines suggested, somewhat imaginatively, that a lengthy and deliberate process of investigation had made the work of The Salvation Army known to and approved by the Russian Government. 'Up to a point, Lord Copper' is the only sensible response to this assumption. Stolypin, presumably, was aware of the Army's existence and character before Stead interviewed him. As already noted, a civil servant in St Petersburg had made enquiries about it. Radstockites and Pashkovites knew of it—but, long before 1908, to be a Radstockite was to lose official favour. Perhaps Prince Galitzin had, as he had told Evangeline Booth he would, sung its praises within Russia, but we hear nothing of this happening. Railton's unauthorized application for permission to begin work lay forgotten somewhere in the files of the Department of Foreign Faiths. These scattered, ephemeral instances of contact between the Army and Russian official consciousness indicate if anything that official Russian interest in The Salvation Army was slight, apart from the work it was doing in Finland,[31] which had,

---

30 Such suspicions were, not unnaturally, widespread throughout the age in which the British Empire was a currently or recently powerful force. Albert Orsborn (*The House of my Pilgrimage*, p. 251), describing a meeting with the 'not unfriendly' but 'unforthcoming' Prime Minister of India, Pandit Nehru, admits the possibility that Nehru shared 'the widely held view that our missionaries were primarily servants of the British Raj'.

31 Finland was a grand duchy within the Russian Empire having been taken from Sweden by conquest in 1809. Its autonomy had been respected until 1898, when a policy

according to *The War Cry*, 'been the subject of frequent official investigation and report to St Petersburg'. Its 'Corps, Rescue Homes, Slum Posts, and Shelters, in the principal towns of Finland' had spoken eloquently 'in the right quarter... of its elevating power among the poor, ignorant, and debased classes of society'. (This, eventually, would indeed prove to be the case.)[32]

But although Finland was within the Russian Empire, it was not Russia proper. It was not Orthodox. What applied in Helsinki did not apply in St Petersburg and Moscow. *The War Cry* listed several factors that, in its view, may have helped turn the key in the previously firmly locked door. Reports of the Army's progress and the General's world journeys and Motor Campaigns had appeared in the Russian Press from time to time. Russian travellers abroad had discovered the 'mysterious Blood-and-Fire Flag' and sent their impressions home. Encountering that flag in Norway, Sweden and Finland, some of them, 'led by our ministry into the liberty and joy of God's great salvation', had testified about 'the people with a strange uniform, happy faces, and a joyful religion'. There had been extensive contacts between Russians and Salvationists in Switzerland and Paris, where scores of Russians—'students, lawyers, doctors, actors and others—have knelt at our penitent forms... a proportion of them has gone forth to prepare, unconsciously, the way for The Army in their great Fatherland'. One 'exalted lady ... a companion of the present Czar when he was yet a youth... embraced the spirit and faith of the Army when she was in Paris'. Back in St Petersburg she circulated Army literature and was a subscriber to the French equivalent of *The War Cry*, *En Avant*, until she died. Visiting London she had attended Army meetings and been delighted by the 'streams of seekers for the blessings of pardon and purity. She would smile, clap her hands, and wave her handkerchief' and 'went so far as to prophesy that ... there were those who would live to behold similar manifestations in the modern and ancient capitals of Russia'.[33]

---

of intensive russification began. During the period covered by this book, apart from the years 1905-10, relations between Finland and Russia were turbulent.

32 Wiggins, in *The History of The Salvation Army, Vol. V*, London, Thomas Nelson & Sons, 1968, p. 74, mentions two instances of individual Salvationists who had conducted unofficial meetings in Russia with considerable success, one a soldier from Hull Icehouse Corps, who was temporarily employed as a foreman on board ship, the other a Russian who had trained as an officer in Germany and been recalled to his native land for military service.

33 This would appear to be the ballerina Matilda Kshensinskaya (1872-1971), Nicholas's first love and (so many assume) mistress before his marriage to Alexandra. Although *The War Cry* does not identify this 'exalted lady' and refers to her being a subscriber to *En Avant*, the French *The War Cry*, 'until the day she died', which in 1908 was 63 years away, Kshensinskaya was the only woman apart from Alexandra for whom he felt affection, which makes it difficult to imagine whom else the exalted lady might be. As with so many matters in Russian history different accounts of the affair flatly contradict each other. Many historians assume that Tsarevitch and ballerina were lovers in the fullest sense. Some however, allow the possibility that the affair may have been platonic. Nicholas himself makes this claim in his diary entry for 1 April, 1892. Yevgenia Glickman (on the internet) allows that Nicholas was infatuated with Matilda for

The War Cry concluded by anticipating that the Army would be received in Russia, as elsewhere, with a mixture of interest, curiosity and goodwill. (Although, on the same basis of previous experience, it might have anticipated some hostility as well, it did not say so.) Its novelty would appeal to the Russians and 'arouse them from hopeless lethargy and the slough of despond'. Commissioner Railton had already visited Russia once and was at present making a further reconnaissance. Before any action could be taken, however, two essential conditions would have to be met: guaranteed supplies of men and money—'the latter always being more difficult to procure than the former'. Until the General was satisfied that Russia would not become a permanent financial burden the Army would not begin work there. Financial caution actually increased during the following years. From 1913 to 1919 the Army's Chancellor of the Exchequer was Commissioner George Mitchell (a complex man who also conducted the International Staff Band, and in doing so sometimes exhibited a flamboyant theatricality at odds with his generally austere, parsimonious character), 'a tight-fisted Chancellor, more than a little apprehensive of our expanding overseas commitments and therefore conservative in philosophy. He was not a spender; he was inclined to be negative, and liked to salt down the money'.[34] Meanwhile, back in 1908, *The War Cry* took a sanguine view:

No one surely can read the above unvarnished... account of what we believe to be the leading of God without being deeply stirred. There are abundant signs that the Lord has called us to, and so far has prepared the way for us in Russia.

WE MUST GO FORWARD, and therefore turn to our friends to come at once to our aid financially. We will provide the men.

---

two years but is firm that that was all there was to it. Perhaps, then, it was the degree of that infatuation which caused the shame which overheated his emotions when, on 8 July, 1894 he made confession of the relationship to Alexandra.

Then there is the question of the attitude of Nicholas's parents. Dominic Lieven, his most authoritative recent biographer, regards the affair as 'a normal rite of passage' about which the emperor and empress had no strong feelings (despite the fact that Alexander loathed loose morals). According to Victor Alexandrov, however, it was widely assumed at the time (and was reported by the St Petersburg correspondent of the influential and objective French daily, *Le Temps*) that Kshensinskaya had seduced Nicholas on the instigation of his father, Alexander III, who wanted her to make a man of his chaste, retiring son. William Gerhardi, contrariwise, states that Alexander deplored this relationship with a mere dancer and took Nicholas on a cruise to distract his attention from her, while on 17 May, 1896, the Dowager Empress was reportedly most unhappy that Nicholas, in 1896, two years after his marriage, went to the Bolshoi for a gala performance during which Kshensinskaya danced a new ballet, *The Pearl*. See Victor Alexandrov, *The End of the Romanovs*, London, Hutchinson, 1966, pp. 115 and 149; William Gerhardi, *The Romanovs*, London, Rich and Cowan, 1940, p. 483; Lieven, *Nicholas II*, pp. 24 and 37; Maylunas and Mironenko, *A Lifelong Passion*, London, 1993, pp. 22, 80 and 145. See also pp. 312-13, below.

34 Orsborn, *The House of My Pilgrimage*, p. 25.

The references to 'hopeless lethargy' and 'the slough of despond' are no doubt arrogant and condescending, but the belief that lethargy and despondency were rife in Russia was The Salvation Army's principal justification for going there. Those supposedly most affected by this spiritual gloom were the peasants and urban workers, whose needs, the justification continued, were not catered for by Russian Orthodoxy. The Church's paucity of doctrinal and biblical teaching, its formal and ritualistic services, the toleration with which heavy drinking, illiteracy and other personal shortcomings (in priesthood and laity alike) were viewed, all seemed at best regrettable, at worst scandalous to western evangelicals fervent for the Ministry of the Word. It is easy to imagine the snorts with which Booth and Railton would have greeted the story of the young Orthodox priest who had said to a western theological student that he could not understand Westerners who were always wanting to *do* something for God while the Russian idea of religion was to be still before God and let him do things for them.[35] The Salvationists would have endorsed the need to be still before God, but would expect stillness to be followed by vigorous action.

They also believed that Orthodoxy had done no more than sprinkle a very limited form of Christianity on top of the paganism it had failed to eradicate. The Church's mainstay was, Vidler remarks, 'the devotion, not unmixed with superstition, of the mass of the uneducated peasants'[36] (although he might have added that its interdependent relationship with the state was also important). But, in an age of urbanization and displacement, whatever its theological authority and traditional standing, the Russian Church left many people and problems untouched. The Salvation Army saw no reason to suppose that Vereshchagin had been mistaken when he remarked to Stead that if its own 'bright, brotherly, social religion... were to enter Russia, it would spread like a prairie fire'.

Railton Again

This 'bright, brotherly, social religion' was still the driving force in the life of George Scott Railton, who was now, as *The War Cry* announced, in Russia again, to conduct a two month 'reconnaissance'. He revisited Odessa, the port towards the western end of the Black Sea that he had passed through in 1906, in the aftermath of the 1905 Revolution. It was calmer now, but still under martial law. It had been a centre of Anarchist activity since 1903 (a group calling itself 'The Uncompromising Ones' was formed in November of that year), and during 1906 and 1907 anarchist-syndicalists blew up several commercial steamships and killed two unpopular sea captains. There had always been tension between Jews and Slavs in the city, and it

---

35 Alec Vidler, *The Church in an Age of Revolution*, Harmondsworth, Penguin Books, 1961, p. 230. Vidler comments that this 'was a kind of spirituality that could enable Christians to endure terrible ordeals with heroic patience, but that would not and did not give them any sense of obligation to work for social justice or political reform'.

36 Vidler, p. 229.

had become notable not only for anti-Semitism but as a centre of Jewish radicalism.[37]

Catherine the Great founded Odessa in 1794, as a southern counterpart to St Petersburg, through which, so long as the Dardanelles remained open to Russian shipping, trade with Western Europe could continue during the icebound months of the northern winter. Its heyday as a free port was the first half of the Nineteenth Century, during which it became a centre of Hebrew and Yiddish literary culture and enjoyed a varied and significant musical life.[38] Its consciously elegant buildings included an opera house and imitation classical villas. For all that, when Railton arrived from Constantinople in 1908, he was puzzled all over again, as he had been in 1905 by its extraordinary mixture of ancient and modern. Its massive stone-built houses and stone-paved streets, boulevards and gardens were such that no city in England could be compared with it—but its trams were pulled by horses, which struck him as extraordinarily old-fashioned.[39] Very poor people mingled with well-dressed ladies but even at the coal wharves he saw less of rags and dirt than he had expected. Soldiers, there to prevent any further revolutionary disturbances, abounded at every turn.[40]

Railton met the 'energetic' Governor Tolmachev, whose life was still under threat but whose 'simple seaside mansion' had a single policeman on the door, who 'made no sign of objection to the entrance of a uniformed Salvationist'. Railton complimented his host on the good order and quiet, which provided a marked contrast with conditions during his previous visit, but in letters home he reported that the Post Office was closely guarded by soldiers, who were, nonetheless, unable to prevent robberies. He enquired into the question of religious liberty and found, to his astonishment, that for years there had been large Baptist churches in Odessa, 'situated upon main thoroughfares, with announcements on their fronts, and without the slightest interference in their worship'. (The Baptists had told him, he wrote privately, that they were freer in Odessa than they were in Germany.) As well as churches attended by foreigners there was a Russian Baptist Church—its members all 'seceders from the national church'[41]—on Kerson Avenue, almost next door to the magnificent public library, and there was a German one near the Post Office. The singing of lively western tunes ('profane to Russian "orthodox" ears') was audible

---

37 Geifman, *Thou Shalt Kill*, pp. 103,123, 135, and 140.

38 The internationally celebrated violinists Mischa Elman and Jascha Heifetz were born and educated there.

39 Before 1907 he would have found the same thing in St Petersburg, where a private tram company had negotiated a contract giving it exclusive rights to ground transport. Each winter, however, a more modern transport company circumvented this contract by laying rails for electric trams on the frozen Neva.

40 *The War Cry*, 2 May, 1908.

41 If this is true, it may be that, as was also true of the central bureaucracy, the Church's power diminished in proportion with distance from the capital. Alternatively, Odessa, with its frequent contacts with the outside world, was exceptional. Legally, foreign confessions in Russia could only serve non-Russian adherents living there.

outside both, but there was no sign of public annoyance. Railton concluded that freedom of worship was 'a grand reality' in Odessa, and that Russians were eager for non-Orthodox religion. There was new Russia, and Odessa was its greatest port. 'If once we got going,' he wrote to his wife, 'on the big scale I'm advocating in Odessa we may easily become a very great power in a very little time...'.[42] He accepted, however, that Odessa was not representative of Russia at large.

Because Odessa was far more exposed to contact with Western Europe than was St Petersburg, and a wide range of foreigners jostled each other in its lively streets, there was genuine religious tolerance. A governor of the city had said that there were ten different nationalities under his jurisdiction, with 'ten different religions and all ten are practised freely'.[43] Catholicism and Protestantism were both to be found there, and parts of the western Ukraine had even been to some extent affected by the Reformation.

Railton described the religious practices of the Russians with diligent interest. He thought Orthodox funerals such as one he saw in the Cathedral 'really a terrible ordeal for the bereaved'. The deceased lay exposed while his loved ones stood through a long series of chants and prayers. 'Then each one must go up and kiss the cross fixed in dead hands, and only after the priest has read out, and laid on the dead man's breast, the bishop's certificate that all his sins, known or unknown, against God, the State, or individuals, are pardoned, is the coffin-lid brought forward and made fast.' Otherwise he was torn between approving the apparent depth of Russian faith, and deprecating its (as he thought) superstitious and idolatrous practices. Even these, however, he mentioned partly in order to praise the Orthodox Odessans' toleration of other faiths. 'One must have seen all the fervent kissing of pictures in every part of every church, the buying and lighting of tapers by the richest as well as the poorest of the congregation, the kneelings and prostrations of both men and women of every class, to understand all it means for this people to witness with perfect patience the opening on their main streets of places of worship where they know that all these practices are not only abandoned but denounced.' Railton was not unaware of Russian anti-Semitism, although he supposed Governor Tolmachev had eradicated it from Odessa. ('Away inland, I am told, it is still the custom to celebrate Easter by attacks on Jews.').[44] Oddly, but entirely typically, Railton spent a Saturday night 'inspecting' some of the city's 83 synagogues. (Each Jewish trade guild had its own.)

---

42 Letter to Mrs Railton, 21 April, 1908. I have corrected an apparent error ('allocating' for 'advocating') in the typed transcript.

43 Anna Reid, *Borderland: A Journey Through the History of Ukraine*, London, Orion, 1997, p. 59.

44 It should be noted, however, that the prominent Jewish writer Isaac Babel, born in Odessa in 1894, featured both pogroms and Jewish gangsterism in his *Odessa Tales*, which were published in 1921 and 1922. Babel fought with the Red Army after the revolution and worked for a time for the Cheka. Nonetheless, tarred with the brush of Trotskyism, he was later arrested by the NKVD, and died in a Siberian prison camp in 1941.

In the hour devoted to worship he had time to visit only four and was disappointed by the moderate attendance 'on what was reckoned to be one of their greatest Sabbaths'.[45] The first, 'a splendid place' was 'occupied by comparatively few... I was at once ushered into a front seat, keeping, of course, my Army cap on, for to remove it would be the equivalent of keeping it on elsewhere. I hope the sight of it did somebody good, for many did not seem by any means absorbed by anything the gilt-cloaked rabbis or the splendid choir did.' Another synagogue was smaller and 'stricter', but the congregation was also sparse. The third was 'what in America would be called a "reformed Synagogue". That means here more genteel fashions, especially in the ladies' gallery, whose low gilt rail gives them as much opportunity for display as the ordinary Christian young lady likes in her place of worship.' The fourth was working class, plain and large, 'where nearly all dressed no better than you may see them in Whitechapel'.

He found little to choose between Judaism and Orthodoxy. 'The same gilt-gated holy place, which only rabbis and priests may enter, and in which the Holy Book is kept, in each place the same ceremonies, the bringing of it out and the holding of it up, and the parading of it round through a bowing, document-kissing crowd, with the same splendid choir singing all the time, and the same termination after the closing of the holy gates and the rapid dispersal of the voluble crowd.' He remarked that the Salvation Army custom of parading around the hall derived from the worship Christ and the apostles 'were accustomed to witness... long ago, only that such outbursts with us are, I think, almost always special and spontaneous, and show an enthusiasm greatly in contrast with the stately, formal, Jewish style, and more in keeping with the eager Russian genuflections that mark every step of the march with the opened gospel round their churches'.

Unsurprisingly, the visit he enjoyed most was not to a formal service, but to a 'blessed hour and more in the mission room, crowded by 60, mostly men, eager and generally believing listeners. A young man full of conceit about his "philosophy" wanted to speak at the finish but was kindly suppressed'.[46] Railton found this experience 'really valuable' and his sense of what was missing in Russia that The Salvation Army could supply is implicit in all his comments. Formal religion seemed to work for some people but for many it choked off true, immediate and continuous joy in the presence of God. For great masses of the uneducated and working classes, to whom spontaneity was infinitely more important than aesthetics and a theologically precise liturgy, The Salvation Army, with its lively music, utterance from the heart, services made up of short and varied elements and, above all, its overwhelming sense that Jesus Christ was the sole mediator between God and man, would satisfy an obviously felt need.

---

45 *All the World*, 1908, pp. 583-84.

46 We may recall Railton's reaction to the officer who read Dante (see p. 98, above): he viewed academic education as irrelevant to religion and a potential source of dilution and confusion in its practice. It was undesirable to turn people who might become useful Salvationists into 'gentlemen'. He was distressed when his sons went to Oxford.

Railton travelled north to Riga and St Petersburg before going home to Margate via Odessa. In Riga he was probably the guest of Baroness von Frank, who was to make contact with Colonel Karl Larsson, leader of the embryonic Salvation Army in Russia, early in 1914. In Lodz he attended a Sunday School Convention with representatives from all over Russia and Siberia, speaking to large congregations in various churches.

On his way back to Odessa he stayed for a period on a small estate at Tolstoye, south-west of Kiev, belonging to a converted Salvationist, Mary von Weisberg. This woman, who was to play a large if occasionally enigmatic part in Salvationist affairs, was described by Colonel Karl Larsson, after he met her in 1914, as:

> ...a warm admirer of The Salvation Army and at the same time a faithful adherent of the Orthodox Church. It is not easy to judge her spiritual attitude, but sometimes her experience appeared slightly nebulous... [Yet] she was willing to do her utmost to enable us to get firmly established in Russia.[47]

Until the revolution she spent most of her time on her estate, so it is unlikely that she had fallen under the spell of Lord Radstock although it appears that his successor, Colonel Pashkov, was active in Kiev in 1876 or 1877. She may have been influenced by the evangelical movement called Stundism (from *stunde,* the German for 'devotional hour'). This originated with a Bible study group near Odessa and spread through the Ukraine about 20 years before Radstock began preaching in the capital. (The connection with Odessa suggests a means by which Railton might have been put in touch with her.)[48]

Railton puzzled the peasants and villagers of Tolstoye. Who was he; why was he there? He astonished them by being the only person to attend a series of early morning requiems for a deceased woman (paid for by her well-to-do family). The priest, disconcerted by having this curiously uniformed, wispily bearded, closely attentive Englishman watching him morning after morning, cleaned and dusted the church: something his parishioners had been demanding for months. After a day or two it became generally understood that he was 'a warrior of Christ' and an instance of a familiar traditional type, the mendicant pilgrim, travelling across country, fed and sheltered by those who homes lay in his path, bringing in exchange an intense, otherworldly spirituality.[49]

---

47 Larsson, Karl, *Tio År I Ryssland*, p. 41.

48 The Stundists were at first influenced by Lutheran and Mennonite leaders; after 1871 they separated into several groups; later still they came increasingly under Baptist influence.

49 Railton had much in common with the late Eighteenth Century figure Gregory Skorovoda, a native of the Ukraine who reacted vigorously against Catherine the Great's westernizing materialism. Ascetically indifferent to the things of this world, he gave up academic life, packed his knapsack with a Hebrew Bible and books in many languages, and wandered in search of full inner knowledge of himself, which could be obtained only through personal contact with God. He, through 'the sincerity and intensity of his quest... commanded respect even among those unable to understand his ideas or

Miss Weisberg, for her part, was alarmed when he determined to attend a potentially drunken and violent feast day in a nearby village. He returned leading a group of girls and young men, all singing the only Salvation Army song of which he knew the Russian words.[50]

Before he left Russia for the last time Railton, without consulting London (indeed in defiance of what he knew would be the reaction) once more applied to the authorities for permission to begin Army work there. He cabled the Tsar, craving an audience.[51] He received only polite official replies.

His farewell from Odessa was characteristic. Addressing a Baptist prayer meeting through an interpreter, he urged them to

> go in for soul-saving seven evenings of every week... The fervent prayers that followed, as well as the address of the German Baptist pastor, gave me every hope that this will come yet.

> The conclusion of it all was that after the benediction the handsomest elder present came up to me, and, after publicly saying how grateful they had all long felt for the gifts and kindnesses they had so often had from England, he gave me several kisses on behalf of the whole nation!

He gave free reign to his optimism in one of his *War Cry* articles:

> I... found myself in a country full of hunger for religion and full of liberty to spread it everywhere. But, Oh, how full of other, and contrary influences! ...Fancy, if you can, a population three times as great as that of the United Kingdom, with at least as much open drunkenness as in England in Wesley's days, and no large temperance society in it, the idea of teetotalism almost entirely unknown in its churches, and many of its priests anything but safe examples![52] ...I am confident that it is our

---

language... [he was] the untitled outsider in aristocratic Russia, the homeless romantic and passionate believer unable to live within the confines of any established system of belief. He stands suspended somewhere between sainthood and total egoism, relatively indifferent to the social and political evils of this world, thirsting rather for the hidden wellsprings and forbidden fruits of a richer world beyond'. (Billington, *The Icon and the Axe*, pp. 238-42.) Railton would have differed with Skorovoda on many points of belief, but temperamentally they might be twins.

50 Eileen Douglas and Mildred Duff: *Commissioner Railton*, London, Salvationist Publishing and Supplies, 1920, pp.179-82.

51 Watson, *Soldier Saint*, pp. 226-27. During a (physically very uncomfortable) tour of the Far East in 1904-05, Railton, on no authority but his own, had begun Salvation Army work in China, news which he communicated in a telegram which caused a stir of astonished displeasure at '101': 'Opened China with a rescue home—Railton' (Watson, p. 220). Bramwell Booth did not regard China as having been 'opened' and the flag did not officially fly there until 1916.

52 In an article published in *The War Cry* on 3 October, 1908, Railton described a fire that broke out after three days and nights of revelry during a village festival and commented on the frequency of such conflagrations and the lack of educational and

Father's good pleasure to give us this Empire to an extent He has given us no other in this world yet. In two months I have had more to do with titled people than in all my previous life;[53] and everywhere they have received the Salvationist in simple uniform with a warmth we rarely expect in such circles anywhere else... I have yet to meet with, or hear of the first Russian aristocrat, knowing anything of our Army, who would not like to see it at work amongst his people... In two months I have rarely had an evening without a crowded meeting of poor people, eager enough to listen even to a translated speaker; but far more eager to pray, or to sing such songs as we delight in. Yet I have been nearly all the time just in these places where the stormiest scenes of revolution passed... This very morning I was startled to notice the soldier with bayonet fixed, inside the grand post office where they take such special pleasure in serving the Salvation man. I had never noticed the bayonet before, so little does the 'state of siege' affect us!

This being so, and noticing as he does much that is bright and kindly, he regrets what he sees as a disproportionate emphasis in English newspapers on murders, arrests and executions, but:

I can contradict, alas, none of these sad reports. They are only too true, and I cannot wonder that we had in this one city [St Petersburg] 250 suicides in the first three months of this year, twenty-six of them people under age... On Sunday I saw the 'Slum' Sunday-school that one of our oldest friends (who has gone herself to live in the 'slum') has gathered, and the next day I went to see 728 dinners served out to unemployed families by another warm friend of ours in another district... There are, alas, only too many drunken parents here, and no doubt some are ragged and dirty; but that sight is comparatively rare in the very poorest alleys. There are said to be many families that cannot even afford one entire room for themselves in the cities. Yet, riding with them in the trains and mingling with them in the streets and on the river boats, I have wondered to find them so rarely anything but the clean, kindly sort that, even when down ever so low, fill you with hope for their future, once they can get hold of a strong, helping hand.[54]

Since the revolution of 1905 the incidence of suicide had indeed increased, alongside an unprecedented escalation of terrorist activity, and according to

---

recreational facilities in the Russian countryside. It is clear from these two articles that he endorsed the need for improvement in social conditions, but that he expected such improvement to follow naturally once the peasants, whom, like the townsfolk, he found 'kindly, intelligent and capable', had undergone religious conversion.

53 A titled person whom Railton did not meet was Count Leo Tolstoy, who was at the time, as Watson points out (*Soldier Saint*, p. 227), assailed by conflicts similar to those that troubled Railton. In 1901 the Orthodox Church had excommunicated him as a heretic. His rigorous but eccentric interpretation of religion put him at odds with his wife who (as Marianne Railton did George) thought him feckless. His children supposed him a candidate for a lunatic asylum. Like Railton, Tolstoy was to become in effect a homeless wanderer. Both died at railway stations. Anyone who relishes the idea of improbable but oddly appropriate encounters can only regret that Railton and Tolstoy never met.

54 *The War Cry*, 27 June, 1908.

psychiatrists these phenomena were intimately connected. The young people of the time were described by the poet Alexander Blok as 'the children of Russia's dreadful years'; many became terrorists and expected to be executed or otherwise killed sooner or later, adding an element of long-term suicide to that of political protest. 'Suicide, murder, sexual perversion, opium, alcohol' were, as Lincoln remarks, integral to Russia's 'Silver Age' at every level of society. Many of the strikingly turbulent people of the era, having sought in vain for definitive answers to age-old questions ('What is art, and what is its relation to life? What is sin, and could a sinner still find salvation? Who (or what) is God? Is there any God at all?') thought often of sublimating their unsuccessful search in a poetic death.[55]

Having given his account of the (for the Army) very promising situation in Russia, Railton leaves our story. The rest of his life followed the pattern established after 1894: he travelled almost continuously, ever optimistic, enthusiastically promoting Salvationism as he understood it. Meanwhile, his influence at '101' declined. He died in 1913, in Cologne Railway Station as he boarded a train he had run to catch. He had recently turned 64.

His contribution to The Salvation Army's attempt to establish itself in Russia encapsulates the ironies of the enterprise. Railton looked at Russia and saw a country where the established religions, whatever their virtues, were not touching great numbers of the people. The Army would fulfil this crying need. What in Railton's view it was not called upon to do was deal in a socially ameliorative way with the homeless and the physically sick, orphans and widows regarded simply as orphans and widows, the human flotsam and jetsam created by a period of urbanization, war and revolution. These people were souls to be saved, and that was The Salvation Army's only proper concern. Clearly, however, had the Russian authorities seen The Salvation Army in this light they would never have extended even the heavily conditional welcome they eventually did. William and Bramwell Booth, however, were pragmatists– which is why they were running The Salvation Army and Railton was not. They knew that it was not in the nature of countries (nor even, often, of individuals) to welcome evangelists who came empty-handed. Something else had to be on offer and that something in the Army's case was its willingness to work amongst the outcasts of society. That was clearly what Stolypin found interesting and possibly useful, and what attracted the attention of concerned (and frightened) members of the Russian aristocracy and upper classes.

The Booths, nonetheless, knew that Railton was an experienced, realistic, if ever-optimistic evangelist. If he thought that the Army could make an impact upon the Russians he was probably right. His opinion and Stolypin's apparent *laiser passer* made the next step obvious. In March 1909, William Booth, Founder and General of The Salvation Army, visited St Petersburg.

---

55 See Geifman, *Thou Shalt Kill*, pp. 19 and 168, Lincoln, *In War's Dark Shadow*, pp. 350-51, and Heier, *Religious Schism*, p. 15.

The General Speaks

St Petersburg was a grand, ceremonial city, its centre a vast parade ground. As the capital and administrative hub of the Russian Empire, it was, to Booth's mind, the place where the Army's work must begin.

Even when, a few years ago, many of its buildings and roads exhibited the crumbling disrepair of the late Twentieth Century, it remained stupendous, fascinating and beautiful. Italianate baroque and neo-classical public buildings evoke its former imperial splendour. Its churches are imposing, elaborate and charmingly delicate in turn. Its avenues and squares are spacious and frequently elegantly laid out. Its canals are crossed by attractively gracious or folksy bridges. Its gardens, in season, can be enchanting. The expansive River Neva flows through its heart, separating the Winter Palace from the slender golden spire of the Cathedral of St Peter and St Paul and providing a natural open space to compliment the vast open-air assembly hall of nearby Palace Square. In winter it freezes over, which makes spring a noisy and spectacular season as the ice breaks and the floes jostle their way to the sea.

The city was created out of nothing by Peter the Great, who decided at the beginning of the Eighteenth Century to build a capital which would face west, provide a link with the rest of Europe and be the envy of the world. He and three of his successors—Catherine the Great (d. 1796), Alexander I (d. 1825), and Nicholas I (d. 1855)—did their best (and, in their treatment of labourers and craftsmen, their worst) to make and keep it so. But for all its imperial solidity, its frequent fogs and summertime white nights (when the sun barely sinks below the horizon) make it a place where solid shapes can appear to dissolve into ghostly outlines, stimulating the imagination and exciting dreams and nightmares. 'Spectral', 'abstract', 'illusory', and 'phantasmagorical', the adjectives routinely chosen, are by no means merely metaphorical, as the Salvationists would discover.

Dostoyevsky, who lived in the city and set two of his greatest novels there, described it as 'the most abstract and contrived city on the entire earthly sphere'.[56] Some thought it a megalomaniac's folly, wrongly sited and wrongly designed (the Marquis de Custine complained in 1839[57] that 'You need hills to support Greek peristyles'). Others thought of it as spiritually and artistically as well as geographically an exotic creation, perched on the extreme edge of the Russian Empire—stretching eastwards across Asia to the Pacific, north beyond the Arctic Circle and South to the Black Sea and Transcaucasia—which it ruled but with which it was at odds. Its magnificence was costly and troublesome to maintain. Year by year, as the ravages of icebound winter were revealed in the candid light of spring, plaster, gilt and colour-wash needed restoration. Its spaciousness could seem bleak (Railton had thought so) since, apart from the usually bustling Nevsky Prospect, the streets and squares were often empty. Above its flat marshy plain, scarcely higher

---

56 Quoted in Billington, *The Icon and the Axe*, p. 417.
57 de Custine, *Letters from Russia*, p. 35.

than the nearby Gulf of Finland, a huge hemisphere of sky exposed it to weather that at any season of the year might change radically and abruptly several times a day.

Many people died during its construction and were, it was rumoured, buried in its foundations. Even for its subsequent inhabitants, St Petersburg could be a death trap: it had the highest mortality rate of any city in Europe.[58] It was regularly inundated by snow, ice and the Neva. The water, although plentiful, was unsafe to drink because of the swampy, stagnant terrain and because the intake for the supply was downstream from three large industrial suburbs. Tuberculosis, typhoid and cholera were rife: in the 1880s, according to the junior British diplomat, Lord Frederick Hamilton, 'the death rate... was far higher than that of Calcutta'.[59] In 1908-09, years in which Railton and Booth visited the city, 30,000 were struck down by cholera. Poor people lived in appalling squalor.[60]

Nonetheless the city provided an elegant and magnificent stage set for those Tsars who wanted to make Russia part of Europe and provided, from their point of view, an instructive contrast with medieval, traditionally Russian Moscow, the cities of the Golden Ring, peasant villages and country estates. But by the mid-Nineteenth Century the pro-western, urban ideology that had induced Peter to build the city which he named after himself as well as after the apostle, was losing its popularity. Slavophile belief in the non-European destiny of Russia revived. Russia's rural landscape, the essence of 'Old Russia', and daily life in the country at large was at the core of the output of the Wanderers association of painters such as Isaac Levitan and Ilya Repin.

Tsar Nicholas disliked his capital for its non-Russianness and for the exhausting, distasteful and dispiriting intrigues and internecine strife of the governing class, which he, a timid, essentially domestic man, deplored. The Tsarina loathed the place: towards the end of 1916 she was to say (in private) that 'Petrograd society... hates me, the corrupt and godless society which thinks of nothing but dancing and dining and takes no interest in anything but its pleasures and adulteries...'.[61]

For all its non-Russianness, the city struck western visitors as exotic—not always pleasantly so. When Meriel Buchanan, daughter of an incoming British Ambassador, arrived in 1910, she noticed a pervading greyness, of 'dirty, half-melting snow and crowds muffled in heavy coats... regarding the sleepy expression

---

58 W. Bruce Lincoln, *In War's Dark Shadow*, p. 106.

59 Lord Frederick Hamilton, *Vanished Pomps of Yesterday*, London, Hodder & Stoughton, 1937, p. 76.

60 The squalor sometimes had its comic side: when the Winter Palace was thoroughly searched following the assassination of Alexander II, the servants were found to have 'vast unauthorised colonies of their relatives living with them on the top floor... in one bedroom a full-grown cow was found, placidly chewing the cud': see Hamilton, *Vanished Pomps*, pp. 110-11.

61 Maurice Paléologue, trs. Frederick A. Holt, *An Ambassador's Memoirs, 1914-17*, London, Hutchinson, 1973, p. 756.

of the coachmen in their thick, wadded blue dressing gowns, one asked, could this still be Europe?'.[62]

By this time St Petersburg had ceased to be merely an elegant stage set. Factories had been built in central residential areas and the canals and rivers were polluted with their waste. Like other Russian cities it was growing uncontrollably. When war broke out in 1914, three of every four residents were peasants born elsewhere. Half the population of 2.2 million people had arrived since 1894. One result of this rampant growth was a rapidly widening gap between the lives of the rich and poor. Around the corner from the costume balls and the luxury shops subsisted a quite different world: that of the soup kitchen and the doss house. An often reproduced photograph of a soup kitchen shows a crowd of greasy-haired, weather-beaten men—mostly young or in the prime of life—eating what appears to be *kashka*, the traditional Russian buckwheat porridge. They sit on backless benches at rough-hewn log tables under a low ceiling of wooden slats. The bare brick walls are dirty and patched with plaster or cement. Light gleams on large copper tureens; the men dip their spoons into communal bowls.

At night such people had to queue for admission to a doss house under notices that read: 'Don't drink unboiled water. Opens 7 p.m. Show passport. Drunks not admitted.'[63] The establishment at 13 Maliy Bolotniy Street charged five copecks for a night's stay, including bread and beef soup in the evening and bread and a mug of tea in the morning. Inside its guests were required to remove their shoes. No bedding was provided and they slept on a wooden shelf divided into sections about 30 inches wide.

This was the city the salvation of whose 2,200,000 citizens was, on 26 and 27 March, 1909, the central concern of General William Booth. But he was not there primarily to win souls. He needed first to enlist the support of St Petersburg's establishment, of which Dominic Lieven writes:

> The capital's political and social 'world' was a village... From Sergeevskaya, Furstatskaya or Mokhovaya streets, in or around which most of the bureaucratic élite lived, a half-hour walk would take the senior official past much of the history of his life. The flats or houses of his friends; his clubs; the government departments in which he had worked; the Guards barracks in which he had served as a young man; the privileged schools, cadet corps or university at which he had been educated: most of these were to be found a short walk on either side of the Nevsky Prospekt... In this tight-knit community, which had all a village's love of gossip and all its knowledge of the intimate details of one's neighbour's affairs [was] concentrated almost the whole political life of a highly centralized empire...[64]

Booth's intensely active two day visit was tightly organized. He had meetings with members of the Imperial family, leading politicians and functionaries, and

---

62 Quoted in Boris Ometev and John Stuart, *St Petersburg, Portrait of an Imperial City*, London, Cassell, 1990, p. 15.

63 Russians were required to carry internal passports.

64 Lieven, *Russia's Rulers under the Old Regime*, pp. 139-41.

visited the Duma. This demanding programme was probably arranged, at Booth's request, by Count Benckendorff, the Russian Ambassador in London.[65]

In the event these meetings only took place as scheduled after unexpected last minute difficulties. In Stockholm en route for Helsinki, Booth heard that he would not be allowed to enter Russia—including Finland—unless he agreed to conduct no meetings. This would have been 'a calamity of no small importance' since the Finnish officers were already gathering in Helsinki for meetings which had been announced and were eagerly anticipated. The British Minister in Stockholm, Sir Cecil Spring Rice[66] arranged a meeting between Commissioner Higgins of The Salvation Army's Foreign Office, who was travelling with Booth, and the Russian Ambassador, and accompanied him during the interview. Meanwhile 'endless' telegrams were sent, 'all sorts of conferences and wonderments' took place. After a day or two Russian objections to the programme already arranged for Finland were withdrawn, but although Booth was permitted to pass through St Petersburg on his way back to London, he was to conduct no meetings there. Booth was puzzled, since, as he understood it, 'Stolypin, the Russian Prime Minister, had consented to our commencing public operations in the country and approved the publication of the fact in the English *Times* some eight or nine weeks ago'.[67]

Higgins provided an hour-by-hour account of the visit to St Petersburg, which was published in *The War Cry*[68] and shows that the ban on meetings was assumed (possibly wishfully) not to apply to private gatherings in aristocratic houses. The overnight train from Helsinki arrived at 10.15 a.m. at the Finland Station (which would also be Lenin's point of arrival on his momentous return from Switzerland eight years later). The group awaiting Booth was much impressed when he stepped from the train and stood with his eyes closed in silent prayer for the salvation of Russia. A Russian colonel in full uniform greeted him, praised the Army's work and wished it success in Russia. Madam Kamensky and Miss Peuker, Radstockites and friends of the Army who had been praying for its advent for years, were there.[69] Booth was taken to the Hotel d'Angleterre[70] in a car sent by a countess.

---

65 On 20 January, 1917, following Benckendorff's death, *The War Cry* described him as a 'warm friend of the Army'. His wife had visited its social institutions during her stay in London and was reported to have said that the only religious people were Russians and Salvationists.

66 Rice wrote the words of the hymn *I Vow to Thee My Country*.

67 He was presumably not being deliberately disingenuous in referring to Stolypin's cautiously worded remarks as a positive announcement (and it was more that six months since Stead's report had appeared in *The Times*). Booth's letters and journals cited in this paragraph are quoted in Begbie, *Life of William Booth*. Volume II, pp. 421-22.

68 10 April, 1909.

69 Larsson (*Tio År I Ryssland*, p. 44) tells us that Miss Peuker 'had from her very early youth been active in the service of the gospel. For a considerable time she edited a Christian weekly paper. She had considerable poetic gift: the Russian translation of the song "Tell me the story of Jesus" is by her, and many more. Although amongst her friends she could number members of the imperial family, she remained all through her life one of the most humble Christians one could desire to meet. In this respect she was a

At 11 a.m. the interviews began. Railton's hostess, Miss Weisberg, from Tolstoye in the Ukraine, who was, according to Higgins, practical, earnest and much concerned with the lot of the poorer peasantry, pleaded for the Army to begin work immediately, begging to know how she might help advance its coming. Two leading Radstockites, Count Pahlen[71] and Baron Nicolay, a close associate of the German evangelist Dr Baedecker, described the condition of the country and the ripeness of the opportunity it presented. After a sparse, hurried lunch, Booth was driven along the Neva (noticing the hundreds of horse-drawn carriages on the ice) to the British Embassy.

In entering the British Embassy Booth and his party were making the first of three visits that day to palaces built by Catherine the Great for her lovers. The embassy occupied half of the Soltikov Palace, the rest being occupied by the descendants of Catherine's favourite Serge Soltikov.

The encounter between Booth and Sir Arthur Nicolson, like many encounters in the last years of Booth's life, must have been a curious occasion. Nicolson was a small, moustachioed man who had been educated at Rugby and Brasenose College, Oxford. Courteous, urbane, shy, diffident, and almost morbidly reserved, he had been a professional diplomat since 1870. He had come to Russia in 1906, briefed to establish *détente* and bring a long period of hostility and suspicion to an end. Booth, son of a failed builder, had worked as a pawnbroker's apprentice. Tall, flashing eyed, he had been an orator and leader all his adult life. Lately he had grown used to conversations with royalty and the nobility, and soon discovered that Lady Nicolson knew Lord Plunket, who had been Governor General of New Zealand at the time of his visit there. He mentioned (neither accidentally nor disinterestedly, as Higgins indicates with an exclamation mark) that Lord Plunket had subscribed liberally to the Army's funds. Nicolson contented himself with promising support if The Salvation Army was eventually allowed into Russia.

---

worthy representative of the Christian Russian aristocracy. Together with a countess of the same type as herself, she built a hospital in Lesnoy, a suburb of St Petersburg. This was completed just at the time when the war broke out and was taken over by the military authorities. After the revolution it fell into the hands of the new powers and for many years Miss Peuker and her friend had to be content with one simple room, where they lived on the verge of starvation. The countess died a couple of years ago and Miss Peuker obtained permission to leave the country and to settle in Germany.'

70 The hotel (now much altered internally) stands across the road from St Isaac's Cathedral, elegant, but architecturally plain and more modest than the de l'Europe, the de France and the Angleterre's sister hotel, the Astoria, next door. In 1914 full board would have cost from 5 roubles (approximately 55 p).

71 Count Pahlen had blotted his copybook so far as the court was concerned in 1896. He had been appointed to investigate the disaster during the coronation celebrations when hundreds of people died at Khodynka Field on the outskirts of Moscow. Pahlen concluded his report with the words, 'Whenever a Grand Duke was given a responsible post there was sure to be trouble'. Thereafter he received no further substantial appointment. See Lieven, *Nicholas II*, p. 67.

From the Embassy, the General was driven further upstream to the Tauride Palace, where, in what had once been its winter garden, the Duma held its debates.[72] This body, a crumb thrown to those who in 1905 demanded a representative legislature, was largely ignored by Tsar Nicholas II, and generally kept subordinate by Stolypin. For their part, Booth and Higgins were determined to be impressed. From the Diplomatic Circle they heard the Minister of Commerce delivering what appeared to be an important speech. The deputies were 'attentive' and 'earnest': Higgins is clearly eager to find signs that Russia was progressing steadily towards the English parliamentary system and that it would in future be a stable country in which the Army could work.

Back at the Hotel d'Angleterre at 3.30 p.m., the General met another large group: Senator Miassoyedoff, whose daughter was a Salvation Army Officer in Paris; Baptist and Methodist ministers; the editor of the *Russian Christian*; and, once again, Miss Weisberg, with 'a small group of lady friends just to shake hands'. All, writes Higgins, joined in the same chorus: 'Come and help us!'.

At 5 p.m. Booth drove to his third paramour's reward of the day, the Marble Palace, now residence of the Grand Duke Konstantine Konstantinovich, the Tsar's cousin. This stood by the Field of Mars, a large parade ground and public park west of the Summer Gardens. Booth thought it amongst the finest palaces he had ever entered.[73] Here he met the Grand Duchess Konstantinova, an encounter of great potential promise. This branch of the Imperial family had a liberal tradition dating back to the abolition of serfdom in 1861, and Konstantine Konstantinovich and Tsar Nicholas were fond of each other and—insofar as anybody could be close to the vacillating, evasive and devious Nicholas—close friends. The Grand Duke's support would be useful. There is even some evidence that Konstantine might almost have been an eager candidate for the salvation that Booth was preaching. Despite his awareness that he had 'a beautiful wife, who is appreciated and respected by all' and 'delightful children', Konstantine was a practising homosexual, with a predilection for 'simple men', who frequented a bath house on the Moika Canal. He was

---

72 The Tauride Palace was built by Catherine for another of her many lovers, Grigory Potemkin, who had helped her annex the Crimea in 1783. Her son and successor Paul (1796-1801) so detested his mother that he stripped the palace and converted it into a barracks for the Horse Guards. After Paul's death it was restored. Nine years after Booth's visit it was to be intermittently at the centre of revolutionary events, providing the first meeting place for, successively, the Provisional Government, the Petrograd Soviet and the Constituent Assembly, which the Bolsheviks closed down after only one day.

73 Construction of the Marble Palace started in 1768. It took 19 years to complete, by which time the intended recipient, Gregory Orlov, had been dead for some time. One of his services to the Empress was to bring a gypsy choir from Moldavia to perform for her, thus starting a vogue for gypsy music that lasted throughout the Nineteenth Century. Using pink marble and pink and grey granite to an unusually austere effect, the Marble Palace was one of the few buildings in St Petersburg to be faced with natural stone. In 1937 it would become the Leningrad Branch of the Central Lenin Museum. This did not survive the fall of Communism. The palace was later restored and is open to visitors.

distressed by his homosexuality, at least partly on religious grounds. His diary recounts his alternating periods of tortured abstention and even more tortured indulgence, and the 'unclean thoughts and passions' that troubled him, 'particularly in church'. He reflects guiltily that he has been 'called "the best man in Russia"', and 'How appalled all those people, who love and respect me, would be if they knew of my depravity! I am deeply dissatisfied with myself'. In December 1905 he had received a blackmailing letter.[74] These aspects of the private life of the Grand Ducal couple might suggest that the Grand Duchess, like so many royal women then and since, was sublimating personal unhappiness by taking an interest in good works. However that may be, the Grand Duke was not present on this occasion but, Higgins tells us, their conversation with the Grand Duchess was 'carried on with a freedom which in itself is unique and charming'.

Booth returned to the hotel to deal with dispatches and visitors for an hour before addressing a meeting in General Saburov's drawing room. The General and his wife met Booth on the staircase, and escorted him into the salon, crammed, no doubt, like other great St Petersburg houses as described by Lord Frederick Hamilton, with 'splendid tapestries, beautiful china, bronzes and *bibelots,* but with the exception of some most indifferent family portraits, and a few modern Russian landscapes... no pictures worth looking at'.[75] The Grand Duchess Konstantinova attended, and sat in the chair next to Booth's as he addressed 'the most select of St Petersburg's society'. Higgins tells us that these people, all of whom understood English, were captivated. Writing about the occasion a quarter of a century later, Karl Larsson noted that had the hosts for this gathering been of lesser social standing the police would probably have intervened. Gatherings in private houses were strictly limited as to numbers as part of the Tsarist government's attempt to stamp out Anarchism and Socialism.[76]

Booth began with the story of his own conversion to Christ 65 years previously. His account of

> the beginning of The Salvation Army on Mile End Waste, of the development of the war all over the world, of the Army's present position, interwoven with incidents from the battlefield, simply holds every lady and gentleman present enthralled. They not only follow every word, but watch every movement, and catch every expression of the General's face.

> Then, with even greater interest, they await the General's pronouncement regarding Russia. He briefly explains his plans and intentions, and tells with what joy he has long anticipated the commencement of operations in the country, and that it was thought the time had now arrived.

---

74 See Maylunas and Mironenko, *A Lifelong Passion*, pp. 222-72, *passim.*

75 Hamilton, *Vanished Pomps*, p. 85-86.

76 Larsson, *Tio År I Ryssland*, p. 10. In 1919 Larsson was to meet the Grand Duchess Konstantinova, who was by then a refugee in Sweden. He took her messages from Miss Peuker who had greeted General Booth on the Finland Station. She told him of the fate of her two sons, who had faced death at the hands of the revolutionaries with prayers upon their lips.

The General is on his feet for over an hour and a quarter, and there is not a single dull moment; it seems difficult for him to find a stopping place, and it is evident that the sight of his audience draws him out and on. When he does sit down expressions of appreciation are heard all over the room. The consensus of opinion seems to be expressed in the words of a lady who said, 'Russia can no longer do without The Salvation Army'.

Booth, besieged by eager hand shakers—including the Grand Duchess Konstantinova, who was at pains to mention how delighted she was to have heard him speak as well as meeting him in her own home earlier—was not able to get away until almost midnight. Early next morning he spoke to an enterprising and determined reporter, then spent the rest of the day in conferences with 'prominent ladies and gentlemen': an administrator of the 'huge' imperial charities, who asked the Army to show Russia how to control its social institutions; a member of the Duma with positive views on what the Army could do—starting preferably at once—in Russia; Senator Torbiesen, representing the major non-imperial charities; and a princess. He was unable to see Stolypin, as he had hoped, for Stolypin was ill: he had to make do with Kokovitsov, Minister of Finance, who was standing in as head of the Ministry. Stolypin's illness may not have been a diplomatic ailment but he can scarcely have been eager to be questioned by Booth. Opposition to his reforms was growing, and the Tsar had already vetoed two of his reforms which would have liberalized the treatment of Jews and allowed the establishment of non-church schools. Booth did however meet the indisposed Prime Minister's brother, whom he had encountered at the Marble Palace the previous day. A keen businessman who wrote frequently in 'Russia's leading newspaper', this Stolypin assured Booth that the attitude of the Russian press towards the Army would be 'all right'.

After a session at the Hotel d'Angleterre writing brief memoranda to dignitaries he had no time (or no invitation) to visit, the same countess's car returned him to the station, where, as Higgins writes, 'just before the train leaves, two poor women come up to the carriage, saying they have walked a long way to get a glimpse of the General's face. He speaks tenderly to them, then, amid the salutes of friends, the train steams out of St Petersburg and the General's first visit is a thing of the past.'

Booth and his party left proclaiming high hopes. But, as Larsson later wrote,

> After the reception accorded to General Booth on this occasion and the promises and assurances given by persons in influential positions it looked as if the doors of Russia were opened wide and that all we had to do was to enter with music, drums and glad Hallelujahs.
>
> It proved not to be quite as simple as this...[77]

Booth probably suspected this—or at any rate should have—before he left. Clara Becker, writing at some time after 1923, tells us that he had another meeting, not

---

77 Larsson, *Tio År I Ryssland,* p. 9.

mentioned by Higgins, with 'Mr Sabler, a strict conservative, and no hope was given for permission ever being granted'.[78] 'Mr Sabler' was Vladimir Karlovich Sabler, a state councillor, whose career as a religious bureaucrat would reach its apogee in 1911 when he was appointed Chief Procurator of the Holy Synod after the incumbent, the 'decent functionary' Lukyanov, fell foul of Sabler's sinister mentor, Grigory Rasputin. The apparent ability of this presumed holy man from Siberia to control the Tsarevitch's haemophiliac attacks won him the Empress's passionate support, and Sabler's counter-productive promotion marked his first successful intervention in an important imperial decision. 'A man of a nastiness remarkable at that time, but soon to be surpassed by a multitude of Rasputin's nominees',[79] Sabler, widely disparaged as an incorrigible reactionary, survived in post until 1915, when Nicholas (provoking Rasputin's anger and, consequently, although she did not like Sabler, Alexandra's distress) was forced to toss a sop to public opinion following a run of military disasters.[80]

Becker's statement (which she introduces with a typically cautious 'I believe') seems likely to be true. Ambassador Benckendorff in London would have tried to arrange a meeting with a senior figure in the procuracy, since the usefulness of Booth's visit would otherwise be severely reduced. Very possibly he tried to arrange a meeting with the Chief Procurator, the relatively liberally inclined Lukyanov, but was circumvented by those who feared that Lukyanov would take the same line as Stolypin, his mentor; Sabler could be relied upon to reject Booth's overtures, which was what the enemies of Stolypin—Rasputin, Alexandra and Nicholas—wanted. (Significantly, it was only after Stolypin's assassination that Rasputin was able to secure Sabler's advancement to the top job.) If Becker's account is accurate, 'the doors of Russia', far from being opened wide, had been bolted shut as soon as Booth left.

Although this interpretation gainsays Higgins' account it is arguably confirmed by events during the following few years. Booth and Higgins no doubt wished to emphasise what they saw as the positive results of their visit, hoping that at some time in the near future God would see fit to change Sabler's mind. Another possibility is that Booth had disliked Sabler and optimistically discounted his influence over his superiors, none of whom was favourably impressed by him. Sabler was widely despised for his 'personal dishonesty and gross lack of principle' and, by Paléologue, the French Ambassador, for his 'contemptible and servile character'. Even his principal respectable supporter, the Empress Alexandra, on one occasion found him 'a most conceited man' and thought 'how unpleasant it would be to have to do with him'.[81] Booth's visit to St Petersburg had a curious epilogue at

---

78 Clara Becker, *Scrapbook: Russia*, p. 1.

79 This and the preceding quotation are from Edward Crankshaw, *The Shadow of the Winter Palace*, p. 385.

80 Richard Pipes, *The Russian Revolution, 1899-1919*, p. 221.

81 Paléologue, *Diary*, 28 September, 1914. It is only fair to add that the ambassador, whose view of people often changed with changing circumstances, described Sabler three weeks later, on 19 October, as 'a nice, kind man'. Alexandra's comments come from a

Buckingham Palace a few days later, on 6 April. He was commanded (at his own request) to be received by Queen Alexandra and her 61 year-old sister, Her Imperial Highness, the Grand Duchess Maria Feodorovna, Dowager Empress of Russia, widow of the reactionary Alexander III and mother of Tsar Nicholas. She was tough as well as beautiful, having undergone the standard royal test of surviving attempted assassination.[82]

Maria Feodorovna may have wanted to do something for Booth, but since the birth of her grandson, Alexis, in 1904, and the discovery of his haemophilia, her influence over Nicholas, which had been great, if not always constructive,[83] was diminishing. She had to an extent alienated him by expressing her disapproval of Rasputin's increasing influence over the Tsarina.[84]

In any case, her enthusiasm for the idea of The Salvation Army masked a deep-seated ambivalence concerning its prospects in Russia. Like the Tsarina she had been born a Protestant, as Princess Dagmar of Denmark. She retained a simple Christian faith, and this must have made Booth hope that she would exercise helpful behind the scenes influence on the Army's behalf. There is no evidence that she ever did this. She would intervene in specific circumstances such as, to anticipate, a moment

---

letter to her husband in 1915 (see Maylunas and Mironenko, *A Lifelong Passion*, pp. 428-29.) Outside the court it did Sabler no good when, in 1911, rumour had it that he had knelt before Rasputin in gratitude for his appointment. This evidence for the low opinions Sabler attracted post-date Booth's visit by several years, but the elderly General was a sharp, unsentimental judge of character. Higgins' reports in *The War Cry* must count as an exercise in optimistic propaganda.

82 Geifman, *Thou Shalt Kill*, p. 36.

83 Lieven, *Nicholas II*, pp. 27-28, 53, 134-35, and 226.

84 Disastrously, Alexandra and her husband thought of the devious Siberian charlatan as 'Our Friend' and regarded him as the epitome of Orthodox holiness. Throughout the decade their relationship with Rasputin became increasingly close, arousing disquiet within the Imperial Family and provoking scandal outside it. The rift between the Dowager Empress and her son and daughter-in-law, which grew as she tried to open their eyes to Rasputin's degenerate behaviour, promoted the growth of two hostile camps at court, a rift which helped bring about the collapse of the Romanov monarchy. The Tsarina's puritanical Orthodoxy (she had the zeal of the convert—albeit one who had taken a long time to abandon the Protestantism in which, largely in England, she had been brought up) was reinforced by panic during the 1900s, when several Romanovs made unsuitable matches. Marriages were contracted which were either morganatic or to women within the prohibited degrees of consanguinity. Adultery and divorce followed. These scandals divided the family, and the Tsarina felt strongly that her role was to stiffen Nicholas's resolve in asserting, and endeavouring to enforce, rigid Orthodox morality. Compounding her obsession with Rasputin and (ironic as the conjunction may appear) her concern for the good behaviour and name of her family, was her conviction that absolutism was the only workable form of government. All these factors made her increasingly obdurate in her opposition to anything that might diminish the standing of the Orthodox Church. Nicholas, who loved his wife simply and unquestioningly, turned towards her and her mysticism and absolutism, and away from his Danish mother, with her western contacts and relatively liberal views.

in 1915 when the military authorities attempted to requisition a house which had been set aside as a Salvation Army home for refugees. She was kind to any officers she happened to meet, but knew in a very Russian way that what was possible, even admirable, elsewhere in the world was not possible in Russia.[85] Her son's dislike of western ideas and institutions, coupled with his and his wife's passionately Orthodox convictions, would make any request to allow the organization to work there a non-starter. Had she, in 1909, tried to plead the cause of The Salvation Army with the increasingly unresponsive Nicholas, she would have been ignored.

Booth's account of his reception at Buckingham Palace suggests that he was unaware of these factors. It suggests also, for all his protestations of modest inhibition when dealing with royalty, a determined attempt to influence her in the Army's favour. It also illustrates some important characteristics of the ways in which he had become accustomed to work: the (clearly rather winning) combination of gaucherie and ease with which the one-time pawnbroker's apprentice invaded the drawing rooms of the ruling class; his willingness—even eagerness—to play the game of etiquette and protocol according to the rules as he understood them ('I took the Queen upon my arm'); the readiness with which, even in these circumstances, he took command ('Ladies, shall we be seated?'); his, perhaps rather naive, perhaps mock-modest delight in the way he was treated ('The interview... so unlike anything I could have expected... indicating not only high respect and deep interest, but real affection'); his possible misreading of regal *politesse* ('the Queen apologizing again and again for occupying so much of my valuable time'); and, above all, his preference, when talking about the Army and its work, for the concrete instance (nowadays habitually derided as 'anecdotal evidence'), and its effectiveness in his hands.

At Buckingham Palace, he writes:

> After waiting a short time, during which I amused myself by gazing at the stiff angular portraits on the walls... the Queen and the Dowager Empress entered. After the usual assurances of welcome and expressions of pleasure my visit gave them, the Queen seized a chair, asked me to sit down opposite one of the lounges, and[,] with the Empress[,] seated herself in front of me, and the conversation at once began... The Dowager Empress is shorter in stature [than the Queen], and with as dark a complexion as the Queen is light. I should certainly not have taken them for sisters, but the friendly manner of both soon made me forget outward appearances. The Queen led the way in the conversation. I tried to state as well as I could the reason for my desire to see the Empress, referred to my recent visit to St Petersburg, to the individuals whom I supposed were known to Her Majesty, whom I had the privilege of meeting there. We talked about what would happen if The Salvation Army commenced operations. The only difficulty expressed by the Empress was that she was afraid that we should be likely to clash with the Church. She remarked that the Russian was naturally religious, deeply attached to his Church, and she thought it would be expected that the Army would take them away from the Church and lead to the formation of another sect which was very objectionable to the

---

85 She said as much to a friend in St Petersburg: see below, p. 135.

Russian authorities. I remarked that there were multitudes of people who never entered the Church, to which statement she objected. I said, 'Well, perhaps once a year!'. She said, 'Many of them once a day!'. It was neither the time nor the place for me to controvert the Empress's statement, but it was certainly capable of modification. At the same time great masses of the Russian people are slavishly attached to the Church and its forms and ceremonies, although, practically speaking, uninfluenced by its teaching or its example. To instance the necessity for the Army, I mentioned the prevalence of drunkenness. Here it was admitted at once that Church Festivals were often seasons of frightful intemperance. I spoke of our work in Cologne in this respect, and in many other parts of the world. At this time or soon afterwards, the Queen asked Princess Victoria if she would fetch her Album as she wanted the General to subscribe his name. It was brought and my birthday was found. With my fountain pen I wrote my name across the page. In doing so, the Queen noticed that I had inked my fingers and she at once led me to the table where there was a sponge by which I could cleanse them, tearing off a sheet of blotting paper to clean the pen. The Empress then produced her Album and Princess Victoria introduced hers. When I got to Princess Victoria's I got a little bolder, and I wrote over my name, 'Saved to save!'. This pleased her. They all three read it, whereupon I wrote over my name in the Dowager Empress's book, 'Seeking and saving the lost'. This also gave pleasure, and I was vexed that I had not written something striking over the Queen's. However, it was too late. They were busy talking around me; I really felt a little confused as to what should come next. I could not very well say, 'Queens and Empresses,' so I said, 'Ladies, shall we be seated?'. The Queen assented... I took the Queen upon my arm and escorted her to the sofa, and we resumed the position at which we sat before. The Queen said, 'Tell us something more about your work'. It is very awkward that the proper things do not always come at the moment; it was so with me. However, I wanted to show the necessity for divine operation in the hearts of those men whom we wanted to benefit, an illustration of which had been given by Treen the night before, that happened at High Barnet. The testimony of a man, who, holding the handle of a door of a public house, was about to enter, when he heard the Army singing:

> See from His head, His hands, His feet,
> Sorrow and love flow mingled down!
> Did e'er such love and sorrow meet
> Or thorns compose so rich a crown?

He stopped to listen, and, he said, a strange feeling came over him. 'Ah!' said the Queen, repeating the words. And a voice said to him, 'Play the man, put your foot down, now's your time!'. He turned away from the public house and he followed the Salvationists to the Hall, went to the Mercy Seat and was saved with the Salvation of God. Here the Queen, with a wondering look on her face, said 'Saved! That's what we all want.'. 'Did he stand firm?' or some question to that effect, was proposed by the Empress, whereupon I remarked that I believed he did... And so the conversation drifted on, the Queen apologizing again and again for occupying so much of my valuable time. Asking me carefully as to the improvement in my sight, and wishing me safe through the operation which was to follow during the week, and reiterating her expressions of sympathy and goodwill, I withdrew—all shaking me by the hand in the most friendly manner, the Queen doing this over and over again. The interview, so remarkable, so unlike anything I could have expected, indicating not only high respect and deep interest, but real affection, came to a termination.[86]

This amiable occasion had no detectable effect so far as Booth's Russian ambitions were concerned, and the same is true of his subsequent meeting with the Russian Ambassador, Count Benckendorff, on 15 April. The Count was 'most free and friendly, and so far as I could judge quite anxious for the Army to commence its work in his country, and really and truly desirous that the effort should be a success'. The Count appeared to confirm that Stolypin was happy for the Army to work in Russia, although he agreed with the Dowager Empress, as reported by Booth, that the ecclesiastical authorities might prove difficult, adding that 'the reactionary party might be induced to suppress the Movement—that is, if they saw it was likely to become a real power in the country'.[87]

Once again Booth can be forgiven for supposing that the Army had won an influential supporter, who would provide excellent advice and contacts, but as so often in Russian matters, there is a teasing vagueness in the Count's utterances and some ambiguity about his status amongst his fellow Russians. The Benckendorffs were an influential family of long-standing. A.K. Benckendorff (1783-1844) had reorganized the police for the rigid, bureaucratic, repressive Tsar Nicholas I, and Count Paul Benckendorff was amongst those close to the Tsar in 1917. But for many Russians the Benckendorffs were merely German interlopers. Prince Felix Yousoupoff had dined with Benckendorff in London in the autumn of 1908, noting 'with surprise that our ambassador... hardly knew a word of Russian'.[88] In 1923 the Benkendorffs and other families like them would be described as 'pompous, smug [Baltic] Germans who had sunk firm roots at the Russian Court and wielded a peculiar kind of influence behind the stage. The highly placed lackeys were united by a profound contempt for the Russian people. Many of them did not know Russia's past...'.[89]

We must conclude that since the comments favourable to the Army by influential or supposedly influential Russians—Stolypin, the Dowager Empress and Benckendorff —were ambivalent, while the attitude of Deputy Procurator Sabler was unambiguously hostile, Higgins' reference to 'the General's first visit' was over-optimistic: the two days in 1909 remained the only time Booth spent in Russia, and

---

86 Quoted in St John Ervine, *God's Soldier* pp. 795-7
87 Begbie, *William Booth*, pp. 430-31.
88 Prince Felix Youssoupoff, (trs from the French by Ann Green and Nicolas Katkoff), *Lost Splendour*, London, The Folio Society, 1996, p. 112. Youssoupoff is not an objective witness. His father had been dismissed from his post as Governor General of Moscow after a few months, an event which he and his wife attributed to the activities of a pro-German cabal at court. Felix adored his mother and accepted her version of the story implicitly.
89 Kantorovich, in *Byloe* (no. 22, p. 228), quoted in Richard Pipes, *The Russian Revolution*, p. 61.

by the time he died in 1912, his ambitious attempt to enter the Russian Empire seemed to have collapsed. Despite the prayers of Salvationists everywhere for the success of his Russian mission, it was indeed to become a thing of the past, at least in the sense that it had no further visible effect. Whatever The Salvation Army's titled, often Radstockite friends in Russia did in attempting to help it gain official recognition was ineffectual.

Events in Russia immediately took a turn for the worse from The Salvation Army's point of view. Stead's meeting with Stolypin in July 1908 had taken place when the latter was beginning to draw back from the religious reforms which would have made it easier for The Salvation Army to enter and work in Russia; Booth's visit in March 1909 coincided with the beginning of his final capitulation, although this did not become apparent until later. In that month the Duma Commission on Religious Affairs approved several bills giving Old Believers (and other Christian non-Orthodox groups) the right to establish themselves and preach and proselytize freely, and allowing Russians to convert from one Christian religion to another without seeking the state's permission. These were strongly supported in the Duma and fiercely opposed by the Orthodox Church and its allies. The assistant procurator denounced the measures as going far beyond the government's intentions, and called for them not to be debated. The Duma ignored him, but on 2 May an assistant to the Minister of Internal Affairs made it clear that the government had changed its mind. Nowhere in the world, he argued in the Duma, did absolute freedom of religion prevail. The end came on 22 May. Addressing the Duma, Stolypin spoke in generalities about religious freedom until it became clear that he and the government had retreated to the starting line. He wanted, he said, to 'dispel certain misunderstandings that have arisen about my opinions', adding that although the Tsar himself had announced the coming of religious freedom with decrees on 12 December, 1904, 17 April, 1905 and 17 October, 1905, many legal issues remained to be resolved before any of this could be carried through. Teetering on the edge of absurdity, he suggested that the Government had moved too fast. The laws on religion, it must be understood, would 'operate in the Russian state, and will be confirmed by the Russian Tsar, who for more than 100 million people was, is, and will be, an Orthodox Tsar'.[90]

The Duma tried to continue the fight but one by one the reforms fell by the wayside. Stolypin told the Council of Ministers that the Orthodox Church would retain its monopoly on proselytizing. The bill on mixed marriages (which was said to violate canon law) and that on freedom of worship were, in October 1909, withdrawn from legislative consideration and never resubmitted. Extension of the rights of Old Believers was voted out by the upper chamber, the State Council. Early in 1910 new restrictions were placed on the activities of non-Orthodox religions, making it more difficult for them to attract new members.

Significantly, from The Salvation Army's point of view, one of the two principal reasons for the failure of Stolypin's three year campaign on behalf of the Old

90 Waldron, Religious Reform, in *Oxford Slavonic Papers*, 1987, pp. 135-36.

Believers (the other being the opposition of the Orthodox Church) was that the Old Believers lacked contacts and support in St Petersburg and experience and expertise to deal with political circles there.[91]

Booth's attempt to enlist the Russian authorities to his cause had failed. Shortly he would make one last effort, sending two officers to work in Russia more or less under cover, but two considerations prevented him from doing this in greater numbers. One was the financial burden, the other the supposed ferocity and efficiency of the secret police. Booth did not wilfully expose his workers to imprisonment or martyrdom; there was always somewhere else where they could be more usefully employed. We may wonder what would have happened had he sent officers to work undercover in a westernized city such as Odessa, far from the bureaucracy of St Petersburg. There, the Army, while seizing whatever opportunities arose to work with Russians, could have been seen as principally a mission to the foreigners who thronged the busy port. But among the visions still shared by Booth and his *enfant terrible,* Railton, was that of a Salvation Army band marching down the Nevsky Prospect. Besides, he preferred working with rather than against the established powers and believed that the way to gain a country's attention was to establish yourself in its capital.

Undercover Operations

A month after Booth's visit, to quote the *Official History,* 'Lieutenant-Colonel Gerrit J. Govaars, of Holland, was selected by the General to prepare for the opening of the Army's work in St Petersburg'.[92] Sadly, the ebullient Govaars, 'the Hallelujah Dutchman', no sooner enters our story than he exits again. His career record shows no official appointment in Russia. His mission was aborted, but whether because of Russian obstructiveness, his own or someone else's decision that it was not worth pursuing, or simply because International Headquarters had found more pressing need of him elsewhere, is not clear.[93]

The following year, in 1910, another attempt was made. Two Danes working in Finland, Colonel and Mrs Jens Povlsen, entered Russia unobtrusively in an attempt to establish the Army's work by stealth. Finland was clearly the ideal jumping-off point for such ventures. The Salvation Army had been established there since 1889, despite the fact that Finland was part of the Russian Empire, having begun its work during the period when Russia still respected Finnish autonomy. In 1898, however, a deliberate campaign of russification began. The constitution was suspended in 1903, but in 1906, following the Revolution the previous year, the Finns were allowed to elect a Diet chosen by universal suffrage of both sexes. During this time

---

91 Waldron. p. 138.

92 Wiggins, *History*, p. 75.

93 One of the Govaars' grandchildren was Robert Simpson, the prominent English composer and writer on music, particularly that of Bruckner, Nielsen and Sibelius. His works included, not entirely coincidentally, a number of substantial pieces for brass band.

The Salvation Army functioned with some freedom, but repression began again in 1910 and conditions deteriorated sharply. A quarter of a century later, widowed and a Lieutenant-Commissioner, Agnes Povlsen recalled, for the *Officers' Review*, her 'five blessed years in Finland' which were, clearly, excellent preparation for what they were to find in Russia itself. '*The War Cry*, uniform, and military titles were forbidden; Meetings were declared illegal; halls were closed, and Salvationists crept through the windows into their meeting place, to have a rousing Hallelujah time behind the back of the policeman who kept watch outside the sealed door.'[94] Colonels Jens Andre and Agnes Povlsen were apt choices for the task of infiltrating Russia. He was level-headed and tactful, well-balanced and variously experienced, an accomplished linguist and translator (he told his fellow Scandinavian, the American composer Erik Leidzen, that he could speak seven languages and keep his mouth shut in all of them),[95] widely-read, and, according to *All the World*[96] 'full of zeal for the Salvation of the unconverted'. His appearance was striking as well: very high forehead surrounded by thick, bushy hair, with finely drawn but prominent features and a jutting pointed moustache. Agnes Povlsen's penetrating but reflective eyes and long, very straight nose were similarly unforgettable. A photograph of the couple exudes vitality, intelligence and determination. Russia, nonetheless, proved even more testing than Finland. Mrs Povlsen, writing in *All the World* in January 1936, continues the story:

> In 1910 the Founder sent us, with his blessing, to St Petersburg, as the capital of Russia was then called. Officially The Salvation Army had no permission to work in Russia, where all international organizations were suspected more or less of being Nihilists or revolutionists in disguise. So we came in quietly, an 'Army' of three Salvationists in plain blue clothes, trusting in God Almighty to guide us to some open door of opportunity. We found a flat, which we made our Headquarters and abode; the furniture, to begin with, consisted mainly of packing cases.[97]

But however unobtrusively they dressed and behaved they were soon aware that they were being watched:

> Every Russian house[98] had... a *dvornik*—a sort of janitor—whose responsibility included reporting to the police any suspicious person living in or visiting the block of flats. One of his assistants kept watch at the main entrance from dusk until

---

94 This followed a period during the later Nineteenth Century when Turgenev and other Russians interested in social reform had looked to protestant Finland as a source of useful ideas, to the extent that a journal which debated such issues, published in St Petersburg, was called *The Finnish Herald*. See Billington, *The Icon and the Axe*, p. 373.

95 William G. Harris, *Sagas of Salvationism*, cited in Will Pratt, *A Funny Thing Happened on the Way!*, Mukilteo, Wine Press Publishing, 1996, p. 63.

96 June 1913.

97 *All the World*, 1936, pp. 18-19.

98 In this context 'house' means 'apartment block'.

morning.[99] Our good *dvornik* evidently felt a bit uneasy about his new tenants. So many Nihilists, plotting to assassinate some member of the government, or even of the Tsar's family, pretended to be 'husband and wife', 'son and daughter', or 'servant'. He would question our little domestic helper if he met her on the staircase. What was her master's occupation? He got many letters from abroad; he had an office at home. Her diplomatic answers only made him more suspicious.

This situation, with its Dostoyevskyan setting and tension, was inherently unstable:

One day our doorbell rang. On the landing stood our good *dvornik* with a tall, German-speaking gentleman, whom he introduced as the new owner of the house, and who 'wanted to see our flat'. We immediately understood that we were in for a regular domiciliary visitation. The gentleman was accompanied by a little 'spy-looking' Russian, who used his eyes diligently as the company went from room to room. The titles of our books were scrutinized, the few pictures on the walls were studied. The 'gentleman' looked into every cupboard, and into the old copper-bath in the little, dark bathroom, as if he expected to find printing machinery hidden away there. Our *dvornik*, meanwhile, stood sentinel at the only entrance to the flat.

Here Mrs Povlsen's narrative shifts genres. Through coincidence or the hand of God a storybook resolution was at hand:

the gentleman asked, quite politely, what had brought us to Russia? My husband told him that we had not been able to start our work yet. And what was that work going to be? Religious and social work? Ah! He was getting nearer to his point. Under the auspices of any organization? Might he ask its name? My husband and I looked at each other. There was no way out, so he answered calmly: 'Yes, The Salvation Army.' I can still see the gentleman lifting his hands and exclaiming, 'Die Heilsarmee!'. We sat quietly waiting for the next 'bomb' and it came: 'I have a daughter who is a Salvation Army officer in Paris!'

'Have we the honour of speaking with His Excellency Mr M?' asked my husband, surprised. 'Yes, it is I.'

This is a splendidly romantic tale, and there is no need to doubt its truth. But it may make us wonder how usefully the Povlsens had been briefed by International Headquarters. The reader will remember that during Booth's visit to St Petersburg, he met Senator Miassoyedoff, whose daughter was an officer in Paris. Why were the Povlsens not given his address and telephone number, since he was evidently amiably disposed? Alternatively—since they clearly knew of the existence of a Mr M who lived in St Petersburg and had a daughter who was a Salvation Army officer in Paris—why had they not approached him of their own accord, giving God a chance to guide them towards some open 'door of opportunity'?

---

99 Many Nineteenth Century blocks of flats in St Petersburg stand within enclosed courtyards with only one exit to the street. Near-total surveillance was easily achieved.

Was there inefficient staff work following William Booth's visit in 1909? Proper briefing might have saved the Povlsen's domestic help the nuisance of being waylaid on shadowy stairways by the good *dvornik,* since, now that they had all been properly introduced, 'His Excellency Mr M.' assured them that he would use his influence to help them obtain official permission to start their work.

Meanwhile, Sir George Buchanan, Sir Arthur Nicolson's successor as British Ambassador, also proved very sympathetic and helpful, and for a time the Povlsens were able to function effectively, if, by Salvation Army standards, somewhat anonymously. The remnants of the Radstockite network of converted aristocrats provided a platform: some had permission to hold evangelical meetings in their homes provided that politics and anti-government utterances were understood to be taboo.

> We were invited [writes Mrs Povlsen], to conduct Salvation Army meetings in several 'halls' they had fixed up. A Princess G.,[100] who used to play the harmonium for us, we called our bandmaster; others, who helped us deal with seekers, were nominated 'Penitent Form Sergeants'. [101] They seemed mightily pleased with their titles.

The Povlsens, according to Clara Becker, conducted meetings 'chiefly in connection with other free missions and the sectarians in Russia, who at the time were much persecuted by the government'.[102] In any case they could not publicly identify themselves as The Salvation Army, but despite this,

> the people seemed taken with the Army's spirit and message, and came in crowds: poor and ignorant men and women, unable to read or write; young, fiery students, despairing of their country; thoughtful, refined people—but oh! so sad; and pale, thin children from the damp, dingy cellars of the city slums. Their faces would light up and their bodies rock to and fro as they joined in the Russian translation of such choruses as 'Let the blessed sunshine in', or 'No, never alone!'. When by and by, we were able to converse a little with them in their own language, how delighted they were!

The Povlsens' work was not confined to these slightly bizarre gatherings in aristocratic houses. They ventured out into the less reputable night-time streets:

> Visitation, often from door to door among the working classes and in the slums, gave us some insight into the awful conditions under which the people lived: sometimes two, three, even five families in one room; six or seven families sharing one kitchen. Morals were low; girls twelve or thirteen years of age were caught

---

100 Possibly one of the the many princesses Galitzin, one of whom was a Radstockite convert and may be the mother of the Prince Nicholas Galitzin who proposed marriage to Evangeline Booth.

101 The penitent form is a plain bench across the front of a Salvation Army hall at which seekers after salvation are invited to kneel.

102 Clara Becker, *Scrapbook: Russia,* p. 1.

soliciting on the streets of St Petersburg at midnight. School children couples would attempt suicide. Some sought to drown their misery in vodka.

While all this was going on, the Army's friends, so the Povlsens were assured, were doing what they could to make its presence permanently acceptable to the government. One such report, as well as partly confirming William Booth's account of his meeting at Buckingham Palace with the Dowager Empress Maria Feodorovna, indicates the layers of ideological and national hostility that lay between the Army and official acceptance by the Russian authorities:

> While we continued our soul-saving work and tried to train our converts for soldiership, some of our friends were 'pulling strings' at the top. One of them, Madame T., one day, in conversation with the Dowager Empress (formerly Princess Dagmar of Denmark), mentioned The Salvation Army. 'Oh, do you also know that Organization?' asked the Empress. 'I met its Founder, William Booth, while on a visit to my sister in London. He is a wonderful man. My sister thinks the world of the Army and its work, and my brother [King Frederick of Denmark] says it has been a real blessing to our little homeland.' But when told that the Army wanted to begin its work also in Russia, and that two Officers of her Majesty's own nationality were in St Petersburg, the Empress shook her head. 'The Army is wonderful', she said, 'and good for other countries, but not for Russia. The Church would not tolerate it!'

Mrs Povlsen thought there was little doubt that but for this consideration of the Church—'reckoned the last bulwark against revolution'—the authorities on the whole would have welcomed the Army, 'especially to help them solve their many social problems'. She felt, too, that the 'common people' would have received the Army enthusiastically. Returning one Sunday afternoon from a meeting in a hospital, she found her husband sitting with a peasant, a man with earnest honest eyes, shoulder-length dark hair and a silky beard covering his chest. He, a rare example of a literate peasant, was from a village in the Ural Mountains, where he had got hold of and studied the New Testament. He asked the village priest whether he knew of anyone who lived according to the precepts of that book, but neither the priest nor anyone else in the village had ever heard tell of such people. One had heard that there were in St Petersburg people called Evangelical Christians who might fit the bill. This man had travelled from the Urals to the capital (a distance of at least 1,000 miles) in quest of them. He had been to all the free churches he could find, arriving finally at the Povlsens' door.

> Now my husband, with his limited Russian vocabulary, was trying to show him the way of Salvation, praying for light to enter this sincere soul. 'I have received much light and help,' said the peasant as he rose to take leave, 'and now I will return to my village to think it all over. I will pray and trust God to guide me in His way of truth and Salvation, and help me to live according to this Book.'

Like the story of a would-be suicide who walked from St Petersburg to Helsinki in search of The Salvation Army, which will be recounted in Chapter Six, this tale, 90 years on, may seem implausible to urban rationalists in the west. It was, however, commonplace for country people in Russia at the time to cover huge distances on foot, many of them engaged in quixotic spiritual quests: peasant wanderers, wise men and prophets, who lived off the alms of the villagers. One such pilgrim, called Abraham, travelled to the Holy Land every year. These pilgrimages had been traditional for centuries and were part of the peasants' preparation for death.[103] Paléologue tells us that 'the great religious drama of the Russian conscience' stemmed from the fact that the nation, deeply evangelical and haunted by the idea of sin and repentance, 'is more sincere, or at any rate more Christian, than its Church'. Christianity appealed less to their reason and conscience than to their imagination and emotions.[104] He also describes a friend's meeting with a woman who had walked from the Urals to Kiev on pilgrimage. It had taken her several months, she didn't know exactly, and when Paléologue's friend expressed amazement that she had travelled not merely so far, but also alone, she said 'Yes, alone... with *my soul*'.[105]

At some point during their stay, according to Larsson, the Povlsens presented a written application for the Army to start work officially. They waited long and patiently for the response of the bureaucracy and were eventually disappointed. Despite (at least as the Povlsens understood it) the preparedness of the authorities to welcome an organization which could help Russia solve its social problems, and the eager interest of those of the 'common people' who were searching for something the Orthodox Church did not offer, in 1912, after the Povlsens had spent 18 months in St Petersburg, the Council of Ministers informed General Booth, via the British Embassy, that the permission requested could not be granted. There can be little doubt that the application had been seen and vetoed by Sabler, who was now Procurator of the Holy Synod. Booth, who was in Oslo, conducting a North European Staff Congress (his last campaign outside England before his death in August of that year), withdrew the Povlsens and sent them to take command in Norway.

Larsson's comments are wry and apposite:

> For anyone knowing conditions in Russia at the time the answer did not come as a surprise. Every application of this kind had to pass through several authorities. It was also well known that any Russian official who might foresee difficulties in recommending any application immediately turned it down. If no one else refused, one could be sure that the Church authorities would do so...[106]

He also attributes the rejection to the easing of tension between government and people which encouraged the former to reconsider promises of religious and political

---

103 Hummel, R. and T., *Patterns of the Sacred; English Protestant and Russian Orthodox Pilgrims of the Nineteenth Century*, London, Scorpion Cavendish, 1995, pp. 42-43.

104 Paléologue, *Diary*, 9 January, 1915.

105 Paléologue, *Diary*, 26 January, 1915.

106 Larsson, *Tio År I Ryssland*, p. 14.

freedom conceded following defeat in the war against Japan and the revolutionary disturbances of 1905. These allowed

> certain evangelical movements... a time of development. But as the Government began to feel reassured, these promises were rescinded one after the other,[107] so that in 1912 only a minimum of the freedom once promised still remained. Simultaneously the people's dissatisfaction grew, and this gave rise to increased suspicion on the part of the authorities, and further restrictions.[108]

These developments, along with the death of Stolypin by assassin's bullet in 1911 and the appointment, after intense, unscrupulous lobbying by Rasputin, of the reactionary Sabler as Procurator, were symptomatic of wider changes. The moment when liberal reform in social and religious affairs appeared possible had passed. The Tsar turned with relief to the circle of reactionary landed nobility that now dominated the Council of State, leaving Stolypin's successor feeling isolated and helpless. Russia had entered a period of growth and prosperity. The revolutionary movement had apparently grown tired and despondent and lost its ability to interest urban workers. Stolypin's land reforms allowed some peasants to join the ranks of the petty bourgeoisie. 'In terms of Russia's political modernization the clock had stopped; it even seemed to have turned back.'[109] No one in power would think of saying, as Stolypin had done, that there was no political reason why The Salvation Army should not enter Russia.

Many thought that an era of disruption and upheaval in Russian history had come to an end: the country could put 1905 behind it. But even from the reactionary point of view not all omens were good.[110] In 1910, Halley's Comet, traditionally a harbinger of cataclysm, had reappeared. Leo Tolstoy had died, along with other artists who had been emblems of their era. In 1911, there was a new wave of anti-Semitism in Russia. People and newspapers talked of the nearness of a Great War. The Russian poet Alexander Blok was to write a decade later that 'one could already sense the smell of burning, blood and iron in the air'. The Symbolist writer Andre Bely began work on his apocalyptic novel, *Petersburg,* which is dominated by the ticking of a terrorist's time bomb, just as the minds of the writer and his friends were dominated by the countdown to European conflagration. 'There will be a leap across history', wrote Bely, who was greatly concerned by (among many other things) the 'Yellow Peril' from the East. 'Great shall be the turmoil... As for Petersburg, it will sink.'[111] *Petersburg* appeared in serialized form in 1913, a few months before the anticipated Great War broke out.

---

107 In 1910 controls were imposed on all meetings held by non-Orthodox groups, and other measures limited their activities. See Waldron, Religious Reform , pp. 117-18.

108 Larsson, *Tio År I Ryssland*, pp. 15-16

109 Lincoln, *In War's Dark Shadow*, p. 348.

110 Lincoln, *In War's Dark Shadow*, pp. 386-87.

111 Andrei Bely (trs. Robert A. Maguire and John E. Malmstad), *St Petersburg*, Bloomington, Indiana University Press, 1983, p. 65.

A symptom of the times was the growth of the organizations known collectively as the Black Hundreds, the largest and most notorious of which was the Union of Russian People, an extreme right wing, anti-Semitic group which had come into existence since 1905. It shared with Nicholas the fantasy of re-establishing personal rule by the Tsar as it had existed in the Seventeenth Century. The idea of a personal bond between autocrat and people had been central (in Nicholas's mind at least) to the canonization of Seraphim in 1903, and was to colour the Romanov tercentenary celebrations in 1913. The URP was built upon racism and xenophobia, anti-western nationalism and, above all else, the supremacy of Orthodoxy.[112] The Council of Ministers, in refusing permission for the Povlsens to continue their work, would have been influenced by these ideas and the shifts in political reality that followed from them.

Even those not fanatically xenophobic were at this time in no mood to do anything that might in any way weaken the Orthodox Church. P.N. Durnovo, who as Minister of Internal Affairs had been central to the survival of the state during the turbulence of 1905-06, continued, as leader of the conservative wing in the State Council, to urge the necessity of maintaining the position of the Church. In May, 1910, he had declared during a debate that

> the cultural weakness of the Russian people does not yet allow the preaching and propaganda of all dogmas to be permitted without distinction. If we want to preserve the unity of the Russian state it would be madness to weaken the force binding it together—that is the Orthodox Church... [It teaches] not only Christ's truth but the need for obedience to the imperial power.[113]

For the Army, in Larsson's words, there was nothing to do but wait.

Astonishingly, the wait was not to be long. Meanwhile, however, one stalwart Salvationist had temporarily lost heart. Staff Captain Rosa Hacklin, a Finn who had assisted the Povlsens during part of their stay in Russia, and had become warmly attached to the country, responded to all suggestions that another attempt might be made with the comment that if the Povlsens had not succeeded, the chances of anyone else gaining a foothold in Russia were very small indeed.[114]

When the Povlsens left for Norway it must have seemed that the door, never more than ajar, had slammed shut in their wake. But within a matter of months, The Salvation Army was back, publicly displaying before the Russian public the social work it was performing in Finland. Very little time would elapse before it would be allowed, albeit in a circumscribed and ambiguous manner, to begin work in Russia itself.

---

112 See Figes, *A People's Tragedy*, pp. 245-46.
113 Quoted in Lieven, *Russia's Rulers under the Old Regime*, pp. 225-26.
114 Rosa Hacklin later relented and served in Russia once again.

CHAPTER 6

Messengers of Salvation

A Viking Warrior, a Death and an Exhibition

The next attempt to establish The Salvation Army in Russia was made once more from Finland. The commander there after 1912 was Colonel Karl Larsson, an austere, fair-haired, straight-backed son of a railway-crossing attendant from Sandjö in Sweden.[1] Like some who would be his female colleagues in Russia he had had a difficult childhood: his father was a drunkard and, although he 'thirsted after knowledge' the school he attended was open for only four months of the year because its teacher was also responsible for two others elsewhere. After his father was converted during a religious revival, Karl's life (and that of his eight siblings) became physically more comfortable, but the sudden death of two neighbours induced him to agonize over whether or not he himself was saved. He turned the problem over to a higher authority: 'O God, save me before I die'. A man with an iron constitution he nevertheless lived his life in the consciousness of approaching death: one of his two mottoes, and a frequent subject of his preaching, was 'Work, for the night is coming'.[2] At 16 he was rising at five, working a 12 hour day as a lithographer and devoting a further five hours to studying art, engraving and German.

He became a Salvation Army officer in 1890 and his devotion to the organization overruled all else. Before they married, he wrote to his wife-to-be, Captain Anna Dahlbom, from Malmö, that:

> ...there are two things which could destroy my good opinion of you... The first concerns my love to God... the other my position as regards the Army. If you should try to draw me from these my obligations or hinder me from fulfilling them, I would tear your heart from my breast even if a piece of mine followed with it.[3]

---

1 Discussing the indispensability of missionary endeavour to the life of the Church, Albert Orsborn remarks that Sweden, 'has made a great living offering of her sons and daughters to serve in distant lands... Only so will Sweden continue to be what it has been through glorious years, the strongest Salvation Army in proportion to population in the whole world.'

2 'We must work the works of him who sent me while it is day; night comes, when no man can work'. (John 9.4)

3 Flora Larsson, *Viking Warrior*, London, Salvationist Publishing and Supplies, 1959, p. 7.

Was this written in reply to query of hers, or was he merely making his position, conscientiously and, some would think, brutally clear? His daughter does not tell us, contenting herself with mentioning that her mother's quiet exterior covered a warrior heart.

In later years, when he, Anna and their seven children took their annual 'furlough', he would carry with him two bulky suitcases full of papers and books. While the others enjoyed the beach he would work through the contents of the cases, allowing himself only a ten minute swim each day. If anyone asked him whether he liked being in his current appointment he responded with puzzled asperity: '*Of course I like being here.* A Salvation Army officer always likes to be where he has been sent by God and the Army.'[4] Demanding much of himself, he was a blunt, demanding taskmaster for those under his command.

The Larsson children must, like most 'officers' kids', often have found their parentage a mixed blessing. 'Work, for the night is coming' and Larsson's other, cheerier motto ('If I try, I may succeed. If I don't try, I'll surely not succeed—so I'll try') admitted no compromise for infancy or other human weakness. During the Russian Revolution, for example, when the youngest of the children, Helmy, was two, Larsson took his family with him to St Petersburg, regardless of its maelstrom of social upheaval, epidemic disease and food shortages.

He was 44 and had served 23 years as an officer in Sweden when he was sent to command Finland in 1912—the last appointment made by William Booth, and the first officially effected by his son and successor, Bramwell. Like the Booths—despite having had, while he was in Helsingfors (as the capital of Finland was then known), his first experience of a Russian police raid on his headquarters—he was on the alert for any opportunity to extend the Army's work across the border. The barriers, he notes, were both political and religious:

> In Finland we had more or less succeeded in convincing the Russian authorities of our unpolitical character. The problem remained how to convince the authorities in Russia itself of this fact, as well as to overcome the difficulties put in our way by church authorities. It was, however, impossible so soon after the negative reply of the government to renew any petition. But was there no possibility to enter without first obtaining permission? Had we not heard our friends say many times: 'In Russia one can obtain only those things one does not ask for'.[5]

In anticipation, he had begun to learn Russian,[6] and reopened a corps at Terijoki, a resort close to the Russian border that attracted 10,000 visitors from St Petersburg every summer. Russia was expected to take over the town at any moment—in which

---

4 Flora Larsson, *Viking Warrior*, p. 26.

5 Larsson, *Tio År I Ryssland*, p. 16.

6 Although he was no mean linguist, he apparently succeeded only in mastering the alphabet.

case The Salvation Army would have a working corps within the country and the problem of entry would be solved.[7]

In the event, however, when the Army returned to Russia it was to St Petersburg itself, and by official invitation. The unexpected request came in 1913, at a time when, economically and socially, Russia was in a state of dangerous turmoil. Although the economy was booming, many people were more conscious than ever before of poverty and of the struggle to survive and support their families. From 1890 until 1914, fuelled by foreign financial and managerial investment, the annual rate of growth was the highest in Europe. But in the period immediately before the war, although the economy continued to expand, and some workers were beginning to see their way out of the cycle of poverty, most found that rising wages were constantly outstripped by much more rapidly rising prices. Disease, foul working conditions and unemployment continued to be the significant indicators of a standard of living that for many was actually falling. The resulting discontent found expression in strikes: 466, involving more than 100,000 workers, in 1911 and four times that many in 1912, with 700,000 workers taking part. During the first half of 1914, 16 new strikes began every day.[8] It was by now obvious that Russia's pseudo-parliament, the State Duma, established under pressure in 1905, was being ignored by the Tsar and his most influential advisors. It scarcely retained even its original status, that of a sop thrown to liberal opinion.

In 1913 celebrations were staged to mark the 300th anniversary of the Romanov dynasty. These had less impact than expected (not least because the Tsar and Tsarina appeared distant and aloof and did not always attend events at which they were expected). The festivities, in effect, marked the onset of the twilight of the Romanovs.

Meanwhile, the Booths, that other dynasty with which this history is concerned, had, between the Povlsens' departure from Russia and the arrival of officers from Finland early in 1913, suffered and survived a great loss. In August 1912, General William Booth was, in the Salvationist phrase, 'Promoted to Glory'. His funeral service, at the Olympia exhibition hall in West London, drew 40,000 people, including Queen Mary, consort of the new king, George V (Edward VII having also been promoted to another place, though possibly not to Glory).[9] The Queen was escorted by Lord Shaftesbury, grandson of the man who had so deplored Booth's informal innovations in religious practice, and it was he who reported to Colonel Unsworth the occurrence which supplied the phrase that became Booth's unofficial epitaph. The Queen had come without advance warning and the only seat available was alongside a shabby but neatly dressed woman, who told the Queen that she had once been a prostitute and been saved from that life by The Salvation Army. She

---

7 Terioki has been known as Zelenogorsk since it became part of the Soviet Republic of Karelia in 1923, too late for Larsson's plan to be fulfilled.

8 Lincoln, *In War's Dark Shadow*, pp. 394-95.

9 The King's funeral drew even vaster crowds than Booth's: this was an age of mass public mourning. See Tuchman, *The Guns of August*, London, The Folio Society, 1995, pp. 11-14.

carried a flower, which she placed on Booth's coffin as it passed down the aisle, saying as she did so, 'He cared for the likes of us'.[10] The following day, Owen Seaman, Editor of *Punch*, provided a more public *envoi*, catching the sentiments of the general public. It concludes:

> No laurelled blazon rests above his bier,
> Yet a great people bows its stricken head
>   Where he who fought without reproach or fear,
> Soldier of Christ, lies dead.[11]

Across the Atlantic the 33 year-old poet Vachel Lindsay, who had been struggling along as a tramp and a beggar and lecturer on art and temperance, made his name with a vivid, vigorous and dramatic elegy, *General William Booth Enters into Heaven*. In 1914 Charles Ives would set 32 of Lindsay's lines to music for unison voices and orchestra as vigorous and dramatic as Lindsay's words, in the process composing what is widely considered to be his greatest song. Lindsay's original had been marked 'To be sung to the tune of The Blood of the Lamb' and each section had a designated accompanying instrument—bass drum, banjos, flutes and tambourines.

> *(Bass drum, beaten loudly.)*
> Booth led boldly with his big bass drum—
> (Are you washed in the blood of the Lamb?)
> The Saints smiled gravely and they said: 'He's come'.
> (Are you washed in the blood of the Lamb?)
> Walking lepers followed, rank on rank,
> Lurching bravos from the ditches dank...
>
> *(Banjos.)*
> Every slum had sent its half-a-score
> The round world over. (Booth had groaned for more)...
>
> *(Reverently sung, no instruments.)*
> And when Booth halted by the curb for prayer
> He saw his Master through the flag-filled air.
> Christ came gently with a robe and crown
> For Booth the soldier, while the throng knelt down.
> He saw King Jesus. They were face to face,
> And he knelt a-weeping in that holy place.
> Are you washed in the blood of the Lamb?

---

10 The story survives in various slightly differing versions; this one is derived from that given in one of the books published to mark The Salvation Army's first centenary, Richard Collier's *The General Next to God,* London, Collins, 1965, pp. 247-48.

11 *Punch,* 28 August, 1912.

Seaman and Lindsay expressed in verse a worldwide conviction that someone remarkable had passed from sight, and in some commentaries the elegiac note extended beyond Booth himself to the organization he had founded, since it had been accepted wisdom that when William Booth died The Salvation Army would disintegrate. Bramwell Booth, however, became General within hours of his father's death, having been named in the sealed envelope left by William and opened according to procedures drawn up by the two of them in 1878.

In the late 1920s, Bramwell Booth's abilities as General and the desirability of incumbents in the post naming their successor would be questioned,[12] but for the time being all was well. This was fortunate, because the First World War, which would lead immediately to Salvationists firing at each other across No Man's Land,[13] was about to present the most severe test The Salvation Army's international leaders had yet faced.

In Russia, however, the Great War was helpful to the Army, giving it four years during which its attempt to establish itself there went almost unchallenged. The bureaucrats had other things to do than harass a small evangelical group whose leaders were mostly women. And, as the war continued, it threw up problems—refugees, displaced persons, soldiers' wives and children in poverty and distress—all problems which the Army was willing and available to help solve.

That the Army was in Russia and able to do these things had seemed an impossibility until the spring of 1913, when, out of the blue, Larsson was invited by an Inspector of State Sanitation, Mr Orädd, to contribute to the display in a pavilion which would represent the Grand Duchy of Finland at a Hygiene Exhibition, to be mounted in St Petersburg and provide the core collection for a permanent museum in that city. Although other such exhibitions were mounted in connection with the Tercentenary celebrations (in May the Tsar visited a new Red Cross building in Moscow and an exhibition put on by the *zemstvo*),[14] this one was probably not connected with the festivities. It was almost certainly organized by the government's temperance body, the Guardianship of Public Sobriety, for the Exhibition was in Petrovsky Park, on Petrovsky Island in the mouth of the Neva, the site of a number of its temperance centres. (The Guardianship had contributed anti-alcohol displays to an International Hygiene Exhibition in Dresden in 1911 and an International Industrial-Artistic Exhibition in Turin during the same year.)[15] On Sundays the park was frequented by working class families. Concerts, comedy

---

12 In 1929, after painful controversy and recrimination, Bramwell Booth was deposed as General by a special session of the High Council. His successor, the first of the continuing line of elected Generals, was Edward Higgins, whose report on William Booth's visit to St Petersburg I have drawn on in Chapter 9. See St John Ervine, *God's Soldier,* pp. 815-1139.

13 *The The War Cry,* 7 November, 1914, p. 1.

14 Maylunas and Mironenko, *Lifelong Passion,* p. 377.

15 See Herlihy, *The Alcoholic Empire,* p. 20.

shows, operettas and plays were staged in its numerous open-air theatres and there was a charity kindergarten.[16]

Although the Exhibition was not part of the tercentenary celebrations, the Tsar was expected to attend and Larsson planned to be present on that occasion. 'This high honour,' however, 'did not materialize'. Meantime, Larsson had reported the invitation and his acceptance of it to International Headquarters, which in turn wrote to the Army's friends in Russia. All agreed that the invitation, intentionally or not, provided the Army with the opportunity it had hoped for.

Thus it came about that among the first Salvation Army uniforms seen in Russia since the visits of George Scott Railton and William Booth was one worn by an exhibition dummy. This represented a slum officer, life-sized, standing ready for action, her navy uniform dress protected by a white pinafore. Her flat-brimmed hat did not much resemble the straw poke-bonnet used by The Salvation Army in England, but her high military collar, trimmed in red, was the same, and the badges were similar. Nearby hung large photographs of William and Bramwell Booth, and items used by The Salvation Army in its social institutions in Finland were on display: beds from its shelters, a cot from a Children's Home, needlework done in the rescue homes. Photographs of these institutions and the work done in them were shown, supplemented by statistical tables. Treasurer Phillipson from Stockholm, 'a well-known expert of decorative art' designed the stand in the Finnish Pavilion, a small, low building, with a veranda, set amongst trees.

During the Exhibition Larsson was assisted by the Radstockite aristocrat, Madame Chertkov, sister-in-law of the late Colonel Pashkov. She was eighty, was rather deaf and could not move without help. Nevertheless, he wrote, she had the bearing of a queen, and 'a young soul dwelt in her'. She possessed vast estates in Russia, as well as houses in Switzerland and England. Her house in St Petersburg, however, was simply furnished, although it contained a valuable library.[17]

Madame Chertkov arranged accommodation for Larsson at Pastor Fettler's Gospel Hall. Larsson discovered that this young, energetic Baptist preacher of Latvian origin openly imitated the Army in many of his methods. Indeed some thought it was his ambition to become the General Booth of Russia. He employed large bands and choirs in his meetings (often performing Salvation Army music) and staged musical processions in the streets. Like Salvation Army halls, his had large platforms and penitent forms at which seekers after salvation knelt. During the period of comparative religious freedom that followed the 1905 Revolution, he had built a

---

16 See Ometev and Stuart, *St. Petersburg: Portrait of an Imperial City*, pp. 67 and 222.

17 When, after the Revolution, Madame Chertkov went into exile at Vyborg in Finland, she gave the house to The Salvation Army, which used it as a children's home, corps meeting hall and headquarters. It was the library that delayed confiscation by the Communist government longer than might have been expected, because the commissar in charge feared its despoliation if a local soviet took it over. Madame Chertkov died in England at the age of 90, in 1922. Her son, Tolstoy's ex-secretary and son-in-law, helped the Army after its extension to Moscow in 1917, particularly by obtaining exemption from war service (as conscientious objectors) for male officers.

number of halls, in Moscow, Riga and elsewhere. His Gospel Hall in St Petersburg had an auditorium for 2,000, as well as several smaller halls and some bedrooms, which were offered *gratis* for short stays, although visitors were expected to provide food for the common table and contribute to collections taken during meetings. Fettler seems to have resembled Booth in other ways as well: as Booth had with the Methodist New Connection, he had found himself, Larsson observes, 'owing to his radical opinions and his autocratic principles... in disagreement with the elder Baptists and evangelical movements' and gone his own way. 'However, not all his enterprises were as practical as they were all-embracing.'[18] (Heier blames the idiosyncrasies of Fettler, amongst others, for the formation of splinter groups, which dissipated the impact of what was left of Radstockism and Pashkovisim.)[19]

Whatever ambitions he may have nurtured, Fettler apparently did not object to the official Salvation Army's arrival, and he gave Larsson his first chances to address Russian congregations in some of the smaller halls within his complex, himself and Madame Yasnovskaya interpreting.

When Commissioner Larsson and Lieutenant Olsoni set up their stand at the Petersburg Exhibition they soon learnt the utility of Jesus' exhortation to the disciples: 'Be ye therefore wise as serpents, and harmless as doves'.[20] Quite soon, 'meetings were being held and soldiers enrolled and Salvationists were seen on the streets wearing uniform, although the Army was as yet proscribed'. He and his assistants had permission to live in St Petersburg 'and make any propaganda we desired for the [three months'] duration of the exhibition, but our need was to find a good reason for continued activity after the exhibition was ended'.[21]

Help was at hand, in the person of a converted Jew, Adam Pieshevski. On the evening of Larsson's first day on Russian soil, 'one of those beautiful summer nights that one can hardly meet with anywhere but in St Petersburg', he was sitting in the courtyard of the Gospel Hall considering the day's experiences when Pieshevski (to judge from photographs he will have been punctiliously dressed, his appearance given individuality by a high wing collar and a thick handlebar moustache which appears to link up with his sideburns) introduced himself. He was 26, and had lived in southern Russia, where he had married a Polish girl. A few days earlier he had come to the capital in search of an office job.

Ten years before, passing through Hamburg on his way to England to stay with his uncle and noticing posters announcing that a general was to speak at a religious meeting, he had heard William Booth preach. This had led him to the Penitent Form

---

18 Fettler was soon to fall foul of the Russian authorities, who exiled him to Siberia at the outbreak of the European war on the grounds that he had accepted donations from German colonists and possibly also from people within Germany itself. Influential friends persuaded the Tsar to commute this to banishment from Russia. His later career took him to Sweden and the United States but he never lost hope of being involved in a large-scale evangelical movement in Russia.

19 Heier, *Religious Schism*, pp. 147-48.

20 Matt. 10.16.

21 Larsson, *Tio År I Ryssland*, p. 24.

and, once in England, he had tried to join The Salvation Army. His uncle, taking fright, sent him home at once, out of harm's way. Now, his wish to help the Army unabated, he offered his services to Larsson. They talked, far into the night, about 'the possibilities that this great country offered to The Salvation Army as well as the great need that existed for an activity such as ours'.

The following evening they met again and Larsson gave him a copy of the 20 page pamphlet (*National Health, Physical and Moral. What The Salvation Army does to further the same. Experiences from Finland*) he had written for visitors to the exhibition. A hiatus followed. The opening of the exhibition was postponed for a fortnight because the buildings and stands were not ready, so Larsson went back to Helsingfors. When he returned, Pieshevski had apparently disappeared. He had arrived in St Petersburg so recently that nobody knew him. However, two or three days later, Pieshevski sent a heavily corrected version of the pamphlet, which had been written by Larsson in Swedish and translated and printed in Helsingfors with unfortunate results. Larsson, recognizing that the existing version was a terrible jumble, had 10,000 copies of Pieshevski's revision printed forthwith—while, however, keeping the old version in case of need. All told, some 13,000 copies were given away, 'mainly to the intellectual classes'.

The Exhibition opened on 20 June, before 'a scintillating gathering: Dukes, Counts, military officers in gold-trimmed uniforms...' Like George Scott Railton before him, Karl Larsson felt that 'never before or since have I moved in so illustrious a company'. There was a religious ceremony, after which Orthodox dignitaries sprinkled holy water over the buildings and the illustrious company.[22]

Outside it rained all day. Large crowds attended nonetheless. Some knew the Army's work in other countries and welcomed its appearance in Russia. Others were ignorant of it, and the officer permanently on duty at the Exhibition, initially Staff Captain Rosa Hacklin (she who had assisted the Povlsens and been so depressed by their failure), subsequently Lieutenant Elsa Olsoni, another of the Army's capable linguists, had over and again to answer the question, 'The Salvation Army? What is that?'. Although many of the visitors were fluent in languages other than Russian, Lieutenant Olsoni's previously elementary knowledge of that tongue increased 'apace'. She was beginning what was to become a ten year stay, during which she faced cholera, imprisonment, hunger, and the deaths of several of her comrades.

Whether the officers should appear in Salvation Army uniform had been debated before the opening. Larsson thought it self-evident that they should, but many of the Army's Russian friends feared that to insist upon so radical a gesture might have unwelcome results. But by some bureaucratic quirk permission was granted and Larsson, Staff Captain Hacklin and Lieutenant Olsoni all went on duty in full regimentals. During the weeks that followed, Larsson, who could travel free on

---

22 Larsson, *Tio År I Ryssland*, p. 23. Larsson noted, with Protestant scepticism, that a few drops may have fallen on him. He admits also to nationalist reflections on the fact that the site of St Petersburg had once belonged to Sweden.

Finnish railways,[23] kept in touch with what was happening by making the eight hour overnight journey on a number of occasions.

Meanwhile, although there was no official suggestion that the Army's appearance at the Exhibition implied permanent official acceptance, the St Petersburg press proved friendly. *Ruskoje Snamja* wrote:

> The most interesting and instructive part of the exhibition belongs to The Salvation Army, which has existed in Finland for 12 years, and during that time opened 68 Corps,[24] Homes (for children and women), Crèches, large shelters for men, timber yards (where workless men can work and receive food and shelter). The Shelters have beds with nice mattresses, sheets, cover (felt), and pillow. Officers from the Army are in charge of the Shelters. There are 300 officers in Finland.

> The Army is also highly valuable for its successful fight against the drink traffic.[25]

Raich (Speech), 'a Liberal daily in good standing' wrote in similar terms, noting that the organization seemed to interest the public in a special way.

The War Cry Becomes Vestnik Spaseniya

The exhibition closed at the beginning of October. The Army's exhibit, which had won in effect the first prize for its section, a Diploma of Honour, was retained, with Larsson's permission, to become part of a permanent Museum of Hygiene. At this point, theoretically, the Army should have retreated to Finland. Once successfully in, however, having interested the public in a special way and received congratulations upon its arrival from the dukes, counts and military personnel who knew its work abroad, it was not willing to be easily dislodged and had already devised and implemented a scheme to ensure its continuing presence on the streets of St Petersburg.

Someone (Larsson did not remember who) suggested the publication of a monthly Salvation Army newspaper. This was so apt a device as to appear with hindsight almost obvious. The Pashkovites had been able, through their Society for the Encouragement of Spiritual and Ethical Reading, to publish more than 200 inexpensive pamphlets between 1876 and 1884, developing 'an enormous propaganda machine unparalleled in the Russian Empire at the time'.[26] Russians, particularly workers and the urban lower classes, becoming increasingly literate, were

---

23 Even within Russia proper it was not unknown for evangelists and agents of the Bible Society to be given free travel on railways and river steamers: see Robert Sloan Latimer, *Dr Baedecker and His Apostolic Work in Russia*, London, Morgan & Scott, 1907, pp. 102-04.

24 *All the World* corrected these figures, which should have been 23 and 80, respectively.

25 *All the World*, December 1913.

26 Heier, *Religious Schism*, p. 118.

enthusiastic newspaper readers, eager to understand the world and their place in it.[27] They were hungry for news of almost any sort, foreign as well as domestic. Since 1906 constitutional reforms and article 79 of the new Fundamental Laws had discontinued prepublication censorship of the press. This greatly increased the number of newspapers available and in so doing gave newly literate public opinion a voice and an influence it had not previously had. In the years before the First World War probably a majority of adults in the cities saw newspapers regularly. The importance of this so far as politics and government were concerned derived largely from the fact that the Duma and the political parties were relatively less free. The press kept the government informed about the attitudes and opinions of the governed[28] and in this way often functioned as a substitute for defective parliamentary institutions.

Nonetheless, the new freedoms were comparative, not absolute. Copies of each edition of all publications had to be submitted to an appropriate committee or official, who might decide that its contents violated the criminal code and confiscate the entire issue or even ban further publication. Criminal proceedings might also be taken against editors or owners, and during the years 1907-09 many prison sentences, suspensions and fines were imposed. Nonetheless, the number of publications trebled to 3,111 between 1900 and 1914. This accumulation of printed matter rendered censorship inefficient and incomplete. In any case the editors tended to be more agile than the censors and much of the political press in these years was written in a kind of code, or camouflaged as reprints of reports in the foreign press.

The proposed Salvation Army publication would consist entirely of reports from abroad, but it still had to tread carefully. Preliminary censorship of articles about religious and ecclesiastical matters had been retained.[29]

For all the difficulties, publication of a newspaper would enable the Army to maintain a legitimate presence. Indeed, Russian police regulations worked, somewhat ironically, to its advantage in a way which would reinforce that presence: permission for newspapers to be sold could be taken to imply permission for them to be

---

27 Acton, *Russia*, p. 134. See also Caspar Ferenczi, Freedom of the Press under the Old Regime, 1905-1914, in Crisp and Edmonson (eds.), *Civil Rights in Imperial Russia,* Oxford, Clarendon Press, 1989. In any case, since 1888 the state censor had approved the sale of Salvation Army publications in Russia (*The The War Cry*, 25 February, 1888, cited in Major Jenty Fairbank's *Notes for a Lecture Given in Russia in 1993*). Larsson does not mention any attempt on his part to invoke this ruling in 1913, although, as we shall see, it might have been useful to him.

28 In their different way, of course, so did the secret police: see D.C.B. Lieven, Police, Rights, and the Empire, 1855-1917, in Crisp and Edmonson, *Civil Rights in Imperial Russia.*

29 The Orthodox Church also had considerable powers of censorship. The printing of books pertaining to Orthodoxy without the approval of the church was prohibited. Church censorship could be used 'with telling effect against opposing denominations' and covered all religious writings and translations. See John Shelton Curtiss, *Church and State in Russia 1900-1917*, New York, Columbia University Press, 1940, pp. 35-37.

produced within the country and sold by agents of The Salvation Army, who, as was required of all news vendors, would have to wear distinctive dress—in other words, their uniforms.

Larsson decided to go ahead, even though Pieshevski's office job with a large firm allowed him to work for The Salvation Army only at night and on Sundays. The job, however, usefully acquainted him with the ways of bureaucracy and he soon enlisted support from an assistant to the official Printing Inspector, who had been left in charge because of his superior's illness. One of the duties of the office was to pass applications for publishing licences to the Commissioner of Police, Count Obolenski, together with a recommendation for or against acceptance. Larsson spent an evening discussing the Army's application with this helpful, sadly anonymous, assistant, who told him, in effect, what he could hope to get away with. If the paper were to be called *The War Cry*, the application would automatically be referred to the War Office, which would almost certainly veto it. A less military name might prove acceptable. Larsson, who seems to have had a useful and rather attractive streak of deviousness, came up with *Vestnik Spaseniya—The Herald of Salvation*. This name would appear not only on the paper itself, but on the hat bands worn by the uniformed sellers, and Larsson calculated that, after a period of acclimatization, the authorities might not notice if *Herald* were to become *Army*. He designed vendors' uniforms that were identical with those of The Salvation Army in everything but the name. The scheme for switching names permanently appears never to have worked entirely (indeed attempts to operate it aroused unwelcome attention), so, endlessly resourceful, Larsson had the hat bands made reversible, with *Herald* on one side and *Army* on the other, the latter to be displayed when circumstances permitted.

These subterfuges appear to have been discussed with the former assistant inspector, who had been promoted following his predecessor's death. Larsson continued to meet him in the evenings and as they parted, the inspector would say, 'Tomorrow in my office I will have forgotten all that we have talked about tonight'. He remained a friend of the paper as long as it continued publication, helping with correction of MSS and proof reading.

There was another regulation to be complied with, and that compliance had fortunate long-term effects. All newspapers were required to have registered owners, a role which the non-existent Army could not perform on its own behalf. A man who had already played an important role in the history of The Salvation Army in Finland—one that, however, had led to dissension and his irritated withdrawal and of which Larsson, as a comparative newcomer, seems to have been unaware—appeared out of the blue and accepted the responsibility. Baron Constantine Boije (a member of one of the noblest families in Finland, according to The Salvation Army's official historian) was, as a young man in the 1880s, sent by the Finnish Government to inspect night refuges for the poor in other European countries. He saw The Salvation Army at work in Stockholm, Berlin and London, and, having already previously been influenced by Lord Radstock (who had preached in Helsingfors as well as St Petersburg) decided on his return to begin an evangelical mission on similar lines. Eventually it was proposed that the mission should become part of the international

Salvation Army. Boije and two others went to London for training, while his wife stayed at home with their five daughters and supervised the mission in his absence. After they commenced official operations in 1889 political trouble was not long in coming. The Finnish establishment feared Russian displeasure; the Imperial Senate rejected The Salvation Army's statutes. Boije's preferred solution to this problem was to sever, at least temporarily, links with London, making The Salvation Army in Finland a national rather than an international organization. William Booth, surprisingly, accepted this, but the Salvationists of Finland did not. In 1890 they insisted that the international link be maintained. Boije withdrew and another officer took charge.[30] Disagreement over whether The Salvation Army in one country could or should be allowed to function separately from the international organization was to become important in Russia—although in this case, ironically, partly because of Constantine Boije's officer daughter Helmy's assessment of the situation, it was International Headquarters which rejected the possibility. Meanwhile, having resurfaced, very usefully for The Salvation Army, in 1913, Boije and, later, Helmy played crucial roles during The Salvation Army's time in Russia.

Pieshevski was appointed editor of *Vestnik Spaseniya* and with remarkable speed published the first, eight-page issue in July, a bare month after the exhibition opened. Its cover was devoted to a picture of William Booth, in uniform of course, with the Salvationist 'S' and crest on the collar, and a larger version of the crest visible on the guernsey which could be seen through his open jacket. Inside there was a profile of him and a selection of opinions of his work; 'Restored to Life', an article by Catherine Booth; an account of the Hygiene Exhibition and the Finnish Congress; dispatches from abroad and the text of a song. This became a regular feature, under the heading 'Salvation Songs' and from issue number three onwards the music as well as the words was sometimes printed.

The paper was, of course subject to restrictions and compromises. It could only give news of Salvation Army activity in Finland and elsewhere abroad, since, officially, none took place in Russia itself. This prohibition was, however, ignored in November 1914, when the front page carried three photographs of the Moscow Gate Slum Station in Petrograd and the work which was going on there. Previously, the covers had carried full page portraits of members of the Booth family (men and women in strict alternation) interspersed occasionally with drawings of biblical scenes or scenes from modern life which pointed some sort of moral. Later, photographs or drawings of the Army's work elsewhere in the world were used. The Tsar made the front page in July 1914, while the following month there was a montage of fighting soldiers, and columns of refugees.

The first issue was a success, helped along by Pastor Fettler, who allowed it to go out as an enclosure in his own paper, helping it attract subscribers all over Russia. Larsson kept up the relationships he had already established with the Russian press, visiting several newspapers in company with Pieshevski in his drive to publicize both the new paper and the Army's stand at the Exhibition. Captain

---

30 Wiggins, *The History of The Salvation Army*, vol. 4, pp. 45-48.

Elsa Olsoni and Lieutenant Henny Granström were the initial officer vendors; in August 1914 they were joined by Nadia Konstantinova-Sundell.

'My Best Men Are Women'[31]

Bramwell Booth had been right to believe that should the Army manage to enter Russia it would find devoted, effective officers to do its work there, although in the event none of those he had in mind in 1908 was still available in 1913. But others, by any standards remarkable people, presented themselves when called upon.

One of The Salvation Army's strengths, more unusual then than now, was its willingness to use the abilities of women of strength and character who longed to be up and doing. Like, for instance, Florence Nightingale, 50 years earlier, they most usually gravitated towards some form of humanitarian service. Discontent, divine or otherwise, with things as they were, drove them to find avenues in which they could be both leaders and servants: a course of action which often led to broken or severely damaged relationships with their families. During its ten dramatic years in Russia The Salvation Army was to have great cause for gratitude that such women were available, in Finland and in Russia itself, for although the Army's work there was always under the supervision of a male officer, he, much of the time, was not on the spot but across the border (admittedly at no great physical distance) in Helsingfors. Russian women in general were said by Paléologue, following Turgenev, to 'greatly excel the men in strength of character, temper and decision of their wills'. He described observing 'perhaps one of the most original types of Russian womanhood: a missionary of the revolutionary gospel'.[32] The Russian women we shall encounter who turned to an older, but in its way equally revolutionary gospel, demonstrate the truth of Paléologue's observations, although they did not choose to extend their passionately militant spirit, as some of their socialist and anarchist sisters did, as far as acts of assassination.

We have quite full accounts of the path through conversion to officership of two of these women, and they illustrate with great clarity both the complexities and simplicities of the Salvationist cast of mind.

The first of these, Nadia Konstantinova-Sundell, one of those who came to St Petersburg to sell *Vestnik Spaseniya*, had grown up in Helsingfors, where she worked for 'the Russian Naval establishment'.[33] Her association with The Salvation

---

31 A statement attributed to William Booth, used in 1974 by Flora Larsson as the title of her book on outstanding women officers.

32 Paléologue, 25 January, 1915. Richard Stites, in *The Women's Liberation Movement in Russia: Feminism, Nihilism, and Bolshevism, 1860-1930*, Princeton, Princeton University Press, 1991, p. 154, makes an explicit parallel between The Salvation Army and the revolutionary movement in their use of women: both 'discovered early that sexual equality was not incompatible with either discipline or ideological purity'.

33 Nadia Konstantinova-Sundell, *The Smallness of Man, the Greatness of God* n.d. (The typescript is held in the Russia files at The Salvation Army Heritage Centre.)

Army began on New Year's Eve 1905, when she was 16. Her family was expecting visitors and a festive mood was *de rigeur*. Nadia, however, did not care for the people who were due to appear, and felt so defiantly unfestive that when two young girls who lodged with the family invited her to a Salvation Army prayer meeting, she left with them, surreptitiously, by way of the kitchen door. At the meeting, at Helsingfors No. 4 Corps, Bätsmansgatan, she was moved by what she saw and heard, and 'immediately caught The Salvation Army fever'.

Thereafter, at intervals, she attended further meetings. When her family found out, she was subjected to their 'sermons and scoldings' but she was already well along the path towards conversion.

In a meeting which Nadia attended when her domestic turmoil was approaching its zenith, an officer spoke about 'people who trample the blood of Christ under their feet' (whom she no doubt, however reluctantly, equated with her parents) and led the meeting in 'the song about the little boat on the waves', which moved her deeply.

The song was probably *A little ship was on the sea*, an elementary versification of the story of Jesus calming a storm on the Sea of Galilee, written for children by the early Nineteenth-Century hymnodist Dorothy Ann Thrupp,[34] which would have given Nadia exactly the imagery she needed to interpret her recent experience and spur on her commitment to the Army in defiance of her parents' wishes:

A little ship was on the sea,
It was a pretty sight;
It sailed along so pleasantly,
And all was calm and bright.

When, lo! a storm began to rise,
The wind grew loud and strong,
It blew the clouds across the skies,
It blew the waves along.

And all but One were sore afraid
Of sinking in the deep;
His head was on a pillow laid,
And He was fast asleep...

He to the storm said: Peace, be still!
The raging billows ceased;
The mighty winds obeyed His will,
And all were hushed to peace...

---

34 This song was likely to be known by Salvationists in 1906, although it was not at that time published by The Salvation Army.

This artless ditty, sung to a bouncy tune, was for Nadia conclusive. She 'decided to choose the narrow path and go against the stream. That night I was saved.'

The news did nothing to calm her family's agitation. Soon she was obliged to apply to her troubles one of Jesus's harsher utterances: 'He that loves father or mother more than me is not worthy of me':[35]

> Life at home became unbearable. Tension increased. I prayed much. On return[ing] home from a journey father heard what was happening. There was a family discussion around the samovar. Father said: 'I will show you that I am your father.' I replied: 'If so, I am leaving home immediately.' Everybody wept, father include[d]. After this the tension somehow eased. I continued to attend meetings, and one day I was enrolled as a recruit. Eager to wear a little shield as a witness I prayed to the Lord for help.

At this stage, fortunately for Nadia, her family was visited by a friend who knew the Army's work. This 'old gentleman' advised them not to hinder her Salvationist activities. Remarkably enough, this advice was accepted, and she was permitted to wear the little shield. 'I went now to meetings as if on wings.' When she was enrolled as a soldier, however, a rearguard action was fought against her wish to appear in full Salvation Army uniform. She won the first round when she appeared at home in the blue blouse with white ribbons and a lyre, as worn by members of the string band. 'Only one thing was said: "Are you going to wear that cowl too?" (They meant the bonnet.)' I promised to wear it only [within the Army hall, during meetings].

But when she was appointed Young People's Sergeant Major at the Corps, she decided, after much pondering, that she must wear full uniform. Her father objected violently, but she told him, 'Father, no words can help here. If it is to be then it must be the whole way'. When, the following Christmas, she and her assistants gave a party for about 300 children, most of them from low-income homes, her mother attended it with her.

She continued as Young People's Sergeant Major for seven years, during which time one of her most valued helpers, Lempi Niskanen, dying of tuberculosis, told her, 'Remember, you have to win souls also on my account'. She took this very much to heart: 'Often I remained at the prayer meetings till midnight and even 1 a.m., longing to win a soul.'

She became a candidate for officership but delayed the decision for several years and eventually almost abandoned it. When she finally went to the Training College (or School of War, as it was then known) her defection from the family was considered by her father to have caused the illness which promptly laid her mother low.

Conversions of this type are nowadays often assumed to be attributable to the confused enthusiasms of adolescence and momentary in their effect. At the turn of the century, however, American psychologists accorded them serious attention.

---

35 Matt. 10. 37.

Professor Starbuck of California in his book, *Psychology of Religion*, defined such events as a 'normal phase' but also a necessary stage in 'growth into a larger spiritual life'. In a course of lectures delivered in 1901-02, William James summarized Starbuck's findings:

> The symptoms are the same,—sense of incompleteness and imperfection; brooding, depression, morbid introspection, and sense of sin; anxiety abut the hereafter; distress over doubts, and the like. And the result is the same—happy relief and objectivity, as the confidence in self gets greater through the adjustment of faculties to the wider outlook.[36]

Professor Starbuck did not merely chart the course of adolescent conversions: he also collected statistics from which he judged their permanence:

> ...the effect of conversion is to bring with it 'a changed attitude towards life, which is fairly constant and permanent, although the feelings fluctuate... persons who have passed through conversion, having once taken a stand for the religious life, tend to feel themselves identified with it...'[37]

This certainly proved to be the case with Nadia Konstantinova-Sundell. Her conversion carried her through almost a decade in Russia, years of laborious work, starvation, ill health and, towards the end, nine months in prison. Although she resigned as an officer after her father's death in 1922, in order to look after her mother, who lived on in ill health until 1926, she remained faithful to her calling and only ceased work in her mid-seventies.

The second of these detailed accounts of a path from conversion to officership concerns Clara Becker and will be given when she enters the story.

Gavan

The *Vestnik Spaseniya* sales team lived in Pieshevski's family flat, which became in effect The Salvation Army's headquarters in Russia. This was unsatisfactory because the *dvornik* (janitor) was (as was usually the case) a police agent and other tenants feared that he would report the production and distribution of *Vestnik Spaseniya*, its uniformed vendors and their stream of visitors. Pieshevski had to move house several times in search of a less hostile atmosphere.[38]

This was eventually found on Vasilevsky Island, across the Neva from St Isaac's Cathedral. At its eastern end lay the intellectual and educational centre of the city, encompassing the Academies of Sciences and Fine Arts, the School of Mines, the Naval School, the Zoological Museum, the Historical and Philological Institutes, the physical and chemical laboratories, and several other schools. The rest of the

---

36 Edwin M Starbuck, quoted in William James, *The Varieties of Religious Experience*, *(The Gifford Lectures 1901-02)*, London, Collins, 1960, p. 203.

37 James, *The Varieties of Religious Experience*, p. 257.

38 Larsson, *Tio År I Ryssland*, p. 29.

island, stretching westward towards the Gulf of Finland, was a very mixed residential area.

In the 1890s the area was earmarked for development as a major new region of the Imperial Capital, to be known as New Petersburg. Five hundred thousand people were to be housed there. Only parts of this scheme, however, were built. The mixed society on the island during the period that concerns us is described by E.M. Almedingen, who lived there at the time:

> Vassiliy (sic) Island, seen from a belfry, would have suggested an irregular piece of some check material. It had five horizontal lines intersected by 14 vertical ones, much shorter and more narrow. The wide strips were known as 'Quays' and 'Prospects'. The narrow ones went by the humbler name of 'Lines', and they were numbered... The lines were to be canals, linking the Neva to her small tributary [further north]. The canals were never made, but the breadth of the Lines remained...
>
> The Island had clear caste distinctions: certain of the lines were almost aristocratic, others merely possible, and the rest quite slummy. The distinction was repeated in the Prospects: *'Bolshoi'* was very *comme il faut, 'Sredny'* (Middle) more than doubtful, and *'Maly'* (small) lying furthest from the Neva, housed the human dregs of the Island...[39]

In the general consciousness of Petersburgers, Vasilevsky Island housed workers, revolutionaries and malcontents. In 1903-07, the Gavansky Gorodok, a model housing settlement for workers, was built at No. 47 Gavanskaya Ulitza, a street parallel with the west coast of the Island, some way beyond the last of the Lines; it was at the intersection of this street with elm-flanked Bolshoi Prospect that the Salvationists' modest flat was located. Gavan, adjacent to some of the slummiest parts of the Island might seem an ideal situation for the Salvationists but it was several miles from the political, administrative, commercial and emotional heart of the city, where people of influence with deep pockets could be attracted and even more remote from other working class districts around the extensive periphery. By 1917 Larsson would be eager to find more central premises.

'Gavan' means 'harbour' in Russian, and the Salvationists applied that name to their quarters, as a home or haven for themselves and the needy of St Petersburg. They lived in the basement of a two-storey log building with plenty of windows (including at least one dormer) that also housed a chemist's shop. Its cellar-like vestibule was connected via a small dark passage with two tiny cubicles and a scullery at the far end. To one side of the passage was a long narrow room that was used as the editorial office of *Vestnik Spaseniya* and the editor's bedroom. The women officers presumably occupied the tiny cubicles. There was one relatively spacious principal room, the windows of which, facing the street at the level of the pavement, were protected by iron bars.

---

39 E.M. Almedingen, *Tomorrow Will Come*, London, The Bodley Head, 1961, pp. 12-13.

After a time this cramped officers' quarters and editorial office became a conventicle as well, at which religious meetings were held most evenings. Chairs placed in rows across the largest room, a green sofa against a side wall, a trunk, and boards placed across stools, provided seating. Interconnecting doors enabled all the rooms, including the passage, to become congregational space: seated and standing, about 30 people could be squeezed in for big occasions, such as the visits of Colonel Larsson. (The interconnecting doors, as will be seen, were to play their part in a comic, frightening but, in its most immediate effect, inspirational police raid.) The congregation consisted of a select, specifically invited few (security was as much at a premium as space).[40] Invitations went only to those who had expressed interest and who were thought to be reliably discreet. But even these sometimes behaved in surprising ways: after the outbreak of war, one convert prayed, in what we might consider more an Orthodox than a Salvationist spirit, that the Tsar might be supplied with the machine guns he needed. And, occasionally, there were gatecrashers.

These gatherings were, of course, illegal, since no more than ten people (even for such day-to-day formalities as a christening or a wedding) were allowed to congregate without obtaining police permission. As foreigners, whose only official standing was as publishers and vendors of a newspaper, Olsoni, Granström and Konstantinova-Sundell knew that they were, however intermittently and ineffectually, under the eye of the authorities. To suggest that nothing more than a social gathering was in progress, samovar and teacups were kept prominently on a table in the living room where the meetings took place.[41]

Speculating on why the Salvationists got away with these meetings for so long, Larsson, once again demonstrating an agreeable and realistic streak of deviousness in dealing with hostile authority, quotes a Russian proverb:

'He who has the friendship of the janitor and the police has no need of the Tsar's goodwill':

We were on good terms with the janitor, and the policeman on duty never let on that he saw anything. I almost believe that they were conspirators with us—or at least that they believed us to possess some kind of privileges.[42]

General Bramwell Booth's daughter Catherine (who in her nineties would become something of a television personality in England, appearing to great effect and acclaim on chat shows), visited St Petersburg after the Finnish Congress of 1913, and remembered preaching in a suffocating atmosphere to an eager congregation with

---

40 This sheds new light, favourable to the Englishman, on Meshchersky's scornful attack on Lord Radstock's custom of sending out printed invitations: Radstock too had the police to consider. (See Chapter Three, above.)

41 One may observe that to anyone familiar with The Salvation Army, at least during its first century or so, this particular subterfuge will hardly appear a deception. Wherever a Salvation Army meeting took place, a teapot and cups were never far away. William Booth famously observed that he liked his religion as he liked his tea, 'hot and strong'.

42 Larsson, *Tio År I Ryssland*, pp. 31-32.

huge shutters at the windows and thick curtains drawn to prevent the sound of singing reaching the street outside. An account of these clandestine congregations by Elsa Olsoni concedes with notable honesty the bizarre character of what was going on.

> How could they... night after night listen to those extremely simple testimonies and to the preaching... in very broken Russian? Outwardly they differed much from each other. The simple peasant woman sat side by side with the lady from the intelligentsia. Old and young, working men, students, doctors, now and then a general...

The answer she offers is precisely the one you would expect, and yet the sense she gives of having arrived at it through deduction as well as expectation is difficult to resist: why *would* such an ill-assorted mixture of people gather in horribly uncomfortable conditions to listen to foreigners uttering revivalist simplicities in incompetent Russian, she will have thought, if not for a reason something like this:

> ...they were united in one desire—hunger and thirst after God. In this simple abode they found something of the living waters. Here many a soul for the first time met with its redeemer. Eternity alone will reveal what the spirit of the Lord achieved at dear old Gavan.[43]

Meanwhile, during daylight hours, walking the streets between breakfast and dusk, Olsoni, Granström and their assistants were selling *Vestnik Spaseniya*, work that, as Larsson notes in praising them, was tiring and discouraging. Learning Russian as they went they entered private houses, drinking saloons, billiard rooms, restaurants and cafeterias to sell papers and talk to anyone who showed interest. When circulation reached 8,000 per month (about 2,000 of these were sold to Russians living in Finland), permission was obtained to sell the paper on trams as well. Pieshevski used his connections to spread knowledge of the paper and The Salvation Army and every time Larsson visited St Petersburg he was given a list of people who wanted or had agreed to meet him. *Birsjeviya Vyedomosti* (Stock Exchange News) gave both paper and organization a kindly mention. Larsson visited various Free Church groups, including the Evangelical Movement, heirs of Radstock and Pashkov, which would, in the evanescent freedom of 1917, sublet to the Army the 700 seat Tenishev Hall, in which it held some of its most successful meetings,[44] and *Mayak* (The Lighthouse), an organization similar to the YMCA, about 2,000 strong, led by two Americans (one of whom had been a Salvation Army officer) who were, however, required to leave all religious matters to a Russian priest and could neither announce the Army's existence nor recommend its newspaper.

---

43 Larsson, *Tio År I Ryssland*, p. 31.

44 The hall was part of the Tenishev Commercial Academy, a progressive school for the sons of wealthy families, which rented it out for a wide variety of meetings and events. See footnote 72, pp. 227-28 below.

Thus, under the threat of proscription and expulsion, the Army continued to publicize itself in secret. The secrecy, albeit stimulating, sometimes had near disastrous results. Larsson describes one such situation. A man made despondent by disappointment and misfortune decided to kill himself and bought poison for the purpose. With his last five kopeks he also bought a copy of *Vestnik Spaseniya*. Interested, he visited the office, but when he arrived the officers were out and the woman they had left in charge told him, using the formula she had been instructed to offer all unknown enquirers, that there was no Salvation Army in Russia: the nearest office was in Finland. Surprisingly, the man rose to the challenge by finding his way on foot, through the bleak winter countryside, to Helsingfors, a journey of some three days. He was greeted by the corps officer, fed and taken to a meeting, where he sought salvation. Convinced that he had turned a corner, he handed over the poison, which he had kept with him in case The Salvation Army should prove inadequate to his needs.[45]

Despite such problems The Salvation Army was playing its hand with some skill, not to say low cunning. Its newspaper was selling well and being read. It was holding religious meetings every night under the noses of the Russian authorities. Converts were being made and committing themselves to service in The Salvation Army. The first such enrolment (under, officially, the auspices of the Helsingfors No. 1 Corps) was of eight fully uniformed men and women and took place on 20 December, 1914.

The Salvationists lost few chances to push against the restrictions that bound them. In the week before Easter 1914, as was customary, a large fair was held in St Petersburg. Olsoni and Granström hired a stand on which they could display *Vestnik Spaseniya*. One of the Army's friends, a Madame von Wahl, took charge of the stall and addressed the crowds that gathered, describing the work and beliefs of the Army. Larsson observes, with delight, that the stand

> ...became in everything but name a properly conducted Open Air meeting. People listened intently, the crowd grew until the gangways were blocked, the little shop was stormed by an eager throng. [Madame von Wahl wrote:] 'My heart was touched by all I saw and heard that testified of the longing of these people for God. I felt I had to empty my soul and wholeheartedly to testify about my Saviour. Oh, how they listened! The crowd grew until finally the gangway was blocked. "Hello, what is

---

45 Larsson, *Tio År I Ryssland*, pp. 35-36. A sceptical reading of this story might well deconstruct it virtually out of existence. Those who seek the help of The Salvation Army, as G.B. Shaw suggested in his play *Major Barbara*, sometimes feel the need to dramatize their situation so as to make themselves interesting: it is concomitant with the loss of morale which set them off on their quest. The corps officer at Helsingfors would not have wished to examine either the convert's *bona fides* or his packet of poison in too forensic a manner, lest he desert his new-found faith. On the other hand, we should remember that suicide rates were very high in St Petersburg. Teetering on the brink of the act, a man might have made a bargain with fate: 'Very well—I will walk three days through the snow, but if, after that, no help is forthcoming, life will truly have betrayed me and I can reject it with a clear conscience'.

happening here?'" I heard a voice asking, whereupon somebody answered: "There is somebody here who is telling us that it is but through the love of the Saviour that we can live in a really human way." After this my little shop was absolutely stormed, and the whole of my stock of *Vestnik Spaseniya*, with the exception of three copies, was sold within a few minutes.'

On Easter Monday a group of comrades from Finland staged a kind of demonstration, walking through the main streets of St Petersburg and then holding a meeting for those who would follow. Together with our own friends there were about 20 uniformed Salvationists who on that day several times "walked" through the main streets or St. Petersburg. In conclusion a meeting was held at which twenty-five people were present. This was our largest Army meeting in the capital up till now, and somebody called it 'our first Congress'.[46]

In 1914, therefore, the Army, despite its official non-existence, had made itself a part, however small, of the life of the Russian capital. Europe, of course, was on the brink of catastrophe, but for the Army, paradoxically, that catastrophe would for the time being help stabilize its position.

Interludes in Riga and London

Three episodes intervened before war broke out, all seemingly fleeting in their impact but none in the long run as abortive as it at first seemed. They illustrate Larsson's determination to do anything possible to increase the Army's standing within the Russian Empire and that of the Russian Salvation Army in the Salvationist world at large.

In February 1914 he accepted an invitation from Baroness A. von Pheilitzer-Frank, who owned a small home for drunkards in Mitau, Latvia. Mitau (now Jelgava) was principally notable in Russian history as the place from which the Empress Anna, an autocrat notorious for arbitrary acts and severe punishments, had emerged. Large numbers of Germans had settled in Latvia, dominating the Latvians and creating a predominately Lutheran society. From the 1870s onwards there had been a government-led reaction against this German domination: Latvian education, law and administration were reformed along Russian lines, and Latvians who had converted to Orthodoxy were forbidden to return to the Lutheran faith. The resulting tensions erupted in 1905-06. When Riga's workers assembled to protest against St Petersburg's Bloody Sunday, a Latvian one resulted: 22 were killed and 60-odd wounded by troops. Thereafter, the country became ever more sharply divided on nationalist lines.

Baroness von Pheilitzer-Frank was presumably one of these embattled Germans, and she had additional problems of her own. Her chief assistant at the home for drunkards had died, and the object of her invitation was to pass it on to The Salvation Army. Larsson was enthusiastic: he was able in Mitau to conduct both

---

46 Larsson, *Tio År I Ryssland*, p. 39-40.

private and public meetings before sympathetic and pleasant audiences and when, some weeks later, he returned to celebrate the Russian Easter with 'these dear people', he was asked to open a corps there. The General in London gave permission for this to happen, but the war intervened. Later, after the revolution, Baroness von Pheilitzer-Frank was killed by the Bolsheviks.

Together with hundreds of Mitau's middle class population, she had been interned. When the German army advanced unexpectedly the Reds, unwilling to let their prisoners be taken by the Germans or escape altogether, opened the prisons and drove them like a herd of cattle towards Riga. They were picked off by mounted executioners during the 24 mile forced march and Baroness von Pheilitzer-Frank was among those who died on the way.[47]

From Larsson's point of view the story had a partly happy ending. In 1927, by which time Latvia had become an independent state, he returned to Mitau. The Baroness's home for drunkards had become the living quarters for The Salvation Army officers running the corps that, in 1914, he had been unable to open.

In the months before the outbreak of war he also visited the Latvian capital, Riga, to inspect a Street Mission run by another German (presumably), Mr Junker. The mission seems to have been modelled on The Salvation Army: its members wore uniform and they also marched in the streets. Junker cared for 'homeless children and fallen men and women', had established a farm colony outside the city, and was on good terms with the provincial governor, who had given him financial assistance. Despite all this, Larsson was not impressed. 'The movement had evidently lost some of its earlier power. There was not much religion in it and hardly any organization at all.' Meanwhile, the governor's support had made Mr Junker revise his previous wish to pass the whole concern over to The Salvation Army. Early in the morning Larsson spoke in a tea house near the waterfront to about 200 people most of whom had spent the night (this was in February) in the open air: 'the most awful looking congregation I have ever addressed in my life'. They listened, however, with 'great attention and respect'. Later he addressed a gathering of 137 at Junker's establishment, about half of them children, the rest 'more or less depraved' men and women. Several men came forward to his improvised penitent form. He addressed a church congregation and, in a private house, a gathering of 'as far as I could make out, mostly Jews'.

So far as Junker's mission was concerned, Larsson's efforts proved abortive. Junker spoke no more of passing the mission to the Army and when he was called up after the outbreak of war the concern collapsed.

The third episode that intervened before the outbreak of war was the attendance of a small Russian delegation at The Salvation Army's fifteen-day International Congress in June 1914, ten years almost to the day after the Congress with which this book began. It was, according to the official historian,[48] 'an unparalleled demonstration of international unity and British solidarity'; even in 1968, the year of

---

47 Larsson, *Tio År I Ryssland.* p. 39.
48 Wiggins, *History of The Salvation Army*, vol. 5, pp. 202-03.

publication, the Army's establishment saw no inherent contradiction in such a statement. London in 1914 was still the capital of the world's wealthiest empire, a city to which people from all over the planet were prepared to travel and, so far as Salvationists were concerned, it remained the place where, 48 years before, the Army had begun its work. It was still the home of General Booth, albeit the son rather than the father. One of the purposes of the Congress was to remind members from such far flung places as New Zealand, Indonesia (only six of its 15 delegates were more than five feet tall) and Texas (presumably rather larger) that they were members of an international movement, one of whose proudest boasts was its unity of spirit and purpose. This, of course, was to be put severely to the test within a few months.

National costume was again worn by many delegates, and created much interest among Londoners and the British press. Lieutenant Vera Gorinovich, one of the small Russian delegation, was, Larsson remarks, 'of attractive appearance and, dressed in the colourful Russian costume, attracted considerable attention'. The story of how her family had become Christians was worthy of the attention her appearance and costume created. Her father, N.E. Gorinovich, a Ukrainian, had been a member of the first of two separate revolutionary groups called 'Land and Liberty'. In 1876, at a time when the group was moving towards schism, the leader of one of the factions, L.G. Deich, basing his suspicions on guesses and rumours, accused him of acting as an *agent provocateur*.

What happened next was recorded in an official report:

...several other political processes occupied the activity of government and justice during the course of the year 1878, so fertile in terrorist events. During that same year the court martial at Odessa passed judgment on the doings of a socialist circle in Elizabethgrad and pronounced a verdict condemning three criminals to death by hanging. This was... the affair of the criminal outrage against a young socialist, Gorinovich, which took place on 11 July, 1876... The enquiry lasted a long time, for the accused were numerous (in all 25 people), of whom several had taken flight and proved difficult to recapture. The principal criminals were: Victor Malinka, Victor Kastiourine... Leon Deutsch, Jacques Stefanovich... Jean Maidanski, (a Jew) and the barrister Kraiev. It was proved that the accused had employed various subterfuges to lure Nicolas Gorinovich to Odessa and attempted to murder him. The crime had taken place in the horse market. They had stabbed the victim a number of times and, in order that he should not be recognized, Malinka (according to the evidence given by the assassins) had urged Deutsch to pour vitriol on his face. But Gorinovich was not dead, and his screams put the evildoers to flight. He was a young man of 21, a newly converted adherent, who seemed to have had second thoughts and to have given the police details of socialist activities. He had begun his studies at a gymnasium in Kiev but had left before finishing the course and, somewhat later, enlisted in an infantry regiment. After joining terrorist circles he spread propaganda in a government sugar factory in Kiev, and forged false passports. He was arrested, but repented and was released at the beginning of 1875. In consideration of this change and of the atrocious treatment he had suffered at the hands of his former comrades, he was acquitted in 1878 during the great trial of propagandists. Horribly mutilated, his limbs broken, impossibly disfigured by the vitriol Deutsch had poured over him, he could only drag out a miserable existence, sustained by the charity of Count Alexis Bobrinski and Colonel Basil Pashkov.

On 3 December 1879, the Odessa court martial passed sentence of death against Malinka, Drobiazquine and Maidanski, and of forced labour against Kastiourine, Kraiev, Tourtschanov and Yanowski. The death sentences were carried out on 7 December, at the racecourse outside the city.[49]

Colonel Pashkov had talked to Gorinovich about the love of God, and he became a convert. After his discharge he was nursed by the Countess Bobrinski, another Pashkovite. His sight completely gone, he founded an Institute for the Blind, wrote a short sketch of his life, *He Loves Me*, and testified keenly to others about the change in his life. He refused, however, to testify against those who had maimed him, saying that but for the grace of God he would have done the same thing. For the rest of his life he wore a black cloth over his disfigured face.[50]

His daughter Vera was introduced to The Salvation Army by Mary von Weisberg (Railton's hostess at Tolstoye in 1908, and one among those who greeted William Booth at St Petersburg in 1909). In the late summer of 1913 she was again in St Petersburg and got in touch with Vera Gorinovich, by this time a student there. Vera had never heard of The Salvation Army but was rapidly persuaded by Miss Weisberg that she must become an officer. Somehow Miss Weisberg also arranged for Vera to attend the Army's training school in Berlin, whence, in due course, she arrived in London (accompanied by Mary von Weisberg) for the International Congress. When it was over, she returned to Russia and took up duties in St Petersburg.

The Russian group at the London Congress was small: Olsoni, Granström, Gorinovich and Weisberg. But they were doubtless inspired by the opportunity to participate in Salvation Saturday, when 12,000 Salvationists, led by General and Mrs Booth, marched from Victoria Embankment to Hyde Park, where they broke into groups to conduct 12 simultaneous open air meetings. The *Daily Telegraph* thought that this event would live in the memory of London when many costlier spectacles had grown dim, and the *Evening News* described the procession as more exciting and brilliant than any London had ever seen outside the great state occasions. *The Nation* wrote of 'so many agreeable and happy faces' and called the event 'a famous victory' for the Army, a final answer to the 'contemptuous wit' of Professor Huxley's jibe about 'Corybantic Christianity'. During the Congress, General Bramwell Booth met the new Queen of England, Queen Mary and, as his father had done, the Dowager Empress Marie Feodorovna of Russia.

---

49 Shebeko, *Chronique du mouvement socialiste en Russie*, St Petersburg, 1890, pp. 159-61.

50 See Geifman, *Thou Shalt Kill*, pp. 85-86 (which includes a photograph of Gorinovich after the attack) and 288 (note 5); Deborah Hardy, *Land and Freedom: the Origins of Russian Terrorism 1876-1879*, New York, Greenwood Press, 1987, p. 55; Shukman (ed.), *The Blackwell Encyclopedia of the Russian Revolution*, p. 58, and 318-19; Trotter, *Lord Radstock*, p. 195; and Larsson, *Tio År I Ryssland*, pp. 41-42.

The Congress must have given the small party of Russians (representatives, let us remember, of an organization which did not exist in the country they were representing) a sense of being part of something large, impressive and exciting, and they must often have needed to called upon that memory as a prop and stay during the years to come.[51] They returned to a country and a capital city shortly to be overwhelmed by humiliating military collapse, political upheaval, famine, epidemic, and civil war. They themselves suffered the consequences of these disasters but worked on, sustained by a belief—which few would consider had much evidence to support it—that they were doing God's work in the place where He needed and had put them.

Russia at War

From the outbreak of war until the abdication of the Tsar in March 1917, The Salvation Army in Russia led a curious existence: there, but not there, working in cooperation with local government and war charities whose figureheads were members of the Imperial Family, yet continuing to have no official existence. The war, producing as it did large numbers of transients and homeless, gave the Army, from the government's point of view, a useful ameliorative function—but not to the point of being recognized as The Salvation Army in Russia. Larsson and his colleagues remained representatives of the Army in Finland, permitted for the time being to do social work within Russia but not to proselytize. When they were no longer required they would be sent home.

When the war began, Russians behaved much like the people of other belligerent states: seized by patriotic euphoria, they accepted promises made by leaders whose word they had doubted fiercely during the previous months or years. The St Petersburg mob sacked German shops and hurled the cast-iron horses from the top of the German Embassy into the street below. Without serious debate the name of the city, with its German overtones, was changed to Petrograd, a more Russian form.[52] Mikhail Vladimirovich Rodzianko, chairman of the Third and Fourth Dumas, describes what happened when the Tsar appeared before his people:

> On the day of the manifesto of war with Germany a great crowd gathered before the Winter Palace... the Tsar came out on the balcony to his people, the Empress behind him. The huge crowd filled the square and the nearby streets, and when the Tsar appeared it was as if an electric spark had run through the crowd, and an enormous 'hurrah' filled the air. Flags and placards with the inscription 'Long live

---

51 To suggest an unexpected but not perverse analogy, the Salvationists, like the rural revolutionaries dispersed throughout the Russian countryside, needed a sense of loyalty, warmth and camaraderie with those far away to keep them going. See Hardy, *Land and Freedom*, p. 151.

52 Solomon Volkov, *St Petersburg, A Cultural History,* London, Sinclair-Stevenson, 1996, p. 195.

Russia and Slavdom' bowed to the ground, and the entire crowd fell to its knees as one man before the Tsar...

Coming [later] out of the palace onto the square, we mingled with the crowd. Some workers came by. I stopped them and asked how they happened to be there when not long before they had been striking and presenting economic and political demands almost with weapons in hand. The workers answered: 'That was our private affair. We found the reforms were going too slowly through the Duma. But now all of Russia is concerned. We came to the Tsar as to our banner, and we will go with him in the name of victory over the Germans.'[53]

The contrast between this and the lukewarm Tercentenary celebrations could hardly be more marked.

Like western euphoria, however, Russian enthusiasm for war diminished rapidly when the fighting failed to be over by Christmas and military deficiencies in supply and organization became apparent. The Russian government, like those in Western Europe, expected the war to be short, and had that been the case, Richard Pipes argues, Russia would have been adequately equipped to fight it.[54] It was, however, manifestly ill-prepared for a longer conflict, just as, indeed, Germany was.[55] Before the end of 1914, Maurice Paléologue was hearing 'reports from many quarters that the Russian army is running short of ammunition and rifles'. (By the summer of 1915 the shortage was such that men were sent unarmed into the trenches 'to wait until their comrades were killed or wounded and their rifles became available').[56] The morale of the military had been low for years. The humiliating fiasco against Japan in 1904-05 had followed defeat in the Crimean War (1853-56); a successful but expensive campaign against the Turks in 1877-78 was insufficient compensation. Rank and file soldiers, overwhelmingly peasant in origin, resented the increasing use of the army to suppress peasant revolts and often defied orders: the disturbances in 1905-06 provoked more than 400 mutinies.

In 1914 the Russian armies were driven out of East Prussia following defeats at Tannenburg and the Masurian Lakes in August and September. 170,000 men were taken prisoner. In 1915, offensives by the Central Powers produced a further collapse and retreat, this time from Poland, leaving another million taken prisoner and almost as many again dead and wounded.[57] Within Russia these disasters created a new and large class of widows and orphans, homeless and on the move. At the front, as the retreat gathered speed, clumsy attempts to implement a scorched earth policy

---

53 Quoted in George Vernadsky *et al* (eds.) *A Source Book for Russian History from Early Times to the February Revolution,* New Haven and London, Yale University Press, 1972, vol. 3, p. 831.

54 Pipes, *The Russian Revolution,* p. 201.

55 Alexandra Richie, *Faust's Metropolis: A History of Berlin,* London, HarperCollins, 1999, pp. 272-73.

56 Major-General Sir Alfred Knox, quoted in Vernadsky *et al, Source Book,* p. 837.

57 See Rogger, *Russia in the Age of Modernization and Revolution 1881-1917,* London, Longman, 1983, p. 258.

produced an even more overwhelming catastrophe: a mass of refugees moved eastwards, clogging roads desperately needed by the military. Meanwhile, the pathological anti-Semitism of General Ianushkevich created such outrage amongst Russia's allies that the Jews had to be given permission to leave the Pale of Settlement along Russia's western borders, adding to the streams of people travelling eastwards.[58] 'The whole of the Polish peasantry seemed to migrate from the districts east of the Vistula... Near Bylesk I passed 20 continuous miles of such fugitives.'[59] These people were fleeing in the mistaken belief that the Russians would not allow them to starve.

Their hope was false because Russia was never adequately organized to cope with wartime conditions. In a section of his *Memoirs* published in 1922, Rodzianko wrote:

> During the entire war the country's internal water routes were never adequately used for the cheap transportation of necessary food... In some districts there was an abundance, even a surplus... while elsewhere there was an acute shortage... requisitioning was conducted without any plan and without any correlation to the army's need for meat... cattle... frequently came to localities not provided with feed and found there neither pasture, nor fodder, nor sufficient watering places... Livestock losses from hunger, sickness, and insufficient veterinary and hygienic care numbered in the thousands and inflicted incalculable misfortune on the population.[60]

Meanwhile, Russia's inflation was worse than that experienced by other belligerent powers. (One of the causes was self inflicted: see pp. 174-75, below.) Before long, workers at home, of whom the metalworkers, machinists and electricians were best off, faced price rises of, on average, 300 per cent, while wages had risen, again on average, by only 100 per cent. The Petrograd security police reported in 1916 that 'the impossibility of even buying many food products and necessities, the time wasted standing idle in queues to receive goods, the increasing incidence of disease due to malnutrition and unsanitary living conditions (cold and dampness because of lack of coal and wood) and so forth, have made the workers, as a whole, prepared for the worst excesses of a "hunger riot"'.[61]

These consequences were, of course, still to come in 1914, but their root causes were already well established. When secret police start to sound humanely concerned for their fellow men, it is time for governments to take stock. The government of Tsar Nicholas II, however, had no will to do so.

The Salvation Army, of course, welcomed neither the war nor the government's lassitude, but these factors provided an opportunity for voluntary charitable organizations to work, especially if, unlike those whose charity was a conventional

58 Lincoln, *Passage Through Armageddon*, pp. 141-433, and 156-58.
59 Vernadsky, *Source Book*, pp. 837-38.
60 *Vernadsky, Source Book*, pp. 857-58.
61 *Vernadsky, Source Book*, pp. 867-68.

offshoot of Orthodox religion or a fashionable side-effect of their sense of *noblesse oblige*, they were prepared to live and suffer alongside those they wanted to help. Members of The Salvation Army like to say that 'Man's extremity is God's opportunity', and so, from their point of view, it was to prove in Russia.

Russia's 'Greatest Victory'

Before settling down to charitable war work, however, The Salvation Army joyously saluted what *The War Cry*'s headline called 'Russia's Greatest Victory'. This was the prohibition of the sale of vodka throughout the Empire, a measure conceived and pushed through by Nicholas in defiance of contrary advice. *The War Cry* was in no doubt of the significance of the decision:

> ...the Tsar and the Russian people have done much to defeat one of their worst enemies—the drink habit... His Majesty's act has placed Russia far ahead of all other nations in the matter of practical example in dealing with a national curse.[62]

Ambassador Paléologue—who presumably preferred wine to vodka—noted 'a decrease in crimes of violence and an appreciable increase in the output of labour'.[63] By November 1915, however, while still referring to the prohibition as 'the result of a noble impulse... the first effects of which were so salutary', he was beginning to wonder whether it was not at least partly to blame for the pessimism and defeatism into which the working class and the peasantry had sunk:

> The traditional nutrition of a race cannot with impunity be changed by a sudden decree. The abuse of spirits was certainly a danger to the physical and moral health of the moujiks, but the fact remains that vodka constituted an important element in their diet, the nervous tonic *par excellence*, and a food which was particularly necessary, as the tissue-repairing qualities of their other food are almost always inadequate.[64]

Despite these, perhaps medically unsound, reflections, it was not unreasonable, given the place of drunkenness in Russian life as described in Chapter Four, above, to suppose that Russia's war effort might be improved by a ban on alcohol, but the ban had unintended consequences. It put more money into workers' pockets at precisely the time when a long-term shortage of consumer goods began, fuelling inflation. The ban, the shortage and the inflation provoked resentment, not least because it was known that the legislators had not prohibited the expensive wines and liqueurs that were their own tipples of choice. The improvement in sobriety noticed by Paléologue was short-lived. Soon Russians were imbibing eau-dé-Cologne, methylated spirits, and other vodka substitutes, including a more than metaphorically lethal substance called *khanja*, which was made and peddled by Chinese workers.

---

62 *The The War Cry*, 31 October, 1914.
63 Paléologue, *Diary*, 16 September, 1914.
64 Paléologue, *Diary*, 21 November, 1915.

Vodka itself—or at any rate a raw, throat-searing substance so-named—was soon available again, and by 1916 was so readily obtainable in the cities that peasants stopped peddling their notorious moonshine *samogon,* which they had made for centuries as a way of beating the state monopoly on vodka. Meanwhile, as has already been noted, the financial consequences were severe. The government suffered a 25 percent diminution in revenue, contributing to the endemic economic weakness of the years before the Revolution. As Orlando Figes remarks,

> ...weighing up minor gains in sobriety against the major losses in revenue, controls on inflation, public health and political authority, the ban on vodka was nothing less than a disaster, which in no small way contributed to the downfall of the old regime.[65]

These developments had a further unfortunate outcome: Kokovtsov, the Prime Minister, who might have rescued Nicholas from his follies (and was engaged in negotiating a French loan), was dismissed for having predicted the probable results of prohibition. (Another cause for his dismissal was his attempt to have Rasputin exiled from the capital when his scandalous public behaviour featured damagingly in police reports.)

It would be absurd to expect The Salvation Army, teetotal and proud of it, and well acquainted with the social consequences of alcoholic excess, not to act as cheerleader when Nicholas banned vodka, but in doing so it idealistically ignored a truth universally acknowledged, that prohibition cannot be imposed on a nation without its consent: alcohol is easy to produce, using commonplace domestic equipment, and even those classes in society which have legislated a ban tend to infringe it, in time discrediting it entirely.

Meanwhile, The Salvation Army's practicality in dealing with those suddenly thrown into disarray by misfortune and social upheaval had been confirmed in the experience of thousands of Russians who found themselves stranded all over Europe and had to make their way home as best they could when war broke out. Passing through Sweden and Finland they found The Salvation Army represented on the aid committees and working in the field. In two Finnish towns, Rauma and Tornea, people in the last stages of their journey home were met by Finnish officers who spoke Russian and were helped in various ways, including the provision of warm blankets, padded clothing and special shoes for that part of the route which had to be traversed by horse-drawn sledges.[66] To The Salvation Army's short-term advantage, reports of this work reached the Russian Government from its consuls in Finland and the refugees themselves.

---

65 Figes, *A People's Tragedy,* p. 298; see also Lincoln, *Passage Through Armageddon,* p. 224, and Pipes, *The Russian Revolution,* p. 234.
66 Larsson, *Tio År I Ryssland,* pp. 42-43.

A New Commander

Russia's needs meant that, whatever its official status might be, The Salvation Army's work was expanding. This was not confined to social work; evangelical work was also increasing, albeit more stealthily. At the outbreak of war, *Vestnik Spaseniya* had a regular group of seven sellers (this number was shortly to increase) who were permitted to travel on trams while selling the paper. On the day one of two Russian sellers began work, he sold 72 copies in four hours in the restaurants and teahouses. 8,000 copies of number 7 were sold and nearly as many of number 9. Converts were being made at the unofficial meetings every evening. Larsson, overseeing this growth with satisfaction, was nevertheless conscious that his primary duty, running The Salvation Army in Finland, precluded his becoming a fixture in Petrograd, and decided to appoint an officer of all-round experience and tried leadership who could be on the spot to guide developments.

He chose Ensign Helmy Boije, the energetic and enterprising daughter of Baron Constantine A.L. Boije, nominal proprietor of *Vestnik Spaseniya*. The family had many connections in Russia. Helmy, who enrolled as a soldier following her conversion in 1903, had trained as a teacher and was (or would become) competent in Finnish, Swedish, German, English, French and Russian. In 1905 she spent a year at the Training College for Officers in London. Before being sent to Petrograd in October, 1914, a few weeks short of her thirty-first birthday, she had served in three Finnish corps, Finnish Headquarters and (as principal) at the Training Garrison for Officers in Helsingfors. Larsson intended her to remain in Russia only until the next session at the Training Garrison was due to begin, but in the event, she stayed for more than five years (with two periods of absence, in London and Helsingfors), working heroically in frequently appalling conditions.[67]

Her Russian assignment was open-ended and improvisatory—or, to put it as she would have done, she was to place herself at God's disposal and follow where he led. She had a small force of newspaper sellers, a flat in Petrograd, a useful amount of goodwill (some of it that of influential people), very little money and no legal standing. She was charged with developing, on these foundations, any Salvationist work which became possible, while bearing in mind that, although social work might prove necessary (and good for public relations), the Army's primary purpose was that which had been stated by William Booth and *The War Cry*: to Win Russia for God.

To begin with there was relatively little difficulty in attracting suitable recruits. We have seen that the first enrolment of soldiers took place in Petrograd on 20 December, 1914; eight men and women were sworn in (as soldiers, technically, of Helsingfors No. 1 Corps). Ensign Boije held the flag, Lieutenant Konstantinova read the *Articles of War* and Larsson conducted the ceremony. 'The new comrades,' he

---

67 During these five years Boije was promoted through the ranks of Adjutant, Staff Captain and Major. In 1920 she was appointed to the Order of the Founder, the highest Salvationist honour. (Helmy M. Boije, career record. This document—which appears to have been drawn up in 1939—does not tally at all points with Larsson's account.)

reports, 'were filled with the "Blood-and-Fire" spirit.' Thus, as a calculated risk, *de facto* if not *de jure*, The Salvation Army opened its first Russian corps.

Sisters of Mercy

We have also seen that ten months later, in October 1915, The Salvation Army in Russia opened its first slum station, just outside St Petersburg's Moscow Gate, announcing the fact with pictures on the front page of *Vestnik Spaseniya*. The juxtaposition of gate (a grandiloquent triumphal arch supporting statues of Plenty, Glory and Victory)[68] and slum station aptly symbolized Russia's situation at the time: Imperial rhetoric confronted squalid reality. The Salvationists, connoisseurs of working class conditions in the great cities of industrial Europe, thought that some slum areas in Petrograd were worse than their equivalents in London.

The station was established after Pieshevski received a letter about a family in which 'the father had died, the mother was down with tuberculosis and the children were utterly neglected. Friends gave us a variety of gifts... on the following morning we set out equipped with buckets, scrubbing brushes, food and money.'[69] The building subsequently obtained as a base for such work was modest: two stories with six windows each. The photograph in *Vestnik Spaseniya* shows a sign (possibly a detachable banner) proclaiming the name *Armiya Spaseniya*. Four officers stationed there visited the families of conscripts away at the front, and distributed bread, milk, soup and clothes, provisioning every day about 100 reservists' wives and children. These unfortunates became very attached to the officers, coming to them for help and guidance with a wide range of problems, including the letters they wrote to their absent husbands and fathers. The officers discovered that even when serving food they must understand the cultural preconceptions of the recipients: if there was no holy picture in the room they feared that it would be unblessed.

The Petrograd Council gave the Slum Post a grant of 200 roubles, a sum matched by a donation from a member of the Imperial Family. In February 1915, Larsson met the Petrograd Council's President, Count Tolstoy, the novelist's nephew. A Ladies' Auxiliary League was formed: they made clothing, toys and sweets for children. On 28 April, 1915 the post was visited by Lady Buchanan, wife of the British Ambassador, who promised to send clothing for the children, who were to be given a summer holiday in the countryside.

A Petrograd church newspaper, *Birch Vjadomosti*, published, under the heading 'A Beautiful Work in Petrograd', a piece praising the work of the Slum Station.

---

68 The art historian George Heard Hamilton (*The Art and Architecture of Russia*, Harmondsworth, Penguin Books, 1975, p. 226) remarks that it is 'as cold as the cast-iron of which it was made'.

69 Konstantinova-Sundell, *The Smallness of Man, the Greatness of God*, p. 2.

A considerable number of women members of the English[70] Salvation Army, which up to now has laboured in Finland and partly also in Petrograd for the temperance idea, have now turned their attention in another direction: they are working to relieve the position in which the families of soldiers find themselves.

On their own initiative they have chosen a district situated outside the Moscow gate. Here they visit daily the homes of these families in order to become acquainted with their need. They attend to the sick, assist mothers with big families, clothe, wash and feed the children or take them to their own home while their mothers have to go out... They also arrange courses at home when they teach sewing etc., and have evenings of songs.[71]

Early in 1915, regarding the area outside the Moscow Gate as 'practically speaking in the country', they moved the Slum Station into slightly larger premises nearer the centre of the city. It was near Vasja's Village, one of the city's worst slum tenements.[72] Captain Olsoni described the pattern of visits there. The approaches were deceptively gracious: a beautiful broad street and a side street that was 'neat and healthy-looking'. The entrance was through a white, three-storeyed house, its upper windows dirty, cracked or broken, with cushions stuffed into them. Beyond the lobby, where there were usually a couple of shawl-clad women and two or three ragged urchins fighting, was the courtyard, onto which opened numerous other houses.

Houses and courtyard constituted Vasja's Village, which was said to hold 4,660 people. Entrances were dark and evil-smelling, their ruined concrete floors scattered with piles of filthy debris. To venture inside required courage and a settled stomach. Visitors had to grope their way through a succession of unlit, usually windowless rooms. Surfaces were sticky with filth. The few windows were dirty and shut. Airlessness, the odours from the piles of filth, together with more normal smells of cooking and washing, produced an overpoweringly nauseating atmosphere. Most of the people there refused to buy *Vestnik Spaseniya*. They were illiterate, they said, and neither God nor man was interested in them. But there were ikons in some rooms, lit by red, dimly flickering oil lamps. Olsoni encountered an old woman, clutching her only possession (a cushion), who was grateful not to have been thrown out, since she could not pay her rent. When cooking finished for the night she was

---

70 This identification of The Salvation Army as English (despite the fact that no one from England was serving in Russia) was not to its advantage.

71 This translation, and some other material attributed to Larsson in this chapter, comes from a typescript held in The Salvation Army's archives in London. Since the first page is missing neither author nor date can be confirmed, but internal evidence suggests that it was written by Larsson.

72 The locations of the new slum station and Vasja's Village are impossible to pinpoint with complete certainty but such evidence as I have found suggests that the Salvationists had moved about three and a half miles north along Moscovsky Prospect, the main road south to Moscow, to the notorious cluster of tenements surrounding the Haymarket.

allowed to sleep in a tiny space by the fire. Elsewhere a little girl was apparently alone in a room that turned out to contain a number of sleeping women, one of whom was her mother. Piles of tawdry finery suggested that the women were prostitutes.

Every room was in multiple occupancy. A place near the fire cost more than one in the corner. When the Salvationists arrived, rumours were rife that the landlord, Vasja, had sold the tenement to developers. Come the spring, its denizens would be thrown onto the street. Incredible as it seemed, it was possible for them to be worse off.

Some tenants managed to keep their apartments neat and comfortable, their windows properly washed, and door, fireplace, floor and, above all, the air, 'irreproachably clean'. Two such, seamstresses, welcomed the Salvationists, not least because, in their view, their inhabitants of Vasja's Village badly needed taking in hand. They rejected rumours of sale and eviction. Vasja's Village was, they said, the greatest benevolent institution in Petrograd. Vasja had built the tenements 20 years before and had sworn never to sell them as long as he lived, despite lucrative offers for the site. It was not Vasja's fault that most of them were so disgusting. Many of the tenants were, they said,

> ...the sort of folk who, if they were put in the Winter Palace itself, would turn it into a pigsty. In the beginning the landlord had lamps put in the stairways—they have all been stolen. Each dwelling has double doors, covered with oil-cloth on the outer side. Six years ago, when cholera was raging, a notice containing a list of suitable precautions was pasted on each outer door. That notice in most cases still remains—the doors have not been washed for six years.[73]

The Salvationists were generally better received by those who, although poor, were anxious to keep themselves from falling into the depths represented by the worst aspects of Vasja's Village. Like the seamstresses, such people were in regular work, making do with a bed and a couple of chairs. Olsoni and her comrades were welcomed by this sort of person, there and elsewhere, and listened to eagerly. This applied particularly in the crowded, long-corridored, multi-staircased buildings where the slightly better off poor lived. One such, known as 'Port Arthur', was home to 5,000 people. On each corridor there were 25 rooms, a family in each, and one kitchen. These kitchens were communal, but in any case tea and bread were the staple diet. In the family rooms, anything not in immediate use was pushed under the bed. In some of these private living quarters the officers conducted small prayer meetings three times per week, telling 'in simple, heartfelt words' the story of Jesus, awakening 'in many a breast memories of all but forgotten teaching'.[74]

A third group with whom the slum officers dealt lived in even more primitive conditions than those Vasja's Village, in dirty wooden huts, with earth floors and no furniture at all.

---

73 *All the World*, 1917, pp. 255-58.
74 *All the World*, November 1914.

The Salvation Army's statistics of membership and activities at the beginning of 1915 are impressive for an organization that officially did not exist. It had six officers, one employee, eight soldiers and nine recruits. There were 30 sellers of *Vestnik Spaseniya*, which had a circulation of between 8,000 and 10,000 per month. It had a song book: 20 pamphlets containing ten typed songs each, sewn together by hand. New songs were added as they were written or translated. Twenty additions, translated by Captain Miassoyedoff, the Russian officer serving in Paris, daughter of the official who had searched the Povlsen's flat in 1912, were found among the papers of the late Commissioner Railton. (Some of these, however, were unusable since the tune was not known, or, if known, could not be made to fit the words.)

In March, a second enrolment, in the presence of Major Mitchell, the International Auditor, saw five more soldiers join the ranks, including two Swedes living in Petrograd. A photograph taken at about this time shows 15 uniformed Salvationists (several were absent), including five captains and four lieutenants. *All the World* noted that the majority of those in the photograph, including all the officers, were women, remarking that 'the work has not suffered on that account' but had been done with 'the greatest thoroughness'.[75]

If recruitment was not an immediate problem, money was. At five kopeks, *Vestnik Spaseniya* generated little revenue, and, as Boije noted in 1916, once the novelty of the paper and the uniform had worn off, sales fell. International Headquarters provided some funds and appealed to its wealthy supporters worldwide for further contributions, but Boije was well aware that one of her duties was to make the Army in Russia self-supporting as soon as possible. On occasion *Vestnik Spaseniya* earned a great deal more than five kopeks. Selling the paper in the Hotel de l'Europe, just off the Nevsky Prospect, between Kazan Cathedral and Arts Square,[76] Boije encountered a gentleman, who greeted her with delight: 'You Salvationists, here!'. He bought the paper, rounding the price up to five roubles. A few days later he called at the editorial office and paid 50 roubles for a book advertised in it: the French translation of English journalist Harold Begbie's book about The Salvation Army, *Broken Earthenware*. After another month he called for the last time. He was leaving the city and to mark his departure handed over a further 500 roubles. Thereafter he sent 100 roubles each month.

Although visits to the Hotel de l'Europe could be financially useful, Boije and her officers spent much more of their time in cellars, cabmen's cafes and *traktirs* (taverns). Unlike the swing doors of an American bar, those of *traktirs* were heavy and creaked open unwelcomingly. Their customers sat on bentwood chairs, at tables

---

75 *All the World*, 1916, pp. 217-22.

76 One of the finest pre-revolutionary hotels (now, restored and modernized, it is still among the best in town): in the opinion of the Tsar's brother-in-law Sandro, its coloured barman from Kentucky was an exciting emblem of how cosmopolitan Petrograd had become. (See Maylunas and Mironenko, p. 393.)

with cloths, and were attended by waiters in white blouses and aprons.[77] Most drank tea, the Salvationists assure us, although vodka and beer were available. A large gilt ikon hung in a prominent position. The counter along one side of the room displayed bottles, glasses, sausages and ham and, although drinks might be served there, no-one drank standing or leaning on it, as they would have done in an English pub. Scattered amongst the tables might be a blind violinist or concertina player, haggling pedlars of pies, Bibles, shirts, old clothes and pencils, beggars, cripples and dwarfs seeking alms, drunks and pilgrims from remote parts of the Empire, collecting money to rebuild their parish church.

The most notable element in *traktir* life was talk. Public meetings were forbidden in Russia, but its city dwellers, seated around a table drinking tea, could exchange views with energy and comparative freedom. In the *Yama Traktir* (the Pit Tavern) on Moscow's Rozhdestvensky Street, workers, scholars and philosophers exchanged such unconventional views that the authorities closed it down, but it resurrected itself as the Bay Tavern at another address, where an English writer, Stephen Graham, enjoyed hot cabbage pies and advanced theological debate. According to Morgan Phillips Price, writing in 1917, the Revolution had been long anticipated in the *traktirs*, where 'working men had whispered of it... with bated breath'.[78]

Cabmen's cafes were usually in cellars. Like the Salvationist women, cab drivers were out on the streets in all weathers, and they dropped into such places frequently, removing their thick, padded cloaks, dropping into a chair and summoning a waiter, who brought a cup of tea, or something stronger. The cloths on the tables had long ceased to be white, and the air was steamy and suffocating, but the cabbies were happy, and 'if the clattering automatic piano was set in motion [they] had no further ambitions or desires'. 'Here', Boije observes, 'one must not be fastidious about the atmosphere'. Initially the cabbies were astonished to the point of speechlessness by the 'apparition' of young women with red bands on their fur hats moving from table to table selling a newspaper. After they had withdrawn, however, tongues began to wag as, in the dim light of smoky lamps, the men commented on what they read. Since, of necessity, this described the Army's work in other lands, such conversations had a more international cast than was usual in these cellars.

In time, cabbies and Salvationists became well disposed towards each other. The cabbies bought *Vestnik Spaseniya* quite willingly—some, who could not read, for the pictures—folding it carefully to take home to their families. They shared their tea with the Salvationists, cutting pieces of apple to drop into the cups. These men understood the Salvationist women, as did the habitués of the working men's restaurants, with their billiard tables and mirrors on the walls. The officers did not enjoy going into better class cafés and elegant restaurants, because 'the evil that flourished there had made the people quite deaf and blind to higher interests', which

---

77 A shout of 'Man!' in a Russian restaurant or cafe at this time would attract several waiters, coming at a run. During the Revolution, however, waiters went on strike, demanding to be treated as humans.

78 Harvey Pitcher, *Witnesses of the Russian Revolution*, London, John Murray, 1994, p. 9.

may explain why, as Captain Olsoni reports, the people there tended to mistake the Salvationists for prostitutes.

Meanwhile, following the outbreak of war, the Army's offer to help with one of the most pressing problems thrown up by the conflict led to its receiving a degree of recognition and financial subsidy from two bodies: the Petrograd City Council and, subsequently, a patriotic committee administered in the name of the Tsar's second daughter, Grand Duchess Tatiana.[79] When, in 1915, the German advance compelled thousands of people to evacuate the war zone, the Petrograd City Council was confronted by an enormous influx of refugees. Wagons piled high with household goods, with women, children and the sick perched or clinging on top, creaked and rumbled through the city. As they rolled, people died, children were born and families were accidentally separated. The Army applied for permission to work with the City Council in dealing with the problem and proposed that Adjutant Boije should serve on the official Petrograd committee for assisting refugees. Count Tolstoy, President of the City Council and Chairman of the Committee, replied:

> The Petrograd Committee for Finding Asylum for Refugees has been informed of your desire to be represented on the Committee, as well as of your plan immediately to arrange and support a home for 200-250 refugees. The Committee has accepted your offer and desires to express our thanks to The Salvation Army in Finland.

Larsson comments, with a certain *faux naiveté*, that 'evidently The Salvation Army in Finland was still nominally at the back of our enterprise. We found this to be the safest.' Clearly this was a cover that suited The Salvation Army, the Petrograd City Council and the Grand Duchess Tatiana's Relief Committee equally well. In wartime none of them would gain anything by looking a gift horse in the mouth.

The Finnish connection was useful as well as expedient: an appeal in Helsingfors yielded beds and other equipment. Finding a suitable building in Petrograd was less

---

79 This may have been made easier by William Booth's meeting with Mr Hansen, supervisor of the Imperial Family's charities, in 1909. Tatiana was the Tsarina's favourite daughter, described as reserved, essentially well-balanced and with a will of her own (Maylunas and Mironenko, *Lifelong Passion,* p. 407). At the outbreak of war she was 17 years old and, because of her secluded upbringing, still very childlike. She had some first-hand experience of dealing with the distressed, because the Tsarina had founded a hospital for the wounded at Tsarskoe Selo, where she and her daughters visited the sick and enjoyed doing the bandaging. (Maylunas and Mironenko, p. 402.) This, however, merely embarrassed and shocked Russian soldiers, who thought that the act caused the Empress to lose her dignity as sovereign. (See Lieven, *Nicholas II,* p. 159.) Paléologue, *Diary,* (pp. 149-50, 11 October, 1914) tells us that 'in the front line dressing-stations the finest of society ladies are rivalling each other in courage, endurance and devotion... But it would be vain to ask them to go without their theatres, music and ballets'. Meriel Buchanan, daughter of the British Ambassador, undertook, with a Russian friend, a course of First Aid training, and describes her nausea and helpless despair at what she experienced. (Meriel Buchanan, *The Dissolution of an Empire,* London, John Murray, 1932, pp. 114-15.)

easy, since a housing shortage was another consequence of the war. The accommodation finally rented, a wooden structure set in a garden in industrial Lesnoy, was smaller than had been hoped for, with space for no more than 50 beds. Captain Henny Granström was appointed matron, and moved in with Lieutenant Erna Perlbach and two sisters. But when the house was almost ready for use a colonel in the Imperial Army appeared: the military authorities had requisitioned the house and required that it be empty by a stated date.

Adjutant Boije hurried off to consult Miss Peuker, one of the Pashkovite Russian ladies who were so frequently useful. Miss Peuker introduced her to the Dowager Empress Marie Feodorovna—she who had met William and Bramwell Booth in London—who was visiting a hospital nearby. Consultations and agreements took place. On the day appointed for The Salvation Army to vacate the property, an Adjutant of the Imperial Court arrived in a Royal carriage, and waited quietly in a side street for the colonel to appear. When he did so, swearing because the Salvationists had not left, the Imperial Adjutant stepped forward. Boije was amused as well as relieved by the transformation that followed. The colonel bowed repeatedly, explaining that he was present merely in order to help the Salvationists and protect them from molestation by others. The Adjutant nonetheless reprimanded him. How could he dare interfere with people who had come to help Russia in its hour of greatest need? Bowing lower still, the 'brave colonel' retired, and was not heard from again.[80]

The Home for Refugees was dedicated on 27 September, in the presence of Larsson, other Salvationist officers and soldiers, friends of The Salvation Army, and, encouragingly, representatives of the Petrograd Committee for Finding Asylum for Refugees—some 50 people in all. Coffee was served and the purpose of the home explained. There were other short addresses, a hymn and prayers. A collection was taken. The following day the Committee sent two carriage loads of weary refugees—20 women and 26 children, the youngest only six weeks old—laden with bundles of old clothes. 'You can imagine', writes Larsson, 'the noise and the smell.' They were fed and sent immediately to bed.

The difficult work began the following day. The Salvationists were brisk about hygiene, separating refugees from their filthy bundles (there was 'quite a battle' before these were banished to the loft) and replacing their clothing (which was of poor quality, held together by bits of string, with rags wrapped around their legs instead of socks or stockings). Most had no underwear. The entire intake was sent to the public baths. Some of them, who had previously lived in huts, were bewildered

---

80 Foreign social workers were not the only people subjected to obstruction by bureaucrats and military jacks-in-office. During the same period, Prince Georgy Lvov, chairman of the All-Russian Union of Zemstvos (local authorities) headed a vigorous movement to provide relief for the sick and wounded and procure supplies for the army. Bureaucrats, themselves unable to provide either the medical care or the military *materiel,* did all they could to frustrate him. The President of the Duma, Mikhail Rodzianko, encountered similar impediments when he made a public fuss about the shortage of boots hindering the army at the front. (Lincoln, *Passage Through Armageddon*, pp. 101-05.)

by their improved physical conditions. One woman, when handed a broom, said she had never seen such a thing. Her former home had an earth floor and 'all the etceteras' were trampled into it. The women were expected to make up their beds every morning, a task that, following inspection by the officers, usually had to be done again. The refugees were unused to sheets and saw no point in them, or in housework generally. Larsson observes, rather stiffly, that they had to be 'taught this and other kinds of work'.

Among the refugees were Sina and Nyusha, orphaned girls speaking a strange dialect, who sat at a long table engrossed in their toys, unsure even of their names, afraid to sleep in a room without adults in case the aeroplanes and bombs should come again. A couple in their late seventies and their middle-aged daughters, the Seljenkos, had walked 400 miles to get to Petrograd after their village home had been torched. Others, Old Believers from southern Russia and the Ukraine, would not eat food prepared by the 'unclean', or sleep in 'unclean' beds. One woman sat up all night in a chair and disappeared the following day. Another refused at first to enter the same room as unbelievers and would not allow her six children to do so. And, naturally, she would not even consider attending the Army's meetings (at which in addition to Bible readings and homiletic treatments of Bible stories, there was hearty singing, especially by the children). Nonetheless, during one such meeting the officers noticed her, a shadowy figure behind the glass panel of the door, listening while holding her youngest child in her arms. Her others pushed the door open to find out what was going on. Eventually they tugged her into the room and she sat down. Telling this story to *All the World,* Adjutant Boije gave no further news of this woman, but commented, with restrained optimism, 'That is how it will be with the Army in Russia, I believe. Slowly it will win its way into the hearts of this great and noble people, and many will be brought to the Lord.'[81]

Once the home was running Boije applied for assistance to the Grand Duchess Tatiana's Patriotic Committee, whose brief was to assist refugees and the wives and children of serving soldiers. The Committee requested further details, then approved a subsidy of 500 roubles per month. Beyond the world of committees the Home won further public recognition and approval for the Army. Visitors found it difficult to believe that its clean and well-ordered residents were refugees. The local Orthodox priest collected both money and clothing on its behalf.

In the summer of 1915, 110 reservists' children were taken for six weeks to a Summer Colony at Perkjavi just beyond the Finnish border. (The state railways ferried them there free of charge, and donations from Petrograd friends of the Army, including the wife of the Foreign Minister, totalled 1,600 roubles.) They returned looking so much healthier that their mothers scarcely recognized them. The mother of one girl of three asked for her to allowed to go again the following summer:

> It did her so much good in her body and you have taught her such beautiful things.

---

81 For the details in these two paragraphs see *All the World,* May 1916.

Last night she was tired but very happy after the long journey from the Colony. I said to her, 'Go to bed, my child...'. Then my little one looked towards the picture of Jesus and made the sign of the cross and knelt upon her knees while she sang, 'At the Cross, at the Cross, where I first saw the light'. 'Do help me to pray, mamma', said my child, 'as the sisters did in the Colony'. I wept and my old mother wept. 'Little one', I said, 'I don't know how to pray', and the child sang once more the little song. So please put her name down to go to the Colony—next year.[82]

During the next six months The Salvation Army extended its public work still further and enjoyed the benefit of several public relations coups. The evident usefulness of the Home for Refugees induced a group of ladies from the American Colony in Petrograd, led by the wife of the American Ambassador, to provide funds for a second home for the Army to administer. This, an apartment in an *art nouveau* block erected on Kamenostrovsky Prospect[83] near the Peter and Paul Fortress during the building boom of a few years before, opened a few days before Christmas. With its six rooms, large hall and kitchen, it struck Larsson as 'really far too elegant' for the Army's purposes.

We can only guess at the feelings of other tenants in the block when refugees 'not on a very high intellectual or social plane' were placed amongst them. When Lieutenant Gorinovich visited them at Christmas, she said they were all heathen. None of them knew why Christmas was celebrated, although a few thought it might have to do with 'the life of the Saviour'. Larsson explains their ignorance in one, to him, damning sentence: 'They came from Poland, where the Roman Catholic Church held sway.' This Home, with Nadia Konstantinova-Sundell as its matron, survived war and revolution until the beginning of 1918.

The Army also opened a home in Finland for Russian children whose fathers had been called to active service. This brought the Army into closer contact with the Russian authorities there. At about the same time the world-wide Salvation Army attracted favourable notice in Russia through gifts of an ambulance and first-aid equipment from Salvationists in Canada and the United States respectively.

In the autumn of 1915, Larsson was approached by a Mr Oblei, an Armenian who was converted when the Povlsens were working clandestinely in St Petersburg. A civil servant who gave lectures of a 'religio-philosophical nature' in his spare time, he had been appointed in charge of a government-backed expedition to Persia to relieve the plight of Armenian refugees who had fled there from Turkish persecution. He requested that some Finnish Salvationists accompany him.

---

82 In August 1992 the present writer witnessed a similar incident, when the mother of a child who had just returned from a Salvation Army Music Camp outside Moscow spoke of her feelings in a highly emotional address to a Salvation Army meeting in the then Moscow headquarters, formerly the headquarters of the Soviet news agency, TASS.

83 After the revolution the prospect was renamed Street of Red Dawns. Subsequently, following the assassination of Kirov, the Leningrad Party Secretary, Stalin (privately pleased, it may be, that a dangerous rival had been disposed of) consented that, along with the city's principal opera and ballet theatre, it should be renamed in his honour, and it became Kirovsky Prospect. It is now Kamenostrovsky Prospect once more.

Larsson probably had little knowledge of the of the complicated politics which lay behind the expedition but was uncharacteristically cautious in accepting an invitation to do good. The journey from Petrograd into Persia would be long and difficult and, in its final stages, would take his officers through areas infested by bands of robbers. In dealing with the refugees, of whom there were hundreds of thousands, starving, destitute, sick and dying, the helpers would be exposed to epidemics. Nevertheless, when he asked for volunteers in Petrograd and Helsingfors he had a more than sufficient response. Six officers were chosen along with a cadet who would become Obeli's personal assistant. On the eve of their departure, however, the Russian government, while continuing to subsidize the expedition, withdrew its official status. Obeli, feeling that this would deprive it of all authority, making his task impossible, resigned. A replacement was found, who asked the Salvationists to go along as planned, but Larsson did not feel that he could entrust his officers to a man of whom he knew nothing. The Salvation Army in Russia reaped an indirect benefit: all but one of the officers who had come from Finland to join the expedition were transferred to Petrograd.[84]

The incident, however abortive, was further evidence that by the end of 1915 The Salvation Army enjoyed quasi-recognition in Petrograd, albeit only as temporarily useful guests from Finland. Its commanding officer sat on an official municipal committee. Its distinctive dress (very like the internationally recognized uniform, apart from the round Russian hat on which The Salvation Army crest and the words *Armiya Spaseniya* were prominently displayed) was permitted, ensuring that its presence was visible (to ordinary Russians as well as to gentlemen in the Hotel de l'Europe). Its personnel provided emergency assistance and sold *Vestnik Spaseniya*. A photograph of the period shows 15 uniformed Salvationists, including five captains and four lieutenants.

Despite all this, the Army's religious meetings had still to be held behind closed doors.

That aside, could it be said that The Salvation Army was becoming firmly established in Russia? *All the World* had begun to hope so, suggesting that

> the time has come when comrades who desire to dedicate their lives for the service of Christ within the Czar's dominions, should at once begin to learn the Russian language, familiarize themselves with its peoples and their manners and customs and beliefs, study their literature, and, so far as possible, get into their very hearts

---

84 Larsson, *Tio År I Ryssland,* pp. 74-75.

and then with all the knowledge at their disposal, and with their full enthusiasm for the work they would do, offer themselves for Officership.[85]

---

[85] *All the World*, July 1915. It is not possible to say whether this stirring call had any effect, since by the time that effect would have been noticed, the possibility of evangelical workers entering Russia had diminished still further. In any case, those familiar with The Salvation Army and its sometimes wilfully eccentric way of treating officers with specialist qualifications may well wonder whether anyone who had undertaken the cultural studies listed would necessarily have been sent to the country where they would be most useful. The Salvation Army, like the Communist parties of Soviet Russia and China, liked to keep its intellectuals firmly in their place, and was occasionally arbitrary in its methods of doing so.

CHAPTER 7

Explorations and Reversals

The Salvation Army: International, Foreign or Russian?

From the summer of 1915, then, The Salvation Army's work amongst refugees and the poor was attracting the attention of the Russian public, which, however, customarily referred to its officers as 'the English sisters of mercy'. Recognition was obviously useful, but the identification was double-edged. Not only were they not, technically, 'sisters of mercy', they were not English. If these devoted workers failed during their years in Russia it was not in good works or evangelical fervour but in something ultimately more damaging: they failed to persuade Russians at large and Russian governments in particular, that their organization was in some sense Russian—part of an international movement, certainly, but Russian just the same. Had they managed to effect this shift in perception it might in due course have been harder for the Bolsheviks to expel them. Other non-conformist groups, such as the Baptists, who had initially functioned in Russia for the benefit of foreign adherents resident there, made the transition and were able, after the revolution, to convince the state that their membership was primarily Russian. They were allowed, albeit fearing or actually enduring persecution, to stay on.

The Salvationists' situation, however, was more complex. They knew that the Russians who supported them did so precisely because they came from outside, from a society that they thought, at least in some respects, was more advanced than Russia. The Salvationists themselves repudiated definition as a merely national body. When they sang

> Through the world resounding,
> Let the Gospel sounding,
> Summon all at Jesus' call,
> His glorious cross surrounding...

or

> Salvation Army, Army of God,
> Onward to conquer the world with Fire and Blood

'the world' meant the whole world, not some segment of it. The globe and all its peoples were the field that was 'white unto harvest'. This universal imperative prevailed even when, as in Russia, it was likely to create trouble. It provided, for the officers at work in the front line and for many of those to whose needs they ministered, a sense of apocalyptic struggle watched and supported by a great cloud of witnesses. Those witnesses were symbolized, in Russia as elsewhere, by the trickle of international visitors who brought news and encouragement from the wider world. Officers and soldiers of the unofficial Salvation Army in Russia were heartened when they were visited in St Petersburg by Colonel Kitching (International Secretary for European Affairs), Major Catherine Booth (the Founder's granddaughter) and the English journalist and author, Harold Begbie (whose book about the Salvationists' work, *Broken Earthenware,* was bought by the gentleman Helmy Boije met in the Hotel de l'Europe). Their work was endorsed when Commissioner Whatmore from International Headquarters boarded a Petrograd tram-car and found all the passengers reading *Vestnik Spaseniya.* Missionary officers on their way from International Headquarters to Japan or Korea frequently passed through Russia on the Trans-Siberian Railway. The Salvation Army's international magazine, *All the World* (its title a reminder of the international drive of the organization) frequently published articles, by Larsson and others, about their work.

Despite his own determined internationalism, Larsson was convinced that if The Salvation Army was to be received by the whole Russian population it had to bear the Russian imprint. It needed to show the authorities that it was in no way dangerous but on the contrary necessary and useful, and to convince the Church that it was not an agent of dissension. Above all (Larsson does not notice the contradiction, from the Orthodox point of view, between this sentence and the previous one), it needed to win as many Russian converts as possible to help it do its work.[1]

During 1915 one extraordinarily special Russian convert was won, a woman who would—at first hesitantly, but eventually with total conviction—devote her life to The Salvation Army. Clara Becker was the Russian-born adopted daughter of a wealthy middle-aged Estonian lawyer who had an apartment near the Imperial Palace in Petrograd. Her early childhood was luxurious but lonely and empty. She knew other children and the life of the city only as an eavesdropper, peeping through the first-floor windows of the apartment or those of the family carriage. The great event each month was the visit of the floor polishers, who skated through the parquet-floored corridors and saloons with brushes attached to their feet.[2] Her only companions were the servants, whom she addressed in German or Russian. French

---

1 Larsson, *Tio År I Ryssland,* pp. 62-63.

2 See Vera Broido, *Daughter of Revolution: A Russian Girlhood Remembered,* London, Constable, 1998, p. 33. Vera, the daughter of two Mensheviks, writes: 'Another entertainment of high calibre was provided by the arrival of the floor polishers. All apartment houses in St Petersburg had parquet flooring, as had some of the main streets, and floor polishing was a high art. It was usually three young men who came. They strapped a thick polishing cloth impregnated with wax to one foot and then performed, arms crossed at the back, an intricate rhythmic and to my mind very beautiful dance, gliding forwards and backwards with supple grace. When many years later I saw Fred Astaire, I was reminded of that very different kind of elegant ballet.'

and English governesses taught her their respective languages, so that by the age of 12 she could speak, read and write in four languages—a number that was to increase threefold in the following decades. Her only friend was the dressmaker, who, however, was not always in the house. It was she who showed Clara an illustrated life of Christ and explained the pictures to her.

When Clara eventually went to school she made timid contact with other children and the world at large. She showed intellectual aptitude and determination and a precocious interest in religion. When at the age of 11 she overheard her father (a sidesman in the Orthodox Church) telling someone that he did not believe in Christ as the Son of God, she decided to discover the truth about Jesus. Since there was no Bible in the house and she feared ridicule if she asked for one, this was easier wished for than achieved. She was given no pocket money and never went out alone. If she wanted to buy anything she must ask whichever adult was accompanying her for the money. Her curiosity about Jesus made her wiser than serpents: she asked for regular pocket money (which other girls at her school were given) and saved for two years until she had enough to buy a Bible.[3] Later, her English governess gave her a copy of St John's Gospel in English. This she memorized. When a schoolmistress suggested that she go to Sunday school, her parents, to her surprise, agreed, provided that, as was also the case on weekdays, she was accompanied by a maid.

Some years later, while training as a teacher, she joined the Student Christian Movement, organized in Russia by Baron Nicolay (whom we have met in connection with Radstock, Pashkov and William Booth), and worked for it as a translator. She remained a prey to uncertainties about the Christian faith, which she resolved only when she was urged by a visiting woman evangelist to insert her own name into her favourite Biblical texts: 'If with all her heart Clara Becker truly seeks me, she shall truly find me...'

By 1915 she had become a teacher of English in a college for girls on Vasilevsky Island. On Ascension Day that year, Nicolay arranged a student excursion to Lesnoy, in the industrial area of Vyborg (incidentally, one of the most fertile breeding grounds of revolution). In the evening a group attended a Salvation Army meeting, and Clara was pleased to go with them, since she had heard and read about The Salvation Army (and had even seen International Headquarters while visiting London with her parents) but, timorous as she was, 'had never dared to attend the meetings as I knew they were very small and a new person was conspicuous'.

There were 12 or 15 at the meeting, which took place in a basement flat of three or four rooms. Clara thought it much like other religious meetings, but she was shocked when, at its conclusion,

---

3 Gladys M. Taylor, *Translator Extraordinary*, London, Salvationist Publishing and Supplies, 1969, p. 7. Clara could have afforded a cheaper Bible much sooner, but knew only the most expensive shops.

a sweet-faced officer, who played the guitar and sang, approached me and asked if I was saved. Surely to put such a direct personal question was terribly rude! I merely murmured 'Yes' and fled.[4]

The question troubled her in ways that will seem strange to those unacquainted with the Salvationist cast of mind. She was sure that she had once *been* saved. She had wanted to be a missionary. But perhaps her parents' implacable opposition and her enjoyment of her job had moderated her fervour and she had become a backslider. She was working for the Student Christian Movement and she was an influence for good at the school, where she loved her students and they were fond of her. Might that not be enough? She avoided The Salvation Army for several months, but something eventually drew her once more to Lesnoy; she found herself kneeling at the chair that served as a penitent form. The same sweet-faced guitarist prayed with her in 'very broken' Russian.

Becker stood up a convert but, always prudent, did not immediately join The Salvation Army. Inch by inch she edged closer until, one Friday evening in 1917 Nadia Konstantinova-Sundell, on her way to translate for Commissioner Larsson at a large united meeting in the Tenishev Academy, fell from a crowded tram into the path of a cab-horse. Clinging to the horse's neck, she was accidentally struck by the driver's whip. When she reached the meeting, Larsson, pacing nervously up and down the entrance hall, agreed that she could not appear before the public to translate, shaken as she was, and with a bruised face. He appealed to the congregation for a translator. Clara Becker stepped forward.[5]

Until this time Clara had no intention of joining The Salvation Army, still less of becoming an officer. The latter course, as she later wrote, was an unattractive proposition:

> The Salvation Army in Russia! Of what did it consist? One slum post, one home for children, tiny, almost clandestine meetings in which we scarcely dared to raise our voices—was it worth the sacrifice?[6]

The tug-of-war continued. Her parents were obstructive, particularly her adoptive mother, whose ambition for her was a society marriage. In December, telling them that she was going to buy stockings, which were unobtainable in Russia, Clara went to Helsingfors to see the 'real' Salvation Army. She was horrified by the band, especially the drum. (Musical instruments were not used in the Orthodox Church.) But, 'comforted by assurances' (from what source she does not say) that The Salvation Army would never use a drum in Russia, she sat the examination for candidates for officership and, without yet having become a soldier, filled in the

---

4 Clara Becker, *Life's Golden Moments*, in the Chicago *The War Cry*, 11 February, 1950.

5 Nadia Konstantinova-Sundell, *The Smallness of Man—the Greatness of God*, pp. 2-3.

6 *The War Cry*, Chicago, 11 February, 1950.

application form. What happened after she trained, in 1917, will be told in its chronological place, but we may note here that her conversion was no transient matter: she worked for The Salvation Army without interruption until her death in May 1968. In Russia in 1915 The Salvation Army may have been unimpressive, even to Becker herself, but its appeal to those of self-sacrificial temperament was far from negligible. Given her social standing and level of education, her conversion had a significance even greater than that of her predecessor, the first Russian officer, Vera Gorinovich. Together, the two women made Larsson's 'Russian imprint' appear possible. One day, The Salvation Army in Russia might be led by Russians.

Larsson Meets Some Peasants

Earlier, Larsson's desire to establish The Salvation Army permanently in Russia had led him, during the Russian Easter of 1915, to undertake a difficult journey in search of answers to two questions: was there any realistic prospect of beginning work in Russia's ancient capital, Moscow? Secondly, was there any possibility of expanding outside the cities and engaging with the most numerous and mysterious segment of Russia's teeming millions: the peasants?

He travelled first, taking Pieshevski and Vera Gorinovich with him, to Tolstoye in the western Ukraine. Here Miss Weisberg, hostess to Railton and arranger of Gorinovich's officer training in Berlin, had her country estate, which she had repeatedly invited him to visit.

Tolstoye was close to the Russian border with Galicia, across the River Dniester from the rugged, heavily forested Carpathian Mountains, on the western edge of the great grain-growing region that throughout its history had made the Ukraine a target for invaders. The area was a crossroads: its main towns were connected by river with either the Black Sea or the Baltic and there was access to Hungary across the Carpathians, while the southern routes from Kiev to Cracow and Prague ran through Terebovlya, a few kilometres north of Tolstoye.[7] In the early Twentieth Century the Southwest, along with the Baltic and the Southern Steppe, was among 'the most fully modernized and most prosperous regions of Russian noble agriculture'.[8] (Nobles had been granted land there as Russia extended its frontiers, and populated their new estates with peasants from their old ones in more central regions.)[9]

The picture, however, had its darker side. Tolstoye lay near the western extremity of an arc across southern Russia in which there had been savage violence between peasants and landowners in 1905 and would be again in 1917. The area was ethnically and socially 'an unbalanced, unhappy place. Poles owned the land,[10] Jews the shops and inns. Ukrainians... laboured out of sight in cottages and fields'.[11]

---

7 See John Fennell, *The Crisis of Medieval Russia*, London, Longman, 1988, pp. 12-13.

8 Lieven, *Russia's Rulers*, p. 41.

9 Moon, *The Russian Peasantry 1600-1930*, pp. 51-52.

10 Miss Weisberg was almost certainly of Polish Jewish descent.

11 Anna Reid, *Borderland*, p. 72.

During the agricultural depression of the late Nineteenth Century, much land had been given or leased to the peasants, but when prosperity returned the process was reversed. Since peasant numbers were increasing, many were forced into debt.

Another complication was that many Ukrainians did not regard themselves as Russian. This led to a revival of the Ukrainian language; the government responded by forbidding not only the language itself, but use of even the terms 'Ukraine' and 'Ukrainian'. The peasants were not the only government-provoked group of dissidents in western Ukraine: it was part of the Pale of Settlement where Russian Jews had, before the German victories in 1914, been compelled to live. It was there, in the Eighteenth Century, that Israel Baal Shem Tov founded Hasidism, a Jewish revivalist movement that later extended throughout Eastern Europe and beyond.[12] Peasants and Jews both became targets when the Tsar determined to Russify the entire Empire and all its peoples, a policy whose effect was the reverse of that intended. Peasants and Jews alike resisted. There were peasant rebellions in the Ukraine from 1902 onwards; meanwhile, many Jews joined the Communist Party.[13]

Larsson does not allude to these matters (although, as we shall see, they had a bearing on Miss Weisberg's actions) but even if he knew what a social and ideological minefield he was entering he was borne along by the habitual optimism of The Salvation Army during its first 50 years. He assumed that the peasantry, uncorrupted by the squalid, slum-bound struggle for existence that was the lot of the city proletariat, would prove more open than them to the message of Salvation.[14] In this remote rural district, he would accurately have assumed, the powers of the imperial bureaucracy, such a barrier to Salvationist activity in the capital, were greatly diminished. Figes comments,

> The power of the imperial government effectively stopped at the 89 provincial capitals where the governors had their offices... The crucial weakness of the Tsarist system was the *under-government* of the localities.[15]

Despite its own urban origins the Army was sentimentally drawn towards the Russian peasantry. This was partly the result of a picture-book level of acquaintance with Russia that was not uncommon in the West before the First World War. Even within Russia itself, the educated and administrative classes were said to know more of Africa and New Zealand than of rural Russia or the peasants on whose labour they lived. The Salvation Army, naturally, tended to take an optimistic view of any group it hoped to evangelize, and a matter of weeks after Larsson's visit to the Ukraine *All the World* offered its readers a rather condescending account of the Russian peasant, possibly written by him. The peasant was

---

12 Louis Jacobs, *The Jewish Religion, a Companion*, Oxford, Oxford University Press, p. 218.

13 Figes, *A People's Tragedy*, pp. 77-83.

14 Murdoch, *Origins*, argues that William Booth himself had sought in rural areas more rapid progress than he was achieving in towns.

15 Figes, *A People's Tragedy*, p. 46. (His emphasis.)

a big, strong, simple-hearted, yet gentle fellow. The essence of loyalty, religious and full of good comradeliness he is, so it seems to us, to be the very one to whom, in years to come, the Army is likely to be a means of much spiritual help and blessing. He is of the kind who will share a last crust with a friend—or even an enemy, if he be in need. He is by nature religious, and now that the Czar has abolished vodka from the land, vodka which sometimes transformed the gentle moujik into a fierce, truculent fellow, there is greater hope that a brighter day will dawn for him; and we suggest that the brighter day will come all the sooner if the Army is able to send to him its officers with the message of Salvation.[16]

Any number of disillusioned Russian idealists could have told *All the World* that this was only a partial view. Young people from the Russian cities, eager to improve the peasants' lot by various political, moral and reformist means, had over and again found themselves confronted with suspicion, narrow-mindedness, hostility, malice, and the threat—even the actuality—of violence and murder. Such reformers found that the peasants listened respectfully—as they would to a priest—but were uninfluenced by what they heard. In fact, a more balanced and therefore less comfortable assessment of the peasantry than *All the World*'s, by 'a Canadian writer', had appeared in the *The War Cry* in 1907:

How shall one describe the character of the Mushik (*sic*)? It is such a bundle of contradictions... at once kind-hearted and brutal; dirty and clean; clever and stupid; obstinate and docile; coarse and delicate... The whole village will care for an orphan child, but a man will beat his wife to death. No peasant will eat forbidden food on a fast day [but] he will think nothing of murder... they steal in the most flagrant manner. They shed tears over a dead daughter—more over a dead cow...[17]

Larsson and others were correct to believe that the peasants were intensely religious, but their religion was an amalgam of Orthodoxy, ancient superstition and identification with the land, which the peasants believed belonged to God. They, by working it, lived in a special relationship with Him. It followed that landowners, so-called, were really usurpers, a belief that licensed peasants to employ the deception, cheating and violence that caused them to be thought of as a dark, threatening mass. Mostly illiterate, they were largely ignorant of the Bible.[18] Their unpraiseworthy characteristics would have been attributed by The Salvation Army, more or less automatically, to 'the drink habit' and neglect by the Orthodox Church, explanations

---

16 *All the World*, July 1915.

17 *The War Cry*, 10 October, 1907. Figes, Orlando, *Peasant Russia, Civil War: The Volga Countryside in Revolution 1917-1921*, Phoenix Press, London, 2001, argues that left to themselves in matters which concerned them directly the peasants were, at least temporarily, capable of exercising judgement and united action, even if, when faced with the coercive power of the state, their illiteracy and lack of discipline made them, as they always had been, politically impotent.

18 For a description of the Russian peasantry on the eve of Revolution, see Figes, *A People's Tragedy*, pp. 84-108.

which were valid as far as they went but again at best partial. Peasants were seldom fully understood by non-peasants. Larsson and *All the World* took their place in a long line of the well-meaning, including the Tsar, writers and revolutionaries, who noticed only such evidence as accorded with their own ideological predilections.

Larsson gives us few indications of how Miss Weisberg dealt with the people on her estate. Commissioner Higgins had described her as 'practical' and 'much concerned with the lot of the poorer peasantry',[19] but how far this concern affected her behaviour as a landowner may be questioned. Her religious beliefs might imply benevolence, but, since Larsson also tells us that she could be overbearing with young Salvationists, that may be a false deduction. Her Polish Jewish name would not endear her to any disaffected Ukrainian peasant.

The journey from Helsingfors to Tolstoye might strike non-Russians as an endurance test and the destination as hardly worth reaching. Even today, in the Ukraine,

> half an hour's drive out of the city one enters a pre-modern world of dirt roads and horse-drawn carts, of outdoor wells and felt boots, of vast silences and velvet-black nights... In winter they wrap their two-room cottages in dried maize stalks for extra insulation, and in spring they drown in Bruegelesque seas of knee-high mud.[20]

Twenty hours in a green third-class carriage[21] (changing trains at Moscow) brought Larsson and his party to Ouzonovo, five miles from the estate, where they were met by a coach 'as ancient as the hills,' drawn by two horses harnessed one behind the other. The coachman stood in front and directed the horses with his whip, sometimes on the road and sometimes off it. The spring thaw and heavy rain made either almost impassable.

Such an inconvenient journey, at a bad time of year, with a major European war in progress and Russia thrown on the defensive along its entire western front (which in Tolstoye was relatively close at hand)[22] seems reckless or foolish, and Larsson was neither. In addition to politeness and the possibility of evangelical activity, he had a third reason for his visit: Miss Weisberg had in mind a benefaction (as yet undisclosed) to The Salvation Army, which—given the military situation in the area—should perhaps be considered before it was too late.[23]

---

19 *The War Cry*, 10 April, 1909.

20 Reid, *Borderland*, p. 20.

21 First-class carriages were blue, second-class yellow (see Henri Troyat, trs. Malcom Barnes, *Daily Life in Russia Under the Last Tsar*, London, Allen & Unwin, 1961, p.14).

22 In August 1914 Brusilov's Eighth Army, advancing into Galicia, then under the Austrian crown, had captured the capital, Lvov, 160 kilometres from Tolstoye. The Russians incurred 210,000 casualties and were short of ammunition, so did not advance into the Hungarian plain but spent the winter camped along the ridge of the Carpathians. In May 1915, the biggest German offensive of the war resulted in (amongst many other things) the retaking of Lvov and the approach of German armies to Russian soil.

23 When the war reached the area the following year, there was considerable destruction of buildings and bridges, unhygienic conditions and barely containable

Larsson and Orthodoxy

The offer, however, was not made explicit until the time of his departure for Moscow. Meanwhile, Larsson was exercised in Tolstoye by a problem that would confront him again in Moscow a few days later: what should be the Army's attitude towards remnants of Orthodox consciousness in its converts? Miss Weisberg, despite being a uniformed Salvationist, continued to hold Orthodox services on the estate, which may be why he regarded her beliefs as 'slightly nebulous'. Characteristically, she had fallen out with her parish priest (the man who had been so impressed by Railton's devotion as to tidy his church), and the Easter services were conducted in a hall on the estate by a visiting dignitary (a 'High Priest', Larsson calls him, remarking that his head looked like one of Doré's representations of Samson) and the incumbent of a neighbouring parish. The estate manager conducted a choir of workers and servants.

Miss Weisberg invited Larsson to address a further gathering in the same hall. His coming had aroused some apprehension. He was clearly a dignitary—another 'high priest'—but his doctrines might be doubtful. Accordingly, the hall was packed. Larsson, standing on a high platform, which brought his head very close to the ceiling, was uncomfortably warm. Lieutenant Gorinovich projected lantern slides of the life of Christ and Larsson preached on 'How Christ Attracts Men' before describing the Army's work in Finland and Petrograd and speaking, as was customary in such circumstances, about his own conversion.

Because the hall was so crowded it was impracticable to ask people to come forward and kneel at the penitent form, so he asked those who wished to give themselves to Christ to raise their hands. Several did so, and Larsson met them briefly afterwards. (He was not sanguine about their future progress: '...they could not expect much help from Miss Weisberg, and Lieutenant Gorinovich was rather timid in her dealings with them'.)

Outside, the rain grew heavier. A stream on the estate overflowed, flooding the fields: a photograph taken by Larsson shows two men in a boat, standing upright, paddling past a snow-covered outcrop of rock in an otherwise inundated field. Despite the weather, he visited the priest who had offended Miss Weisberg (with or without her permission he does not say), who told him about Railton's regular attendance at services seven years earlier.

Just before Larsson left for Moscow, Miss Weisberg explained her proposed benefaction: she would bequeath her estate to the Army, on the condition that a home would be built for the old people of the village.

This offer, even as it stood, typified Miss Weisberg's impracticality: the area was a social and political tinderbox and German forces, only a few miles off, were liable to overrun the town. Larsson, who as a historian often keeps his cards very close to his chest, gives little idea of his reaction on the spot, but apparently felt obliged to take her offer seriously. He reported it to International Headquarters, and when, in

---

outbreaks of typhoid, spotted fever and smallpox. See Florence Farmborough, ed. John Joliffe, *Russian Album*, Salisbury, Michael Russell, 1979, pp. 55-70.

July that same year, Colonel Kitching and Major Catherine Booth visited Russia following the Congress in Helsingfors which marked the Army's twenty-fifth anniversary in Finland, they travelled with him to Tolstoye to discuss possible plans for the estate. During the visit they discovered that Miss Weisberg's grasp of legal and financial reality was yet slenderer than they had supposed: her offer was as nebulous as her beliefs since her brother had got into severe financial difficulties and the estate was heavily mortgaged. We hear no more about Tolstoye: Miss Weisberg lost everything in the revolution, and lived thereafter with the Salvationists in Petrograd, not always getting on with the younger members, but welcome as one who had been and continued to be a committed helper.

Meanwhile, Larsson undertook the second leg of his reconnaissance, spending two days in Moscow. Even he, single-minded and mission-driven as he was, spent a little time seeing 'the churches in the Kremlin and other places of interest', but he also looked at slums and overcrowded lodging houses, conferred with people who might welcome the Army to Moscow and help it establish itself there and addressed gatherings of students. These meetings and discussions helped him focus his views about what the Army's attitude to the Orthodox conscience should be, views which, he comments, did not win the approval of 'our evangelical friends, except the most broad-minded'—and might almost be described as a more systematic version of those of the 'nebulous' Miss Weisberg. Whether or not Larsson was fully aware of the degree of intellectual flexibility enjoyed by educated Russians (as well as peasants) in whom orthodoxy, paganism and rationalism could happily co-exist, he was ready to allow converts to retain a surprising number of orthodox practices. Perhaps he felt this was forced on him by necessity. Certainly he hoped—even assumed—that such practices would in time wither away.[24]

Ikons he neither condemned nor dismissed. He knew that Russians expected ikons in places where they lived, ate and worshipped: if none were visible they would not enter. As we have already noted, ikons were displayed in the Slum Post and Home for refugees. The same policy was adopted in connection with the halls in which the Army conducted its religious meetings.

> When No. 4 Corps in Petrograd was opened, a painting of Christ with Joseph and Mary on their way to Egypt was hung up... and a little lamp lit before the picture. This Corps was really the most flourishing... we had in Petrograd.

> We made it however a rule that the ikon must have a picture of Christ and not of any saints. It had to be placed on the side wall between the platform and [the body of] the hall in order that nobody should need to turn his back to it, which was considered very bad.

He also accepted the sign of the cross. This symbolic act, he thought, could be misused but was essentially right and good, and Orthodox comrades would be

---

24 Larsson's account of his attitude to these matters is in *Tio År I Ryssland*, chapter 8 ('Working Guidelines'), pp. 67-69.

allowed to make it in front of the ikon before meetings began. Nor were they discouraged from wearing a cross 'on a chain next to the body'.

Other ways in which Salvationist converts continued to observe Orthodoxy might seem more surprising.[25]

Larsson justified his tolerance by citing Paul's willingness to circumcise Timothy in order to win 'his countrymen's confidence'. However, much later, in the mid-1930s, when it seemed to him that the Orthodox Church had suffered an irreversible loss of prestige under the Communists, he would arrive at the view that if The Salvation Army ever returned to Russia such concessions would not be necessary.[26] But by then he had also been convinced by 'one of our Russian officers', that it might prove impossible 'to exert any influence' on Russians if their love of symbolism was not gratified.

> Should a Russian lose the possibility of satisfying the soul's craving for the mystical it is as if he has nothing to hold onto. He is lost in a waterless desert. Whether this is due to a special quality of soul or is a result of hundreds of years of isolation from other peoples, it is difficult to decide. But it seems to be a case of all or nothing: either becoming a martyr for Christ, like the Stundists, or conducting ruthless propaganda for atheism, as millions now do.[27]

Whether to make confession before the priest and attend Mass once a year, was left to individual choice. One comrade explained her confession in Salvation Army terms: she gave her testimony to the Lord in the presence of the priest. This practice did not survive long; as Larsson wryly noted, comrades attending confession in

---

25 There was a precedent for this approach: until 1870 the Stundists (a Protestant sect of German origin) remained within the Orthodox Church, 'much as the early Methodists remained for a time within the Anglican communion'. See Curtiss, *Church and State*, pp. 164-65.

26 This assumption has proved, in the long run, to be mistaken. After the German invasion in 1941 the support of the Church was invoked by Stalin and he subsequently allowed the reopening of some 20,000 churches, eight seminaries and some monasteries. After the war persecution was resumed, but after the fall of the Soviet regime the 1990s saw a considerable revival of the Orthodox Church, with consequential revival of conflict with religious bodies from elsewhere. The most marked assertion of this revival of prestige and influence was the rebuilding, in Moscow, near the Kremlin, of the Cathedral of Christ the Redeemer (reconsecrated in 1997), which had been blown up on Stalin's orders in 1931. The outside of the building was completed in three years by building teams working day and night. Even given that there has been dispute over whether there was any need to undertake this expensive reconstruction (especially when there were huge modern housing estates with no churches at all), the fact of it was striking evidence of nostalgia for Russia's pre-Communist past and a clear assertion that the Russian Orthodox Church was a force to be reckoned with. See Cross and Livingstone, *Oxford Dictionary of the Christian Church*, pp. 1427-28, and Wil van den Bercken, *Holy Russia and Christian Europe: East and West in the Religious Ideology of Russia*, London, SCM Press, 1999, pp. 216-19.

27 Larsson, *Tio År I Ryssland*, p. 69.

Salvation Army uniform were not always made heartily welcome, which cooled their enthusiasm. Thus, he adds with restrained pleasure, the situation that the Army regarded as proper, of Salvationists leaving Orthodox practices behind them, was arrived at naturally and by consent, without unnecessary trouble.

It was, however, legally required that marriages, baptisms and funerals be conducted by an Orthodox priest. Larsson was accustomed enough to a similar situation in his native Sweden, for in 1915 it was still relatively novel for marriages between Swedish Salvationists to be conducted by anyone other than a Lutheran cleric. Larsson thought that the situation in Russia would change eventually and be largely harmless in the meantime.

Interestingly, Larsson concludes his discussion of the issue with the observation that he 'could not say that the above-mentioned guidelines had the General's approval. On the other hand, neither did he forbid them.'

A Setback

For the moment The Salvation Army felt relatively secure. Its meetings might be clandestine, but converts and candidates for officership were presenting themselves, albeit in small numbers.[28] Twenty officers and soldiers from Russia, led by Helmy Boije, took part in the Congress in Helsingfors and among the seekers after Salvation during the Congress was a Russian bluejacket, who was counselled by a Russian Cadet who had been called up for military service but given special leave to attend. Social work was going ahead in Petrograd, and earning plaudits. Nevertheless, calamity—or, at least, apparent calamity—lay in wait.

As it happened, this was witnessed by a visitor from International Headquarters, the International Travelling Commissioner, Hugh Whatmore. Early in 1915 he had passed through Petrograd on his way to Korea, and noted that:

> With Ensign Boije, who speaks Russian very well, are six officers, three cadets[29] and one employee. The Work embraces: five Meetings weekly at what may be termed the Corps; the daily feeding of 80 children at the Slum Centre; Children's Meetings on Sundays at the Slum Centre; the care of babies, whose unmarried mothers subscribe to their maintenance; the sale of *The Salvation Messenger*; the Summer Colony for Children...[30]

Whatmore addressed about 30 people in Madame Chertkov's drawing room, 'nearly everyone... of noble birth', amongst them the Princess Galitzin, and a meeting at the

---

28 Five young women, converted at this time, trained as officers in Helsingfors (although only one of them, Captain Irberg, continued as an officer for more than about five years): Clara Becker, *Notes on Russia, Scrapbook*, p. 1.

29 I.e. trainee officers.

30 The SA Heritage Centre file on Commissioner Whatmore contains cuttings from a life of Commissioner Hugh Whatmore by Harry W. Williams, serialized in what appears to be the Australian *The War Cry*, in 1974.

slum centre, attended by 'two countesses, a baroness, a doctor of philosophy, a retired government official, and the humbler folk who go to make up our following.' He described the atmosphere at the meetings in the flat at Gavan:

The bedrooms, as well as the dining-room, were crowded. I have seldom been so impressed and really moved. The congregation, about half of whom were men, numbered about 50 persons, and comprised a sprinkling of working people, several professional gentlemen and ladies of high standing, two countesses and a baroness, attended by their maids and footmen.

I gave two addresses... and later spoke to the soldiers alone. After the latter a young woman, evidently speaking on behalf of the soldiers, (of whom there are now 24), said, with convincing power, that she hoped I would convey to the General that his Russian soldiers could be depended upon as foundation stones upon which the future Salvation Army in Russia could be built. A young student in full Salvation Army uniform followed and the little group broke up with thanksgiving. They deeply stirred my heart.

When Whatmore returned, towards the end of October, Russia was in a nervous state. Between July and September, Warsaw, Brest-Litovsk and Vilnius had been lost to the Germans and only in October had the Russian forces been able (largely because the Germans outran their line of supply) to stabilize a front running from Riga through Pinsk to Tarnopol.[31] In Moscow, shops with German names provoked riots and demonstrations. After a period of loyal abstention, strikes and violent industrial clashes increased, a tendency which would accelerate through 1916 and culminate in the February Revolution.

In September the Tsar, acting under his wife's influence (and, at one remove, under that of Rasputin, who wanted Nicholas away from Petrograd so that his influence on the Tsarina could be increased), assumed command of the Russian forces in the field. Although he believed that this improved morale, events suggest otherwise; his euphoria was induced by the stream of praise directed at him by the Tsarina, who constantly assured him at last he was acting as he should, like a true autocrat. (Nicholas, unfortunately for himself, had come to believe that he had sworn to uphold autocracy in his coronation oath, although this was not the case.) At home, the Imperial Family grew ever more divided, with the Tsarina on one side and all other senior royals on the other. Alexandra was convinced that they were ganging up on her and Nicholas and, through her, on Rasputin. In this fevered atmosphere, publication, by the Duma's progressive bloc, of a programme of political and administrative reforms provoked a series of reactionary responses and appointments by the Tsar, one of which was to have repercussions for The Salvation Army. The Minister of the Interior was dismissed for his liberal tendencies and replaced by a protégé of Rasputin, Alexi Khvostov, an unscrupulous gormandizer thirsty for power. He and a new Chief of Police, Beletsky, took to office with such vigour as to

---

31 Tarnopol was about 40 miles north of Miss Weisberg's estate at Tolstoye.

be nicknamed 'the two volcanoes'. Their energy, for the moment, helped improve relations between government and people.[32]

Anything not long established in the mainstream of Russia's traditional Orthodox life came once more under suspicion, and soon after he was appointed, Khvostov's Ministry of the Interior planted a paragraph in various newspapers to the effect that it was once more 'considering' the activities of The Salvation Army. In response to the 'suspicions' voiced by unnamed people, it intended to ensure that Salvationist activities 'harmonized' with existing laws and customs. The announcement may have been intended simply to counter earlier favorable press comments. The 'suspicions' may have been that the Army was an agent of foreign governments, particularly that of Great Britain. [33]

Whatever the purpose of this gnomic utterance, nothing happened for some time. Larsson wondered whether it had been intended merely to placate the Army's enemies within Russia. He does not say who those enemies were, but one obvious candidate is the Orthodox Church. There is another possibility. Rasputin, Khvostov's protector, deplored all things western, was, despite his gross behaviour and accusations of Khlystian heresy, a convinced, not to say rabid, Orthodox, and—although he wanted Russia to get itself out of the war—in his way a patriot. I have found no direct evidence that Rasputin knew anything of The Salvation Army but if he did he would have felt bound to thwart it.

What happened next, however, is well documented. The Petrograd District Commissioners pounced during a meeting at Gavan in late October, which Commissioner Whatmore attended.[34] A member of the congregation, a stranger who had aroused the officers' suspicions, left without farewell or explanation partway through the meeting. Shortly afterwards, during a Bible reading, three policemen arrived. One stood in the street doorway, preventing anyone from leaving. Another approached the reader, Lieutenant Konstantinova, by a roundabout route through the linked side-rooms of the flat, and demanded to be told what book she was reading and what specifically she was reading from it. She quoted one perhaps rather provocative line: 'Thou art weighed in the balance and found wanting'.[35]

The policeman was 'somewhat disturbed'. (Given the prevailing atmosphere of political and military paranoia, he may have detected subversive implications.) He demanded Konstantinova's name and ordered that the meeting be concluded at once. What followed—an investigation in minute detail of what had taken place in the flat

---

32 See Lincoln, *Armageddon*, pp. 205-06.

33 I have lost my note of the source of the information in this paragraph (it came, I believe, from Larsson but he does not include it in *Tio År I Ryssland*). My friend Anatoly Kurchatkin in Moscow, who searched for the Ministry's announcement on my behalf in newspapers of the time, was unable to find it. However, since what follows confirms that something of the kind was afoot, I retain it in the text and crave the indulgence of the reader.

34 My account of this meeting collates those in Larsson's *Ten Years in Russia*, and Williams' life of Whatmore See note 30, above.

35 Part of the writing on the wall that so dismayed Belshazzar. See Dan. 5.27.

that evening—had its comic side. Adjutant Boije gave the names of those who had prayed and spoken about their beliefs and experiences. At the policeman's insistence, she asked all of them to repeat what they had said. The gist of these utterances was passed on by telephone to the District Commissioners who had initiated the raid. During these telephone conversations those Salvationists not under interrogation passed the time by singing Army songs to guitar accompaniment, amusing as well as surprising the police and providing the Commissioners with a musical background to the police summaries of their testimonies. This went on until two in the morning, when everyone's name and address was taken.[36]

When the police and non-Salvationist members of the congregation had left, Adjutant Boije gathered around her the 20 Army officers and soldiers who remained and read to them the Army's Articles of War—a response curiously reminiscent of other dissidents before and since who, in modest Russian flats furnished with green sofas and samovars, have recited defiant manifestos. The strenuous prose in which Booth required his followers to commit themselves to peril and sacrifice can seldom have been spoken in more ominous—or more inspiring—circumstances:

> ...believing solemnly that The Salvation Army has been raised up by God, and is sustained and directed by Him, I do here declare my full determination, by God's help, to be a true soldier of the Army till I die... I do here and now, and forever, renounce the world with all its sinful pleasures... I do here declare that I will spend all the time, strength, money and influence I can in supporting and carrying on this war... believing that the sure and only way to remedy all the evils in the world is by bringing men to submit themselves to the government of the Lord Jesus Christ... feeling that the love of Christ, who died to save me, requires from me this devotion of my life to His service for the Salvation of the whole world...

Fired by Boije's no doubt emotionally charged reading, the beleaguered Russian Salvationists decided that the time had come for the Petrograd Number One Corps to be formally inaugurated. In future they would meet without dissimulation, accepting unflinchingly whatever might be in store for them.

They heard nothing from the police until 11 November, when a squad arrived to carry out a sentence imposed by the Commissioners without further examination or trial. Everyone who had been at the meeting was to pay a fine of 75 roubles or go to jail for three weeks. For Adjutant Boije, as leader of the meeting, and Adam

---

36 In behaving as they did, the policemen may have been applying prohibitions that Pobedonostsev had imposed upon the Stundists in 1900. As in the case of the Salvationists, Stundist meetings were in any case proscribed, but they were specifically not to be allowed 'the group singing of special verses from the Bible and of hymns from the service books of the sect. the reading, by anyone of the gathering, of chosen parts of Holy Scriptures, with explanation thereof in the spirit of the false doctrines of the sect; also, kneeling devotions with improvised "inspired" prayers, without the sign of the cross'. (See Curtiss, *Church and State*, pp. 168-69.) All these, of course, were also Salvationist practices.

Pieshevski, as lessee of the flat, the sentence was 200 roubles or two months' imprisonment.

There was a loophole in the law which, fortunately, Boije and Pieshevski were aware of: a respite of three days was permitted before the fine had to be paid, and no-one could be sent to jail until that time had elapsed. The police left empty-handed and Boije went to consult Madame Chertkov, who sent her in turn to Miss Peuker, the longstanding friend of the Army who, it will be remembered, had enlisted the Dowager Empress against the colonel who had tried to evict them from their Home for Refugees. Once again a member of the Imperial Family was invoked, this time the Tsar's aunt, Konstantin Konstantinovich's sister, Olga;[37] she sent a telegram to Khvostov, who ordered Beletsky to drop the case.[38] After further delay, those under arrest were freed and fines were waived. Those who had already paid were promised reimbursement. But the mills ground slowly: 15 months later, when the Revolution broke out, no money had been returned, nor was it subsequently.

It may be significant that the raid on Gavan occurred shortly after Khvostov came to power. Equally, there may have been no special motive for the police action, which might have taken place at any time during the preceding two years. As Larsson writes:

> Although we had come unharmed through two years' 'law-breaking' and had been forgiven such 'crime' as we had been accused of, our meetings were no more legal than they had been; in fact we were now in a much worse position, since the case had made plain that we stood under no kind of protection.[39]

Perhaps he overstates a little. The intervention of the Dowager Queen implies some possibility of protection—which, however, would only be available *post facto*. If the political and military situation deteriorated it might not be offered at all. For the moment, though, things became easier as the likelihood of occupation of Petrograd and Moscow by German forces faded.[40]

---

37 Olga Konstantinovna, Dowager Queen of Greece, whose husband, George I, had been assassinated at Salonika in 1913, during the First Balkan War.

38 Having in the meantime fallen out with Rasputin, Khvostov was dismissed in March of 1916.

39 Larsson, *Tio År I Ryssland*, p. 81.

40 It might be melodramatic to suggest that there was any significant attempt by, say, the reactionary tendency within the Church, spurred on by the Tsarina and Rasputin, to close down, The Salvation Army while the Tsarina's enemies within the Imperial family countered with the Dowager Queen Olga's telegram to the Minister of the Interior. But, perhaps coincidentally, the only other specific action taken against The Salvation Army by the Imperial government was also handled by one of Rasputin's protégés, Procurator Sabler. This was the rejection, in 1912, of the Povlsens' application to be permitted to begin work officially.

A Self-inflicted Wound

Once again, The Salvation Army was forced to adopt new tactics. From November 1915 onwards, strangers arriving at meetings were warned that such gatherings were outside the law: they attended at their own risk. Unsurprisingly, few not already soldiers or staunch friends dared risk arrest or heavy fines. Some did, however. In December, during Larsson's first visit to Petrograd after the police raid, a man deeply impressed by the ceremony of the service of dedication of Pieshevski's infant daughter Nadjesda to God and Salvation warfare[41] himself sought Salvation. At a subsequent meeting his testimony moved three others to do the same.

But although the Salvationists were determined to recover from the setback, another blow was about to fall, this time from an unexpected quarter. Larsson gives the facts:

> The year 1916 began with a great disappointment. Adjutant Helmy Boije, who was so well equipped and so necessary to our work in Russia, was appointed to England by the General in order to study training work. It was difficult for us to understand this order.[42]

What can General Bramwell Booth, sitting in his office at 101 Queen Victoria Street, London, have supposed he was doing? Boije was clearly the most experienced and able officer in Russia's fledgling Salvation Army. She spoke fluent Russian. Her service on the committee for refugees had won her the respect of the Petrograd City authorities. Wherever she saw any possibility of interesting a potentially helpful person in the Army's work, or of starting a new activity, she did not rest until that chance had been seized. Her decisive reaction to the police raid demonstrated her ability to act calmly, swiftly and effectively under pressure. She was, Larsson convincingly writes, the right woman in the right place. Why, then, remove her from a struggling outpost facing a situation of great and increasing difficulty, which could only be exacerbated by her departure when, we may safely assume, she very much wanted to stay?[43] The difficulties of travel from Petrograd to London in the middle of a great European war suggest further excellent reasons to doubt the utility of such an appointment. And what could Boije (who had already worked at the Training Garrison in Helsingfors) learn in London about training officers that she could not learn, more practically and more usefully, in the field in Petrograd?

---

41 The Salvation Army's equivalent of baptism.

42 Larsson, *Tio År I Ryssland*, p. 87.

43 As an officer, she was sworn to absolute obedience and in 1916 it would have been more or less unthinkable for her to question or reject her farewell orders, or for anyone else, including Larsson, to question them on her or his own or Russia's behalf. More recently it has become relatively acceptable for officers to negotiate over new appointments, on such grounds as health or family matters and for officers in Larsson's position to ask to retain the services of valuable subordinates.

One answer to these questions lies in a tradition established in the earliest years of the Army. To William and Bramwell Booth it was an article of faith that the individual was always subordinate to the organization (unless that individual's surname happened to be Booth, and often even then).[44] They held this view for two complementary reasons: first, because no officer should ever begin to feel that a job or territory was 'theirs'; secondly, because it was unhealthy for any corps or larger grouping of Salvationists to feel that it could not function without the presence of a favourite officer. Since, however, Boije had been in Petrograd a mere 14 months, these considerations cannot sensibly have been in the General's mind—although they would have arrived there soon enough had anyone questioned his wisdom in moving her.

He may, as Boije's subsequent appointments suggest, have supposed that he was taking a longer view of the best interests of the work in Russia, since after a year in London she was appointed Principal of the Training Garrison in Helsingfors, where, as Booth presumably anticipated, she would be training officers to work in Russia as well as in Finland. (By September 1918 she was back in Russia, where she stayed until ill health brought about her final departure in April 1922.) The fact remains that her departure from Petrograd at the beginning of 1916 came at a crucially unfortunate time and was seen by Larsson as a severe blow to the work there.

The End of Imperial Russia

Bearing up under this new trial, The Salvation Army in Russia practised survival and bided its time in depressing circumstances. Only one new initiative was attempted.[45]

1916 was to be the last year of Tsarist Russia, during which disintegration of government and society accelerated out of control. Another short-term prime minister was appointed and sacked. Russia's war effort was revived on the south-western front through the determination and flair of an outstanding general, Alexei Brusilov, but his efforts foundered when his colleagues further north refused support. Nicholas's leadership was widely agreed to be disastrous, and criticisms previously reserved for the Tsarina, Rasputin, and the ineffectuals and Germanophiles in his entourage, were aimed directly at the sacred leader himself. He, however, remained ineffably unaware of the worsening situation. A matter of days before he was forced to abdicate, he expressed happiness over the fact that at the front he could rest his brain, untroubled by ministers with troublesome questions demanding thought.[46]

---

44 Evangeline Booth insisted on remaining in America despite various attempts by her brother to move her elsewhere, but she was unique in this successful defiance of his managerial directives: several of her siblings who had attempted similar manoeuvres and been told that regulations applied as much to them as to other officers, had left the Army as a result.

45 See p. 199 below.

46 See Lincoln, *Armageddon*, pp. 169 and 322, and Brian Moynahan, *Rasputin: The Saint Who Sinned*, London, Aurum Press, 1997, p. 244.

Meanwhile, the government in Petrograd became a conduit for increasingly eccentric policies and appointments ordered by Alexandra but initiated by Rasputin. The formal machinery of state appeared politically bankrupt. The people of Petrograd, depressed and indifferent, longed for an end to the war on any terms. An anonymous rhymster proclaimed

> We do not take defeat amiss,
> And victory gives us no delight,
> The source of all our cares is this:
> Can we get vodka for tonight?[47]

Was Russia destroyed as ally and enemy? No-one knew. It had some successes. Its industrialists were at last producing weapons for use alongside those sent by America and France, delivery of which had been made possible by an astounding combination of organization, engineering and tyrannically driven slave-labour: the Murmansk-Petrozavodsk railway was built, by work gangs sometimes more than 50,000 strong, toiling around the clock. During the snowstorms, sub-zero temperatures and darkness at noon of winter they were lit by flaring torches; in summer by the midnight sun. Meanwhile, an energetic War Minister, Alexy Polivanov, ensured that two million men were drafted and trained and armed to a better standard than anything seen since August 1914.

Decline, apparently inexorable, continued nevertheless. Having offended Alexandra—by criticizing Rasputin, and again by catching Stürmer in the act of embezzling five million roubles—Polivanov was sacked. The rank and file of the Russian Army, deprived by wholesale slaughter of their immediate leaders, the junior officers, were demoralized by being forced to mount repeated attacks across obstructive, dangerous terrain against impregnable objectives. Rumours of starvation and mass civilian cemeteries in Petrograd swept through the trenches. The stories were premature, but only just. 1916's harvest and replanting were devastated by shortage of manpower. Grain supplies ought to have been adequate, since none could be exported, but when villagers, as ever in times of economic crisis, began hoarding it, prices rose—and the overstretched railway system could scarcely transport what there was from southern farmlands to faraway northern cities. Until then, the rouble had been one of the world's soundest currencies; now it halved in value during the year. By May, the war had created 3.3 million refugees—a statistic which puts The Salvation Army's work with refugees into depressing perspective.

Meanwhile, people of every class talked of the possibility and possible consequences of revolution.

Only commitment kept the Salvationists going during 1916. With the authorities inclined to blame spies and foreign agents for Russia's deteriorating situation, they could do little more than survive as unobtrusively as possible. Growth amongst Russians within Russia was impeded by the threat of arrest and fines following the

---

47 See Lincoln, *Armageddon*, p. 215.

raid on the Gavan flat. Many Salvationist men were called up, reducing numbers still further. Larsson (ever in search of light in darkness) comments, 'this was offset by the fact that many other servicemen were reached with the message and became converts, so the Gospel continued to spread'. Over the border in Helsingfors, Open Air meetings in Kaisaniemi Park were attended by large crowds of Russian soldiers (all sermons, speeches and testimonies were translated into Russian) and it frequently happened that up to 20 of them would come forward into the Salvationist ring to pray for salvation from their sin.

In December, shortage of paper curtailed the print run of *Vestnik Spaseniya*. (The 1,500 copies printed sold well, Larsson tells us, despite its price: 50 kopeks for an eight-page paper. 'The hearts of many of the war-stricken people were searching after God, and they found comfort and help in reading its pages.') There were only two more numbers, each reduced to four pages. Subsequently the paper shortage worsened and the paper, which had leant the organization a quasi legal status since July 1913, ceased publication for a period—there is conflicting evidence as to how long—but it was certainly on the streets again in June 1917.[48]

Although the Army behaved more cautiously than it had done before the raid on Gavan it did not become timid. Lieutenant Gorinovich showed one kind of nerve when, returning from a visit to a convalescent sister in the Ukraine, she attempted to change trains at Moscow and was told that at present only officers were permitted to travel by rail to Petrograd. 'I *am* an officer', she said, 'in The Salvation Army.' She was allowed onto the train.[49] As for the Army at large, far from trying to conceal its existence, it asked Beletsky's successor as Commissioner of Police for permission to open a shelter for the homeless. He was sympathetic until he heard that morning and evening prayers would be part of the daily routine. He promised to consult the Church authorities, but before anything was decided he, along with many others and much else, was toppled by the Revolution.

Signs that unpredictable upheaval was imminent grew ever more ominous. In November, at the opening of the autumn session of the Duma, Paul Miliukov, leader of the Cadets (the Constitutional Democratic Party), accused the Prime Minister, Stürmer, of weakening Russia at home and undermining relations with her allies in a way that made victory impossible. 'Is this stupidity, or is this treason?', he had asked, in measured tones but to great dramatic effect. (The imputation of treason was, as he later admitted, unjustified.) 'Choose either one, the consequences are the same.'[50] The Government forbade the press to report or comment on Miliukov's speech, but, as Paléologue noted, it was in circulation nevertheless, its impact enhanced by exaggerations and improvements. In December Nicholas proved himself still capable of sudden, rather pointless gestures: he decreed that all German terms (*Oberhofmarschall, Jägermeister,* and the like) should be removed from the nomenclature of official titles and ranks, to be replaced by Russian equivalents.

---

48 William Nicholson, *The Romance of the The War Cry,* London, Salvationist Publishing and Supplies, 1929, pp.126-27.
49 *The War Cry,* 15 April, 1916.
50 See Lincoln, *Armageddon,* p. 300 and Pipes, *The Russian Revolution,* pp. 252-55.

A sense that crisis and scandal might erupt at any moment produced a poisonous, morally anaesthetized atmosphere in the capital. Robert Wilton, the *Times* correspondent, thought that corrupt officials were being imitated by all classes. All Russia 'seems to be engaged in a whirl of plunder', he wrote. 'Every man is trying to rob his neighbour to the utmost of his capacity'.[51] Siberia was said to be overflowing with food while Petrograd was starving. Pogroms were threatened. Rumours of spies and treasonable activity abounded. Rasputin and his circle were not the only Petrogradians to indulge in orgiastic drunkenness and debauchery. In *Can't Stand It*, the poet Vladimir Mayakovsky wrote of '...the scream of a thousand and one tortured days' and, in an *envoi* to the poem, headed *For History*, he announced

> When all are distributed through heaven and through hell,
> conclusions will be drawn about this earth—
> remember well:
> In 1916
> the beautiful people disappeared from Petrograd.[52]

In December, the long-running soap opera of relations between the Imperial Family and Rasputin, so widely known, so widely thought to be profoundly damaging to the standing of the monarchy, came, too late, to an end. The *starets* had grown increasingly indiscreet and dissolute during the course of the year, and, with Nicholas absent at the front, Alexandra had interfered increasingly in the processes of government, invariably after taking advice from the dark bearded man with hypnotic eyes who, according to scurrilous rumour supported by forged pornographic letters, was nightly enjoying her sexual favours.[53] The Prime Minister and Minister of the Interior had both been replaced with candidates proposed by him. The Okhrana agents who shadowed him recorded in unemotional language the extreme and increasing levels of drunkenness he repeatedly achieved. He himself noticed his own deterioration, admitting on one occasion that his healing powers were deserting him. Various schemes to kill him had been mooted during the year, some more seriously than others. Rasputin heard the rumours, and alternated between nervousness and fatalism in his response to them.[54] The assassination itself, by Prince Felix

---

51 Quoted in Moynahan, *Rasputin*, p. 299.

52 Translated by Bernard Meares, in Albert C..Todd, and Max Hayward (eds), *Twentieth Century Russian Poetry*, London, Fourth Estate, 1993, p. 243.

53 This was entirely untrue, but he was nightly—oftener than nightly—enjoying the favours of a stream of women ranging from the nobility and bourgeoisie through to courtesans, mistresses of ministers and bureaucrats, and prostitutes. These women all knew about each other and positively insisted that new paramours join their number. Those who had husbands found them for the most part complaisant. See Orlando Figes and Boris Kolonitskii, *Reinterpreting the Russian Revolution*, New Haven and London, Yale University Press, 1999, pp. 13-14, and illustration 1.

54 For the activities of Rasputin and his enemies during 1916, see Brian Moynahan, *Rasputin*, pp. 275-313.

Yousoupoff and others, need not be recounted here. It came too late to save Nicholas (who was reported to have seemed relieved by this event—although this may have been nothing more than his habitual, widely misunderstood, fatalism on the receipt of bad news), and in any case its significance should not be exaggerated. Nevertheless, it was in effect an announcement that the successive, increasingly reactionary administrations he had appointed in defiance of more moderate advice, their inefficiency in prosecuting the war and dealing with social and economic discontent at home, together with the scandal of Rasputin's character and influence over the Tsarina and therefore over the Tsar, had finally alienated not only the natural opponents of autocracy but also many of those who looked to it as the fount and guarantor of their own status. Soon Moscow regiments would be talking openly of proclaiming another Tsar. There were rumours of similar intentions within the Imperial family itself. Intended by its perpetrators to bring the Tsar to his senses and to drive a wedge between him and his wife, the murder of Rasputin had the opposite effect: he was as uxoriously cocooned in family life as ever, and his fatalistic religious faith blinded him to everything else. V.V. Shulgin, a loyal Tsarist, summed up the despair of the rest of the country in a diary entry: 'How terrible is an autocracy without an autocrat'.[55]

At the turn of the year the Russian climate took a hand in events. The previous two winters had been relatively mild; that of 1916-17 was unusually harsh. The average temperature in Petrograd during the first three months of 1917 was minus 14 degrees centigrade, 16.5 degrees lower than during the equivalent period in 1916. Moscow was colder still, and in parts of European Russia the temperature was 50 degrees below freezing. Peasant women refused to cart food into the cities. 'Sixty thousand freight cars with fuel, provisions and fodder lay buried beneath the snowdrifts,' as Protopopov, the inept Minister of the Interior, later admitted.[56] Discontent, fierce or sullen, arising from hunger, cold, defeat and disillusionment, became universal: at the front, in the cities and across the countryside. Seen in retrospect it might seem that the outbreak of revolution was imminent and inevitable, but when it came, a mere seven weeks into the new year, Lenin, in exile in Switzerland, was as much surprised as anyone else. But, naturally, he welcomed it and took steps to exploit it for his own purposes. So, in its own way, did The Salvation Army.

---

55 Lincoln, *Armageddon*, p. 282.
56 See Pipes, *The Russian Revolution*, p. 272, and Lincoln, *Armageddon*, p. 316.

CHAPTER 8

1917: A Transient Freedom

Revolution

The February Revolution was a bloodier affair than the Bolshevik coup, which followed in October. What happened in February was a spontaneous uprising, growing out of riots occasioned by shortage of bread, the threat of rationing and the rigours of an exceptionally cold winter, followed by a sudden sense of release and joy when, on 23 February, the temperature rose to minus five degrees. Beginning with bread riots and becoming (when peasant soldiers refused to fire upon other peasants) a military mutiny, events on the streets were for some time well ahead of the leaders of the socialist and democratic parties who were thought by the tsarist authorities to be organizing them. A Socialist Revolutionary leader, Sergei Mstislavsky, said in 1922, 'The revolution found us, the party members, fast asleep, just like the Foolish Virgins in the Gospel'. Those who were not asleep were in prison, in exile, or abroad.[1]

In the absence of the most energetic revolutionary leaders the turbulence which was unleashed was too great and too various for any one of those available to control it usefully. The 'Provisional Executive Committee of the Soviet of Workers' Deputies'—holed up in the left wing of the Tauride Palace conducting wildly disorganized debates during which everyone spoke at once—assumed that Russia must pass through a period of bourgeois capitalism before the revolution proper could take place. Faced with the possibility of seizing power, they temporized, then backed away. By contrast, in the right wing of the palace, the centre/right remnants of the Duma conducted orderly debates, which, however, served only to expose their divisions. Unable to decide whether to revive a radically modified tsarism or search for some other, democratically stable form of administration (they knew not what), they formed a Provisional Government, which was ridiculed as indistinguishable from its numerous predecessors, to the particular derision of the workers and peasant soldiery on whose behalf it was supposed to speak for being led by Prince Lvov.[2] But Lvov, for all his rank,

---

1 Figes, *A People's Tragedy*, p. 323.

2 In Lvov's case the mirth was possibly undeserved: he had a long and distinguished record as a social reformer who consistently defied efforts by bureaucrats to silence and obstruct him. However, we should note Iurii Vladimirovich Got'e's enthusiastic commendation, in 1919, of Tikhomirov's comment that Lvov was 'a political deaf-mute'. See Iurii Vladimirovich Got'e (trs. and ed. Terence Emmons), *Time of Troubles: The Diary of Iurii Vladimirovich Got'e*, London, I.B. Tauris, 1988, p. 315.

presided over the passing of a dazzling series of reforms during the first weeks of the Provisional Government... Freedoms of assembly, press and speech were granted. Legal restrictions of religion, class and race were removed. There was a general amnesty. Universal adult suffrage was introduced.[3]

These freedoms were deliberately granted but there was, as Figes observes, 'a general crisis of authority'. A multiplicity of local and sectional *ad hoc* committees ruled the equally innumerable factions. Suddenly, as Lenin remarked, Russia had become the freest country in the world.

In due course he would exploit that freedom, but was not the first to try. The most immediate opportunist was Alexander Kerensky, a flamboyant defence lawyer whose principal political talents were for inflammatory oratory and (what would become his greatest handicap) running with the hare and hunting with the hounds. During the period that followed the February uprising, he kept seats warm in both wings of the Tauride, wearing a morning coat with a starched dress shirt and collar when he addressed the Duma, tearing them off as he sprinted through the corridors to harangue the Soviet as a man of the people.

Another who exploited the new freedom was Karl Larsson.

News of the uprising on 27 February/12March[4] did not reach Larsson in Helsingfors until 16 March (the Petrograd telegraph office had been closed down for three days),[5] when, 'towards evening... the streets buzzed with rumours'.[6] Writing a decade and a half later, he indicates that he believed at the time that the worst was already over. A few police stations had been burnt along with files on criminals or political dissenters that they had housed (often by those still awaiting trial).[7] Other documents were stolen, or left to blow about in the windy streets.[8] Policemen, military officers, soldiers and civilians had been killed, but given the degree of upheaval the number of deaths was surprisingly low and the disturbances and street fighting appeared to have ceased. It is significant that he should err so far on the side of optimism. As a Salvationist he was bound to take the cheerful view: if such far-reaching changes had indeed taken place with relatively little violence then God, whose will must be operating somewhere within them, was to be praised. As a member of a non-political organization, he was bound (even if what he wrote in the

---

3 Figes, *A People's Tragedy*, p. 358.

4 The disparity between old and new style dates (which replaced the old in February 1918) is relatively important during 1917, when events took place in quick succession.

5 Phillip Knightley, *The First Casualty*, London, André Deutsche, 1975, p. 144.

6 Larsson, *Tio År I Ryssland*, p. 94.

7 In Krestovsky Prison and the adjoining District Court, valuable archives covering many centuries were destroyed: see Pitcher, *Witnesses of the Russian Revolution*, p. 25.

8 Destruction of the prisons was regarded by some revolutionaries as a 'Christian mission', since there was no criminal who could not be reformed. (See Figes and Kolonitskii, *Interpreting the Russian Revolution,* p. 55.) This followed a tradition that dated back to the Nineteenth Century, when Nicholai Morozov, the terrorist, had compared 'the dedication and heroism of the assassin with that of the early Christian martyr'. (See Hardy, *Land and Freedom*, p. 139.)

1930s had been influenced by hindsight and the passage of time) to avoid passing political judgements.[9] Or he may, also with hindsight, have wished to see the February Revolution as essentially benign, in contrast to the Bolshevik *coup* in October, which, although almost entirely bloodless, had far less desirable consequences for The Salvation Army. For Larsson, the most important event of early 1917 was not the abdication of the Tsar but the abolition, on 20 March/2April, of all restrictions relating to religion. Now the Army could preach the gospel and do its work. The oxygen of publicity, denied it for four years, could be administered. Anything was possible.

The day on which Larsson received news of the upheaval was also Russia's last day as a monarchy. Nicholas brought his reign to an end in much the same manner as, for two decades, he had conducted it: like a man sleepwalking through a world of delusion.[10] On 26 February, when, in Petrograd, the army had fired into crowds of demonstrators, causing casualties, the Tsar, at his military headquarters in Stavka, wrote in his diary:

> At ten o'clock I went to Mass. The reports were on time. There were many people at breakfast, including all the foreigners. Wrote to Alix and went for a walk near the chapel by the Bobrisky road. The weather was fine and frosty. After tea I read and talked with Senator Tregubov until dinner. Played dominoes in the evening.

Next morning he received a cable from the President of the Duma describing the desperate urgency of the situation: it begged him to 'take immediate steps... tomorrow it will be too late'. Nicholas glanced at it and told Count Fredericks, 'That fat fellow Rodzianko has again written to me with all kinds of nonsense, which I shan't even bother to answer.'[11]

Three days later, under pressure from politicians, but also from generals (who feared a disgraceful termination of Russia's contribution to the war, and whose opinion weighed far more heavily with him), betrayed (as he saw it) by his people, he abdicated, on behalf of both himself and his son, in favour of his brother, Grand Duke Michael. The following day, as Larsson in Helsingfors was hearing news of the uprising, the Grand Duke, surprised and annoyed at having thus been promoted without prior consultation, and all too aware that his safety could not be guaranteed

---

9 Later, it seems that Commissioner Henry Mapp, who was briefly appointed in charge of the Russian Salvation Army, as it burgeoned during the early months of 1917, publicly expressed his opposition to Bolshevism, an act that was regarded by some senior Salvationist leaders as the cause of the Army's eventual expulsion.

10 According to Stolypin's brother-in-law Sazonov, Nicholas regarded himself as 'destined for terrible trials' because his birthday was on 6 May, the Saint's day of the Patriarch Job. (See Paléologue, *Diary*, 20 August, 1914.)

11 Pipes, *Russian Revolution*, p. 282.

by the Provisional Government, declined the honour. Three hundred and four years of Romanov rule came to an abrupt and ignominious end.[12]

Larsson seized his earliest opportunity to visit Petrograd, acting as the pathfinder for a group of Swedish and Finnish officers who were about to cross Russia on their way to missionary posts in China. He arrived on 19 March/1 April and looked upon the city with an uplifted heart:

> Trams had not yet begun to run but on that clear frosty morning I walked with a lighter step than ever before to our headquarters. We had freedom now and could do as we liked just as in other parts of the world.[13]

A Petrograd Spring and Easter: Public Meetings at Last

When Larsson's Swedish and Finnish missionary colleagues arrived they were able to attend the large public meetings that the Petrograd Salvationists could now organize without hindrance. For the moment a sort of spiritual free market had stumbled into being. The leader of the Swedes and Finns, Staff Captain Richard Sjöblom, wrote:

> How can I describe the three days we spent in Petrograd? It is impossible. They brought so much joy and blessing. It was all so new for us.
>
> The hurricane of revolution had swept through the city. Now everything was calm. Here and there we saw people demonstrating their joy over what had happened. Russians had become a free people. God grant that this measure of freedom may be rightly utilized, for only then can freedom bring blessing.
>
> For us foreigners the meetings were marvellous. What must they have been to our comrades who for so many years had struggled on in fear and trembling. Now we could invite whoever we liked to our meetings, in the two halls we hired for the purpose in the centre of the city. The military governor had told Staff Captain Hacklin, 'We cannot provide you with a place but if you can find one, hold as large a meeting as you like'. Despite the short time we had to advertise, many people came. The Holy Spirit worked and souls sought salvation... Tears and outbursts of joy alternated.[14]

Sjöblom's prim remarks about freedom being 'rightly utilized' reflect the fact that in the days following 27 February/12 March the behaviour of the crowd which had

---

12 For the abdication and the end of the monarchy and the quotations in my account, see Figes, *A People's Tragedy*, pp. 339-53, and Pipes, *The Russian Revolution*, pp. 309-20.

13 Larsson, *Tio År I Ryssland*, p. 95. From the Finland Station on the Vyborg Side, past the Peter and Paul Fortress and along the length of Vasilevsky Island is about four miles.

14 Larsson, *Tio År I Ryssland*, p. 95.

taken over the Petrograd streets, previously surprisingly well-ordered and unified in purpose, lurched towards the kind of peasant riot on a huge scale described by Alexander Pushkin in *The History of Pugachev*: a vengeful and merciless orgy of destruction of the property of those whose wealth allowed them to exploit the lives and labour of others.[15] The soldier mutineers brought with them weapons and a penchant for direct physical action; simultaneously something approaching 8,000 common criminals were released from prison. Serious minded and nervous citizens, including the democratic intelligentsia, retired indoors. Burglary, sexual assault, muggings and accidental or casual shootings increased. People had sex in the streets and there was mass intoxication following the looting of the Winter Palace wine cellars. (This and many other similar expropriations were probably in part acts of revenge for the fact that the wealthy had been able to go on drinking, in their homes and their first class clubs and restaurants, during the prohibition years from 1914 onwards.)

But Sjöblom's words also suggest a real sense that from the Army's point of view something necessary had been achieved. Unfree people cannot freely choose to follow Christ. Sjöblom and Larsson were carried along by the spirit at least of one of the many instant mythologizations of the February revolution, which interpreted it as a spiritual and moral resurrection of Russia and its people: 'perhaps the most Christian act in the history of the world', according to Merezhkovsky, the radical thinker who had written on 'Christianity without Christ'. People compared the revolution explicitly to Easter, greeting each other with the traditional Easter greeting 'Christ is risen', or 'Russia has risen'. Crowds gathered in the streets to offer prayer and praise in thanks. Suddenly the streets were full of people singing the *Marseillaise* and, to a lesser extent, the *Internationale*. Booklets of political songs similar to the Army's collections of religious ones appeared. Red flags abounded. 'Day and night across the whole country a continuous disorderly meeting went on from February until the autumn of 1917'.[16] Such an atmosphere might have been made for The Salvation Army. The street assemblies were, of course, very close to the sort of Open Air meeting the Salvationists longed to conduct. Although the Army deplored political anarchy, in such respects as these it found the atmosphere of the time congenial to its purposes. For Larsson, for Helmy Boije, Clara Becker,

---

15 Yemelyan Ivanovich Pugachev was a Cossack pretender to the Russian throne who led a mass rebellion against Catherine II in 1773-74. See Pushkin, Alexander (trs, Earl Samson), *The History of Pugachev*, London, Phoenix Press, 2001, pp. 85-87 and *passim*. (When the book was first published, in 1833, Tsar Nicholas I insisted that it be renamed *The History of the Pugachev Rebellion*, on the grounds that a rebel could not have a history.)

16 The quotation is from the memoirist Konstantin Paustovsky. See Figes, *A People's Tragedy*, pp. 352 and 368-69, and Figes and Kolonistskii, *Interpreting the Russian Revolution*, pp. 39, 41, 62-65 and 69. On Vasilevsky Island on 20 March Paléologue noted that he found 'meetings' in progress everywhere. 'One of the company mounts a stone, or a bench, or a heap of snow and talks his head off, gesticulating wildly. The audience gazes fixedly at the orator and listens in a kind of rapt absorption.'

Rosa Hacklin, Nadia Konstantinova-Sundell, Elsa Olsoni, and the others, this was the dawn in which it was bliss to be alive.

The meetings in late March mentioned by Sjöblom were the Army's first public meetings in Petrograd. The congregations consisted of 'working people, military men and others of the better class'.[17] These people bought copies of the Army's Song Book and their singing, in a mixture of languages but with Russian most prominent, was accompanied by 'a good string band'.[18] The stage was filled with uniformed Russian Salvationists, the officers working in Petrograd, and the nine missionary officers. Could this, Larsson asked himself, really be happening?

These meetings were advertised as a farewell to the Finnish and Swedish officers on their way to China: a cunning ruse, one might suggest, for reminding Petrograders that the Army, a novelty in their city, had already a busy, established life elsewhere. Testimonies given by Swedes and Finns were translated into Russian. Two Russians also spoke, and,

> as soon as the Prayer Meeting began five volunteers came forward to the penitent form. One of these, directly he got through, stood up and gave his testimony, and urged the military men present to give themselves to God. One did so. In half an hour 13 seekers were registered, all volunteers.[19]

> We were delighted. The Missionary Officers' eyes were filled with tears. At the close of the meeting the outgoing comrades came forward, and with the whole congregation standing, the blessing of God was called down upon their life's work.[20]

The Russian Easter Sunday fell on 2/15 April in 1917, then as now a week later than in the western world. For Larsson and the Salvationists, it provided an occasion for their second series of large public meetings in the Russian capital: a busy attempt to achieve public notice and dispense information. The weekend did not begin well. Larsson miscalculated, realizing too late that Russians hardly thought of Good Friday as a Holy Day, focussing their attention on Easter Sunday. Consequently the Friday congregations were small. On the Saturday the trams stopped at six o'clock, which kept many soldiers away. On Easter Sunday the trams were again at a standstill, compelling cancellation of the morning meeting.

Things picked up in the afternoon. The meeting was to be held in a theatre just off Nevsky Prospect and, as a preliminary to it, the Salvationists organized their first

---

17 *The War Cry*, 5 May, 1917.

18 This implies guitars rather than orchestral stringed instruments.

19 Larsson presumably means that these people came forward to kneel at the penitent form without being spoken to by Salvationists seeking to influence them.

20 *The War Cry*, 5 May, 1917. The Salvation Army continued to work in China despite enormous difficulties and governmental hostility until 1952, when all foreign missionaries were expelled and native Chinese Salvationists were required to cut themselves off from the international body. See the Army's *Official History*, vols 5, 6 and 7.

street march. Parading through the streets with banners and bands, the Army's traditional method of attracting attention in Britain and other countries that (however reluctantly in some cases) permitted it, had previously been entirely out of the question in Russia.

Some 20 Salvationists who had managed to assemble despite the difficulties set off on a route that took almost an hour. At their head was the flag—the Finnish Salvation Army banner over whose stars had been fastened a piece of gold cloth on which were painted the Russian words 'Blood and Fire'. Next came the band, which as Larsson cheerily notes consisted of 'me and my concertina', then, two by two, the rest, each with an open songbook in front of them—since most were foreigners and did not know the words of the songs in Russian. Carrying a placard announcing the indoor meetings to come, they marched from the headquarters at Gavan, along the Bolshoi Prospect on Vasilevsky Island, across the Neva and up the Nevsky Prospect, singing, 'with all their hearts', to the accompaniment of Larsson's concertina,

> Rouse then, Soldiers, Rally round the banner!
> Ready, steady, pass the word along;
> Onward, forward, shout aloud Hosanna!
> Christ is Captain of the mighty throng![21]

The small procession attracted the good-natured attention of thousands out walking in the spring sunshine, although most lost interest when the Salvationists turned into the side street where their hired hall stood.[22] Nonetheless its 450 seats were filled.

Most of that 450, Larsson supposed, had not the remotest idea what sort of meeting they were attending. The task of explaining The Salvation Army fell to two native Russian speakers, Miss Weisberg (whose estate at Tolstoye would by July be in the thick of the fighting) and a male recruit called Ilyashenko. Both were applauded, Ilyashenko particularly, because he brought greetings from soldiers at the front line in the European war. Larsson, with some trepidation, allowed members of the public to speak. A military officer asked for a statement of the Army's attitude towards the Church and the war. Could Salvationists be relied upon to do their duty at the front? Larsson gave cautious answers, which 'seemed to satisfy those present'.

Larsson had misgivings about the evangelical aspects of the meeting. Could God produce spiritual results from a congregation composed of such varying elements, he wondered, but his doubts were overwhelmed when 20 adults and several children

---

21 When quoting songs, Larsson gives the lyrics in Swedish and, doubtless for metrical reasons, they usually differ slightly from the English originals. Since it seems clear that they were in any case sung in a medley of languages, I give the English versions.

22 A fortnight later Paléologue noted that during that period he had seen processions of Jews, Mohammedans, Buddhists, working men and women, peasants of both sexes, orphans, deaf mutes, midwives, prostitutes and the *mutilés* of the war (who were protesting against pacifism). See Paléologue, *Diary*, p. 907.

knelt at the penitent form, coming forward simultaneously and being obliged to stand and wait until room was available at the improvized Mercy Seat. Only in Russia, he rejoiced, had he seen people queue up to seek Christ.[23] It was nine in the evening before the Salvationists, tired out, returned home.

At noon on Easter Monday they were back for their largest meeting of the weekend, for which the ornate, brightly windowed, 800 seat Alexander Hall of the Petrograd Duma on Nevsky Prospect was thrown open. Full-length portraits of Nineteenth Century civic leaders gazed down on the proceedings.[24] Once more the meeting was preceded by a street procession, which, with Larsson's concertina and the banners and placards, helped to attract a large gathering. Again there were questions about the Army's standpoint *vis-à-vis* politics and the Orthodox Church. When, at the end of the meeting, the Salvationists knelt and sang 'I give Thee all and go the way Thou hast commanded', eight people knelt at the penitent form. In the evening they held a crowded Salvation Meeting in the more modestly sized headquarters at Gavan: five people sought salvation.

That evening, Easter Monday 1917, was a fateful moment for Russia. At ten minutes past eleven another, much larger demonstration, with a full-sized band, banners and interested, partly hostile, partly cheering, crowds, was staged in Petrograd. At the Finland Station a 'thunderous *Marseillaise* boomed forth on the platform and shouts of welcome rang out'[25] when, in a sealed train (which had run very late), Vladimir Ilyich Lenin arrived home from exile in Switzerland, brought by the Germans, who hoped that he would gain power and take Russia out of the war.[26] Entering the imperial waiting room almost at a run, carrying a magnificent bouquet, 'he stopped in front of Chkheidze [a Georgian Menshevik] as though colliding with a completely unexpected obstacle. Chkheidze pronounced a speech of welcome which had 'not only the spirit and wording but also the tone of a sermon'. Lenin 'stood there as though nothing taking place had the slightest connexion with him' until Chkheidze had finished, then delivered a call to arms which was 'really no reply to Chkheidze's welcome', full of phrases such as 'vanguard of the worldwide proletarian army', 'piratical imperialist war' and 'any day now the whole of European capitalism may crash'. His words were 'a bright, blinding, exotic beacon', to be sure, but also 'a voice from outside...novel, harsh and somewhat deafening...' and 'far from enough. It was not enough to acclaim the worldwide Socialist revolution: we had to understand what practical use to make of this idea...' Lenin left the station in an armoured car, from the top of which, at every traffic light, he harangued the crowd.

---

23 In 1917 Russians were less used to queuing than they later became.

24 Seven months later the building would be a rallying point for anti-Bolshevik forces.

25 This and the following quotations are from Sukhanov (ed., abr. and trs. Joel Carmichel), *The Russian Revolution 1917: A Personal Record*, Princeton, Princeton University Press, 1984, pp. 272-76.

26 It will be remembered that William Booth had arrived at the same station almost exactly eight years previously. The two arrivals were in some odd details rather similar, but Lenin's support base grew far more rapidly than did Booth's.

'Preceded by [a] searchlight and accompanied by the band, flags, workers detachments, army units, and an enormous crowd of private people' he was taken to the Bolshevik headquarters near the Peter and Paul Fortress, the former home of Kshesinskaya, the ballerina, widely supposed to be the former mistress of the deposed Tsar.[27] From the second floor balcony, 'by now hoarse', he made yet another speech. This time his attack on Russian participation provoked one of the accompanying soldiers to shout 'Ought to stick our bayonets in a fellow like that... Must be a German... Eh, he ought to be!'. Many people had little idea what to make of him. Possibly a mere trouble-maker, very possibly a German agent, uttering inflammatory sentiments which had little to do with the revolution for which they had been fighting while he was safely abroad, installed in the palace of a former royal mistress: who was he, and why had he been given so thunderous a welcome?

When he arrived Lenin's power base was exceedingly small and German hopes can only have seemed excessive, but within a year he was able to oblige his sponsors by doing both the things they hoped for.

Meanwhile, Larsson, who does not mention Lenin's arrival in his account of these days, was busy on behalf of the revolution he was himself trying to bring about. On Tuesday morning three new soldiers, including Ilyushenko, were enrolled, and in the evening, a soldiers' meeting (a kind of consciousness-raising exercise at which non-Salvationists will not have been present) moved Larsson deeply. In plain, straightforward, powerful testimonies, he tells us, beaming, happy converts spoke with sincerity, enthusiasm, and assurance of victory.[28]

On the same day as Larsson's converts recounted their experiences, Lenin, with armed escort, went to the Tauride Palace a few miles away, where he delivered his *April Theses* to the Soviet. He demanded a Russian withdrawal from the war, withdrawal of support from the Provisional Government, creation of a republic of soviets, transfer of all land to the peasants' soviets, and the creation of a revolutionary international. Three days later the *Theses* were published in *Pravda*.

---

27 Kshesinskaya (1872-1971) is, according to the *International Encyclopedia of Dance* 'generally recognized as the last great Russian ballerina of the imperial age' (although Nijinsky dismissed her virtuoso dancing as 'vulgar acrobatics'). She liked roles that allowed her to display 'bravura, cheerfulness and refined classical form'. Her house was one of the first to be sacked by the insurgents. Paléologue attributes her unpopularity to the fact that one day during the severe winter of 1916-17 four military lorry loads of sacks of coal had been delivered to her house at a time when the temperature was minus 35 and even Sir George Buchanan, British Ambassador, had been unable to obtain any. Sir George, who saw what was happening, thought it 'a bit thick'. (Paléologue, 13 March, 1917.) See Selma Jeanne Cohen, (Founding Editor), *International Encyclopedia of Dance*, Volume 4, New York and Oxford, Oxford University Press, 1988, and pp. 111, n. 33, above, and pp. 312-13, below.

28 *The War Cry*, 2 June, 1917; Larson, *Tio År I Ryssland*, pp. 94-101. These testimonies are discussed in detail under Trophies: Conversions and Testimonies, pp. 226-31, below.

Like his speech at the Finland Station the *Theses* were widely seen as the utterance of a man completely cut off from the realities of Russia's situation. Some of his enemies confidently supposed that he had destroyed his credibility for ever. Paléologue reports:

This morning Miliukov[29] gleefully remarked to me:

'Lenin was a hopeless failure at the *Soviet* yesterday. He argued the pacifist cause so heatedly, and with such effrontery and lack of tact, that he was compelled to stop and leave the room amidst a storm of booing. He will never survive it.'

I answered him in Russian fashion: 'God grant it!'.

But I very much fear that once again Miliukov will prove the dupe of his own optimism. Lenin's arrival is in fact represented to me as the most dangerous ordeal the Russian revolution could have to face.

Three days later he added:

Lenin's influence seems to have been increasing greatly in the last few days. One point of which there can be no doubt is that he has already gathered round him, or under his orders, all the hot-heads of the revolution; he is now established as a strong leader.[30]

The First Open Air Meeting: Trouble on Vasilevsky Island

The following Sunday 9/22 April, Larsson made his own next move, a more than usually daring application of his motto 'If I don't try, I can't succeed'. It happened almost by accident. He had travelled from Helsingfors to meet Commander George Mitchell, who was to pass through Petrograd on his way back to London from the Far East, but the Commander's train was delayed. With time on his hands which he could not bear to waste, Larsson decided that since the Army had marched twice down Nevsky Prospect, it was time to go one step further and hold a fully-fledged Open Air Meeting with testimonies, Bible readings, exhortations, and, of course, singing. The attempt ended in near riot.[31] The Provisional Government's regulations allowing freedom of assembly were still a month away, and Larsson, operating from Helsingfors, may not have realized quite how volatile the atmosphere had become

---

29 Leader of the Constitutional Democratic Party and Minister of Foreign Affairs in the Provisional Government.

30 Paléologue, *op. cit.*, 14 and 17 April, 1917.

31 Larsson, *Tio År I Ryssland*, pp. 108-10. Like all Salvation Army activities open air meetings are covered by Orders and Regulations. The responsibilities of the officer in charge include the avoidance of obstruction of traffic and annoyance to the public, and cooperation with the police and other authorities.

since the publication of Lenin's *Theses*. Another factor was that Nevsky Prospect on a holiday Sunday afternoon was a freer, more tolerant place than Vasilevsky Island at 6.15 in the evening.

It was then that Larsson gathered his forces—about 30 officers, soldiers and recruits (those who had not yet been sworn in as soldiers)—at Gavan. Led by the flag-bearer and Larsson with his concertina, they marched for about ten minutes up Bolshoi Prospect towards the University, turned into a side street and formed a circle. Within minutes they were surrounded by about 1,000 people. Clara Becker, now a candidate for officership, stood on 'an old stool, broken and patched up with boards nailed on crosswise', embarrassed and disturbed because she 'was a teacher at one of our larger schools, situated just a few streets [away], to translate for [Larsson], give out songs, pray, in short do most of the meeting except for two testimonies'.[32] The songs she read out were English songs that had been translated into Russian by Konoplieva, a Russian woman officer who had trained in Finland in 1915. Becker thought her 'wonderfully gifted'. She certainly seems to have had some talent for improvement. One of the songs Becker read out had a chorus (a jolly little march), which ran:

> If the Cross we boldly bear,
> Then the crown we shall wear,
> When we dwell with Jesus there,
> In the bright for evermore.[33]

Konopliva's version of the last line translates (in Larsson's Swedish version at least) as 'O, what eternal delight', which may well be thought more satisfactory than the original.[34] Becker and one other of the Salvationists led the meeting in prayer and a further song printed in *Vestnik Spaseniya* was sung, followed by testimonies.

Perhaps it was this shift from praying and singing to direct personal expression that provoked trouble. Although most of the crowd was friendly and well-behaved, one man made noisy objections and demanded to be allowed to speak. Larsson, thinking it unwise to permit someone completely unknown to speak in an Army meeting in the open air, announced, somewhat obscurely, that they put not their trust in preachers, but in Christ alone. Another song was sung and a collection (17 roubles) taken, then Larsson preached on the text, 'What a man sows, that shall he also reap'.

The crowd's agitation increased. The man who wanted to speak repeated his demand and, when Larsson (who was beginning to suspect him of being an *agent*

---

32 Clara Becker, *Notes on Russia, Scrapbook*, p. 2.

33 *Salvation Army Songs*, London, Salvationist Publishing and Supplies, 1923, p. 288.

34 Becker notes that Konoplieva 'sang well and was a fearless, energetic Salvationist, a good speaker—but with an absolute lack of discipline', a criticism which may or may not relate to Becker's further comment that Konoplieva 'left in 1919 and is now, so it is believed, a nun'. (Clara Becker, *Scrapbook*, p. 1.)

provocateur of the Orthodox Church) again refused permission, shouted, 'These people belong to the Black Hundreds', (any of the right-wing paramilitary groups which fought in the streets with socialists, liberals and Jews), which suggests that he had not understood much of what the Salvationists had been saying and singing. Whether he was lying or merely confused, his assertion aroused aggressive hostility in the crowd.

This was no time to linger. Larsson ordered his forces to form into ranks and march off. The crowd parted to let them through. Becker thought this procession 'both touching and funny', with Larsson 'leading with big steps and we following after, single file or in pairs, as best we could'.[35] In the crush Larsson could not see what was happening behind him but learnt later that those at the rear of the march had been jostled and threatened all the way back to Gavan. Once there, because there was space for no more than 70 people, only a fraction of those struggling to get in and refusing to believe that space was so limited, could be admitted. The multitude was too excited and indignant to listen to explanations and wanted to see for themselves what this secret organization was up to behind its closed doors, which they attempted to storm. Two young Salvationists, one of them a woman student, 'a sweet spirit' in Larsson's words, stood outside and did what they could to calm the mob.

Thanks to their youthful powers of persuasion, our first open air meeting in Russia ended without any serious consequences. We, meanwhile, remained completely ignorant of what was happening outside and were conducting a meeting for those who had succeeded in getting inside.[36]

The Salvationists decided not to conduct any further open air meetings for the time being. The risks were great, and the Army was not yet sufficiently known to the public for its activities to be understood.

A month later Prince Lvov's Provisional Government issued new regulations concerning meetings and gatherings in the open air. From the Army's point of view the most important points were:

All Russian citizens have the right to hold meetings indoors without any restrictions and open air meetings except in streets with tramlines. All Russian citizens have the right without separate permits to form associations and societies not of a criminal character, and are also permitted to keep up correspondence with similar associations abroad.[37]

This marked the beginning of an encouraging time. During the summer they held meetings in the city's parks without creating disturbance.[38] By June, perhaps earlier, eight page monthly editions of *Vestnik Spaseniya* were again being sold in the

---

35 Becker, *Notes on Russia*, p. 2.
36 Larsson, *Tio År I Ryssland*, pp. 109-10.
37 Larsson, *Tio År I Ryssland*, p. 110.
38 This was to continue into the following year.

streets. The sellers chose a likely spot, sang a song or two and gave an explanation of the paper's contents. Passers-by were still interested and a dozen papers could be sold in a few minutes. During the same period 200 songbooks and 200 copies of The Salvation Army brochure were sold. The print run of *Vestnik Spaseniya* was increased by 250.

The membership was also growing. Converts from the Easter meetings were a various group: workers, students, soldiers, single women, people of all classes, young people and the middle-aged. Backsliders returned to the fold. Members of other denominations encouraged the work. The Salvationists looked forward with hope to the revival, as they saw it, of Christianity in Russia. But Larsson, never satisfied that things were going as well as they should, notes with a certain divine discontent that although the opportunities before them were marvellous and the Russians had a profound yearning for the living word of God, some words of Jesus to his disciples remained apposite: 'The harvest truly is plenteous, but the labourers are few; pray ye therefore the Lord of the harvest, that he will send forth labourers into his harvest.'[39]

Trophies: Conversions and Testimonies

What sorts of people joined The Salvation Army in Russia during this heady period in the summer of 1917? What were they looking for and what did they find? How sustained were their conversions?

Larsson tells us that the testimonies delivered during a meeting on the Tuesday after Easter illustrated 'the seriousness, openness and straight-forwardness which reveal the Russian character—here it is all or nothing'.[40] He sensibly distinguishes between those whose 'conversion' constituted a return to a faith they had lost, and those whose backgrounds were apparently non-religious. These latter he calls 'trophies'.

One of the former group, a student in military uniform, said that ten years previously he had attended a conference of Christian students at which The Salvation Army was discussed. The conclusion had been that it was unsuited to Russian conditions, particularly because of its 'outward form'. Later, by reading 'philosophical books' he had been led 'step by step away from God'. But now his conscience had been troubled by what he heard during the Good Friday meeting, and again on Easter Monday. He had walked home without coming to a decision. There he was visited by 'a brother in Christ'. They prayed together and he made a new and successful attempt to find God. He felt transformed.

A second speaker, wanting, as a Christian, to live a useful life, had studied nursing and 'walked in good paths for some years'. More recently she had begun to visit theatres, the world had exerted increasing influence over her and her faith had cooled, a fact she had kept from her Christian friends. When the invitation for people to go to the penitent form came, she wanted to, but held back for fear of what her

---

39 Matt. 9. 37-38.
40 Larsson, *Tio År I Ryssland*, p. 101.

Christian friends would say. Finally she took her courage in both hands and went forward. This restored her peace of mind.

The third testimony, according to Larsson, showed how a simple middle-aged workman understood the question of salvation. He had knelt at the penitent form three times during the series of Easter meetings. God brought him through, and on the morning of Easter Sunday he had been enrolled in The Salvation Army.[41] His testimony took the form of a letter to his mother and sister, which he read out. It attributed his interest in the Army and his conversion to his reading of *Vestnik Spaseniya*, a copy of which he enclosed, imploring his sister to read it so that she too might be saved and led into the way of truth and learn to love the whole world. He felt that 'Jesus Christ has not forgotten me and that he will be glad to help me in The Salvation Army'.

A soldier on leave gave an account of his life. He had once been condemned to death (we are not told what his offence had been, nor when it took place) but after the intervention of a sympathetic officer the sentence had been commuted to ten years' penal servitude. Now, in Petrograd on leave, he had wandered the streets in deep distress, finding no welcome anywhere. He was rescued from despair by the sight of The Salvation Army's procession in the Nevsky Prospect. At the meetings he had met people who loved him and had found Christ.

The death penalty aside, these are standard stories of spiritual turbulence, and their confessional vein is no more pronounced than anything that might have been heard in London or New York, then or since. The association of reading and the theatre with wordliness is commonplace. What these Russians had to say at Easter 1917 embodies the standard concepts of western evangelicalism. Why should this be? Perhaps Larsson's summaries emphasize this aspect since to an extent he would have heard what he expected to hear and in passing it on would express it in terms that his readership would immediately recognize. Perhaps the speakers had some idea what was expected and sought to provide it—some Russians often tend as a matter of politeness to play whatever role seems to be expected of them in any particular situation. There remains, however, the possibility that these Russians were using such language to express what they actually felt: that, in other words, the conversion experience they claimed was what they were looking for and they thought it was not available within Orthodoxy.

Two of the four were clearly renewing a faith they had already once embraced, and it is possible that the others were in the same category: the middle-aged workman expected his mother and sister to be pleased by his conversion. (The soldier who had been saved from the death penalty may or may not fall into this category.) These support Murdoch's contention that Salvation tended to be sought by people who had been 'raised as evangelicals' but fallen away.[42]

---

41 The process would take longer nowadays, but these were unusual times.
42 Murdoch, *Origins*, p. 87.

The three 'trophies'—those who wanted to escape from what had been totally irreligious lives—form a less predictable group.[43]

Eugene Vladimirovich, 'the man in the flame-red jersey' was the son of a woman who in her youth had been a doctor in Petrograd's largest hospital but had later 'slid into the lowest depths'—Vasja's Village (as already noted) the worst slum in Petrograd. The boy too had become 'a wretched outcast'. Late one spring afternoon he went to a loading ramp on the Neva, where the ice had broken and great bergs from Lake Ladoga were drifting slowly downstream 'like white spectres in the faint light from the street lamps'; he intended to throw himself into the river. But 'some inner power' deterred him and led him instead, clad in a ragged jacket, under which could be glimpsed a brilliant flame-red jersey' to a meeting at Gavan. Later he became a Salvationist and a keen seller of *Vestnik Spaseniya*.

Marusja, a slum child, had been thrown onto the streets at an early age. She earned her living as a bare-footed beggar, singing melancholy folksongs. Later she moved indoors, becoming the city's most celebrated teahouse singer. After performing she would pass the night over bottles of beer and glasses of tea, drowsing the days away on some convenient floor. When her voice had burnt down to little more than a sibilant whisper, the teahouses closed their doors to her. Eventually she found her way to The Salvation Army Corps in a house at 22 Petergovsky Prospect near the Narva Triumphal Arch in the south-western corner of the city. There she learnt to sing a 'love song to our God'. Stocky, enveloped in a white shawl, with a white cloth on her head and a worn Bible under her arm, she had, Adjutant Raino tells us, a 'negligent liveliness of manner', which was 'a kind of request for indulgence of what she had been'.

Trophy number three was by some distance the most remarkable. A short, middle-aged man, a shift worker, he appeared at meetings once every other week, taking a seat by a window. One Sunday evening, as people were leaving, he asked for a few words with the officer in charge.

'I want to know what it is that brings me to these meetings', he began. 'That is your penitent form. It has a special magnetic power for me, but it is after all only for Christianizing, and I, I am a heathen, a Samoyed.'[44] He had on his conscience, he

---

43 Larsson takes his accounts of them (*Tio År I Ryssland*, pp. 102-07) from articles written for the Finnish *The War Cry* by Adjutant Lydia Raino.

44 Samoyeds are Mongolians from the extreme north of Asia, near the Barents and Kara Seas; the name implies 'cannibal' in Russian. In apparently choosing to live beyond the forest line the Samoyeds 'seemed to transgress the outer limits of savagery...'. The Finnish philologist Kai Donner visited them in 1911, dressing as they did, in a coat consisting of two layers of elk fur to keep out the cold (as low as minus 40 degrees Fahrenheit). In the only dwelling resembling a building, 'a half subterranean shack with beam walls and a chimney of clay and branches, 30 people slept packed together on the floor'. It was too cold for anyone ever to undress; 'the place bred vermin and stench'. Russians viewed Samoyed as a blend of savage nobility and sub-human barbarity. See Felipe Fernández-Armesto, *Civilizations*, London, Macmillan, 2000, pp. 38-40.

said, something his people considered a crime, but felt he had no right to bring his guilt to the Army's altar, since the crime would not be recognized as such by the Salvationists. Yet every time he had a free evening that altar drew him irresistibly.

Ten years before one of his people had committed a ghastly crime. The punishment required by Samoyed ancestral law was that his nose and ears be torn off and crushed. Lots were cast to find the person who should carry out this punishment. The lot fell on him, but he could not bring himself to do it. Instead, he fled his father's hut, pursued by his family's curses. He had never returned to the icebound Siberian shore that was the land of his fathers. For years the curse had hung over him. Now he felt that something was available at the Army's penitent form that could make amends for everything. But that form was for Christians and he was a heathen. Was there really a power which could forgive every crime?

The officer spoke of the depths of Jesus's forgiveness for all mankind, heathen as well as Christian. When the would-be penitent prayed with the officer at the penitent form he underwent some sort of powerful cathartic experience. Adjutant Raino describes it thus:

> ...light burst into his soul, scattering the darkness of heathendom. [He] quaked at the touch of the Holy Spirit, and when he opened his mouth, it was with a wonderful power, which I had never known at any time before in our work: his whole being was radiant. When he had risen from his kneeling position, he said: 'I have never before bent the knee to any man and never been beholden to anyone. The Creator is the first, in His presence I will humble myself, and He has atoned for my guilt. Now I can return to my homeland, for He has wiped out the law of my ancestors.

Did he survive his return to the ice-bound Siberian shore or did his people's vengeance strike him down? We do not know.

What can be deduced from these converts and trophies? It is clear that The Salvation Army offered a message and an atmosphere that some Russians welcomed. It must also be said that (although most of these testimonies to religious awakening or re-awakening are much like those which might be heard in other countries) Russians have always had a special passion for self-projection and self-dramatization, for joining in any kind of public debate or confrontation. It was said of the Emperor Nicholas I that 'he postures incessantly, with the result that he is never natural even when he is sincere'. Revolutionaries jeered at others who they claimed would adopt any position that might win applause. De Custine dismissed the whole of Russian civilization as pure play-acting: 'They are much less interested in being civilized than in making us believe them so.'[45] To quote these judgements is not necessarily to suggest that those who spoke at the Army's Easter meetings in 1917 were insincere: the comment on Nicholas I is sufficient warning against that. Russians loved to embrace a position without restraint and to argue and defend it passionately. They had a strong distaste for rational calculation in spiritual matters.[46] Larsson's

---

45 Ronald Hingley, *The Russian Mind*, London, The Bodley Head, 1977, p. 73.
46 Hingley, *The Russian Mind*, p. 108.

remarks about their seriousness, candour and all-or-nothingness may be taken as true, so far they go, but he may not have understood how socially predisposed the Russians were to project those qualities.

Did the 'trophies', those who found release from destructive situations in their own lives, really need The Salvation Army in order to make their escape? The distressed Samoyed might have been able to obtain a similar sense of release by talking to an Orthodox priest and opening himself to the Orthodox liturgy, but as a self-styled 'heathen' and a member of a 'savage' race he would not have been made welcome by most Orthodox. Marusja, the teahouse singer, whom one is inclined to think of (following in the footsteps of the Hallelujah Dutchman) as the Hallelujah Edith Piaf, illustrates another feature which the Army offered and Orthodoxy did not: as a lay person she could participate, using such of her skill as she retained, in what she regarded as the service of God. Similarly, Eugene Vladimirovich, the man in the flame red jersey (his taste in clothes suggests that he was virtually a natural Salvationist), found an outlet for energies that his former life had frustrated. These encounters and conversions may be a little less remarkable than Larsson would have us believe, but they can be listed amongst what Roy Hattersley calls the 'million little miracles' that The Salvation Army has to its credit.[47]

Commissioner Mapp and the Bolshevik Revolution

After spring 1917, Larsson writes, the future was full of hope. An expansion of Salvationist activities was widely anticipated, by the Salvationists themselves and by others who wanted them to take control of existing charitable institutions. For the time being their efforts continued to be concentrated within Petrograd. There they were permitted to hold public meetings[48] that need no longer be surreptitious conventicles of 20 or 30 people but gatherings permitted to attract hundreds or even thousands. Their previously published songbooks soon sold out, and an expanded edition was in preparation. *Vestnik Spaseniya* was printing 20,000 copies each month.

Russian Salvationists continued to enjoy encouraging contacts with the Salvationist world outside. When Rosa Hacklin had to take a second period of sick leave, Staff Captain Richard Sjöblom, who had accompanied the contingent of Scandinavian officers to China, was appointed to Russia. During Whitsun a band from Helsingfors visited Petrograd. After a march along Nevsky Prospect, a morning meeting was held in a concert hall. Then the band travelled several miles to the *Cirque Moderne* in Kameneostrovski Prospect north of the Peter and Paul Fortress, for an afternoon meeting. The day was warm and, given a widespread holiday atmosphere, the trams were crowded, which made it a long, tiring journey for the

---

47 Hattersley, *Blood and Fire: William and Catherine Booth and Their Salvation Army*, London, Little, Brown, 1999, p. 441.

48 As they were to discover, this permission did not necessarily apply in other Russian cities.

band and greatly delayed their arrival. This large venue was nonetheless almost full.[49] A 'believing brother from the fleet' made an inspiring speech and 'many sought salvation'. Larsson noted that 'by the end there was a powerful feeling of brotherliness and the traditional farewell kisses were not lacking'.[50] During the weekend the Army had also staged two meetings in its own hall, a second march along Nevsky Prospect, and a further meeting in the 800 seat Alexander Hall of the Petrograd Duma, as they had done on Easter Monday. Larsson was overjoyed to see so many soldiers on the platform (he does not specify the number) and, all told, there were 40 'petitioners for mercy'.[51]

These meetings, described as 'glorious' by Clara Becker, had difficult consequences for her. Because she had to translate for Larsson, she had to postpone entering the Training Garrison in Helsinki as she had planned. This meant that for a period of some weeks after she had resigned her teaching post at the end of the summer term she had to remain in the home of her disapproving adoptive parents: 'Those weeks spent at home after school was closed were the most difficult ones I had'.[52]

The political, sometimes quasi-religious, excitement in the streets of Petrograd continued during late May and early June and was caught by Harold Williams, a polyglot New Zealander reporting from Russia for the *Daily Chronicle*. He was not enchanted by The Salvation Army. His remarks about the excitement in the streets of Petrograd cast an interesting light on Larsson's account of the enthusiastic meetings he was able to conduct. 'Once stiff, taciturn and rather morose, [Petrograd] has suddenly become loquacious and noisy', Williams wrote, on 8 June:

> The hum of argument never ceases day or night... You cannot buy a hat or a packet of cigarettes without being enticed into a political discussion. The servants and house porters demand advice as to which party they should vote for in the ward elections. Every wall in the town is placarded with notices of meetings, lectures, congresses, and electoral appeals, and announcements, not only in Russian, but in Polish, Lithuanian, Yiddish and Hebrew.

> Meetings are crowded, and who does not speak at meetings now? There are ministers, workmen, returned exiles, soldiers, officers, students, escaped prisoners of war, cripples, sailors, Englishmen, Frenchmen, Serbs, Belgians, Italians, Americans. There is a fierce argument between the parties, violent applause, violent hissing. The battle of the meetings flows over into the unceasing buzz and murmur and perpetual cut and thrust of the streets and the trams and the workshops and the

---

49 In October the *Cirque Moderne* would be packed to the doors for a meeting addressed by Trotsky. Kameneostrovski Prospect was the street where the Army's 'American Home' was situated.

50 These kisses were part of Russian, not Salvationist tradition.

51 Larsson, *Tio År I Ryssland*, p. 111-12.

52 Clara Becker, *Scrapbook: Russia*, p. 2.

barracks. Two men argue at a street corner and are at once surrounded by an excited crowd. Even at concerts now the music is diluted with political speeches...[53]

The Nevsky Prospect has become a kind of *Quartier Latin*. Book hawkers line the pavement and cry sensational pamphlets about Rasputin and Nicholas, and who is Lenin, and how much land will the peasants get. Returned exiles flit through the crowd, recognizable by the Rue Bertholet cut of their clothes and their hair.

Newsboys used to carry papers in a bag. Now there are so many papers and such a demand for them that the hawkers have had to improvize stalls at the street corners, and one may pause there and watch the play of political sympathies and antipathies as the hard-faced young workman buys the [Bolshevik] *Pravda* or the dreamy student buys the [Menshevik] *Den*, or some stout, elderly gentleman buys the [right-wing] *Novoe Vremya* with a melancholy air of resignation.

Then on certain days the streets fill with processions, and the pulse of disputation beats more strongly. Last Sunday crossing from the other side of the Neva I saw near Kshesinskaya's house a meeting of Leninites. Next door The Salvation Army were holding a service. Crossing the bridge was a long church procession with icons and crosses and glittering banners and a sweet, slow chanting of ancient prayers. But in front of the procession the red flag was waving.

On Nevsky the scene changed again. Here was a procession of armed but tame-looking Anarchists with black flag and black coffin, while a troop of laughing Cossacks followed at a distance. Further up near the City Hall a Salvation Army band was crashing out some sickly Western air, and a plain clothes militiaman leaned on his gun and listened.

I have been absent from Petrograd for a time, and listening to the talk in the streets I notice a change. The frank joy of the early state of the revolution has given place to bitter party strife, and growing resentment against the extremists and disturbers of order. The desire for order is becoming a passion with the crowd, and the national instinct, at first baffled and stunned by the vehement outcry of preachers of immediate social revolution, is beginning to reassert itself. I sometimes begin to fear the reaction may be too violent.[54]

---

53 Colonel Knox, Military Attaché at the British Embassy, had noted in April the invention of a new verb, '*mitingovat'*', to attend meetings. A man would ask his friend what he was going to do that evening, and the reply would be: 'I will attend meetings a little' (*ya nemnogo mitinguyu*). (Pitcher, *Witnesses*, p. 72.)

54 Quoted in Pitcher, *Witnesses*, pp. 102-03. According to Phillip Knightley, Williams 'was so personally involved with the anti-Bolshevist forces [his wife, Ariadna Tyrkova, was a member of the Central Committee of the Kadet (Constitutional Democrat) party] that he should never have been given the assignment': see Knightley, *First Casualty*, p. 138. None of the western newspapermen working in revolutionary Russia was notably objective. Robert Wilton of *The Times* sympathized entirely with the upper classes (and is much pilloried on the internet in the early Twenty-First century for

This was equally a tempestuous time for the new Provisional Government, which had been formed on 5/18 May, with Prince Lvov as President and Alexander Kerensky, who in July would succeed him, as Minister of War. The oppositions were extremely active. Meeting on 24-29April/7-12May, the Seventh Bolshevik Party Conference had, despite strong internal opposition, adopted the main points of Lenin's April *Theses*. The Mensheviks and Socialist Revolutionaries held party conferences. At the First All-Russian Congress of Soviets of Workers' and Soldiers' Deputies (3-24 June /16 June-7 July), Lenin, leading a Bolshevik contingent of 105 (out of 822), announced that the Bolsheviks were ready to seize power. On 10/23 June the Ukrainian *Rada* proclaimed the autonomy of the Ukraine. In Galicia General Brusilov was preparing for what proved to be Russia's last major attempt to influence the course of the war. Its failure would give impetus to Lenin's determination to withdraw from hostilities as immediately as possible, and hastened the demise of the Provisional Government of Lvov and Kerensky.

Larsson saw these events from his own perspective. While able to 'make good use of our freedom to bring salvation to the Russian people', he was beginning to feel that freedom had its drawbacks. 'Freedom was a huge gift and certainly not to be misused.' Its effects

> to an extent made our pursuit of our aims more difficult... There were disturbances and even street fights both in the centre of the city and in the outskirts, together with looting of wine cellars, accompanied by shooting. The law-abiding part of the population accordingly stayed at home in the evenings, which had the effect of closing down our meetings.[55]

Meanwhile, in London, General Bramwell Booth decided that with the Army's work in Russia apparently about to expand rapidly, it was no longer sensible to expect Larsson to run Russia as well as Finland, his official command, which was itself in the grip of revolution. It was time to send in someone of recognized international standing. Booth appointed Commissioner Henry W. Mapp as Pioneer Commissioner and Territorial Commander in North Russia, looking forward to the day when a second Salvationist territory could be established further south.[56]

'rabidly anti-Semitic' views). Morgan Philips Price, of the *Guardian,* and the American John Reed clearly supported the revolutionaries. Even Arthur Ransome, representing the Liberal *Daily News*, was thought to be a dangerous Red, partly because he had fallen in love with Trotsky's secretary.

55 Larsson, *Tio År I Ryssland*, p. 112.

56 The English transcription of a television programme produced by The Salvation Army in Sweden in 1992-93, *Frälsningsarmén I Ryssland*, makes it clear (p. 3) that the appointment of Mapp rather than Larsson is still regarded as inexplicable by the latter's compatriots. It concedes, however, that Mapp 'was good at fundraising, and the times were opportune'. However, he 'did the silliest thing you can do with money in a time of revolution and inflation: he put it in the bank'. This was almost certainly not the only silly thing Mapp did while he was in Russia.

Henry Mapp had had to date what the English *War Cry* called 'an interesting career'.[57] Born in India of English parents, he had, as a schoolteacher still in his teens, been converted at a Salvation Army meeting. 'Don't be so enthusiastic,' a dismayed friend had told him, but enthusiasm and energy remained central elements in his make-up, elements that made him a useful friend and a tenacious opponent. As with many male Salvation Army officers of the period, photographs suggest a certain dandyishness in his appearance: thick, dark wavy hair, which gave his head in frontal silhouette the appearance of having sprouted wings, and a prominent moustache. Hair and moustache paled and thinned with age, but his eyes retained an intensity and glitter that made him appear slightly manic.

Still in India, he became an officer after the usual struggle against the idea. His early years of service were marked by 'loneliness, privation, trials and disappointments'. Nonetheless, he saw 'whole villages give up their idols and turn to the Living Christ'. He achieved promotion, married and transferred to International Headquarters, where he was the Assistant Social Secretary for India and Ceylon before returning East in command of Ceylon. His wife's health confined him for a time to less arduous posts in England and Canada. Then he was sent, alone (Mrs Mapp, whose health continued to be poor, remained in Canada) as Territorial Commander to South America (then one large territory, now divided into two) and, later, Japan. His stay in Russia was not expected to be lengthy, merely deferring for the time being an earlier appointment as Trade Secretary at International Headquarters, which would allow him to be reunited with his wife.[58]

Mapp's task in Russia was to inject energy and worldwide experience into what (in conjunction with the recent commencement of operations in China) would have been the greatest expansion of activity in The Salvation Army's history. For the moment the territory was a small one. There were 12 corps (the largest with no more than 60 soldiers, the smallest with 12) and outposts—a term which Mapp said was the best available for small groups, brought into being by people who had been converted by their reading of *Vestnik Spaseniya*, hundreds of copies of which were sent to towns no Army officer or soldier had ever visited. This happened, for instance, in Odessa, on the Black Sea. (Early the following year, the man who organized the outpost in Odessa would write to the Army in Petrograd, saying that he could not continue unless he had further instructions, and a course of training was arranged for him.)[59] Mapp considered the spirit of the officers and soldiers was zealous and courageous, but did not underestimate the various and formidable obstacles he would have to overcome.

Had he succeeded in building, upon these tiny foundations, a firmly established Salvation Army, accepted by the State and the Orthodox Church (although in June 1917 the latter seemed relatively unimportant), it would have been a triumph both for him and the organization he served. He was well qualified for the task. In South

---

57 *The War Cry*, 30 June, 1917.
58 *The War Cry*, 23 June, 1917.
59 *The War Cry*, 16 March, 1918, p. 5.

America, Ceylon and Japan (all countries in which the Army has survived to this day) he had dealt with non-Christian or Catholic authorities and people, useful preparation for coping with atheistic revolutionary Russia as well as with its Orthodox Church. He was not entirely unacquainted with the country, either, having visited St Petersburg in 1907, when he called on Baron Nicolay.[60] He was experienced, as Larsson's disappointed compatriots would grudgingly acknowledge, in the necessary craft of persuading supporters and sponsors to subsidize the Army's work, and his energy and commitment were at least as great as those of anybody else in a notably energetic and committed organization. Nonetheless, his time in Russia proved shorter even than had been expected, and at least one future general of The Salvation Army would hold him largely responsible for the Communists' eventual refusal to allow it to stay.

Mapp's welcome meeting in Petrograd took place on Sunday 25 June/8 July, 1917. The omens seemed auspicious. Twenty officers, some Russian, some Finnish, who more or less knew the language and were familiar with The Salvation Army's spirit and methods, were already at work. Twenty more, from Finland and Sweden, were promised. There were a number of recruits and soldiers. The Army had the use of a hall holding about 150, space for editorial work on *Vestnik Spaseniya*, two social institutions and a slum post. A great many songs and choruses had been translated and printed and were available for visitors to meetings. Much of the detailed work necessary for the establishment of a Salvation Army territory had already been done. The cradle, as Larsson put it, was ready for the newborn child.

Immediately following the welcome meeting, Mapp travelled to Helsingfors to conduct the Finnish Congress (2-6/13-17 July), taking with him a substantial contingent of Russians. When he returned to Petrograd, with Sjöblom in attendance and a Captain von Wahl as his translator (Clara Becker having gone to the Training Garrison in Helsingfors) he asked Adjutant Olsoni to find a flat in the city centre for use as a headquarters: the apartment at Gavan was too small and too remote. She found one, just five minutes' walk from St Isaac's Cathedral: six rooms and a kitchen at 22 Voznesensky Prospect (Ascension Street), a 'good street', Olsoni tells us.[61] Vacant flats were hard to come by in Petrograd and Mapp and Olsoni were inclined to see God's hand in their success—although the current occupant, a lady with an aged husband, forced by his ill health to leave her rather splendid home, may

---

60 Wiggins, *History of the Salvation Army*, vol. 5, p. 75.

61 Olsoni: *Russian Pictures* (typescript of extracts in S.A. Heritage Centre's Russian files). Voznesensky Prospect ran southwards from St Isaac's Cathedral and two of the city's leading hotels: the Astoria (one of Rasputin's haunts) and the Angleterre (at which William Booth had stayed in 1909). The prospect itself had a much seedier aspect. Dostoevsky had had a flat nearby in the period before he was arrested and sentenced to death, and mentions the street frequently in *Crime and Punishment*. Suicides frequently jumped from the bridge over the Griboedev Canal, and in the novel the murderer Raskolnikov, himself contemplating suicide, watches a woman attempt to take her life; she is, however, rescued by a policeman. (See Anna Benn and Rosamund Bartlett, *Literary Russia: A Guide*, London, Papermac, 1997, pp. 306-07.)

have been less inclined to read divine intervention into the circumstances. There was one drawback: it was a condition of the agreement that the furnishings ('a little too luxurious for our needs') must be bought for 5,000 roubles. Mapp decided to go ahead, even though the contract had to be signed the same day, and he did not have 5,000 roubles. He began what turned out to be an impressive demonstration of his powers as a fundraiser. Money promised by International Headquarters had not yet arrived, but he had a telegram of introduction to a Petrograd banker. When he presented this document and explained the situation, the manager let him have the money. The transaction took only ten minutes and even he was amazed at the confidence shown in the Army by people to whom it was little more than a name.

Once he had his headquarters, Mapp looked for halls for the seven corps he intended to establish throughout the city. For the Number One Corps, he hired, for three meetings per week, a large room in a People's Dining Room near the flat at Gavan. Number Two, the most centrally situated, was a temperance hall in Nikolsky Pereulok, which held about 300. Number Three was in another People's Dining Room not far from 'Port Arthur'.[62] Number Four, a disused restaurant near the Narva Gate on the southwestern edge of the city, was to prove one of the most successful: self-supporting, with a strength of almost 100 soldiers. Numbers Five and Six were in the revolutionary industrial district of Vyborg, northeast of the Neva. (Finnish Salvationists living in Vyborg attended Number Six Corps.) Number Seven Corps was on the town side of the Neva opposite the Ochta district, in a boarding house for elderly women that had been put under its supervision. Nearby stood the 'graceful smoke-blue cupolas of the Smolny Convent outlined in dull gold', next to the Smolny Institute, to which the Soviet had transferred while the Tauride Palace was redecorated (having suffered much wear and tear since the revolution). There, in a lofty white ballroom lit by glazed white chandeliers, a 'monstrous dun mass' of soldiers and workmen, 'deep-humming in a blue haze of smoke,'[63] conducted their debates, not yet aware that Russian parliamentary democracy was tottering. From this room, very shortly, Lenin would order the Bolshevik seizure of power.

Mapp calculated that in addition to the money necessary for the hiring of corps premises the Army needed a 'War Fund' of 100,000 roubles. His account of how he obtained it indicates that institutions and companies, well-to-do citizens and others far less well off were alike eager to give money to the Army. The first bank he approached gave 10,000 roubles, which was matched by two large firms. Some Austrian prisoners of war had sent a nurse with 25 roubles they had collected. A woman appeared out of the blue to donate 700 roubles. By the time of the official opening of the North Russian Territory, which took place in September, within two months of his arrival, he had assembled his fund.

---

62 Port Arthur was a very large lodging house for the respectably employed working class. I have tried, and failed, to discover its location. These 'People's Dining Rooms' were almost certainly connected with the temperance centres, known as 'People's Houses' established by the state Guardianship of Public Sobriety. (See above, Chapters 4 and 6.)

63 See John Reed, *Ten Days that Shook the World*, Harmondsworth, Penguin Books, 1974, pp. 54, 55 and 84.

He was confident that if the Army could find the necessary officers it would soon be at work throughout Russia. There were frequent, all expenses paid invitations to conduct meetings all over the country. A children's home, debt free and with a fund of 13,000 roubles, was on offer, as was another on an island in the Neva, with an endowment of 53,000 roubles, and an invalids' home near the Winter Palace, which had considerable reserves of money and firewood. A gentleman had offered 80,000 roubles to the orphanage the Army had already established. An architect, Conradi, had offered control of a seven-storey, 600 room building which housed over 4,000 working class people. The Army would have to take responsibility for a mortgage of 50,000 roubles, but in addition to the income it would generate, it would allow the establishment of a further slum post and corps. 'A great manufacturer' whom Mapp visited, hoping for a donation, did not wait for him to ask. 'I have a large business in Finland, and some of my men there are Salvationists, exerting a good influence over their fellows', he said. 'I know all about your work. I hope that many of my men in Petrograd will become Salvationists, too.' He handed over 'a handsome donation'.[64] Precisely how much of this promised money ever reached the Army's bank account is not clear. Most of what did, however, was to be rendered valueless by circumstances, as we shall see.

Meanwhile, Mapp was anticipating meetings with the Minister of Religious Affairs and Prime Minister Kerensky,[65] but had an odder encounter than either of these would have been when he attended a lecture given by a 'little, kindly old lady with nearly white hair and pink cheeks',[66] called by the Social Revolutionaries the 'grandmother of the revolution', Katerina Breshko-Breshkovskaya. When Mapp introduced himself she welcomed him joyfully. 'Salvation Army!' she exclaimed. 'I'm so very glad The Salvation Army has come to Russia after all!' and she put her arms about Mapp's shoulders and kissed him.[67]

---

64 *The War Cry*, 26 January, 1918, p. 5. It is obvious enough that the 'good influence' the Finnish Salvationist employees exerted on their fellows would have the effect of making them more docile, well-disciplined and honest. It is also relevant that industrialists in tsarist Russia paid very little income tax, which allowed them plenty of scope to subsidize charitable and cultural activities. See Lincoln, *In War's Dark Shadow*, p. 88.

65 Olsoni, *Russian Pictures*, pp. 5-6.

66 Arthur Ransome, in his autobiography, quoted in Pitcher, *Witnesses*, p. 80.

67 *The War Cry*, 26 January, 1918, p. 5. There were elements of Breshko-Breshkovskaya's political past that Mapp must have deplored but also some he would have admired. Born in 1844, she had witnessed the evils of serfdom at first hand. Strong religious convictions led her into legal, educational and social work amongst the peasants (who had been disappointed by the Emancipation of 1861) until, in 1872, such work was declared subversive. She responded by helping to set up a socialist commune in Kiev, and in 1878 became the first woman to be exiled to Siberia. Returning to Russia in 1896 she helped establish the Socialist Revolutionary Party. In 1907 she was exiled to Siberia once more, this time in perpetuity. She returned to Petrograd in triumph in March 1917 to attend the first All-Russian Conference of Workers' and Soldiers' Deputies. By the time she met Mapp in October she 'was afraid that that something terrible was going

Mapp interpreted this encounter as an indication that the Army was appreciated in 'powerful places', but Breshko-Breshkovskaya, once internationally famous, had become a marginal figure in the Russia of 1917. It is diverting nevertheless to think of this disparate pair, the dashing, moustachioed Salvationist and the cherubic, head-scarfed, 'highly cultured and noble' babushka and terrorist, briefly touching cheeks and making common cause during the heady, disastrous month of October. In very different ways they had devoted lifetimes to agitation on behalf of others.

But whereas Mapp anticipated the expansion of The Salvation Army, Breshko-Breskovskaya was pessimistic about the outcome of the revolution. The political situation had become ever more volatile. In July, the economic and social state of the nation had deteriorated. Industrial production declined steeply. Unemployment was aggravated by lockouts, inflation became still more serious, and violence and theft increased across the countryside. Workers, soldiers and sailors from the nearby Kronstadt training base staged violent demonstrations against the Provisional Government. The Bolsheviks, after a pause for calculation, supported their action. Loyalist troops suppressed these demonstrations and the Bolsheviks were denounced as agents of Germany and a number of their leaders were arrested and charged with high treason. Lenin took refuge in Finland for two months, urging immediate armed revolution on his colleagues the while. The Orthodox Church, bent on reform and restoration of the Patriarchate, launched outspoken attacks on the Left. Prince Lvov resigned as President and Kerensky formed a second coalition government. Eventually, the Seventh Bolshevik Party Congress declared that a carefully planned armed insurrection (not the dare-devil sort promoted by Lenin) was the only way to take power, and elected a Central Committee that included Lenin, Kamenev, Zinoviev, Stalin and Trotsky. The offensive in Galicia, which had begun successfully in June, petered out. The Commander in Chief of the Russian forces, Brusilov, was replaced by Kornilov.

Meanwhile, Kerensky's histrionic appeals for loyalty increasingly failed to disguise 'his growing isolation, his weakness of will, his paralytic fear of the Left, and his fatal indecision in taking suitable measures against it'.[68] This last flaw was vividly illustrated by his failure to send Trotsky, recently let out on bail and using

---

to happen'. She supported Kerensky—who had visited her in Siberia in 1912 and whom she adopted as her political heir—and the 'democratic counter-revolution' against the Bolsheviks in 1918. Unsurprisingly, Trotsky denounced her as the godmother of the counter-revolution (Leon Trotsky, *The History of the Russian Revolution*, London, Victor Gollancz, 1934, p. 246), while from an anti-Bolshevik perspective, Got'e described her as '...pretentious... the blind, utter fool...' (Got'e, *Time of Troubles*, p. 422.) See also Harold Shukman (ed.) *The Blackwell Encyclopedia of the Russian Revolution*, Oxford, Blackwell, 1994, p. 311, Geifman, *Thou Shalt Kill*, p. 72, Katerina Breshko-Breskovskaya, *Hidden Springs of the Russian Revolution: Personal Memories of Katerina Breshko-Breshkovskaya*, Stanford, Stanford University Press, 1931, p. 300, and Figes, *A People's Tragedy*, p. 456.

68 Figes, *A People's Tragedy*, p. 456.

his freedom to incite the masses to 'murder and pillage',[69] back to jail. In August Kornilov, following mass desertions, called for a strengthening of army discipline (he had already reinstated the death penalty at the front), and, later, having sent soldiers into Petrograd, allegedly in order to prevent a Bolshevik insurrection, demanded the resignation of the new government. His troops were opposed by workers and soldiers. Kerensky, now confronted by a German advance that had taken Riga and ·was threatening Petrograd, dismissed Kornilov, taking command of the army himself. Precisely what was going on during the Kornilov Affair remains a matter of controversy. That conspiracies were afoot is not in doubt, but who was conspiring with and against whom and to what end remains undecided. In the weeks and years that followed, Kerensky repeatedly denied complicity in Kornilov's revolt: perhaps he protested too much. Whether he and Kornilov were working together or in opposition to each other, neither emerged as a winner from the events of August. Victory went, in October, to the Bolsheviks.

In September, Kerensky arrested Kornilov, proclaimed a republic and, following the resignation of the moderate Kadet ministers,[70] formed a directorate of five who were to govern until a new administration could be formed. Constant tension and sleepless nights were taking their toll and he 'lived with the aid of morphine and cocaine'.[71] Katerina Breshko-Breshkovskaya moved into the Winter Palace to lend him moral support (wags called her his 'Nanny'), but he was a spent force. His energy and his oratory, previously effective weapons, deserted him. He was a tired, sick man, and knew it. His decrees were ignored and the question being asked was no longer whether he could save himself and his country but who would fill the power vacuum that he had allowed to form. Late in the month he announced a third coalition government, but he had by then lost the cooperation of the Bolsheviks as well as the Kadets.

It was during this agitated month, two days after Kerensky proclaimed a republic and arrested Kornilov, that The Salvation Army in Russia staged its official opening.

The meetings marking the inauguration of the new territory were held in the Tenishev[72] auditorium, a large amphitheatre shaped hall at 33 Mokhovaya Ulitsa, on

---

69 The British Ambassador, Sir George Buchanan, wondered how 'any self-respecting government' could allow this: see Pitcher, *Witnesses*, p. 187.

70 The Kadets were by their own definition constitutional democrats, which meant in effect that they were on the right wing of those groups that looked for significant political change in Russia. They regarded the government as a traditional enemy and all revolutionaries as their temporary allies. They professed to adhere to the law; they also, however, accepted terrorism as a legitimate and necessary tool of political change. Although they tended not to practise it themselves, they supported its use by other groups, and could not have survived themselves as a force in pre-revolution politics without the background threat of anarchist and socialist violence. See Geifman, *Thou Shalt Kill*, pp. 207-22.

71 Figes, *A People's Tragedy*, p. 456.

72 Olsoni and others refer to the auditorium as the Tenisheva Concert Hall, which strictly speaking it was not. It was part of the Tenishev Commercial Academy, a 'modern,

3/16 September. The circumstances were so unpredictable that Mapp, as he later told English Salvationists, considered deferring the meetings. Then he reflected that The Salvation Army had always had to fight against adverse circumstances: history was merely repeating itself.[73] He pressed on, taking what comfort he could from a welcome strengthening of his forces. Staff Captain Hacklin and another resting officer had returned. Ten new officers from Finland had arrived. Staff Captain Sjöblom, accompanied by his wife, had been appointed Mapp's ADC.

In the event the opening meeting was a great success. The hall was packed, the reinforcements gave a lift to proceedings, and a band from Finland created an air of festivity. There was, Olsoni tells us, a buzz of anticipation as the Salvationists took their places, the soldiers in the body of the hall with interested members of the public, the officers on stage. At the climax of the meeting, amidst euphoric enthusiasm and optimism, the officers were dedicated beneath the flag and their appointments to the city's seven corps and the social institutions were announced. At a subsequent soldiers' meeting, Mapp directed the soldiers who had attended meetings at Gavan to attend the new corps nearest to their homes, thus ensuring that each new corps began life with a group of existing, experienced soldiers. Every Friday the seven corps united for a meeting led by Mapp in the Tenishev School.

Clara Becker, having finished her training in Helsinki, returned and was appointed Mapp's translator[74] and secretary, and secretary in charge of candidates for officership. For six weeks, she reports, 'things went with a swing'. In one corps, in a working class district, 40 recruits signed up within a month. The difficulty, so enthusiastic and willing to help and serve were they, was to stop them wearing uniform before they had been properly prepared for the responsibilities that change of dress would imply. Staff Captain Boije's father came over from Finland to conduct meetings. Becker accompanied him as translator, and was with him when he carried a sandwich board 'through the most squalid streets in Petrograd'—places she had never seen, although she had lived in the city for 24 years.[75]

---

forward–thinking institution attended by the sons of the liberal intelligentsia....The amphitheatre-shaped auditorium...was often rented out for meetings.' (See Benn and Bartlett, *A Guide to Literary Russia*, pp. 260-61.) The poet and novelist Osip Mandelstamm was a pupil there starting in 1900. A still better known alumnus, who began there in 1911, was the lepidopterist extraordinaire Vladimir Nabokov, author of, among many other novels, *Lolita, Pale Fire* and *Pnin*. Mandelstam, having publicly recited a poem critical of Stalin, was arrested in 1934 and died in the Gulag in 1938. Nabokov, soon after graduating in 1917, went with his family into exile in America and, later, Switzerland.

73 *The War Cry*, 26 January, 1918, p. 1.

74 During the course she had added Finnish and Swedish to her repertoire of languages. Her parents, like those of Nadia Konstantinova-Sundell, had found the idea of the bonnet a particular sticking point, having been told that it looked like a coal scuttle. However, when eventually her mother (who had wanted her to become a socialite and marry well) saw it, she liked it, although she thought it would look better with a little lace frill inside it.

75 Becker, *Scrapbook*, p. 2.

She writes enthusiastically about the new recruits.

Many... became marvellous soldiers, local officers and officers. For instance, there was Seligman, a Jew. He was married with five children. He could cope with any situation! He had the ability to force his way through, wherever it was necessary. When he had to apply for permission to travel by train, which was very difficult, and he was last in the queue, he would make his way right to the front and show his 'S's, which in Russian could also mean 'Soviet'... and people thought he was some high-ranking person and let him pass.

Then we had a man called Tsuber. He came forward in a meeting, and as soon as he got up from the mercy seat, he wanted to give his testimony. He was truly converted and was so reliable that in the marine barracks where he served, he was entrusted with the distribution of bread—possibly the highest sign of trust a person could be shown. It would have been so easy to remove one or two loaves and sell them at a high price, instead of distributing them properly. Tsuber later became corps sergeant major and was later imprisoned with us.

Another turned up in the middle of the night. Next morning he was lying on a mattress on the floor, fully clothed in military uniform. But he had taken his boots off —and his feet were clean! It was so unusual to see clean feet at a time when soap was so scarce that we could not even wash our clothes or ourselves! We were so surprised. When he woke, he wanted to go immediately and be really saved at The Salvation Army. This happened, he was given a recruit's ribbon, and then he continued to his home village, a tiny place in the interior of Russia. He had never seen a two-storey house until he joined the military—he intended to spread the good news of the gospel in his home village.[76]

Thus, in a matter of weeks, under Mapp's energetically autocratic hand, one corps had become seven, and what was—in appearance at least—a large Salvation Army had sprung up throughout St Petersburg, still at this stage Russia's capital. A Swedish Salvationist editor, who visited Petrograd in the late summer, described the fanatical and emotional enthusiasm of a meeting at Number Two Corps:

The meeting had drawn a packed house. People of all classes were there: students, soldiers and civilians, rich and poor, men and women—the hall presenting a lively picture reminiscent of scenes from Gorky and Dostoyevsky. They were all eyes and ears, and nothing in the meeting escaped their attention. Officers and soldiers gave fiery, passionate testimonies, like arrows fired into the heart. When, finally, the Commissioner, his voice like the edge of a sword, preached a powerful sermon, we witnessed a marvellous sight: some 30 people rushed to the penitent form. In floods of tears, people cried out and prayed, kissed the floor and crossed themselves. And after all this—what radiant faces! This was one of the most moving scenes we had ever beheld—a scene which taught us far better than anything we had seen before

---

76 Becker, *Scrapbook.*

how deeply the people in the great land of Russia yearned after true and real salvation.[77]

In the political world outside, events paused while the Bolsheviks, frantic to choose the exact best moment for their insurrection, laid plans and disputed amongst themselves. On 7/20 October Lenin returned from Finland, disguised to the extent of having shaved off his beard and donned a workman's cap. Meanwhile the weather and standards of living deteriorated. As the American radical and war correspondent, John Reed, who arrived in Petrograd at this time, wrote,

> September and October are the worst months of the Russian year—especially the Petrograd year.

> Under dull grey skies, in the shortening days, the rain fell drenching, incessant. The mud underfoot was deep, slippery and clinging, tracked everywhere by heavy boots, and worse than usual because of the complete breakdown of the Municipal administration. Bitter damp winds rushed in from the Gulf of Finland, and the chill fog rolled through the streets. At night, for motives of economy as well fear of Zeppelins, the street lights were few and far between... It was dark from three in the afternoon to ten in the morning. Robberies and house-breaking increased. In apartment houses the men took turns at all-night guard duty, armed with loaded rifles...

> Week by week food became scarcer...Towards the end there was a week without any bread at all... There was milk for about half the babies in the city...

> Of course all the theatres were going every night, including Sundays. Karsavina appeared in a new ballet... Chaliapin was singing... there were weekly exhibitions of paintings. Hordes of the female *intelligentsia* went to hear lectures on Art, Literature and the easy philosophies. It was a particularly active season for Theosophists. And The Salvation Army, admitted to Russia for the first time in history, plastered the walls with announcements of gospel meetings, which amused and astounded Russian audiences...[78]

For the Salvationists, work continued in its established pattern. Reinforcements from Sweden, whose arrival would allow expansion, were awaited. Plans were laid to establish a 'War School' for the training of Russian officers in a splendid house on Vasilevsky Island, placed at The Salvation Army's disposal by Madame Chertkov, who had left for Finland. Madame Chertkov was not, of course, being wholly altruistic. The difference between the houses of rich and poor was very marked in tsarist Russia (Richard Stites remarks that 'The Russian city before the revolution was inequality carved in masonry') and particularly so in St Petersburg. Confiscation of the houses of the wealthy began soon after the February Revolution. In part this

---

77 Captain Marie von Wahl-Hubbenet reported in a letter to the Finnish *The War Cry* in November that this Number Two Corps had registered 200 new converts.

78 Reed, *Ten Days*, pp. 37-38.

was motivated by a genuine wish to house more people in better conditions, in part it was a mixture of doctrinaire egalitarianism and class-driven revenge.[79] Confiscated houses were sometimes occupied by the owners' former servants, sometimes they simply decayed. (This, of course, could happen to houses left empty or nearly empty without having been confiscated.)[80] Madame Chertkov could reasonably calculate that giving her house to the Army would ensure not only that it would continue to be occupied in her absence, but also that its inhabitants would clearly not be members of the privileged classes.

On 25 October/7 November Larsson had 'pressing reasons' for visiting Petrograd. The 'pressing reasons' are not specified, although we may note that Becker, in her *Scrapbook,* says that he obviously longed to be in Russia permanently. Arriving before midday, walking through the long streets from the Finland Station to the Headquarters on Voznesensky Prospect, he was unaware that during the previous night, the Red Guards, along with soldiers and sailors sympathetic to the Bolsheviks, had taken control of the city (apart from the Winter Palace, to which the ministers of the Provisional Government had withdrawn) and Kerensky had fled, in search of reinforcements, while at nine o'clock that morning the Astoria Hotel, just down the street from Salvation Army Headquarters, had been commandeered. Before the end of the morning the banks had closed their doors.

During a discussion that afternoon, he and the other Salvationists were suddenly aware that silence had fallen. Looking down from the windows they saw that barricades had been erected at either end of the street and soldiers lying behind them were apparently ready to shoot although in fact no shots were exchanged. Miss von Weisberg reacted very emotionally, begging the group to go on their knees and pray for Russia, whose fate, she said, would now be decided. Larsson confesses that neither he nor the others were well enough informed to take the situation so seriously, but he added, with the benefit of hindsight, that it was Miss von Weisberg who was proved right. Furthermore (again very much with the benefit of hindsight), it was not only the fate of Russia that was about to be settled but also that of the Army's work there.[81] Miss von Weisberg, however, was not so much better informed as more emotionally involved. It was not immediately clear to anybody other than Bolshevik triumphalists that anything very important had happened.

That night, with ineffectual assistance from the gunners of the Peter and Paul fortress and the cruiser *Aurora*, the Winter Palace was stormed, falling at 2.30 a.m. Thereafter events moved swiftly. During the next day and night a new, Bolshevik, government was proclaimed. Revolution spread to Moscow the following day, and soon thereafter to Baku, Tashkent, Jaroslavl, Tver, Smolensk, Nizhni Novgorod, Kazan, Samara, Saratov, Rostov and Ufa. Kerensky, meanwhile, had returned with his reinforcements, an unimpressive and reluctant band of Cossacks, to attack

---

79 See Richard Stites, *Revolutionary Dreams*, New York and Oxford, Oxford University Press, 1989, pp. 128-30.

80 For a particularly bizarre example of this, see Almedingen, *Tomorrow Will Come*, London, 1961, pp. 133-53.

81 Karl Larsson, *Tio År I Ryssland*, pp. 120-21.

Petrograd. The attack was halted at the Pulkovo Heights and the attacking army was persuaded to go over to the Bolsheviks. Kerensky narrowly escaped capture by dressing up as a female nurse and went underground. Later he fled to the West, where he agitated against the Bolsheviks until his death in 1970.

Although the October revolution would in time be presented by the Bolsheviks (not least in Sergei Eisenstein's masterly but fictional propaganda film, *October*) as a heroic struggle, with a cast of thousands, many of whom met a heroic death, it was in fact a small-scale event. Far less blood was spilt than in February. Theatres and restaurants functioned normally throughout. Even during the bombardment of the Winter Palace by the guns of the Peter and Paul Fortress, the British Ambassador noted that trams were running as usual over the Trinity Bridge, which crossed the Neva between the Embassy and the Fortress.[82] Nor was Larsson, when he arrived next morning, the only person in Petrograd unaware of the momentous happenings of the night before. Even the 'storming of the Winter Palace' was not the spectacular event the phrase makes it seem. Most of its defenders, their morale low and their stomachs empty, had already given up and gone home before the attack, such as it was, began. The building suffered little exterior damage. The shells fired by the *Aurora* were blanks. Of the 30 to 35 live ones fired from the Peter and Paul Fortress across the Neva only two struck the Palace, chipping a cornice and breaking a window. (The remainder fell into the Neva.) This low-key, revisionist account of the 'storming' (few lives lost, little damage to buildings) has been accepted by most recent historians,[83] but some pro-Bolshevik journalists who were eyewitnesses tended to dramatize the occasion. According to Bessie Beatty, correspondent for the *San Francisco Bulletin*, the cobblestones of Palace Square were, a quarter of an hour after the Palace fell, carpeted with broken glass from its smashed windows.[84] This exuberant 'I was there' touch would be characteristic of Beatty's friend John Reed, except that in his case you would expect it to be true. Reed himself does not mention broken glass, only a barricade of firewood and a pile of rifles abandoned by fleeing defenders, while present day historians disappointingly report but one window broken in the entire Winter Palace. The southern side of the Palace, abutting on Palace Square, faces away from the river and the fortress and could not have been hit by shells from that source. Furthermore, Palace Square is 59,964 square metres in area.

The performance of those who masterminded the coup tends nowadays to be seen as a model of comic inefficiency, but in the weeks and months that followed, the Bolshevik leaders became less comic and more brutally effective. Lenin, 'a strange popular leader—a leader purely by virtue of intellect; colourless, humourless, uncompromising and detached, without picturesque idiosyncrasies'—announced to a packed hall of deputies at the Smolny, 'We shall now proceed to construct the

---

82 Quoted in Pitcher, *Witnesses*, p. 200.

83 See, e.g., Figes, *A People's Tragedy*, pp. 484-85, and Pipes, *The Russian Revolution 1899-1918*, p. 494-95.

84 See Pitcher, *Witnesses*, pp. 206-07.

Socialist Order!'.[85] Thereafter, he and his colleagues, by means of manoeuvres and stratagems that lie outside the scope of this book, set about establishing a one-party dictatorship. It was this consequence of the October revolution that was to spell disaster for The Salvation Army.

For the moment, however, Mapp and Larsson had little conception of the consequences this second revolution would have for them. In London, General Bramwell Booth was expecting the work in Russia to expand, and two days later (27 October/9 November) he telegraphed Larsson, giving his detailed thoughts on the situation and asking whether he was willing to accept the appointment of Chief Secretary for North Russia, and hoping that soon the way would open for the Army to work in South Russia. (This suggests that Mapp was not expected to stay long and Larsson would be asked to succeed him, or, alternatively, would be asked to command the hoped-for new territory to the south.) Larsson did not hesitate. 'I placed myself entirely at his disposal. What this might mean for me I did not consider. The spread of God's rule through The Salvation Army's work was what I thought of first.'[86]

On 4/17 November Larsson received another telegram. The General was pleased by his willingness to co-operate. Meanwhile Commissioner Mapp was to visit London immediately to confer with the General and during his absence Larsson was to supervise the work in Petrograd while remaining as leader in Finland.

Larsson, therefore, was once more, as he had been before Mapp's arrival, in charge in two countries simultaneously. In the interim, however, travel had become more difficult and both countries concerned had lurched towards civil war. Even Salvationists, accustomed to the idea of autocratic powers wielded by a single General in London, may think it strange that after less than four months in his post, Mapp should be commanded to undertake what could only be a difficult journey across Europe merely in order to confer with his leader. What conference could they have face to face which could not be entrusted to the lengthy telegrams Bramwell Booth was in the habit of dispatching all over the globe?

It is possible that Mapp was summoned not so much to confer as to be given a stern warning. I take the hint that this may have been so from a letter written on 27 May, 1947, by the then General, Albert Orsborn, to Colonel Robert Sandall, author of the first three volumes of the Army's official history:

This is to thank you for yours of the 22nd, in which you tell me about the trouble caused with Russia by the then Commissioner Mapp expressing his opinions on "Red Russia."

Yes, thank you, I remember the incident quite well, and have all along understood that this was the cause of our being thrown out of Russia. What a pity![87]

---

85 See Reed, *Ten Days,* pp. 128-29.
86 Karl Larsson, *Tio År I Ryssland,* p. 121.
87 Held in the Russia Files at The Salvation Army Heritage Centre.

Could Mapp's remarks have had this effect? In a letter to the present author, dated 2 February, 1998, Karl Larsson's granddaughter, Colonel Miriam Frederiksen, then under-secretary in The Salvation Army's Europe Department, wrote that 'it is likely that Commissioner Mapp's expressed opinions were the reason for him being recalled...' She adds, however, 'I doubt that Commissioner Mapp's comments had anything to do with our eventual closure in 1923. *I believe my grandfather would have hinted as much in his writings, had this been the case.*' (My italics.) This seems entirely probable, although (or possibly, not least because) the utterance, whatever it was, the existence of which is revealed by Orsborn's letter, has, apart from that reference, disappeared from the historical record. It does not appear in Larsson's book, nor in the appropriate volume of the Official History,[88] in the English *The War Cry*, in *All the World*, in the slim file on Mapp kept at The Salvation Army International Heritage Centre, nor (I am assured) in the confidential files relating to the premature termination of his career which are held in the office of the Chief of the Staff at International Headquarters.

There cannot have been any Salvation Army officers who actually approved of the atheism of the Communist regime in Russia, but they were bound by regulation to keep their disapproval to themselves. As it happens, Albert Orsborn, whose letter is quoted above, had direct personal knowledge of how the Army's leaders reacted when officers infringed this rule, and these give us a clue as to what may have happened to Mapp.

In January 1888 the future General's father, Staff-Captain Orsborn, pioneered the Army's work in Norway and in nine months established it successfully. Then, as the Official History puts it, 'the Orsborns left for England'.[89] The volume containing this uninformative statement was published in 1964, yet in 1958 General Orsborn had published his own, far more illuminating account:

My father's love for fighting minorities led him to take sides with the Norwegians in their struggle for political independence. In so doing he committed The Salvation Army to political bias. This was clearly against our rules. We are definitely non-political. We co-operate with Governments, and with law, but we declare no political policy, in any country, nor do our officers ever direct others in their voting... In this ruling our Founder was most wise. Few things aroused his anger more than narrow, partisan feelings when manifested by his people. 'Silence!' I heard him shout to a vast, excited crowd at the Crystal Palace, demonstrating in favour of Japan after their victory in the Russo-Japanese war. 'Silence!' he roared. 'We know no blood and fire, except for the salvation of souls.' He was instantly obeyed. He was determined to keep out of politics and he detested war. It is not surprising that he relieved my father of his command in Norway, and brought him home to take an English division, with headquarters in Sheffield. This

---

88 Frederick Coutts, *The Better Fight*, London, Hodder & Soughton, 1973.
89 Wiggins, *The History of the Salvation Army*, vol.4, p. 42.

was a mortal blow to a sensitive and capable man. He never recovered from it; 17 years later he resigned.[90]

Something of this sort could well have happened to Mapp at the hands of Bramwell Booth. Ten days elapsed between the Bolshevik seizure of power and the second telegram Larsson received from London. This would just about allow time for Mapp's indiscretion and for news of it to reach London (might not Larsson himself have sent a telegram?) and for the General to summon him for consultations. It is possible, of course that Mapp's remarks were made subsequently—while he was in London, or even after he had moved to his next appointment. But if he was reproved—and Bramwell Booth's sense of duty and propriety would have required him to do it—this would go some way towards explaining the hostility towards his General which Mapp increasingly exhibited during the decade following his five month command of the Territory of North Russia.[91]

The following year, General Booth would have had no need to look as far from home as Commissioner Mapp to find a Salvationist officer vigorously attacking Bolshevism in public. His own wife did so, vigorously, in her regular column, International Notes, in *All the World*. In December 1919, following two articles and a number of letters in *The Times* about religious persecution in Russia, she quoted with warm approval a letter, published in *The Times* on 14 November, from an officer serving with the British Army in Russia. The letter had originally been written to his wife, who had sent it on to the newspaper. It is a remarkable letter occupying almost two full columns, which recounts horrific atrocities described in what must have been unusually explicit detail. He urges his wife to

...spend one hour... daily, in doing the Bolshevist *harm*. With your typewriter. In thought, word and deed. I want you to put heart and soul into helping General Denikin [leader of the White forces from October 1918] and his cause. For if ever there was a crusade it is his...[I will send you] such information and photos as I hope will set England blazing with indignation and disgust... And much that is unprintable, but MUST BE KNOWN... And I hope and pray that I shall rouse you, and all our friends, to such a white heat of enthusiasm for this crusade and holy hatred for the Bolshevist that you will do everything in your power to enlighten people at home.[92]

---

90 Albert Orsborn, *The House of My Pilgrimage*, p. 5.

91 After his time in Russia Mapp was, in succession, in charge of the Army's work amongst Allied troops, International Travelling Commissioner, and International Secretary. During this period he became one of General Bramwell Booth's most vocal critics—to a degree which some historians of the Army think was in excess of any evidence which he could cite in support of his attitude—and a leader of the group of Commissioners which, in 1929, sought Bramwell Booth's resignation.

92 *The Times*, 14 November, 1919, pp. 13-14; *All the World*, December 1919, pp. 531-32.

In 1919 Mrs Booth would quote extensively from an appeal sent by 'the women of Russia' to the people of England. This had been forwarded by Colonel Larsson after he had left Russia for the last time, on 18 December, 1918. It spoke well of the work of The Salvation Army and attacked the Soviet's anti-Christian education policies, and 'morals undescribable' in the now mixed schools, the punishments meted out to those who criticized the state, and the distribution of 'the worst poison... something that makes the heart shudder with horror', blasphemous parodies entitled *The Red Gospel* and *The Red Christ*. Exactly who these 'women of Russia were' is not clear, perhaps for understandable reasons. (*All the World's* concluding comment is that 'This appeal bears no signatures, for it can bear but one, which is LEGION'.) In one sense, Mrs Booth would have been in dereliction of duty had she not publicized this appeal and the officer's letter. Nonetheless, it is hard to imagine what Mapp might have said that could have been any more likely to attract the hostile attention of the Russian government to the Salvationists within its borders. Her denunciations make the off the cuff remark of Miss Kangur, which apparently precipitated a wave of arrests in 1921, seem innocuous—yet Miss Kangur's moment of spoken indiscretion and folly is routinely deplored, while Mrs Booth's printed opinions attract no such reproof.[93]

Meanwhile, to return to late 1917, a month elapsed between the receipt of Bramwell Booth's telegram announcing Mapp's departure and the actual event. Larsson tells us that Mapp was unable to leave any sooner. This may simply have been because of the difficulty of obtaining an exit visa from a new and doubtless suspicious government. Some tsarist bureaucrats had been inclined to assume that the Salvationists were English spies; the Bolsheviks were unlikely to be any less wary. At that time, in any case, all bureaucratic procedures required repeated applications over a period of weeks, and extra money, on a rising scale, was often required to change hands.[94] Becker tells us that 'to get the Commissioner's passport we had to go right to the Bolsheviks, and the Commissioner was aghast at the women we saw there. But, of course, that was nothing to what we saw later on'.[95]

Events in Petrograd were increasingly tinged with garish melodrama. The last large meeting Mapp conducted before his departure was bizarrely sensational. It was one of the Friday night gatherings in the Tenishev School amphitheatre, at which soldiers from all seven corps met together. Mapp was speaking when

there entered, by a door near the platform, a gloomy-looking individual who stalked across the open space before the penitent form, passing thence up the central aisle

---

93 See pp. 281 and 283 below.

94 E.M. Almedingen, *Tomorrow Will Come*, p. 97. Foreign travel documents were traditionally an object of suspicion and obstruction in Russia: see, for example, Oliphant, *The Russian Shores of the Black Sea*, pp. 266-67.

95 Clara Becker, *Scrapbook: Russia*, p. 3. Perhaps one of the women who caused Mapp's perturbation was the pioneer feminist and advocate of free love, Aleksandra Kollontai, who was an excellent linguist and might well have lectured him and Becker on such matters had they chanced to meet.

right to the top-most row of the tiered gallery. Then, facing the platform, he drew something from his coat and began to take aim at the Commissioner. Everybody waited for the sharp crack of a rifle, but none came, and the Commissioner went on talking.

Again and again the menacing figure of the lunatic, for this he was found to be, assumed the war-like attitude, but nothing else happened, and, to show how the Spirit of God triumphs over distracting circumstances, we have but to add that 30 people knelt at the mercy-seat...[96]

On December 16th, the atmosphere in Petrograd had become so disturbed that when, having taken Mapp's luggage to the station ready for his departure next morning, Becker and Captain and Mrs Sjöblom joined him for a last public meeting, only the four of them were present. They returned to the flat for tea and home-made pies filled with porridge ('something very extraordinary in those days of scarcity', Becker tells us). Next morning they made their way to the station through unlighted streets, with shots being fired on all sides. Despite this, a number of Salvationists had gathered at the station to bid Mapp farewell.

Mapp left Russia apparently expecting to return, and full of optimism that The Salvation Army, with its bright meetings, was bound in the long run to appeal to the workers in the cities and towns. It could claim, he told an interviewer, at least one miracle of physical, as well as many of spiritual healing: a woman who had been unable to speak above a whisper for three years, all manner of treatments having failed, succeeded, at her fourth attempt on consecutive days following her conversion, in addressing an Army meeting in a strong, clear voice. There was nothing else like the Army in Russia. One day, he was perfectly assured, the painter Vereshchagin, who years before had told W.T. Stead that the Army's style of service would exactly suit the Russian peasant, would be recognized as a prophet.[97]

Mapp's departure on 5/18 December coincided with German raids on British Scandinavian convoys, which inflicted serious losses and forced Admiral Beatty to use a squadron of battleships as cover.[98] Consequently Mapp's journey to London was delayed by two weeks, which he spent stranded in Bergen. The raids continued into 1918 and by the time he was ready to return to Russia the sea route to Finland was closed.

Larsson received another telegram from London (he gives no date):

Commissioner Mapp's return will remain impossible for some time. The General decrees that you are to become Chief Secretary for Northern Russia. When the Commissioner leaves you will continue as Chief Secretary in charge. I will name

---

96 *The War Cry*, 26 January, 1918, p. 5.

97 *The War Cry*, 26 January, 1918, p. 1, and *All the World*, 1918, p. 108.

98 R. Earnest Dupuy and Trevor N. Dupuy, *The Collins Encyclopedia of Military History from 3500 B.C. to the Present*, Fourth Edition, London, HarperCollins, 1993, p. 1068. See also George C., Schoolfield, *Helsinki of the Czars: Finland's Capital 1808-1918*, Columbia, Columbia University Press, 1996, pp. 251-64.

your successor in Finland as soon as possible. So farewell from Finland
immediately. I assure you of our high estimation for the work you have done. We
will arrange a war council in Finland, promote Boije to Staff Captain and instruct
her to take charge of the Training College. Staff Captain and Mrs Sjöblom will
return to Finland.

Uproar in Helsingfors

Larsson, however, informed the General that he could not leave Finland immediately.
The political situation in Helsingfors had deteriorated, making it impossible for him
to go. He does not say what made it impossible but it was not because he was not
permitted to travel, since he visited Petrograd from Finland several times during the
time when he remained there (and one of those journeys took him much further
afield). He appears, indeed, to have decided that his primary duty was to remain in
Finland to hold The Salvation Army there together. If so we can only conclude that
on this occasion the unquestioningly obedient Larsson actually avoided obeying a
direct order.

Certainly the situation in Finland was becoming daily more chaotic. In February
1917 many Finns had seen the upheaval in Petrograd as an opportunity for them to
overthrow Russian rule. Hundreds of Russian officers were killed in Helsingfors, on
warships in the harbour, on the streets, and in the barracks. The government, having
rid itself of the nonentities appointed by Nicholas, pursued a pro-German policy that
led inevitably to a rupture with the western European Allies. Marauding bands of
soldiers roamed the countryside. Unemployment increased, inflation took hold and
strikes in agricultural areas caused food shortages. In July the Finnish parliament
declared the country's partial independence from Russia (it was immediately declared
'dissolved' by the Provisional Government in Petrograd), proceeding to full
autonomy on 24 November/7 December.

At that stage Lenin, desperate for peace, let it appear that he recognized Finland's
independence, but late in January 1918, when the threat of a White counter-
revolution loomed in Russia, he had the Russian army and navy assist the Finnish
Communists in taking control of Helsinki and much of the southern part of the
country.[99] They dissolved the Finnish Senate and Diet and set out to transform the
country into a Soviet republic. Food became yet scarcer and more expensive. A full-
blooded civil war raged until the Germans, fearing the arrival of western
reinforcements for the anti-Bolsheviks (which would have created in effect a new
Allied Eastern front) sent in troops who captured Helsingfors on 12 April and
Vyborg at the end of the month. Despite this, however, upheaval within the country,

---

99 As it happened, the White Russians, driven by an unrealistic desire to restore the
former Russian Empire, refused to accept the Finns' already proclaimed independence,
scuppering what might have been an important alliance.

bound up as it was with events in Russia and the rival ambitions of the Germans and the Western Allies, continued.[100]

During the two months when the Communists held the south, an estimated 6,000 Finns, including some of the influential friends and helpers of The Salvation Army, were killed, often very cruelly. A Lutheran priest was crucified in his own church under a blasphemous inscription. Larsson, as he describes it, was 'kept as in a sack'. He lost contact with Salvationists in the north of Finland as well as with those in Petrograd. There were no newspapers and no post, and telegraph and telephone services also closed down for a time. Male Salvation Army officers had to go into hiding to avoid being conscripted into the Red Guards. Public gatherings and travel were both restricted. The Salvationists pursued throughout their policy of helping those in need regardless of the political situation. Larsson, in the Finnish *The War Cry*, castigated both sides for cruelty and foolhardiness.[101] Salvationists assisted with medical services and distribution of food and were allowed by the Reds to visit White prisoners. Correspondingly, when the Whites regained control, they were permitted to visit Red prisoners held in concentration camps and Fort Sveaborg. Many of these latter were political prisoners under sentence of death, and one of the Salvationists, Joakim Myklebust, later described an intensely emotional meeting conducted for these condemned men when he preached on the text, 'Behold the lamb of God which taketh away the sin of the world', and the singing of the song,

> Shall we gather at the river
> Where bright angel feet have trod...

The prisoners' heartfelt thanks reduced the visitors to tears.[102]

Larsson Travels South

In the depths of this grim period, in a manner almost humorously characteristic of his extreme devotion to duty, Larsson decided, in February 1918, to undertake a long, difficult, uncomfortable and possibly dangerous journey from Helsingfors to the village of Domnino, 15 kilometres from Orel, itself some 350 kilometres south of Moscow.[103] Larsson had been intending for some time to revisit middle and

---

100 See Pipes, *Russia Under the Bolshevik Regime*, London, Harvill, 1994, pp. 92-93, D.G. Kirby, *Finland in the Twentieth Century*, London, Hurst, 1979, pp. 40-63, Shukman, *The Blackwell Encyclopedia of the Russian Revolution*, pp. 228-30, and Schoolfield, *Helsinki of the Czars*, pp. 251-64.

101 Transcription of video *Fräslsningsarmén I Ryssland*, p. 4.

102 Larsson, in *All the World*, 1918, pp. 511-14 and Emerik Olsoni, in *The Officers' Review*, 1938, pp. 539-44.

103 Orel, a fortress town (the name means 'eagle'), was the birthplace of Ivan Turgenev, who used it frequently as a setting for his novels, most particularly as 'the town of O' in *A Nest of Gentlefolk*. It was also the boyhood home of Nikolay Leskov, who wrote so searchingly about Lord Radstock (see Chapter 2, above). In Stalin's time it

southern Russia, and had drawn up a provisional itinerary: Moscow, Orel, Kiev, Yekaterinoslav, Odessa and Nikolayev, but the troubles in Finland and, once the Russian Civil War got under way, in the Ukraine, forced him to trim it severely.

He was anxious to visit Orel because, late in 1917, the earlier established of the two Petrograd children's homes—the one set in a garden in industrial Lesnoy, on the Vyborg side beyond the Finland Station—had (because of the shortage of food in Petrograd) been moved to Domnino, a village near Orel. The matron, Captain Granström, and the other officers had had no contact with colleagues for four months.[104] As well as bringing encouragement to his juniors, Larsson wished to assess whether the chances of extending the Army's work into southern Russia had improved since he had travelled, in less extreme but nevertheless difficult conditions, to Moscow and Tolstoye at Easter 1915.

The move to Domnino had come about when a Miss Ascherkov offered the Salvationists the use of a manager's house attached to disused oil wells (formerly worked by the Nobel family) in the village. The relocation, which required 34 people, mainly children, to undertake a 67 hour journey, accompanied by their furniture and effects, had been the chapter of accidents customary for all Russian travellers at that time. Two carriages were commandeered, one for people, one for furnishings and baggage. When they arrived at Orel, it was discovered that the second had gone astray. Seligman, the resourceful young Jewish trainee officer who was in charge of the move, talked his way onto the locomotive of a train making the return journey and examined carriages standing in the sidings at every station until he found it, then persuaded another driver to attach it to a train bound for Orel. Local Russians thought him a miracle worker.

Larsson left Helsingfors for Petrograd on 11 February.[105] He spent the 12th at a desk then met Captain Konstantinova and a 12-year-old girl, also bound for the home, at the Moscow station.[106] Two thousand would-be passengers, most of them soldiers laden with sacks and bags, were crammed onto the platforms, storming the

---

was the site of a 'Special Psychiatric Hospital', to which, among others, many political dissidents were sent. See Benn and Bartlett, *A Guide to Literary Russia*, pp. 362-74, and Archie Brown, Michael Kaser, and Gerald S. Smith (Eds.), *The Cambridge Encyclopedia of Russia and the Soviet Union*, Cambridge, Cambridge University Press, 1994, p. 377.

104 In the summer of 1918, the other Children's Home, the 'American' one near the Peter and Paul Fortress, would likewise find refuge in Vologda, 400 kilometres north-east of Moscow. These removals solved the food and fuel shortages that had severely affected both homes, but other difficulties, unsurprisingly, arose all too soon. At about this time America and some other nations, anxious to show how low they ranked Bolshevik pretentions to legitimacy, moved their embassies to Vologda—which had the advantage, it has to be said, of two possible escape routes to the sea, at Archangel, north of the Arctic Circle, and Vladivostok far to the east. (See W. Bruce Lincoln, *Red Victory*, London, Sphere Books, 1991, pp. 182-83.)

105 The Russian calendar had been switched to new style 11 days earlier.

106 Larsson wrote two differing accounts of this journey, in Through Russia in War-Time, in *All the World*, 1918, pp. 467-70, and *Tio År I Ryssland*, pp. 123-28. I collate the two.

carriages whenever a train arrived, fighting like madmen for seats and shouting themselves hoarse. Most of the carriage windows so far unbroken were smashed in the struggle to board the train. Larsson and his companions were in some danger: with the war coming to an end in near-total confusion, soldiers who, legitimately or otherwise, had fled the front line, were a menace everywhere in European Russia. The situation was especially bad in Petrograd. Taking into account the resident garrison, along with others who had deserted in order to 'support the revolution', more than 100,000 uniformed men were roaming the streets, armed and out of control. At gunpoint they demanded money, food, and possessions, punishing resistance with death. [107]

Larsson's and Konstantinova's own uniforms perhaps provided some degree of protection. Konstantinova and the girl had seats in a carriage without intact window panes, light or heat; Larsson perched, constantly dislodged, on a sack in the corridor.

In Moscow he discovered that he could not conduct the meeting he had planned because the disorders had been used as an excuse to raise hall rentals to prohibitive levels. He and Konstantinova went to the station to catch an evening train to Orel, losing and recovering the girl in doing so. Five hours in a queue achieved nothing. They watched trains arrive and depart, with passengers who could not force their way inside clinging to the roofs of the carriages, perching on the couplings, the tender or the locomotive. A bitterly cold but less crowded midnight train took them to Tula, halfway to Orel, where they caught up with a train they had seen leave Moscow the evening before. Their onward journey to Orel was the worst, Larsson tells us, he ever endured. The corridors were choked with wildly debating passengers. The Salvationists' densely packed compartment was unventilated (the window, miraculously unbroken, was jammed shut). When sweating passengers succeeded in opening it, frozen travellers clinging to the roof tried to slide in through it and had continually to be repulsed.[108] The train arrived at Orel during the small hours and passengers had to fight their way off against an inrush of hundreds of soldiers. Then they were imprisoned in the station by a night-time curfew, drowsing on any available horizontal surface, disturbed at intervals by armed patrols carrying out random passport checks or body searches. Frequent verbal confrontations threatened to erupt into fisticuffs or gunfire. But eventually, after a third night without sleep, daylight released them and they arranged for a horse-drawn sledge to take them to Domnino.

Their visit achieved its aim: Captain Granström and the officers were encouraged. So was Larsson. The women had won the confidence of local people and the home

---

107 See Lincoln, *Red Victory*, p. 54.

108 Bad as Larsson's experience was, later Salvationist visitors to Orel suffered worse; the fate of those riding outside the train. Staff Captain Boije was obliged, at each station on one of her journeys, to clamber onto a carriage roof as the train was moving off. She and others in her situation were driven down on arrival at the next stop; then the whole process started over again. Another woman Salvationist was forced to stand throughout a 24 hour journey.

was generally admired. A priest had said that 'a breath of the great world's civilization has reached our backwater'.

Nevertheless, all that remains is to describe the institution's melancholy end:

> The history of this home for the following three years is a history of a handful of Finnish women fighting a heroic battle against superstition, sickness, [official] ill will and death until the day they could return [to Finland], unfortunately having to leave both children and inventory [furniture and effects] in hands far less capable of doing the work.[109]

The civilization they had brought with them was no longer required.

Cut Off

Their return journey was a further catalogue of delay, crush, cigarette smoke, alcohol fumes, body odour and non-stop political oratory. Larsson hoped to stop off at Yasnaya Polyana, in response to an invitation to visit the Tolstoy estate, but they arrived there well after midnight and he abandoned the plan. In Moscow Mr Anderson, Secretary of the American YMCA, discussed with him the Army's chances of success in that city. Anderson reported that he met new difficulties and obstructions daily. After further delays (caused by fears of the approaching German Army and Konstatinova having mislaid her identity papers) Larsson arrived back in Helsinki. Soon after his return the border between Finland and Russia was closed, and for three months he had no contact with the Salvationists in Russia.

---

109 The quotation is from an eight-page typescript, by either Larsson or Olsoni, held at The Salvation Army Heritage Centre.

CHAPTER 9

Disease, Death, Terror, Endurance

Socialism, Civil War and a Poet's Despair

During the three months when Larsson was unable to visit The Salvation Army in Petrograd and other forms of communication were equally impossible, the officers there were cut off from the world outside. The Sjöbloms had stayed on in Petrograd as leaders but they were only the most senior of a group of relatively junior officers, none of whom felt competent to take important decisions, at least until circumstances forced them to. When Larsson was finally able to visit Petrograd in May 1918, what he saw indicated that The Salvation Army had lost most of what it had gained during 1917. It was financially much less well off and the new regime was actively hostile to religious organizations, particularly foreign ones.

Revolution and counter-revolution had spread over a vast area outside the Russian capital, and for the next three years Bolshevik attempts to implement Lenin's triumphalist pledge, 'We shall now proceed to construct the Socialist order', took place against a background of bitter civil war. Meanwhile, at Brest-Litovsk at the end of January, Trotsky declared that Russia was no longer at war with the Central Powers—who, however refused to accept his conditions. A further offensive against Russia was mounted in mid-February before the peace treaty was finally signed on 3 March.

Many Russians, particularly metropolitan intellectuals, were still trying to convince themselves that the Revolution had been for the best. Disillusionment, however, was looming. In January 1918, Alexander Blok, the outstanding literary figure of the Russian symbolist movement, wrote what is by common consent his greatest work, *The Twelve*. This vividly descriptive poem blends sacred and profane in capturing the mood of St Petersburg following the October Revolution, which it both celebrates and mourns on its way towards an ambiguously religious conclusion.

In darkness and snow 'you cannot stand upright for the wind: the wind scouring God's world'.[1] An 'old weeping woman is worried to death' about a banner proclaiming Power to the Constituent Assembly. Such a length of cloth could have made leggings for so many children without clothes. A long-haired scribbler whispers that Russia has been sold down the river. A cleric is taunted. A lady in a fur 'slips up—Smack!—on her beam end'. The wind rejoices. Twelve Red Guards

---

1 I quote the translation by Jon Stallworthy and Peter France given in Albert C. Todd and Max Hayward, (with Daniel Weissbort) (eds.), selected with an Introduction by Yegeny Yevtushenko, *Twentieth Century Russian Poetry*, London, Fourth Estate, 1993, pp. 71-81.

march through the streets, having 'a crack at Holy Russia' and shouting 'Down with the cross!' A whore is murdered; violence becomes endemic.

> The bourgeois with a hangdog air
> Stands speechless, like a question mark,
> And the old world behind him there
> Stands with its tail down in the dark.

The weather worsens and, keeping 'a Revolutionary Step',

> Abusing God's name as they go,
> All twelve march onward into snow...

> And wrapped in wild snow at their head
> Carrying the flag blood-red—
> Soft-footed in the blizzard's swirl,
> Invulnerable where bullets sliced—
> Crowned with a crown of snowflake pearl,
> In a wreath of white rose,
> Ahead of them Christ Jesus goes.

This attempt to see Red Guards as unwitting disciples of Christ and the bloodletting of the Revolution as 'a necessary sacrificial offering to redeem the sins of Russia's past [from which] Russia would arise... its horrors purified'[2] drew criticism from both right and left: the former because he found any good at all in the revolution which had overtaken Russia; the latter because he hearkened back to the supposedly discredited leavings of the ecclesiastical past in order to interpret it. He lived long enough to realize that the cleansing and revival he had hoped for would not happen, and died in July 1921, hoping that art would somehow survive but despairing in that he was being prevented from contributing to it by 'bureaucrats who plan to direct poetry through their own channels, violating its secret freedom...'. His fatal illness has never been identified, but according to one who observed him in the last months of his life, he died 'because he wanted to die'.[3]

Salvationists Garrison a Palace

In this unstable situation The Salvation Army's need to be visibly staffed and run by Russians was greater than ever. Before his departure for London Commissioner Mapp had talked of opening a Training Garrison for Russian Salvationist officers (to be called a Military Academy) and, despite his absence, political upheaval and

---

2 Victor Terras, *A History of Russian Literature*, p. 431.
3 Blok's speech in honour of Pushkin (February 1921), and E. Gollerbakh's comments on Blok's death are quoted in Todd and Hayward, *Twentieth Century Russian Poetry*, p. 45.

increasingly inauspicious omens, and a sense that for the moment the Army was not so much marching as marking time, the plan was not allowed to die—indeed almost took on a life of its own. There was obviously a need for the Army to train Russian officers. Although some of the existing officers had been born or brought up there and knew Russian, the majority were foreigners, inexpert in the country's language and customs. In any case, candidates (volunteers for officership) needed to be instructed in Salvationist beliefs and practice: there was a limit to how much could be learnt on the job, and some danger in relying totally on improvization.

These dangers were perhaps illustrated when one of the most promising of the seven corps opened by Mapp in September closed within a few months. The commanding officer, Ensign Rytkönen, had worked hard and effectively, despite the absence of a lieutenant to assist her and a large working-class church across the street which generated considerable opposition. After a couple of months there were about 40 soldiers and the corps appeared to be thriving. Abruptly, Ensign Rytkönen was baptized into the Orthodox Church, married one of the soldiers at the corps—a young man of less than 20, until then a candidate for officership—and vanished. She was replaced immediately but permission to use the hall was withdrawn and the corps disintegrated. Later references suggest that the disintegration may have been temporary.

Where the Training Garrison was concerned, political and social upheaval smoothed the Salvationists' path. As has been mentioned, the Radstockite Madame Chertkov fled to Finland, placing all but the second floor of her splendid four-storey Petrograd mansion at the Army's disposal until she should return. This elegant house at the aristocratic end of Bolshoi Prospect on Vasilevsky Island, with its spacious hall, broad staircase decorated with busts, urns and mirrors, secluded courtyard and garden and necessary outbuildings such as laundry and woodshed, was socially and architecturally a world away from the apartment at Gavan, at the other end of the street.[4]

The first people to benefit were the officers from Sweden, who lived in the house while learning the language, with Staff Captain Hacklin, former manager of the 'American' children's home, as Matron. However, a married couple with a small daughter left after a few weeks because of the poor food. (Becker observes sharply that 'they had better food by far than we had at H.Q.') Candidates from the various Petrograd corps were told that the building would open as a Training Garrison in March. Meanwhile they would have to be patient and prepare themselves as best they could.

It was decided that the Chertkov residence should house not only the Training Garrison but also Number Seven Corps, whose accommodation on the banks of the Neva near the Smolny Institute and the Tauride Palace was for some reason no longer available. (This may have been a revival of the corps that disintegrated after

---

4 Much of what we know about the Chertkov mansion and the Salvationists' use of it is derived from Olsoni's memoir *Russian Pictures*, which Larsson quotes extensively. Olsoni, as it happens, had a very soft spot for 'dear old Gavan'.

the defection of Ensign Rytkönen to Orthodoxy.) The corps officers were Elsa Olsoni and one of the cadets, who 'felt like drops in the ocean' in this large, fine house. When they held their first meetings in the elegant, parquet-floored salon they felt relieved that the gold coronets, pictures and the furniture were shrouded in white tulle. They placed salon chairs in rows and improvized a platform, but they and their congregations felt uneasy; the first meetings there must have been stiff and inhibited. It was one thing for General William Booth to address a royal, aristocratic and bourgeois drawing-room meeting at the home of General Saburov in 1909, in the unimaginably distant days before the revolution, another for junior officers to evangelize the humble, poor and outcast in a room where ghosts of the departed upper classes lurked among shrouded busts and portraits. But once people began to feel at home in these palatially spooky surroundings, there were 'many blessed meetings' at which 'souls sought salvation'.

Meanwhile, the Training Garrison began its work rather sooner than expected when a cadet arrived unannounced from the provinces. Despite having been requested to await instructions, more soon followed. As so often in Salvation Army history, leaders had to move swiftly in order to keep pace with the keenness of the led. Housekeeping was the most obvious difficulty and it was a considerable triumph when Staff Captain Hacklin obtained some ten-pound packs of horsemeat. A barrel of pickled cabbage was found elsewhere, and together these formed the staple food of the cadets in the 'Preparatory Training Garrison'.

The city in which this institution began its short life was enduring worse conditions than any in its 200 year history. Shortages of food, fuel, goods and services threatened to overwhelm it; sufferings occasioned by economic collapse and bitter winter storms were intensified by social uncertainty. In a topsy-turvy world, former 'haves' lived on the streets as beggars and prostitutes whilst ex-'have-nots' colonized their houses and palaces as slum-relief housing or social clubs, for good measure running riot in their wine cellars. The Government did its bit to disrupt the old order, abolishing church marriage, making divorce available on demand and confiscating, without feeling the need to explain why, precious metals, jewellery, money, factories and private houses. As blizzards produced mountains of snow, fuel supplies failed and the lights went out. Drunkenness, theft and murder became commonplace.[5]

In May, the border reopened and the long-awaited reappearance of Larsson took place. His mere arrival apparently blew away their feelings of uncertainty and isolation, reviving their joyous belief that they enjoyed God's guidance and protection.

'Now how are things with the Training Garrison?' was one of his first questions. When he heard that there were 18 candidates eager to become cadets in training, he decided that further preparation was unnecessary. The College must open immediately. The six cadets already informally in training, men and women of varying nationalities and professional backgrounds, helped set everything in order.

---

5 See Lincoln, *Red Victory*, pp. 52-56.

Within a few days the Colonel arranged a commissioning meeting at which the Swedish officers were told where they would be working and the Training Garrison staff was announced. Staff Captain Per Åstrom, who had earlier been on the staff of the Swedish Training Garrison, was to be principal, assisted by officers from Sweden, Finland and Russia. The College opened on 21 May, for a session that was to last four months.

As it happened, this was the only group of cadets The Salvation Army in Russia was able to train. Most were Russian and what happened to them after The Salvation Army was driven out in 1923 is not known. One of them, however, Rakel Holm, was Finnish. She spent her life as a Salvation Army officer and described the events and atmosphere of the time many years later.

She had arrived in Petrograd in the autumn of 1917 with the party of Finnish officers. During the following eight months she worked alongside Elsa Olsoni (the woman, she reminds us, who was the first and also the last Salvationist officer in Russia during the years 1913-23), an experience that prompted her to become one of the 18 cadets offering themselves for full training.

She thought her fellows fascinating and unusual. Two medical students from the remote interior had found a copy of *Vestnik Spaseniya*, which had made them eager to 'belong to this Army'. There were two trained nurses, a teacher and an office worker. The group bonded well and adjusted readily to Salvationist methods. They had no textbooks (apart from the Bible), making do with notes taken during lessons and lectures. She had kept her carefully hand-written Bible lessons, and enjoyed looking occasionally at the Russian text.

She remembered without sentimental affection the sour, rancid cabbage soup, served without bread, morning, noon and night and the relief when headquarters, after great efforts, procured potatoes and rye flour. The first morning they found real potatoes on their plates, 'Grace became a resounding song of praise!' In those days potatoes were not peeled in Russia. We ate, as was said in Russian, 'kartoshski mondeerie—potatoes in uniform'.[6]

The cadets attending the Training Garrison did domestic chores as well as attending classes. They conducted open air meetings, attracting 'hundreds of people', in the Summer and Tauride Gardens across the Neva. Large crowds followed their processions to the indoor meetings, and 'many souls sought God'. They also conducted indoor meetings at the other six corps in the city and, such was their exuberance, held impromptu open air meetings on their way there as a trailer for the indoor meeting they were about to conduct. Home and hospital visits were also integral to their work.

Seligman Faces a Firing Squad

Once again it was bliss in that dawn to be alive—but they were not left wondering for long what consequences the Bolshevik seizure of power would have for them.

---

6 Transcription of Swedish video *Frälsninsarmén I Ryssland*, p. 6.

Once more, as under Nicholas II, The Salvation Army became the object of
unfriendly official interest. An incident involving Otto Ljungholm and the cadets
illustrates the uncertainties and risks of the period and—as Larsson glossed his
account—'the spirit of adventure and self-sacrifice by which these people lived'.[7]
Ljungholm's own comment was: 'Uncertainty was our watchword'. The group was
conducting an open air meeting when it was surrounded by a crowd of armed soldiers,
who forbade them to continue and insisted that a representative Salvationist should
go with them to the Commissar's office. Cadet Seligman—he who had searched
railway sidings south of Moscow for the American Home's missing
luggage—offered himself (presumably on the spur of the moment, without
consulting Ljungholm, who would surely have demurred). The soldiers hailed a
passing droshky and took him away.

The immediate worry was Seligman's 'fragile little wife', who was not out with
them. How would she react to her husband's abrupt and ominous disappearance?
Ljungholm, who feared the worst, prepared to break the news carefully, but some of
the cadets, in their excitement forgetting all other considerations, ran ahead and, in
the doorway of the Chertkov mansion, shouted the news that Seligman had been
arrested. When Mrs Seligman appeared, Ljungholm thought that she would faint or
give way to self-pity and despair for her five children. Instead, he tells us, she raised
her eyes to heaven and exclaimed, 'Thank God! Thank God! How wonderful to be
counted worthy to suffer for Jesus' sake!'. That sort of willingness to suffer,
Ljungholm comments, 'speaks loudly to the Russian soul'. We may simply note
that he tells the story without self-consciousness and without any notion that it
might be disbelieved or received with disapproval.

They all prayed for Seligman that night and next morning he reappeared. He had
been cross-examined about the character of the meeting, his attitude to God, and
other matters. We can only conclude that his interrogators were casual young men
who felt no need to consult anyone more senior, since, having heard Seligman's
replies, they sentenced him to death by firing squad. He was placed against a wall,
but, as they raised their rifles, he shouted: 'Before you shoot, listen! I am not afraid
to die.' He pulled up his guernsey, with its Salvation Army crest and its all too
appropriate motto, 'Blood and Fire' and bared his breast. 'I am saved and will go to
heaven. I was a party zealot, once, but then I was saved and now all I want is to get
other people saved.' The squad commander decided that the death penalty could be
postponed for the time being. Seligman was taken back inside and an all night
discussion began. Having debated his beliefs with him until morning they released
him, but ordered him to report at 12 noon. At 11, accordingly, he took leave of his
wife and comrades and presented himself punctually to the Commissar. But the
Commissar, who had things to attend to (or had perhaps merely lost interest in the
game), told him merely to report again next morning. This continued for several
days before he was told not to bother.

---

7 Ljungholm told Larsson this story some time later: see Karl Larsson, *Tio År I
Ryssland*, pp. 131-33, and SA International Heritage Centre file on Ljungholm.

This incident perhaps suggests little more than a taste for sadistic byplay and religious debate among revolutionary soldiers, but we cannot doubt that Seligman was both courageous and fortunate. The killing of a suspected counter-revolutionary would not have exposed his captors to disciplinary action. Seligman may well have been only seconds from death.

Starvation and Epidemic

Death could strike in other ways. Food was scarce in Petrograd and throughout Russia during the summer of 1918. Peasants hoarded grain (or distilled it into vodka) in protest at low prices and the unavailability of agricultural tools and equipment. Many rich grain-producing areas had been lost to the Whites, or the Germans following the peace treaty concluded by Trotsky at Brest Litovsk in March, when Russia signed away 300 years' worth of territorial gains, including, as well as important food producing areas, coal mines, iron foundries, steel mills, and 60 million people.

In what remained of the former empire, the situation became worse than desperate: total starvation was only averted because of the activities of black market traders known as 'bagmen' who took tools and other goods into the agricultural areas and bartered them for grain, which they took back to the cities for sale. Bagmen were vilified as greedy bourgeois capitalists and enemies of the people by the Soviet authorities, who nevertheless were forced to leave them free to function. As a survivor, Sorokin, remarked, the rule was 'to each man nothing unless he gets it by transgressing the laws of the Communist government'.[8]

In the streets, horses died from starvation and lay decomposing where they dropped. With everyone weakened and Petrograd's water supply as impure as ever, infectious diseases—smallpox, cholera, typhoid fever and typhus—were rife. Soon the Salvationists suffered a crushing personal loss.[9]

For weeks together our Cadets lived on sour cabbage, morning, noon and night. Hardly anybody had any bread; milk, butter and sugar we never dreamt of. Our chief food consisted in soup made of dried vegetables. The only place that was a little better off for food was the American Refuge, seeing they got food there from the government for the children. Thither the Swedish officers used to go for a cup of coffee, and especially the men officers were often there... One day [Major Hacklin, who was in charge] noticed that a Swedish man lieutenant... had some kind of spots on his face and... hands. She... asked him not to come for fear of contagion for the children. Nevertheless some days later [he returned] ...he and Captain Olsen, a woman, were having some fun on account of some bit of food. Two days later we heard that Captain Olsen was sick...

---

8 See Lincoln, *Red Victory*, pp. 64-72.

9 The account that follows of Olsen's illness, death and funeral and the quotations come from Becker's *Scrapbook*, pp. 3-4, and Larsson, *Tio År I Ryssland*, pp.134-37.

Like several other Swedish officers (who eventually recovered) Captain Olsen had contracted smallpox. She was taken to a hospital, then to another, where she died. Becker and Sjöblom went to identify the body on a 'fearfully hot' July day:

> When the door was opened an overpowering smell met us, so the Brigadier could not proceed further. There were some 40-60 corpses, naked, covered with dirty sheets, upon which thousands of flies were sitting. There was a small passage along which one could not go without touching the corpses. There were two men who were handling these corpses like so many pieces of wood. At our entrance the flies buzzed up. I passed along that passage up to our dead comrade, the sheet was lifted and I saw an unrecognizable face—black and disfigured by the disease, but by her fair hair I knew it was she.

They ordered a coffin and handed over some of Olsen's clothes—which they expected to be stolen forthwith.

It was out of the question for a Salvation Army officer who had been 'promoted to glory' not to have a proper funeral. But, among many other problems, for reasons that will be explained later, they could not draw money from the Army's bank accounts to pay for it. It happened, however, that Becker's adoptive parents, whom she had so angered and disappointed by becoming an officer, had left Petrograd the previous May, having first made it possible for her to draw money from their account. 'What I would never have done for myself', Becker records, 'I did for the Army'.

Larsson, who had been visiting Moscow to explore the possibility of beginning work there, conducted the funeral. 'I was alone at home (H.Q.) when he came,' Becker writes. 'I will never forget telling him the news.' The funeral took place in the hospital chapel, in which there were numerous coffins, open and closed, and some naked bodies 'distorted by the cramps of cholera'. Larsson had insisted that a flag should be made for the occasion, although the materials were hard to come by and 'cost a fortune'. Olsen's coffin was draped with the flag, which had wild flowers pinned to it, during the service. Afterwards it was held aloft as the Salvationists marched behind the hearse to the cemetery, as Becker records:

> For some reason or other the driver took us along the most awful streets. Dead horses were lying about, dogs were tearing pieces out of them, and our hearts were filled with horror and an inexpressible fear for the comrades that were sick. I will always remember standing at that grave. The smell coming up was sickening, and as I translated for one after the other I had to fight against physical sickness along with the heartache...

> Captain Olsen was the first Salvation Army martyr on the Russian Missionary Field. She rests in an unknown grave...[10] But the Lord knows the place and He

---

10 Sjöblom later wrote about visiting Olsen's grave in the Lutheran cemetery, so its whereabouts was remembered at least for a time.

stands watch until the day when all the mists roll away and every 'why' will receive its answer.

Mapp's Bank Accounts, Lenin's New Society

The officers in Petrograd could not draw money from any of The Salvation Army's recently opened bank accounts because all were held in the name of the absent Mapp. Since his departure from Petrograd for 'consultations' in London had been delayed for several weeks, he had had time to make other arrangements. His failure to do so, and London's apparent failure to instruct him to do so, indicates that The Salvation Army's system, which was supposed to ensure institutional efficiency independently of individuals, was on this occasion ineffectual. The fact that Mapp never returned made matters worse: The Salvation Army simply lost much of the money. Becker gives two conflicting versions of what happened: one, that by the time the money could be withdrawn it had been so far devalued by inflation as to be virtually worthless; the other, that in 1921 the Salvationists were informed that their money had 'been nationalized'.[11]

Nationalization on a large scale was already under way in 1918, enforced by the beginnings of totalitarian terror. The principle of socialization of land, decreed two months earlier, was reaffirmed in February 1918. Foreign trade was nationalized in April, followed, in late June, by all major industrial sectors, in August by urban dwellings, and, in November, domestic trade. Lenin proclaimed the need for a strong state and followed this up by taking action against Anarchists, rightist (then leftist) Social Revolutionaries and Mensheviks, and, eventually, 'bourgeois' journals. On the night of 16-17 July, six days after the first Constitution of the Soviet State was ratified, in an attempt to eliminate the most obvious potential focus of potential opposition, the Imperial Family—Nicholas, Alexandra, Olga, Tatiana, Maria, Anastasia and Alexei, together with their attendants—were 'executed' during a 20 minute bloodbath in Yekaterinburg, in the Siberian foothills of the Ural mountains, where they had been imprisoned.

Six weeks later, a Social Revolutionary, Fanny Kaplan, shot Lenin, seriously wounding him. The attack was made the occasion of a government announcement that the response to this 'White terror' would be 'Red terror'. This continued a process already under way, the replacement of the rule of law by a concept called 'revolutionary conscience'. The state took to itself the freedom, indeed the duty, to judge terrorist acts according to whether they favoured or were hostile to the revolution. Henceforward the death penalty was applicable to a catch-all ragbag of offences, roughly divisible into crimes against the state—treason, espionage, desertion, mutiny, issuing false exemptions from military service, insubordination, and counter-revolutionary activity—and infringements of revolutionary morality—looting, theft, intoxication, prostitution, and contracting syphilis.[12]

---

11 Becker, *Scrapbook*, p. 4.
12 See Lincoln, *Red Victory*, pp. 160-61.

Larsson's Last Stand

Against this background of bloodletting, and despite the financial and other difficulties already mentioned, the small band of Salvationists carried on working. Russia's first and only Training Session lasted four months, at the end of which Larsson, at last free to leave Finland permanently, arrived to take command of the Territory, bringing Staff Captain Boije and other officers with him. Since Larsson had his wife and six children (aged from three to 16) with him, his wisdom in going to live in Russia was questioned by a Finnish frontier guard. 'You will soon be returning from there', he said. Larsson thought not.

In Petrograd the Larssons lived in the house at 22 Voznesensky Prospect, which had formerly been the headquarters. (The new headquarters was in 26 rooms and two halls of a former Dutch schoolhouse near St Isaac's Cathedral.) The Sjöbloms, who were about to return to Finland, were there to welcome them; when Mrs Sjöblom saw the six children she wept. 'She knew,' Larssson comments, 'what was awaiting them'.[13]

Larsson's son, Sture, then 12, almost 13, remembered vividly some aspects of their short stay. He and the other children had been excited by the prospect of going to Russia. In Finland they had awaited their father's return from visits to 'the great, war-torn country in the east' with tales of long journeys in the interior in terrible conditions. Once in Russia, they were able to appreciate more fully his restless enthusiasm and the remarkable amount of work he put in. They soon understood that their father's hopes of success were fading. Although he had received invitations to begin work in Novgorod (as we shall see) and Kiev, among other cities, such offers seemed ever more chimerical while the signs and portents of persecution to come grew ever more real. On the morning of 11 November, 1918, Sture (who, because there was no school for him to attend, had been given several small jobs at headquarters to occupy his time) arrived there with his father, to find that the police had sealed most of the doors. A few nights later two officials appeared at their flat and searched it. The children watched the two strangers go through everything, look into every drawer, open every cupboard, search every pocket and read every letter. A few documents were taken away for further investigation. This was exciting but frightening as well.

The children were also aware of their mother's self-sacrifice. When they gathered for an evening meal, usually tea and a piece of Russian sour dark bread, she would go into the dining room first to share out the piece of bread they were having. When they were called in and saw the tiny piece on her plate they protested, often in tears but always in vain.

Sture's final memory, of course, was of the farewell scene at the railway station when they left Russia for ever on 18 December, 1918: the pale faces of the Russian Salvationists as they said goodbye to their leaders, his parents, shedding many and bitter tears.[14]

---

13 Larsson, *Tio År I Ryssland*, p. 138.
14 Transcription of videotape, *Frälsningsarmén i Ryssland*.

This is to anticipate, but it emphasizes that Larsson's last days in Russia were brief (just over three months) and increasingly desperate. Their short stay, however, began with optimism and intense activity. Plans to make a start in Moscow provided stimulation and focus, as the Russian diary kept by Otto Ljungholm between 8 September and 14 October indicates. It opens with his thirty-third birthday, which was also the third anniversary of his marriage to 'little lovely Gerda'. The following day, newcomers from Sweden brought coffee and cakes, rice pudding and wild lingonberries.[15] He mentions numerous enthusiastic meetings and sessions of prayer, leading up to the dedication, on 11 September, of the new headquarters, in time for Russia's first Salvation Army Congress, which began next day.

A series of confusions and farcical accidents almost caused the Larssons to miss the inaugural meeting. First they were accidentally locked into their fourth floor flat and could leave it only through a neighbouring flat, occupied by puzzled Russians whom they were meeting for the first time. (One of the more surprising things about the methodical and conscientious Larsson is that although he knew the Russian alphabet he never learnt to speak the language. Indeed, on at least one occasion—when a soldier on a train demanded to see documents it would have been embarrassing to produce—he used his ignorance to his own advantage.) Then, through a further mishap, the party had to travel on different trams, and Mrs Larsson, having not been in Petrograd before, did not know where to get off. The meeting itself, held in the Tenishev School, where Mapp had conducted his weekly united meetings, was a little disappointing: 'only about 300' had gathered. Street-fighting, dilatory trams, inflation and large-scale exodus from the city had begun to take effect.

The cadets sang a song of welcome, which ran in part:

Russia, the land of our fathers, has been starving in darkness and dirt, has suffered and waited for centuries for light that would shine over its expanse. In this hour of joy Russia welcomes you, who have come from distant lands to take part in the fight. May God himself stand by your side and give you grace to save us from suffering and evil.

Including the cadets, no fewer than 52 officers attended the Congress to confer and be urged on to greater activity. Larsson said that he was totally committed to the salvation of Russia, and Mrs Larsson apologized for the size of her family—a burden, she felt, imposed on the Russians, who had so little to begin with. At the public meetings some 30 came to the penitent form. (Only about a third, however, actually sought salvation.) The climax of the Congress came on the Monday night, when the newly commissioned cadets and some older officers received their marching orders, to Moscow (a group under Ljungholm's command)[16] and other cities as well

---

15 A small, dark red, sour-tasting berry, beloved in Scandinavia, where it is used in deserts and (sweetened) in a sauce for pancakes.

16 Shortly before they left Petrograd for Moscow, Ljunholm and his wife attended an Orthodox service at the Cathedral of the Saviour on the Blood. His measured but largely favourable response indicates how far he and others had come in recognizing that the

as within Petrograd. The Congress was, according to Becker, 'a very blessed time', after which things looked brighter. But, although it was not yet apparent that the frontier guard's prediction would all too soon prove accurate, Larsson, despite his innate optimism and his response to the frontier guard, despite the opening of new corps in Moscow and at Orel, was beginning to feel, as he would later write, that

> 1918 was in every respect a dark year for our work. Despite all our hopes, all our strivings after triumphant faith, in spite even of our occasional successes, it was becoming clear that the tide was on the ebb.[17]

By the time the Ljungholms left for Moscow on 15 October (after much prayer and preparation, two days spent mending shoes and the visit to Emma Olsen's grave), the cost and shortage of food was a severe problem. Small amounts of cabbage, greens and potatoes constituted their dinner; a sparse breakfast was their only other meal. Flour could only be obtained illegally. Bread was available intermittently, two grams at a time. Once, in the small hours, Ljungholm was woken by stomach pains from a dream of eating Swedish bread with baked ham.

As well as hunger, officers had to endure random persecution by the authorities. Captain Holm and Lieutenant Labanobe spent five days in jail for singing and selling *Vestnik Spaseniya* on the street. It was two days, during which they were totally without food, before they were able to inform headquarters. A sergeant, sent to the jail to look into the matter and give the prisoners food, was also jailed for three hours. Three days later, equally without explanation, Holm and Labanobe were released. Meanwhile, the Swedish consul in Moscow was urging all Swedes to leave the country. Even Larsson found this ominous.

In these depressing and debilitating conditions, only someone as determined as he could have been 'tormented' by the question of whether to proceed with the inauguration of a Salvation Army corps in Moscow. Anyone less single-minded might have thought that the issue had been settled by forces beyond his control. Money was perilously scarce. Russian friends, including V.G. Chertkov and the Countess Tolstoy, who put Larsson up when he visited Moscow, suggested postponement. A telegram from International Headquarters urged the same rational course of action. But his will to try and to succeed, compounded of stubborn faith in God and in himself, made him inclined to ignore such sensible advice. The officers were already in place and, after many difficulties, arrangements to rent a hall (at 9 Pokrovka Street) and quarters were in hand. He himself had determined and promised in the firmest possible terms to open fire in the ancient capital, having been told by Commissar Bonch-Bruevich (a former temperance campaigner, now, for the time being one of Lenin's most trusted colleagues) that since there was religious freedom

---

religious experience of Orthodoxy was authentic. Nevertheless, he passed on his passion for the Salvation of Russia to his descendants: 73 years later, in 1991, his grandson, Sven-Erik, was appointed to re-open the Moscow corps.

17 Larsson, *Tio År I Ryssland*, p. 123.

in Russia there was nothing to prevent The Salvation Army beginning its activities in Moscow.

This, even if it might be revoked by some other official at a moment's notice, was encouraging; better still, while plunged in an uncharacteristic fit of near-readiness to give up following a tea-time conversation about the state of the country with Countess Tolstoy and the Chertkovs, Larsson received some good news: a considerable sum of money had been deposited in The Salvation Army's account on behalf of a family living abroad. It appeared that God's wishes and those of International Headquarters might on this occasion be at variance. On 18 October, despite a police raid on his flat in Petrograd, which forced him to endure two further uncomfortable overnight train journeys, he led the inaugural meeting in Moscow. 'In God alone is my confidence,' they sang.

Their first weeks' operations were encouraging. Meetings were full, there were converts and many Bibles and copies of *Vestnik Spaseniya* were sold. Against that, meetings with the Communist city authorities led nowhere, although Larsson was always treated with great civility. But when he asked whether the city was going to do anything for the homeless children who lived on its pavements, the answer was chilling: 'We are not interested in street people.'[18]

Lack of whole-hearted official recognition was not Larsson's greatest problem. The political and economic chaos into which the country had fallen was increasingly threatening The Salvation Army's survival. Russia's economic difficulties were partly caused by the war but the actions of the government played their part. The Salvation Army could not but be affected and Larsson was soon reporting disastrous financial losses to the Chief of Staff. The first was the subsidy it had received for two years from the Grand Duchess Tatiana's committee; the money had almost covered the upkeep of one of the children's homes. Soon afterwards, the American colony, which had supported 'the American Home', left Petrograd. Many others who had contributed to The Salvation Army's funds were now paupers. Such people had been deprived of their possessions and were allowed to take only 1,000 roubles per month from their bank accounts. They were in the fourth category for ration cards, which meant that they were charged 20 times as much as others for food. They had to pay high taxes and were of necessity selling such of their possessions as had not already been confiscated.

By decree, people were required to supply one or more complete military uniforms according to a sliding scale based on their business profits, the amount they paid in rent or other financial indicators. The Salvationists hoped to be exempted because they were foreigners (a plea which proved double-edged). Meanwhile Larsson had on one occasion to use money borrowed from a relative by Miss Weisberg to pay his fare to Moscow.

At last, with the help of the Swedish Legation, Larsson succeeded in withdrawing money from Mapp's inaugural fund, held by the Anglo-Russian Bank. A second attempt, to get 8,000 roubles (7,000 of which was needed to pay the fuel bill of one

---

18 Larsson, *Tio År I Ryssland*, p. 144.

of the children's homes), encountered renewed bureaucratic obstruction. Mapp had also deposited (in his own name) 51,000 roubles with the Don-Asorff Bank. None of this was ever recovered, the authorities arguing that a state of war existed between the Soviet Union and Great Britain (which supported the Whites and of which the account holder was a citizen).[19]

Rampant inflation made survival the most burning question of all. It was prohibited to import food into cities but thousands of people travelled into the countryside every week in search of supplies. The prohibition was enforced only intermittently, but sometimes very severely. There were cases of women who, having borrowed money or sold their last possessions to buy potatoes for their children, committed suicide when these were confiscated. As we might expect, the enterprising and indefatigable Seligman, accompanied by another male Salvationist, travelled far south to beg potatoes from the peasantry. He gathered enough to fill two full railway wagons, in which he concealed a few small sacks of flour. At the border of the Petrograd district the wagons were uncoupled from the train and Seligman went in search of an official willing to issue an import licence. The head commissar said he would confiscate everything. 'Then I will send them back,' Seligman retorted. Later he found a sub-commissar willing to issue a conditional permit. Taken first to the Chertkov mansion, the supplies were later distributed piecemeal around other Salvation Army buildings under cover of darkness. Another food gatherer, Captain Lydia Konopljova, carrying half a sack of foodstuffs, jumped off a train into a snowdrift rather than risk having it confiscated by soldiers on guard at the station, making her way home through unfrequented side streets.[20]

Initially, the Larsson family was regarded as unproductive and was allowed only third-class bread cards. (First-class card holders received half of a pound of bread per day, second-class, a quarter pound, third-class, an eighth, and fourth-class, two whiting per day.) Later, Mrs Larsson, for her work in the children's home, was classified as a manual labourer and given a first-class card. The eldest daughter rose to second-class, and the younger children received children's cards. But Larsson himself and another daughter remained in the third-class, the unnecessary ones. (These classifications, however, were largely irrelevant, for the shops had little food to sell.) The family subsisted on minute portions of rye porridge, coffee or tea (without milk or sugar), bread, potatoes and salt fish. Meat was an occasional extra. The three-year-old was allowed one cup of milk per week.

Meanwhile, *Vestnik Spaseniya*, which had given The Salvation Army its foothold in Russia, faced demise. While Bolshevik bureaucrats produced an avalanche of papers and documents, non-governmental publications faced shortages. Printing costs had risen by 50 per cent. In October 1918 the Baptist newspaper, *The Guest*, ceased publication. *Vyestnik Spaseniya* struggled on until January. By then the

---

19 This 'state of war' was never formally the case, although an Allied force fought in north Russia between 23 June, 1918, and September-October, 1919: see Dupuy and Dupuy, *Collins Encyclopedia of Military History*, p. 1095.

20 Rakel Holm, *Memories from Russia*, p. 8.

Swedish Red Cross contingent had gone home, leaving their remaining stock of food for the Salvationists, who lived off it for a few weeks.

Food shortages affected The Salvation Army in other ways. Congregations were dwindling. 'Starving people', Larsson reported tersely to the Chief of the Staff at International Headquarters, 'do not attend meetings'. The cost of a tram ride had risen to one rouble. Previously, the Salvationists had been able to advertise their existence and the times and places of their indoor meeting by conducting short informal meetings on street corners but since the assassination of People's Commissar Uritsky on 30 August, 1918, and, on the same day, the attempted assassination of Lenin, such gatherings were strictly forbidden.

A month later, at around midnight on Sunday 27 October, the Ljungholms' quarters was searched by two armed men, who accused them of being counter-revolutionaries. (Such an accusation could have arisen from several causes: Mapp's anti-Bolshevik opinions, if indeed he had made them public; the fact that The Salvation Army was often thought of as principally a British organization and British troops were in Russia fighting on the on the White side; or simply the fact that all Christians were presumably ideologically bound to be anti-Bolshevik. Protestations that Salvationism was non-political fell on deaf ears.) At 1.30 a.m. the revolver-toting inspectors departed, leaving behind an ineffectually sealed drawer containing various unimportant papers and the Ljungholms' supply of sugar. During further encounters during the next two days, at the Commissar's office and at the flat, it became apparent that it was Ljungholm's foreignness and *Vestnik Spaseniya* (with its mentions of General Booth) that principally aroused Communist disquiet. Ljungholm was told that 'We have no generals, we are all comrades. We have no Tsar and we don't want a god either.' The Salvation Army's certificate of registration for Moscow was recognized, but it made no mention of selling newspapers. That they were allowed to sell them in Petrograd did not apply in Moscow. After discussion they were allowed to sell songbooks (since without them they could not conduct meetings).

In Petrograd, meanwhile, attendances had also picked up, but official harassment was increasing ominously. The Commissar for Education was starting to take an interest in the children's homes because of the religious instruction that the children were given. (The Commissar in Orel had declared that the state should take over the home there and instruct the children in the principals of Socialism.) Similarly the other (formerly 'American') children's home, now in Vologda, was told that an inventory of its effects had been taken and that the house would shortly be requisitioned and the children dispersed elsewhere. The inevitable was postponed for the time being by the response that the home, run by Swedish officers, was now Swedish rather than American but it was the issue of children's homes which finally brought to fruition repeated pressure to make the Salvationists give up Madame Chertkov's house on Vasilevsky Island. (It had been possible to resist this pressure thus far only because the house contained a large library and valuable paintings, of which the Salvationists were probably the most reliable available custodians.) The fact that Captain Liljebad had taken in some 30 children, mostly orphans, who had survived the cholera epidemic in the summer, gave the commissars their excuse. The group was dispersed and the house and all its contents confiscated. As usual the commissars were wondrously inconsistent in their behaviour. Captain Lijebad was told several times during examination that she should be shot, but was subsequently offered one of the paintings ('which naturally, she refused to accept') as a memento.

When Miss Peuker offered Larsson a new thirty room hospital, rent-free, to be used as a social institution, the offer had to be declined, because any arrangement concerning the renting, possession and use of property was liable to be overruled by the authorities, without warning and without right of appeal. Attempts to negotiate with them were invariably time-consuming and frustrating, consisting largely of waiting to keep appointments that were not honoured.

In November, the offices at the headquarters were sealed (the cashier hurried out with the cash box, so that was saved) and requisitioned; the Salvationists were allowed to remove only their personal belongings. Two corps and a slum post were closed down. Larsson spoke (Miss Weisberg acting as translator) to a Mr Stepanov at the Cheka ('Special Commission for the Struggle against Counter-revolution and Sabotage', as the secret political police were known between 1917 and 1922) who subjected him to a formal examination concerning the Salvationists' work and plans. The result was a characteristic inconsistency in official behaviour. Meetings continued to be held in a small hall within the building but the larger one and the offices remained sealed. 'I don't know how many times', Larsson writes, 'I stood outside the sealed door of my office, needing something that was locked inside, tempted to slide a thread between the two wax seals! It would have been the easiest thing in the world to renew them so that no one would have noticed anything. But I triumphed over the tempter.' There was even a threat that the Larssons' living quarters would be sealed off, on the grounds that it had been the editorial office of *Vestnik Spaseniya*, which was now proscribed by officials in Moscow. The malicious appearance of the police emissaries (who were eventually persuaded that the address was now a private house) provoked debate, after they had gone, as to whether Larsson should sleep elsewhere that night. He stayed put and no arrest took place, but 'it was not soothing to the nerves to know that fifty metres away was a building to which many prisoners were taken for examination. Every morning at about four we were woken by revolver shots from that direction, and knew that some of those arrested and examined had been sent to Eternity'.[21]

A few more weeks passed in fruitless discussions. The authorities in Moscow announced that only the existing stock of publications could be sold, and only to those who attended meetings. With Larsson's permission, the Ljungholms left Moscow and returned to Sweden, along with a number of other officers. *Vestnik Spaseniya* would cease publication in January. With the children's homes and slum posts broken up and with only two corps still functioning, The Salvation Army in Russia had almost ceased to exist.

---

21 Larsson, *Tio År I Ryssland*, pp 158-60.

Larsson became increasingly conscious that the Swedish legation, which had for some time been urging Swedes to leave Russia, was becoming impatient with him. The officials themselves would be leaving in mid-December. In what he calls his most difficult choice he decided to leave. Had he had only himself to think of he would willingly have stayed on, but he could not ask his family to endure another Russian winter in penury (the Army's bank accounts were once more in effect frozen, and it was frequently impossible to exchange Swedish money). Without diplomatic protection, as he now was, he was under almost continuous threat of arrest. When Captain Boije (who had returned to Russia as Larsson's second-in-command when the Sjöbloms left for Sweden) said that she would remain and take charge of whatever work could be done, he made up his mind. He felt, he writes, like a deserter. He announced his decision to the soldiers, to 'universal sorrow'. They had understood that he must go but had hoped that he would nevertheless stay. He packed, taking very little, leaving a number of trunks of books and clothes. (Two years later these were ruined by floods.)

The day before he left, Lieutenant Becker, who had been in Estonia visiting her elderly father and had been prevented from recrossing the frontier, unexpectedly returned.

Early in the morning of 18 December, while it was still dark, those officers who were staying behind trekked with the Larsson family through the deserted streets of Petrograd and across the Neva to the Finland Station. They felt compassed about by a great crowd of bitter enemies. During their brief farewells they prayed that God would keep them from sin and that no sufferings might push them into compromises and denials. Larsson said to Olsoni (who had served in Russia since the Hygiene Exhibition in 1913 and was nicknamed 'the Gavan captain'), 'You were the first and will also be the last'.

When they reached the frontier, the guard recognized them. 'Didn't I tell you', he exclaimed, 'that you would return soon?'

'Quite right,' said Larsson, 'but we'll be back again another time.'

He seems to have meant this and supposed that it would occur in about six months but, when he died in 1949, the time when return became possible was still fifty-one years away. Many times before his death he reflected on a passage written by Meriel Buchanan, daughter of the British Ambassador in St Petersburg during the revolution:

Only those who have lived there know what it means, or can understand the nameless charm with which Russia holds one, the homesickness that makes one long for her strange waywardness. I remember being often told, 'Oh, yes, you may grumble at Petrograd now, but you will want to come back. Once you have lived in Russia you will always want to come back. She will never let you forget her.'[22]

---

22 Larsson, *Tio År I Ryssland*, p. 166. I have not been able to find the source of the quotation.

Boije's Countryside Campaigns

With Larsson gone, Boije characteristically initiated a scheme that made it seem, neither for the first or quite the last time, that The Salvation Army might have a continuing future in Russia. Parties of three 'village warriors', of whom Boije herself was often one, would set off with musical instruments, Bibles and song books, to conduct 'campaigns' of about a fortnight's duration amongst the peasants living in villages within easy reach of Petrograd and Moscow.[23] In the former case much of the population was of Swedish descent and spoke Swedish, which made evangelism easier for those officers who were themselves Swedish. Those who did not, often understood Finnish. Like the Russian townsfolk, the villagers were friendly, kind and hospitable and were always pleased to have the Salvationists visit them. (To non-Salvationists there may seem an element of desperation in such expeditions, in carrying the Gospel to groups of strangers whom they would in all probability never see again. Salvationists, however, would prefer to invoke the Parable of the Sower.) On occasion in fact these visits were in response to specific invitations and it would appear that there were advantages for both inviters and invited. From the point of view of the Russian inviters there was still, outside the main revolutionary centres, a large religious shaped hole waiting to be filled. The Orthodox Church was virtually proscribed, making formal religious services in churches difficult to find and dangerous to attend. The Salvation Army's services, on the other hand, taking place in any available public hall, or even in private houses, fulfilled a need. Equally, from the Salvationists' standpoint, when established corps in Leningrad and Moscow were subjected to arbitrary visitation, harassment and closure, a more peripatetic strategy offered an opportunity to spread their message widely, hoping that some of the seed would fall on fertile ground, while they stayed one step ahead of the authorities.

We may note, in parenthesis, that this strategy was very like the 'flying propaganda' employed by the majority of the Russian students who had participated in the spontaneous 'to the people' movement in the summer of 1874. Moving rapidly from village to village, they preached socialist ideas. We may note also that the Salvationists, whose beliefs were already familiar to the peasants, were more welcome. The students' use, sometimes of vernacular parables, but more often of rather academic paraphrases of their favourite socialist works, left the peasants bewildered, indifferent or hostile.[24]

That The Salvation Army might have found this strategy successful in the long term is illustrated by what happened as a result of one of the earliest of the invitations, which had come in October 1918, before Larsson's departure, from the Abbot of a monastery and other leading citizens in Novgorod. One hundred miles

---

23 This account is derived from an interview with Brigadier Boije by the journalist Arthur E. Copping, printed in *All the World*, 1926, pp. 49-52 and 121 and Larsson's use of it in *Tio År I Ryssland*, pp. 170-72.

24 Barbara Alpern Engel, and Clifford N.. Rosenthal, *Five Sisters: Women Against the Tsar*, New York and London, Routledge, 1992, p. xxvi.

south of Petrograd, Novgorod had a claim to be the oldest city in Russia, and had rivalled Moscow during the Fourteenth and Fifteenth Centuries until 1478, when it was defeated and its vast territories annexed by Moscow's ruler, Ivan III, 'the Great'.[25]

Larsson asked Boije and three young captains (including the ubiquitous Seligman) to take up the invitation. Permission to travel was as ever difficult to obtain and their overnight journey, sitting on parcels of *Vestnik Spaseniya* in the corridors of a crowded, dirty, smelly train, uncomfortable and sleepless. On arrival on Sunday morning, Boije tells us, they were greeted, not by the Abbot but by

> a friend who took us to his humble little home. We very much hoped to get some food but he was only able to give us a cup of 'tea,' made from dried black-currant leaves and a piece of cured herring. We had been longing for bread, but there was none to be had.

> This brother had secured the Town Hall for our meeting, but, as we knew, there had been no opportunity or facilities for making the gathering known. So we had each come provided with a rubber stamp, with which, on a corner of each copy of *Vestnik Spaseniya*, we invited readers to the meeting, which had been fixed for four o'clock that day. Having stamped the 800 papers, we mapped out Novgorod into four sections [then] ...went off to sell [the papers]. It was a wonderful experience.

Since Salvationists had never been seen in Novgorod before it was not difficult to arouse interest. Everyone who saw them asked questions. The association of the words 'army' and 'salvation' caused surprise. Some people asked them whether they were part of a new Red Army. They spent several increasingly hungry hours selling papers and inviting people to the meeting. They tore themselves away to be given another cup of black currant tea and piece of cured herring before going to the town hall.

As four o'clock approached they were dismayed that no one had appeared but shortly after the appointed hour a few figures peeped around the door. Within minutes there was a crowd of 400 or 500, some sitting on window ledges or the backs of chairs. In the front row sat the Abbot and a number of other monks. Nervous about what they might think, Boije began, with the assistance of guitar and concertina, to teach the gathering 'Jesus, the name high over all'. This went down well and soon the rafters were ringing to the Russian equivalent of

> We have no other argument,
> We want no other plea;
> It is enough that Jesus died,
> And that He died for me.

---

25 See Robert O. Crummey, *The Formation of Muscovy 1304-1613*, London, Longman, 1987, pp. 87-89.

After a prayer (with the 400 or 500 kneeling on the floor) the younger men and women, who had been asking each other quietly what was going on, since they were puzzled by what appeared to be a religious gathering but was not taking place in a church, fell silent and listened with the others to Boije's account of what The Salvation Army was. Following a vocal solo and Seligman's account of his conversion and the changes it had brought into his life, which elicited audible comments of surprise and appreciation, the Abbot rose and asked if he might say a few words. Boije's nerves fluttered again but she invited him onto the platform ('that holy place' he called it). He won her encomium ('a most delightful old man') when he proved to know a great deal about The Salvation Army and William Booth. He told the gathering that 'I want to recommend these brothers and sisters to you very warmly. They have come to this country to help us and bless us, and you must not look upon any of them as foreigners with a foreign religion.' Turning to the Salvationists, he concluded, 'I would like you, when you go back to England, to convey to General Booth our warmest greetings, and thanks for having sent you to us.'

There was a collection to which everyone, however restricted their means, tried to give something, then Boije read from the Bible and delivered a sermon. At the conclusion when she asked if there were any who had resolved to follow Christ, the entire congregation at first stood, then knelt. Having begun shortly after four, the meeting went on until eight, with most of those present eagerly continuing discussion with the Salvationists and shaking their hands. (All this, it will be remembered, was done by the Salvationists on two cups of black currant tea and two pieces of pickled herring.) Amongst the last to approach Boije was the town commissar, who asked her to visit his office the following morning. His manner was cordial and friendly, so she did not assume that he meant to cause trouble. Since she had to return to Leningrad by the night train she deputed Seligman to visit the commissar in her stead. The commissar told Seligman that he was giving The Salvation Army formal authority to start work in Novgorod and would give every kind of assistance he could. Seligman explained that it was impossible under the existing circumstances for The Salvation Army to establish a permanent presence in Novgorod.

These events, and Boije's account of them, raise pertinent questions. Might it have been possible for the Salvationists to establish a series of centres, run from week to week by the locals, which they themselves would visit on a frequent, if not absolutely regular basis? This would have helped dispel the charge of Russian nationalists (Orthodox or Communist) that Salvationism was foreign. (We may note that the Abbot in Novgorod, despite his eagerness to establish that it was not foreign, assumed automatically that the visitors were from England.) It would also have been, at least marginally, less likely to attract the disapproval and interference of the Communist authorities. It is possible, however, that the need for Salvationists to have permission to travel would have obviated this seeming advantage. The bureaucracy would have been able to keep track of them—and, if it wished, obstruct them. Also, of course, they had to find the money for fares.

Nevertheless, such a free-floating strategy might have allowed The Salvation Army to continue working in Russia when the day came when all foreign officers had to leave the country.

We have to remember that certain factors inherent in the situation might have constituted insurmountable obstacles. The Russian system of internal passports and travel permits would probably have stymied any attempt by the Salvationists to become free-floating, while their own sense that a trained officer ought always to be in charge to ensure maintenance of correct doctrine, discipline and style would have proved an equal inhibition from their own side. And in considering the reception they had in Novgorod, we must also remember the Russian tendency to behave as they suppose visitors would wish them to. Some words of the Nineteenth-Century westernizing socialist, Alexander Herzen, are pertinent:

> Our attitude towards Europe and Europeans is still that of provincials towards the dwellers in a capital: we are servile and apologetic, take every difference for a defect, blush for our peculiarities and try to hide them, and confess our inferiority by imitation... Western nations talk of our duplicity and cunning; they believe we want to deceive them, when we are only trying to make a creditable appearance and pass muster. A Russian will express quite different political views in talking to different persons, without any ulterior object, and merely from a wish to please: the bump of complaisance is highly developed in our skulls.[26]

And, as has already been noted, Russians liked to embrace a position or belief in order to test it out and to engage in a large theatrical event with singing and concerted mass movement while doing so. We do not know whether the visits of other guests of different persuasions to Novgorod were welcomed with equal enthusiasm.

But even if we do not take Boije's glowing account of what happened in that city entirely at face value there does not seem to be any reason for outright scepticism. She nowhere comes across as a vainglorious person eager to establish her own prowess as preacher and evangelist. Faced, as she was in 1926 when Copping's article appeared, with the sorry facts that The Salvation Army had been unable to build upon what had happened in Novgorod and had subsequently been expelled from Russia, a less honest person might have been inclined to underplay the townsfolk's response. She tells it, if not altogether—in some putatively objective sense—as it was, then at least entirely as she understood it to be. When Copping asked her whether there was anything exceptional about the response of the Novogorodians, she said that fervour and readiness to accept the Salvationist message were a constant experience, not only in cities and large towns, but 'more notably in the constant succession of two-week campaigns we prosecuted, right up to the last, in surrounding villages'.

---

26 Alexander Herzen, (trs. J.D. Duff), *Childhood, Youth and Exile*, Oxford, Oxford University Press, 1980 p. 101.

In the first weeks of 1919, for instance, two lieutenants were sent to Pskov, the ancient city on the River Velikaya, about 150 miles south-west of Petrograd (where Nicholas II had renounced the throne) to conduct meetings in the villages nearby. It was hoped by those who had invited them that the Salvationists would help to counter the evil influence of 'low, blasphemous' literature that the Bolsheviks circulated in the countryside.[27] These visits also offered a chance to escape temporarily from unhealthy Petrograd (35,000 deaths were registered there in January 1919, about a twentieth of the population) and to gather food.

On these village expeditions the Salvationists travelled on foot, tramping in winter through miles and miles of snow. Frequently they met peasants, who greeted them in the traditional way: 'May God be your help.' Arriving in a village, they chose a large house and asked the occupants whether they would like a meeting to take place there. The suggestion was apparently always welcomed, and children were sent to alert the rest of the village. Congregations assembled rapidly.

When the largest room in the house was crowded, they would start with a song. Many of the Russians proved to have beautiful voices. Anything the Salvationists said was listened to with rapt attention, with comments and interjections of 'That's right, sister!' When one of the party prayed everyone knelt, carefully avoiding turning their backs on the icon.

Because of the solemn nature of peasant piety the Salvationists felt obliged to be less free and easy than was natural to them, and they positively dreaded the sort of rural interruption—a sudden moo or cock crow at an untoward moment, or an irruption of piglets which got entangled with the children's legs. 'If anything funny happens, don't look at me,' they implored each other before beginning. Afterwards the samovar and rye bread cut into small pieces appeared. 'All manner of questions' were asked, and the visitors were implored to talk to relatives about drink and other problems. A young woman begged Boije to find out from her boyfriend why he had lately been inattentive. He proved 'rather a rough lad' and was distinctly offhand.

At the end of each day they slept at the last house at which a meeting had been held. These were terrible nights, especially in winter:

> The entire peasant family sleep on top of the brick oven. It is very hot and stuffy up there, and the smell is awful. But it was better to be half suffocated on the oven than frozen to death on the floor. And being half suffocated was only a minor part of the tribulation. The place was apt to be alive with cockroaches, bugs, fleas and lice. Those insects and the terrible fumes and perspiration made for a truly nightmarish experience, but—well, anyone who knows those simple, good-hearted Russian peasants would willingly endure that, and even worse tribulation, to serve them.

Thus it was, in the line of duty, that Rakel Holm and Helmy Boije contracted typhus.

---

27 Larsson, Letter to Brigadier Catherine Booth, March 1919, in Larsson file.

The Valley of the Shadow

'Even worse tribulation' turned out to be no idle phrase and the question of a possible Russian successor to Boije also proved far from academic.

During the hungry spring of 1918, disease had joined the scourges suffered by the Russians. Typhus was rampant, carried by the lice that lived on chronically unwashed servicemen on their way home and city folk fleeing to supposed safety. Lice were further encouraged by a breakdown in cleaning cities that had begun when war broke out and worsened rapidly. One louse bite could mean death. Conditions were worst, perhaps, in Petrograd.[28]

Rakel Holm was the first Salvationist victim. She was on the point of leaving Russia, because she was a Finn and the Finns, having massed counter-revolutionary forces near the Russian border, were *personae non gratae*. (Boije, also a Finn, was for the time being determined to stay in her post as leader.) Holm hovered between life and death for several days but recovered in time to leave on the last day for which her travel permit was valid.

Boije's struggle to survive took longer. As her account of the visit to Novgorod makes clear, she, in common with her comrades, was hungry for most of 1919. At one point 26 Petrograd Salvationists succeeded in forming a food company, which allowed them to obtain fortnightly rations from official stores at a comparatively reasonable price. But this proved merely a temporary palliative. Come the summer, Boije was seriously malnourished and suffering from boils. When she recovered she called the officers together and because of the seriousness of their economic position, urged those who could to find ordinary jobs and earn some money. Clara Becker found work, first in the Post Office, later in the Ministry of Agriculture and her salaries helped to feed her comrades and cover the various costs associated with Boije's subsequent illness. Others also obtained work. Boije went to the Vologda children's home for a fortnight's rest. She also visited Moscow and Domnino and a report written rather guardedly by Miss Peuker on 18 September was the first inkling Larsson had that something was seriously amiss. This mentioned enormously rising costs in all the homes but asserted continuing faith in God. It was written by Miss Peuker because there was an immediate chance of getting a letter through and Boije had 'a severe headache, caused by an attack of influenza, and therefore cannot write herself'. The same post brought a later letter from Becker referring to Miss Peuker's letter and clarifying the real position: Boije had for six days been fighting a virulent form of typhus; in that time she had had no more than ten hours' sleep. Two Salvationists, trained nurses, were helping look after her and 'God be praised, for the moment we even have money'. She seemed to be improving but it would be months before she would be fit for work.

Meanwhile, the Children's Home at Domnino, near Orel, had been taken over by the Soviet authorities a couple of weeks before, but the doctor did not think it advisable to tell Boije so. (The home, as Larsson subsequently explains, had been in 'White' territory for a couple of months but when the White forces retreated the

---

28 See Lincoln, *Red Victory,* p. 64, and 362-64.

Communists confiscated the building.) The officers stayed on in the village for a time, earning a living by sewing and nursing the sick. But The Salvation Army in Russia had been haemorrhaging officers since the beginning of the year as those who could take no more fled to Finland, crossing the border, at considerable risk, without permission or documents.

Becker concludes her letter with a timidity that perhaps casts light on Boije's doubts about her as a potential leader:[29]

> I have been uncertain whether it is right of me to write this letter, but I feel it is my duty to inform you of the situation.[30]

The Salvationists who provide our accounts of this period were not inclined to dwell graphically on the details of their suffering but the writer Edith M. Almedingen, who grew up on Vasilevsky Island, has left us a vivid picture of her experience of typhus in Petrograd at this time:

> A louse must have bitten me somewhere. They suggested to Esther [her room-mate] that she should send me off to one of the typhus hospitals and, had she agreed, I might not have come out. People died like flies in those hospitals. There were not enough doctors. The supply of medicines was negligible.

In the early stages, Miss Almedingen shrieked so frighteningly that a pregnant woman living in the same building gave birth almost a month prematurely. On one occasion she wrenched the window open and clambered onto the window ledge to throw herself out. When Esther tried to restrain her she fought back violently.

> For three weeks I was unconscious. When this was over, I wondered whether my body was made of frangible spun glass. At the least movement the glass seemed to break with an exquisite pain. During those weeks of convalescence, [my] temperature fell to normal in the morning. In the afternoon I was plunged back into a furnace, and talked 'most varied nonsense', as Esther told me much later.

Later still, she persuaded someone to let her look into a mirror.

> I picked it up and was glad to be alone. I saw a stranger's face, white skin drawn tight over the bones and the eyes grown to the size of two Bavarian plums. I stared, wondering where I had last seen something like the face before me. I remembered soon enough. A blurred picture of a mortuary near Moscow came into my mind, the mirror fell on the bare boards...[31]

Not long after Becker had written to Larsson her finances seem to have deteriorated again, although she continued to work as a state official during the day,

---

29 See p. 270 below.
30 Larsson, *Tio År I Ryssland,* pp. 180-81.
31 E.M. Almedingen, *Tomorrow Will Come,* pp. 226-27.

sawing wood and doing the washing and snatching sleep after work, sitting up with Boije on alternate nights. She also conducted the weekly corps meeting, formerly Boije's responsibility.

The term of Boije's typhus stretched into months rather than weeks[32]. Towards the end of November she suffered severe back pain. The doctor hedged his bets for a time before advising that she be taken to hospital for an X-ray. We have seen Miss Almedingen's report that few who entered the typhus hospitals came out alive and it is echoed by Becker's grief-stricken statement: 'It was like giving the dearest one I had into the hands of the executioner'. Telling Boije what was to happen was 'hard work', but she agreed. A place at one of the large hospitals was arranged, as was an ambulance, which was to arrive on Sunday morning.

Sunday is necessarily a busy day for Salvationists. When the ambulance failed to arrive during the morning Becker and others had to attend a music festival at the corps. When they hurried back it had still not come. They sat up (through six or seven hours of darkness without electric light) until ten, when they went to bed.

They were awoken two and a half hours later. The ambulance was waiting, four floors down. Since all front doors were sealed by government order, the back stairs—narrow, steep, dirty and unlit—had to be used. Boije was carried on a stretcher at an acute angle down four floors to the street, then through snow a foot deep to the vehicle. The snow concealed deep ruts and holes in the streets and the journey, which took an hour, was 'torture for the invalid'.

The hospital was in near total-darkness, lit only by the simplest of oil lamps–jars of oil with a floating wick—which did not stop those receiving their new patient being rigorously bureaucratic. When Boije was finally given a bed in a large, crowded ward she rejoiced at her new found comfort. Becker, who saw springs sticking out of the mattress on a neighbouring bed, was sceptical, and before long Boije was noticing her own bed's unevenness. Becker procured, by what form of bullying or cajolement she does not say, a horsehair blanket, sheets and pillows. There was no sign of medication or treatment. Becker went to another hospital some blocks away where their doctor was on night duty. He returned with her and did what he could.

For the next five nights they sat with Boije, wearing winter coats, high rubber boots and headgear. No doctor came and there was no news of the X-ray for which she had been admitted. Hot water could only be had after a trek though sludge, snow and darkness to a kitchen (lit by one small oil lamp) several buildings away. Two obstacles stood in the way of the X-ray: shortage of doctors and absence of electric power. Becker asked another officer to stand in for her at the Ministry of Agriculture and spent two days in search of a doctor. She found one, but he could do nothing without an X-ray. Becker heard that the power would be on briefly the following Saturday night. The doctor, the operator and the stretcher-bearers bowed to her

---

32 The following account is drawn from an untitled, undated typescript in the Becker File at The Salvation Army Heritage Centre, London and Larsson, *Tio År I Ryssland*, pp. 179-89.

importunities and it was arranged. Boije was carried across yards and gardens (half-way the bearers put her down to rest themselves) and the X-ray was taken. Once she was back in bed there was a rumpus in the passage outside. A patient in the ward above had been waiting three months for an X-ray and operation and the nurse in charge, incensed, demanded that he receive at once the same treatment as the Salvationist. But the stretcher-bearers were weary. The doctor in charge told Becker next day that she was a hero. No one in the three months he had worked there had achieved anything comparable.

Boije underwent surgery finally on 18 December, to what end is unclear. Her kidneys were diseased but neither was removed. The two Salvationists who were trained nurses looked after her for two agonizing nights until she was taken back to the theatre to have her stitches inspected and her bandages renewed. A hiatus of nine days followed. Becker went once more into persuasive mode but when the doctor came, after two in the afternoon, the stretcher-bearers had finished work for the day. Becker helped the doctor carry another patient (a young girl, one of 140 in the surgical wards) up to the theatre, while Boije's stitches were removed in her own bed.

After ten more days her fever abated and, armed with the doctor's promise to tend her at home, Becker had her discharged. No ambulance being available,

we put a large spring mattress on a big sleigh, added the other bed clothes and took the Staff Captain home in state, carrying her upstairs ourselves on a borrowed stretcher.

Boije appeared to improve, then suffered a series of heart attacks. Becker gave up her job to look after her, another officer taking her place permanently in the Ministry of Agriculture. For the rest of the winter Boije's illness seemed poised to overwhelm her. She lay, drifting in and out of consciousness in a half-world that was disturbed from time to time by police visitations. Ironically these were always signalled by a resumption of the electricity supply. At some time around or after midnight the lights would go on in the block and heavy footsteps would thunder up the stairs. The Salvationists, like all the other residents, were required to awake and show their papers. The women among the inspection parties were usually harshest in their treatment of the women Salvationists. Male or female, however, once they were informed of Boije's presence and condition, and asked to be as quiet as possible, 'always behaved decently'.

Larsson had not heard anything since September or October and was shocked when, at the end of March 1920, Sjöblom received a postcard from a Miss E. Dick, a member of the English colony which was now finally leaving the Soviet Union. Having just crossed the border on her way home, she was in the quarantine centre at Teriyoki. She wished Larsson to be informed (in Czechoslovakia, whither he had been transferred) that, following typhus and a kidney operation, Boije had blood poisoning and was dying. She mentioned various other illnesses and deaths among the officers and the confiscation of the children's home at Orel.

Miss Dick also carried a letter from Boije to her father, who called at the quarantine centre to collect it. Written in Miss Dick's presence on 27 March, when Boije was thought too ill to survive the journey to Finland and was not expected to live more than two weeks, it expresses firm belief in the afterlife.

Very soon I will go home to God and then all will be well. Rejoice with me! In company with Mother I will await you all. If God wills that I recover I will return as soon as I can. Send word especially to Colonel Larsson that I tried but was not able to work as I would have wished. He will understand. I shall be with you, closer than I am now, and see everything from up there...[33]

A little later in the spring, however, there was better news. Arthur E. Coping, of the *Daily Chronicle*, became the first non-Communist journalist to enter Russia since the Soviet seizure of power. A friend of The Salvation Army, he enquired into the welfare of its personnel. In both Moscow and Petrograd he was told (an earnest of things to come rather than the truth) that The Salvation Army did not exist in Russia. He persisted, suggesting that if the authorities did not give him an address for the Salvationists he would tell the world that the Bolsheviks had killed them. He was put in touch within a few minutes. He arranged, in Petrograd, a permit for Boije to leave but, since the authorities would not allow any of her comrades to travel with her and they would not entrust her to strangers, there was a stalemate. Meanwhile, however, Dr Martini of the Danish Red Cross had, in Moscow, arranged another permit, which included a nurse. Now everything went smoothly. In an ambulance provided by the authorities, with Captain Tapaneinen as nurse, the sometimes unconscious, sometimes delirious Boije was taken to the border and carried by stretcher to her waiting father. She was admitted to a private ward in a leading hospital and, in time, overcame the worst effects of her illness.

Could The Salvation Army Have Survived in Communist Russia?

Boije's illness came during an ongoing debate about what would happen when she and all other Finns had to leave Russia. She does not say whether she thought of the informal campaigns in villages and provincial towns which she initiated as a strategy for survival and even expansion, with local cells of Salvationists meeting unobtrusively until times should improve. It seems likely, however, that the idea at least crossed her mind.

Even in Petrograd and Moscow, however, another possible strategy was emerging—that of increased cooperation with some Orthodox clergy and other sympathetic Russians. In the summer of 1919 the Salvationists were invited to visit one of the Orthodox parishes in Moscow by the priest, whom Boije describes as 'a really converted man'. They sang their songs in the church. The same priest visited The Salvation Army hall and addressed the congregation. Another visitor who asked to do this was a professor, the leader of the Students' Association. When he arrived

---

33 Larsson, *Tio År I Ryssland*, p. 188.

he had brought a group of students with him and it appeared that he intended to deliver a formal lecture. Boije suggested that the meeting should begin in the normal Salvationist way. After singing and a prayer, two converts, one of them an elderly former drunkard, testified to their new beliefs. Boije noticed that the professor and students were listening intently. When she invited the professor to speak he, in tears, abandoned his lecture in favour of his own testimony. This led to a further session of prayer during which nine of the students knelt at the penitent form.

Another group with which the Salvationists formed close link was the Tolstoy disciples. One of them,

> a fine looking Caucasian with a large beard... came to us and talked, talked, talked. At first he wouldn't entertain the idea of prayer, but at last we got him on his knees. Then he prayed indeed and got greatly excited and had a beautiful spiritual experience. It was good after that to see him at street corners, still with the rope around his waist and with other details of the Tolstoy dress, but now selling *Vestnik Spaseniya* and delighting to tell the simple gospel story to the knots of people who gathered around him.[34]

Behind these possibly encouraging developments lay others more ominous. It had been clear at least since the beginning of the year that quite soon all foreign Salvation Army Officers would be forced to leave Russia. Even in advance of Boije's illness, International Headquarters raised the question of whether it would be possible to leave behind a functioning Salvation Army consisting entirely of and led by native Russians. It appears that Brigadier Catherine Booth (General Bramwell Booth's daughter) asked Larsson whether any of the Russian officers were of sufficient experience and standing to be appointed in charge. In his reply, written in March 1919, Larsson had no practicable suggestion to offer:

> for me to propose anybody of our young Russian officers to take charge of our work in Russia seems to be utterly hopeless. We have two or three men who would [see themselves] as the only one who could be thought of for such a position. But I cannot depend on them. And who is it among the women who can take up the position? Lieutenant Becker is the only [one] with some common sense, but I am afraid that the staff captain [i.e. Boije], would not trust her.[35]

Larsson's remark that he 'could not depend' upon the men is probably not intended as a reflection on their character and commitment (although he clearly indicates that the two not appointed might be less than eager to take orders from the one who was) but a reflection of the fact that all Russian men were liable to be called up at any time. His remark that Boije would not trust Becker requires more examination, and the fact that Becker would shortly nurse and sustain Boije during a life-threatening illness makes of it a melancholy enigma.

---

34 *All the World*, 1926, p.123. This and earlier references to *Vestnik Spaseniya* of course pre-date January 1919 when the paper finally folded.

35 Larsson, Letter to Brigadier Catherine Booth, p. 3.

Like all the officers under consideration, Becker was young and inexperienced. And there was what had already become, after only 53 years, a question of Salvation Army tradition. Evangeline Booth was the only single woman ever to command a territory and in normal circumstances no one of the rank of lieutenant would have been considered for such an appointment. Further, Becker's own account of herself suggests that she was a shy, rather timid person who, far from wanting to lead, looked to others for leadership. Had she been placed in charge she would certainly have taken the responsibility very seriously—so much so that she might well have been crushed by it. She was tough but possibly not robust. Even so, she had proven capacity for devoted hard work and was a competent linguist who, as it turned out, served The Salvation Army untiringly for the rest of her life.

We may wonder, therefore, what might have happened had she been asked to take command during Boije's illness and after her departure from Russia. The Salvation Army could then have been presented as a Russian organization with a Russian leader, answering one of the larger objections which Russians, Tsarist and Communist, had to it. Instead, The Salvation Army, at crucial points during its last two desperate years in Russia, had no physically fit and officially recognized commander, creating a situation in which improvising individuals served, *de facto*, in the role at different times. As we shall see, it was the Finn, Elsa Olsoni, who conducted the final negotiations with the Soviet authorities.[36]

36 Olsoni was a woman of powerful emotions who was deeply and permanently affected by the eventual failure of The Salvation Army to survive in Communist Russia. In 1972, when she was living in retirement in Helsingfors, it was said of her that '...she would rather not speak of the hard, bitter years when she gave her youth for the salvation of Russia, but she reads her Russian Bible and prays for the Russian people'. See video, *Frälsningsarmen i Ryssland*, and the English transcript of it, p. 10.

CHAPTER 10

The War on Religion

The End of the 'American' Home

The report on the state of affairs in Russia that Boije was eventually able to write and was forwarded to Larsson in Prague by Colonel Joachim Micklebust, the chief secretary in Finland, made grim reading. A number of officers had died of typhus, including a Lieutenant Zinovsky, whose widow was expecting a child and, at the Children's Home in Domnino, south of Orel, Captain Hilda Tuomanien who remained fully conscious until the end, calling 'Father, lift me higher!' as she lay dying. Two women officers and a male soldier 'hammered together a coffin', dug a grave and buried her. Soon afterwards five other officers went down with the disease but recovered.

Some male officers had been drafted into the army. Some officers had, as Boije had urged them to do, taken jobs, which naturally reduced their availability for Salvation Army work. Others had returned to their homes. After the departure of the Finnish officers forced the Army to close the home at Domnino, a mere 15 of their colleagues remained, with a few employees, in Petrograd, Moscow and Vologda.[1]

The 'American' children's home was the last substantial centre of Salvation Army work to be closed down and its loss signalled the end of everything. The home, it will be remembered, had begun in a palatial flat in Petrograd. When, in March 1918, the Bolsheviks declared Moscow to be the capital of the new Russia, American and other diplomats relocated their embassies, not to Moscow but to Vologda, a sleepy provincial town of some 40,000 people, 560 kilometres east of Petrograd. In doing so they distanced themselves from the Communist government, established contact with the White Russians and found a place from which they could if need be escape—either by sea from Archangel or by railway to Murmansk. Other allied institutions also moved to Vologda, including the New York City Bank, which subsidized the 'American' home. Shortage of food and the administration's hostility to The Salvation Army had made the home ever more difficult to maintain in Petrograd. Therefore, helped by officials from the bank, Staff-Captain Rosa Hacklin found suitable premises in the countryside fifteen miles from Vologda. They had scarcely settled in, however, when political developments placed them under threat. In August allied troops landed at Archangel. The Soviets were understandably annoyed. (The Soviet authorities may also have been aware that Salvationist officers were working

---

1 Larsson, *Tio År I Ryssland*, pp. 189-90.

with the British and American forces in Siberia and Vladivostok.)[2] Hacklin was called into the bank to be told that because, as the commissars chose to express it, American celebrations on the Fourth of July had greatly angered the Soviet people, the bank was to close at only 24 hours' notice. The bank manager handed her 1,000 roubles, promising to send more from Moscow, if he could, before departing for the USA.

The home housed a few officers and almost 40 children. One thousand roubles would last about a week. The additional sum the manager was able to send from Moscow lasted a little longer. Then, once again, help came from an unexpected quarter. Most of the foreigners still in Russia were anxious to leave but were allowed to take only a limited sum of money with them. Thus, as the Russian aristocracy had done with their houses, many decided to deposit their surplus money with The Salvation Army in the hope that they would be compensated abroad. (The exchange rate of the rouble stood at one penny; such compensation would not have been unduly expensive.) Well over 100,000 roubles accumulated in this way. By the spring of 1919, however, the shortages and continuing inflation had made even the possession of money almost irrelevant. Food could only be obtained by bartering other useful objects or materials for it. For a period they had only pickled cabbage for dinner. (It smelt so bad that the children would not eat it, but sat there, 'playing with their spoons'.) Breakfast and supper were better, with oat porridge and good rye bread smeared with cod liver oil.

Fortunately the local commissar was a friend of the Salvationists and allowed the officers and children to take part in the potato harvest. Also, when it was announced that the home should be closed because of its connection with America, he accepted the argument that since it was now run entirely by Swedish officers from Finland with local money, that connection no longer existed. His friendship arose from a favour they had done him. Although he was a Communist, he and his wife retained some elements of Orthodox practice. The day before their firstborn was due to be christened they had heard from the dressmaker that the cloth from which the baptismal robe was to be made had been 'spoiled'. The Salvationists hurriedly contrived a dress out of an old red sash and some blue ribbon. Having cast their sash upon the waters they found it coming back as potatoes.

Meanwhile the girls in the home had been taught to sew (what the boys were taught goes unrecorded) and a sale of work fetched a further 3,000 roubles. More money was raised at Christmas, when people came to hear the children sing and recite. For a time all seemed to go well: the home was registered without fuss or interference. But in the autumn of 1919 the premises were requisitioned for use as a school. The home moved into a house belonging to a general's widow who wanted to avoid having soldiers billeted on her. She had a supply of firewood that she was forbidden to sell, which obviated the need to collect fallen branches and dead trees from the nearby forest. In the summer of 1920 the home acquired a pig, two hens and two rabbits. But the end was in sight. The general's widow was evicted from the

---

2 *The War Cry*, 4 January and 31 May, 1919.

two rooms she occupied and a soviet official moved in. He noticed that the officers conducted evening prayers with the children and gave them a kindly warning that the authorities would not tolerate this much longer. Curiosity grew in the village. Most foreigners had left Russia. Why were these Finns still there? Surely it was not merely in order to look after 40 Russian orphans. A policeman for whom they had sewn and embroidered a shirt warned them that the local Soviet had discussed them. They would not be allowed to stay much longer.

Captain Konstantinova from Moscow and another officer spent a couple of weeks with them on holiday. Konstantinova invited Hacklin to conduct the harvest celebrations in the capital. She agreed, apparently in a somewhat fatalistic spirit, thinking that she would never see the home again. She and others prayed in the fields on the way to the village station. Clara Becker, who had moved to the home for rest and recuperation after Boije's departure, tells us what happened next. Lieutenant Polsova, the home's lawyer, who had obtained Hacklin's travelling permit, travelled as far as Vologda to see them off. When she returned to the home after nightfall she had with her a Communist detective who had come on the same train from town as she, and the village policeman. They had come to arrest Rosa Hacklin. The detective behaved courteously and refrained from searching or sealing Hacklin's office.

Next day a male officer, alerted by Hacklin, arrived to slaughter and butcher the pig. The meat was hidden. The day after that the chickens were to meet the same fate but the villagers had got to them first: only their heads remained. During the week that followed the officers prepared to leave. At the end of that time Lieutenant Polsova went into Vologda to hear the final decision of the authorities. She returned accompanied by the detective. This time he searched Hacklin's office and took some papers. When doing it he saw a guitar hanging on the wall and asked whether anyone there could play. Captain Kokonen was prevailed upon to play and sing 'Let the blessed sunshine in'.

A few days later the home was officially closed. The officers went to Petrograd and in time some of the children who had distant family connections in that city also returned there. The rest were presumably taken to a state children's home to be taught atheism and take part in processions that parodied Orthodoxy. One or two officers stayed in Vologda, eking out a living as nurses and seamstresses.

The Salvation Army in Russia was dying the death of a thousand cuts—but the agony was not to be prolonged. A more implacable enemy than typhus, starvation or financial stringency was poised to hasten the outcome.

'Spiritual Gin…Unutterable Vileness'

This was the War on Religion. Victory in the Civil War, suppression of rebellion by the 14,000 sailors of the Baltic fleet on Kronstadt (who in 1917 had been the Bolshevik's vanguard), elimination of all other political parties and the introduction of the New Economic Policy (limited privatization and decentralization of industry and encouragement of foreign investment) put Lenin in a position in which he felt strong enough to attack the Orthodox Church. (Fearful of arousing large-scale organized opposition, he had avoided troubling it during the Civil War.) His hostility towards it had, however, long been clear. At the time of the revolution the first draft of a constitution for the Soviet Republic had stated that 'Religion is the private affair of citizens' but Lenin insisted that this be replaced by what became Article 13 of the RSFSR Constitution of 10 July, 1918, which guaranteed 'freedom of religious and anti-religious propaganda'. This was bound to be—was intended to be—an unequal struggle: ranged against the forces of the state and the Communist Party were Churches 'weakened, if not crippled by discriminatory legislation'.[3] Lenin was reviving, in a much harsher form, Marx's definition of religion as 'the opium of the people'. Marx wrote that

> Religion is the sigh of the oppressed creature, the heart of a heartless world, the spirit of soulless stagnation. It is the *opium* of the people.

Lenin's take on this was less measured:

> Religion is a kind of spiritual gin in which the slaves of capital drown their human shape and their claims to any decent life.

Later, he wrote, yet more bitterly, that

> Every religious idea, every idea of God, even flirting with the idea of God, is unutterable vileness... vileness of the most dangerous kind... *Every* defence or justification of the idea of God, even the most refined, the best intentioned, is justification of reaction.

Elsewhere he develops this last notion:

> All modern religions and Churches, all religious organizations, Marxism always regards as organs of *bourgeois* reaction serving to defend exploitation and to stupefy the working class.

The Marxist-Leninst objection to religion thus united a number of separate but complementary ideas. First, religion was false: a mere comforting fantasy designed to alleviate the sufferings of the oppressed. Secondly it was a conspiracy by the oppressors to keep the masses in subjection. Thirdly, its notion of rewards to come in a future life for the sufferings and distresses could only reduce the hunger of the people for change here and now; it was by definition opposed to change and social improvement. The 1919 Party programme stated that

> The Party strives for the complete destruction of the ties between the exploiter classes and the organization of religious propaganda; it furthers the actual

---

3 Robert Conquest, *Religion in the USSR*, London, 1968, The Bodley Head, p. 13. See pp. 13-16 and 7-9, on which my discussion is based and from which the quotations from Marx and Lenin are taken.

liberation of the toiling masses from religious prejudices and organizes the broadest scientific-educational and anti-religious propaganda.

There was also, it must be said, a fear that the Orthodox Church was the one force within the country that could and would rally resistance against the atheistic Bolsheviks.

Such were the overt motives behind the anti-Christian propaganda (often of a crude, simplistic sort—pictures, for instance, of a pregnant Virgin Mary asking for an abortion) with which the state bombarded its citizens. There were other, less explicit motives, which were greatly influenced by the religions the Communists despised. Writing in the early 1940s, Bertrand Russell pointed out that Marx's eschatology is directly derived from the 'Jewish pattern of history... [which] is such as to make a powerful appeal to the oppressed and unfortunate at all times' and from St Augustine's adaptation of that pattern (in *The City of God*) to Christianity. 'To understand Marx psychologically', he argues, 'one should use the following dictionary:

> Yaweh = Dialectical Materialism
> The Messiah = Marx
> The Elect = The Proletariat
> The Church = The Communist Party
> The Second Coming = The Revolution
> Hell = The Punishment of the Capitalists
> The Millennium = The Communist Commonwealth

The terms on the left give the emotional content of the terms on the right, and it is this emotional content, familiar to those who have had a Christian or Jewish upbringing, that makes Marx's eschatology credible.'[4]

Under Lenin and Stalin this emotional content was given outward form by the adaptation of traditional religious symbols and customs to Soviet purposes. 'Socialist Realism' in the visual arts developed an iconography of socialist struggle and aspiration, reinforced by omnipresent idealized portraits of the glorious leaders. When Lenin died in 1924, Stalin ensured that his corpse became the focus of a quasi-religious cult. Against the wishes of his wife and family (and certainly against his own, often stated, denunciations of the cult of personality) it was embalmed and kept publicly visible at great trouble and expense[5] in a mausoleum (initially of wood but from 1930 of red granite) designed by A.V. Shchusev who, before the revolution had designed Moscow's Church of Martha and Mary.[6] Respectful crowds came to this

---

4 Bertrand Russell, *History of Western Philosophy and its Connection with Political and Social Circumstances from the Earliest Times to the Present Day*, London, George Allen and Unwin, 1957, p. 383.

5 For a full, entertaining account see Zbarsky, Ilya and Hutchinson, Samuel, *Lenin's Embalmers*, London, Harvill, 1988.

6 Hamilton, *Art and Architecture of Russia*, pp. 282 and 316, note 49.

place of pilgrimage to file past the body in solemn silence. Lenin had become, in the terms of Russell's lexicon, the crucified Messiah who had given his life that the people might be redeemed, redemption in this case being understood as 'the electrification of the Soviet Union'.[7] Many revolutionaries had been religious in their youth and their expectations of the revolution were millennial in tone, Some, as we shall see, had spent time and energy during the 15 or so years before the revolution trying to find the God in the Marxist machine. Even the new cult object, Lenin himself, had once been described as a 'religious thinker', albeit in a pejorative sense, 'using the word "religion" as a synonym for clericalism, dogmatism, dualism and authoritarianism...'.[8] If Communism was indeed to become a religion it could of course brook no rivals. Christianity had to go.

In the nationwide campaign against religion that followed, The Salvation Army was of course a relatively insignificant target. From the Soviet point of view, however, it was provocative on a number of counts. It was foreign and, worse, was associated with England, an imperialist nation. Within Russia, it had been supported, however distantly, by members of the former ruling class, including members of the imperial family. It ran children's homes, thus demonstrating that all was not well in the workers' paradise. It taught its charges to believe in outdated myths. Furthermore, although, like Communism, it preached universal salvation, it dealt with people one at a time as individuals whereas for the true Marxist, 'salvation could only be universal, not individual'.[9]

The principle object of attack was, of course, the Orthodox Church, which was deprived of the material and legal basis of its existence when all church land was nationalized without compensation and clergy were disenfranchised. Services were permitted to continue but church buildings were often used for secular or even anti-religious purposes: courses of instruction, lectures, concerts, film shows, political meetings and dances. Church marriages were refused legal recognition. Much church property, particularly artistic treasures, was confiscated and resistance was met with violence. When senior clergy complained, they were put on trial on charges of counter-revolutionary agitation. A number were executed amid accusations that the leaders of the Church had declared war on the government.

7 See Acton, *Russia*, pp. 201-02, on 'the cult of the departed prophet'.

8 See Christopher Read, *Religion, Revolution and the Russian Intelligentsia, 1900–1912*, London, Macmillan, 1979, pp. 57-94.

9 Read, *Religion, Revolution, and the Russian Intelligentsia*, p. 89.

Larsson Meets the Cheka[10]

Harassment of The Salvation Army had, as we have seen, occurred at random intervals throughout its time in Russia but before Larsson left it was formalized. On 13 November, 1918 he had had a conversation with a Cheka official, Stepanov, who later sent minutes of the meeting, which read as follows:

> Owing to the dangerous influence spread by the organization, The Salvation Army, and in view of the fact that it is supported by citizens of America, England and Sweden, and seeing its activities are at war with the interest of the Soviet government and detrimental to the rights of the working population, its activities are prohibited in the district of Petrograd, including the holding of meetings, the work with the Children's Home, and the publication of the newspaper *Vestnik Spaseniya*. The premises will be confiscated and sold.[11]

When Larsson appealed against this decision he was told that the matter had been handed over to Lunacharsky's Commissariat of Enlightenment (in effect the Ministry for Education and the Arts) and would be dealt with by Zlata Lilina, wife of Grigory Zinoviev, a member of the Triumvirate (the others were Stalin and Kamenev) that dominated the Politburo.[12] Lunacharsky had been one of those who, while in exile during the 1900s, attracted criticism from Lenin as 'God-seekers' or 'God-builders' because of his wish to interpret Marxism as a man-made substitute for theistic religion, which, in addition to providing a critique of social and economic conditions and a blue-print for political action, would satisfy the deeper levels of human nature. He was still so inclined at the time of Lenin's death in 1924, and was among those who supported Stalin in promoting the Lenin mausoleum as the centre of a religious cult.[13] Religion, he thought, could only be destroyed if it was also replaced. He wrote that

> Religion is like a nail: if you hit it on the head you only drive it deeper... Here one needs pliers. Religion must be *grabbed*, squeezed from below; you do not beat it but pull it out, pull it with its roots. And this can be achieved *only by scientific propaganda, by the moral and artistic education of the masses.*[14]

---

10 Communist Russia's political police force, operating outside the law as an instrument of terror, was established in December 1917 as The All-Russian Extraordinary Commission to Combat Counterrevolution, Speculation and Administrative Crimes (later 'to Combat Counterrevolution and Sabotage'). Power struggles within the Communist Party led to its being renamed many times, its most famous acronyms being OGPU, NKVD and KGB.

11 Larsson, *Tio År I Ryssland*, p. 175.

12 Stalin later turned against the other two and both were executed in 1936 in the wake of the first great show trial.

13 Stites, *Revolutionary Dreams*, p. 120.

14 Quoted by Pipes, *Russia under the Bolshevik Regime*, p. 338.

If Lunacharsky was inclined to at least a pseudo-religious view of life (albeit he would have accepted none of the beliefs of The Salvation Army) and, uniquely amongst the Soviet leaders, was benevolent and generous by nature, the official into whose care he gave the organization's fate, Zlata Lilina (Madame Zinoviev), was a secularist hard-liner. The Salvation Army's children's homes which aimed to replace their charges' lost parents, would have attracted her particular scorn, for she insisted, on anti-parental grounds, that all children should be raised by the state.

> Is not parental love to a large extent harmful to the child? The family is individualistic and egoistic and the child raised by it is, for the most part, antisocial, filled with egoistic strivings... Raising children is not the private task of parents but the task of society.[15]

With Lilina in charge and, given the attitude to Salvationism already stated by the KGB ('its activities are at war with the interest of the Soviet government and detrimental to the rights of the working population') and the Soviets' now secure hold on government, it could only be a matter of time before The Salvation Army was disbanded ('liquidated' was the term eventually used). The Salvationists, however, had to face further trials of their faith and endurance before that came to pass.[16]

Famine and Freezing Weather

Starvation was rife. The ration card system had broken down. Official food supplies consisted of potatoes (usually at least half rotten and often frozen) and some oats. The waywardness of the railways and the arbitrary behaviour of 'requisitioners', who were authorized to confiscate any food not officially accounted for, made the traditional device of travelling into the countryside to buy food from peasants difficult, dangerous and more often than not futile. The Salvationists were in a double bind. Not only could they not feed themselves, they could not feed others. One day, before her illness struck, Helmy Boije was accosted in the street by an elderly woman. 'You are The Salvation Army', she said. 'Cannot you help me? Give me a piece of bread. I have had no food for two days.' Boije had to confess that she had nothing to give. Somewhat unfairly, one feels, the woman gave Boije a look that she would never forget and said, 'You call yourselves The Salvation Army and you cannot do as much as that'. Boije felt almost ashamed to be wearing her uniform.

Sometimes the cold seemed even worse than the hunger. Firewood, like food, was in short supply and any empty buildings, with official permission and under official regulations, were soon stripped of wooden fittings by licensed scavengers with handcarts, axes, and saws. Obtaining such permission required queueing to see

---

15 Quoted by Pipes, *Russia under the Bolshevik Regime*, p. 331.

16 The account of the privations of these years comes largely from Elsa Olsoni's *Russian Pictures*, as quoted extensively in Larsson, *Tio År I Ryssland*, pp. 191-97.

numerous functionaries: the time so spent could be anything up to 18 hours. Whereas hunger weakened and depressed people over time, the cold, as Elsa Olsoni describes it, 'with its icy fingers gripped every atom of our being in an extraordinarily painful way'. New clothes were unobtainable. So were thread and wool, which made mending and patching difficult. In the summer people had got by with shoes made from sacking but in the Russian winter felt boots were necessary.

The electricity supply was intermittent and people lived in darkness for a large part of most days.

Trying as these physical deprivations were they were less destructive, Olsoni tells us, than the overriding condition of the time: 'continuous insecurity with regard to property, freedom and life.' This drove some to despair, madness or suicide; the Salvationists were 'driven by it more than ever to the foot of the cross'. One of them, in Petrograd, walking home from the food committee carrying some herring wrapped in paper, was arrested and cross-examined about her right to the fish. Having been kept up most of the night she had to return next day with a written affidavit before the herring were given back. On trains, agents of GPU (State Political Administration, later OGPU) might demand to inspect papers. Even if the papers were in order GPU men might decide that the traveller was on the wrong train and arrest them, thus beginning several days in custody at the next major railway station before the accusation was resolved by an arbitrary decision one way or the other. Night-time visitations continued, resulting more or less automatically in a month's penal servitude followed by enforced employment by the state. In this way a number of Salvationists became student nurses, charwomen or clerks. In the prevailing climate of suspicion evangelical trips to the countryside were no longer so carefree; several officers found themselves appearing before local magistrates on suspicion—of what they were not told.

In part, such arrests, arbitrary charges and imprisonment arose from Lenin's decision to use terror as an instrument of control. In the case of The Salvation Army the war on religion was an additional factor.

Apart from the small groups in Moscow and Petrograd there was very little of The Salvation Army left to destroy. During the winter of 1920-21, seven officers and five children (those left unaccommodated after the closure of the two children's homes) lived in a six-roomed flat in Petrograd. Three of the women worked in the city's hospitals. Captain Belevsky (the pork butcher) and his wife were left to continue The Salvation Army's more normal work, travelling into the countryside to conduct meetings and obtain food.

The children went to school despite difficulties getting clothes and footwear. By some means

> a pair of new galoshes came into their possession. The oldest girl was the lucky one whom they fitted and she was given them for Christmas. 'And she, normally a very self-possessed girl, kissed those galoshes!'.

As winter became spring, the situation in Petrograd worsened rapidly. The Kronstadt rebellion resulted, *inter alia*, in the city being placed under martial law. Foreigners, particularly if wearing uniforms, became more than ever objects of suspicion. The officers agreed among themselves that it was becoming impossible to carry on Salvation Army work there, as well as increasingly dangerous merely to be there at all. Several prepared to leave the country, including Clara Becker, who intended to visit Estonia, where her father, now a widower and to whom she was partially reconciled, was living.

Elsewhere, despite the loss of the children's homes and despite the fact that many officers had to work full time for the state, there was once again an air of optimism. Elsa Olsoni was seriously considering the possibility of starting one or more new corps in the interior of the country, where continuing fortnight-long campaigns with officers moving from village to village had given encouraging results. In Moscow, Nadia Konstantinova conducted meetings every weeknight and twice on Sundays. The hall was usually full and people continued to surrender to Christ. 'We now have 21 soldiers and five local officers', she wrote, 'besides which we have 20 recruits who are soon to be enrolled as soldiers while, of our 350 converts, a number are about to be made recruits.'

Prisoners for Christ

Konstantinova also wrote, however, that 'we feel as if we are living on a volcano'. Nonetheless, it was in Petrograd that the volcano first erupted and—albeit the Salvationists had felt for some time that they were under threat of summary arrest—the eruption was provoked by an ill-considered remark by one of their own, Miss Kangur, a nurse and a member of the Petrograd string band. This indiscreet young woman and the sister-in-law of one of the officers were out walking on the evening of 24 February and fell into conversation with a soldier on guard outside a military barracks near St Isaac's Cathedral. In the hearing of a group that had gathered to listen Kangur told him, 'You ought to use your bayonets on your own government'. One of the listeners was an informer in the pay of the Cheka, who arrested the two women and took them to a police station. The officer's sister-in-law turned out to be disastrously ill-disposed towards The Salvation Army (for which reason Larsson can only bring himself to identify her as 'N'), giving all the information demanded of her, including addresses where Salvationists could be found. She was then released. Sister Kangur was put into solitary confinement at Cheka headquarters for two weeks, after which she was sent to Spalernaya prison.

Next morning, at five and ten o'clock, raids were made on the two addresses 'N' had revealed and by lunchtime Corps Sergeant-Major and Mrs Tsuber, Helmy Manainen, Rosa Hacklin, Henny Granström, Captain Belevsky (whose wife was in hospital, having given birth to their first child two days earlier) and Elsa Olsoni were all in custody. The Red Guards searched Olsoni's room and took letters she had received from Finland: one of the charges levelled at the Salvationists was that they were counter-revolutionary agents in touch with foreign countries. The guards tore The Salvation Army flag to pieces, arrested those of the Salvationists who did not have children to look after and took them away, again leaving a soldier on guard to arrest anyone else who should appear. Before they left, all the Salvationists, whether staying or departing, sang, 'God be with you till we meet again.' The Bolsheviks laughed, saying it was a fine, sad song. Tsuber, however, reduced them to tears with 'I carry the flag of the Saviour, the flag of the blood and of fire'.[17]

At Cheka headquarters the men and women were separated and taken through labyrinthine passages and stairs, undergoing sundry examinations. The women's cubicles were on the top floor, where they were greeted with curiosity by a mixed group of people who at once became comrades in misfortune, wanting to know 'Why are you here?' and 'Who are you?'.

After a few days they were removed—by night, in a fast car, through empty streets—to the well-known Spalernaya remand prison, where the women's section consisted of six large rooms with bitumen floors and metal gratings in windows and doorways.

Clara Becker had not been arrested, having been to Lesnoy to say goodbye to her friends at the hospital where she had worked as a nurse, before leaving for Estonia. The curfew had had forced her to stay with relatives overnight. On her way home next morning she encountered a girl from the house who warned her that a soldier was waiting at the flat to arrest anyone who called. For several days she busied herself caring for Mrs Belevsky. She sent a telegram to International Headquarters, beating the censors with the message that 'a number of our families are with Paul and Silas in Acts 16'.[18]

She was eventually arrested when, having heard that the helpers left in the flat were not being allowed out to get fuel and food and two of the children were ill, she wrote a note to her father telling him not to expect her for some time and presented herself at the flat with supplies. She was immediately arrested but was allowed to stay there overnight to sort things out. For almost farcical reasons the flat was more crowded than she expected.

> A little girl had come to visit one of ours and had been arrested. When she did not reappear at home, her mother, getting worried, sent first one brother, then another. Both were detained. Finally, the father came to fetch the children and he too was arrested. Then a former recruit of ours came and he was arrested.[19]

The following afternoon Becker was taken to Cheka Headquarters and placed in solitary confinement in a cell five-and-a-half by three feet. A dirty sack filled with

---

17 *All the World*, 1925, p. 194.

18 Acts 16 tells the story of the apostles being arrested, whipped and imprisoned by order of the magistrates in Philippi, the town in Macedonia where Brutus and Cassius were defeated by Antony and Octavius in 42 B.C.

19 Larsson, *Tio År I Ryssland*, p. 212. Larsson's account of the arrests and of what followed, on which mine is closely based, is on pp. 208-24. I have also taken details from the Swedish video, *Frälsningsarmén I Ryssland* and from Flora Larsson, *All My Best Men Are Women*, pp. 54-58. Some of the details in my account of Becker's time in prison come from a memoir, *Three Prison Cells and What Their Walls Taught Me*, a shortened, unsigned version of which was published in *All the World*, 1926, pp. 199-200.

what had once been straw lay on a narrow wooden bench fastened to a wall. Opposite was a tiny wooden table. Assessing the cramped conditions she wryly thanked God that she was very short. There was an opening, seven inches square, in the door, through which food was passed and which allowed her to see the board on which hung keys to the 29 cells, subdivisions within a large room.[20] High up an electric light shone day and night. She and the blank white plaster walls, untouched by graffiti, were under 24 hour surveillance by male warders.

As a precaution, in case it concealed something important, her thick, plaited hair was unwound. She had taken a few things with her from the flat—a blanket, a needle and thread, a knife, a New Testament in English and a small mug. Twice daily, the mug, which she was allowed to keep throughout her time in prison, was filled with warm, unidentifiable liquid.

She was kept at Cheka headquarters for ten days before being transferred, abruptly, at 1 a.m. to the Spalernaya prison. She still had a small pencil (though nothing, of course, to sharpen it apart from teeth and nails) and before she left, knowing that the words would be scrubbed off as soon as they were noticed, she wrote on a wall, 'God is love'.

In Spalernaya, a huge building with long corridors and a profusion of iron bars, she was once again 'in solitary', although her cell was much more spacious.

I thought I was seeing the stars for the last time. There, after a thorough search, everything was taken from me—my New Testament, needle—everything except my tiny mug. I was led to a cell where there already was another woman, but she was taken away, and I fell asleep. One great advantage in this prison was that they turned the light off at night...

The stone floor was damp. The painted walls had not been kept clear of written messages from her predecessors in captivity—messages of despair, of fear, some blasphemies—but over and again, the word 'Why?' She glossed one of these appeals for an explanation with part of Daniel's hymn of praise to God's omniscience (and his willingness to share it with those who have striven after wisdom and understanding): 'He knoweth what is in the darkness'.[21] Elsewhere on the walls she drew a Salvation Army crest and, with much labour, wrote out a song, 'I'm giving my all to Jesus'.

During her third night in Spalernaya she was awakened when the door opened, the light was switched on and another prisoner was pushed into the cell. It was Sister Kangur. Despite Kangur's role in provoking the arrests Becker seems to have been pleased to have her company. They assumed that they would be separated when the connection between them was realized, but they were moved together to another cell, with a sloping floor two inches deep in water at its lowest point. Here too, there were many inscriptions, including an ill-spelt, faltering 'Lord's Prayer'. Becker once

---

20 The other 28 cells were occupied by men, all, she learned, called Becker: someone with that name had committed some offence, hence the mass arrest of male Beckers.

21 Dan. 2. 22.

more added a gloss, a phrase that became the motto of her time in prison: 'peace like a river'. [22]

This cell also had a window, and when they heard voices down below they could with some physical contortion see the other inmates exercising in the yard below. Becker waved her red guernsey through the bars to attract their attention and some elementary communication in dumb show was established. About a month after they had all been arrested they discovered by this means that Sergeant-Major Tsuber and his wife had been released. Becker later heard that shortly before his release Tsuber had been questioned for five hours (another account gives 'more than two hours').[23]

Tsuber had knelt at the penitent form the second time he attended a meeting at the Petrograd Second Corps. Employed by the food commissariat at the marine barracks in Petrograd, he soon made himself indispensable to the Salvationists in his free time. We are told that 'when difficult days came, his joyful "Hallelujah!" was as full of faith as in brighter days'. He was as fearless and lively a debater as Seligman and disarmed his interrogators with a defence based on *Romans* 13: 'All authority is from God'. A few days before the arrests, his wife rejoined him from the country after a separation imposed by the war. When she was taken to prison she knew very little about The Salvation Army and indeed resented his membership of it. Only slowly after a month 'herded together with unspeakable characters... the company of the [Salvationist] officers... was that of angels, by comparison' did she come round.[24]

Tsuber described his encounter with the examining committee in a letter written to Colonel Sjöblom in Helsinki after his release. The examination began with this dialogue:

> Chairman: You are a seaman, and, it seems, stupid enough to have joined The Salvation Army. Come to us and we will put you to the university, and you will become an educated man.

> Tsuber: I am learning in the University of Jesus Christ and (taking his New Testament from his pocket) here is my book. I advise you to read it.

> Chairman: It is easily seen you are quite mad.[25]

---

22 Becker may have taken the phrase from H.G. Spafford's hymn, written in memory of his children drowned at sea, which begins:
> When peace like a river attendeth my way,
> When sorrows like sea-billows roll,
> Whatever my lot, Thou has taught me to know
> It is well, it is well with my soul.

Alternatively she may have taken it direct from Spafford's source, Isa. 66.12 (in the Authorized Version; some later translators replace 'peace' with 'prosperity').

23 *All the World*, 1925, p. 195.

24 *All the World*, 1922, pp. 349-50.

25 *All the World*, 1925, p. 194.

Having questioned him about The Salvation Army's purposes and suggested to him that the Bible account of Jesus' death and resurrection came from Satan rather than God, the examining committee passed on to The Salvation Army's attitude to politics. What, in particular, was The Salvation Army's attitude towards the Soviet Government? This is when he cited St Paul:

> Let every soul be subject unto the higher powers. For there is no power but of God: the powers that be are ordained of God. Whosoever therefore resisteth the power, resisteth the ordinance of God: and they that resist shall receive to themselves damnation.[26]

This amused the President of the Examining Committee who exclaimed (with an oath), 'How he can answer!'.

When asked whether the power of the Bolsheviks was from God, Tsuber affirmed that it was, refusing to be distracted by remarks about differing forms of government in different countries: 'All power whatsoever', he argued on the strength of St Paul's dictum, 'is from God'.

He was perhaps, a little uncharitable when, having announced that he and The Salvation Army took no part in politics, he was questioned about Miss Kangur and her remark to the guard. He alluded to Kangur's youth and inexperience, no doubt justifiable points to make, but to suggest that she was comparable to Judas, as he went on to do, seems unduly harsh, since she fairly obviously had no intention of betrayal and said no more than, one would imagine, many Salvationists may have thought, or even said, privately, sentiments that Commissioner Mapp may well have articulated in public. Miss Kangur, who paid for her folly by spending far longer in prison than any other Salvationist, emerging only after The Salvation Army had been closed down, has in general been unkindly treated by Salvationist writers. In their defence it has to be said that Miss Kangur was a soldier in an army and she and her fellows had almost certainly been ordered many times not to say anything that might provoke official anger. Given that near certainty and given the situation Zuber was in, he had little choice but to distance himself from her views. But the episode reminds us that The Salvation Army's claim to be apolitical is a vexed one, particularly in situations where all the other parties involved—in this case all Russian governments of whatever stripe and the Russian Orthodox Church—regard religion and politics as inseparable. Reference has already been made to Mrs General Booth's attacks on Bolshevism in *All the World* during 1919; these, although they dealt only with religious and moral concerns, would certainly have appeared politically motivated by any Bolshevik official to whom they had been reported.

The examiner seems finally to have decided that although Tsuber had clearly been thoroughly brainwashed, he was relatively harmless; he told him to abandon the Bible in favour of some other teaching before he found himself in the madhouse. According to differing reported versions of his letter, Tsuber replied either that he

---

26 Rom. 13.1-2.

needed no other teaching than Christ's, or else remarked that God would surely look after 'his fools'. If the latter, was he, consciously or otherwise, alluding not only to St Paul's discussion (in the first Epistle to the Corinthians)[27] of the virtues of 'foolishness' in the service of Christ, but also to the traditional Russian reverence for the peripatetic 'holy fool'? Were his interrogators, consciously or otherwise, influenced by this quasi-instinctive ploy? We cannot say. Whether because of his irrepressible vivacity in argument or because his captors had lost interest, Tsuber and his wife were released at six o'clock the following evening.

Meanwhile, those Salvationists who were free, who included four officers, were doing what they could to help the ten who were in prison, getting food in to them every three days, boosted, in time by supplies sent from Finland. They also persuaded the Finnish legation to discuss their situation with the Russian authorities. These diplomatic efforts may have borne some fruit, for on Easter Day, 27 March, 1921, two days after the Zubers' release and just over a month after they had all been arrested, Becker and eight other Salvationists were also freed, the sole exception being the unfortunate Miss Kangur, who was to be dragged from one prison to another for three more years. Larsson remarks that nobody could quite believe that the Salvationists' release had been so casual. An incarceration of several years had seemed increasingly likely. They could not but be aware that prisoners other than themselves were subjected daily to hostile examination, during which any statement or indication of emotion could have the gravest consequences: the death penalty, banishment or the concentration camps. For the Salvationists also, such fates might be just around the corner.

Their release, therefore, came almost as an anti-climax. And, indeed, imprisonment itself, once they adapted to it, had not been unmitigated suffering. Despite the gratings in all the inside walls and partitions, prison was much warmer than the apartments they had lived in when free. Similarly, although the food was spartan at best, it was no worse than that available outside, and additional food parcels, arriving on Mondays and Fridays for those who had people on the outside able to help them, alleviated the situation, even allowing for the insistence of prison staff that they should enjoy some of the benefit, and, more agreeably, sharing with other prisoners less fortunate than themselves. They had the choice, too, of either eating everything at once, so that they felt satisfied once daily, or eating a little at a time at set hours.

Rather to their surprise, the Salvationists found many of their fellow prisoners very congenial. There was a lively crowd of students from the women's medical institute, (who had been declared 'counter-revolutionary' and interned *en masse*), whose cells rang with chatter and undergraduate songs. There were school mistresses, doctors and a university professor, all of whom conversed freely with the Salvationists. Other women found imprisonment more trying: those who were there because their husbands, sons or sons-in-law were under suspicion, or who were unfortunate enough to share names with known or suspected opponents of the state.

---

27 See 1 Cor. 4.10: 'We are fools for Christ's sake'.

These people, plunged into previously unimaginable circumstances that they felt they did not deserve, could not defy depression with singing and laughter, as did the students, or with objective or abstract discussions, like the intellectuals.

Despite these mitigating factors, days were long. Sometimes they were set to mending prison clothes. Some gave language lessons; there was even a lecture on the French Revolution. A news summary (perhaps tendentious) was read out each day. Other than those in solitary confinement, prisoners were allowed 20 minutes to walk in the small garden (from which, it will be remembered, the Salvationists were able to exchange sign language messages with Clara Becker and Miss Kangur).

At night the overcrowding was all too obvious. Thirty prisoners occupied cells with ten bunks. Every inch of floor was covered by straw mattresses, which even extended along the balcony outside the top floor windows.

The Salvationists were naturally bound to find God's will and grace in these discomforts: Clara Becker was moved to write that her four weeks in gaol had been amongst the happiest of her life. She was relieved of her customary pressing responsibilities (most immediately for Boije's welfare, but for other matters as well) and she had time for communion with God. She felt, as she wrote on the cell wall, 'peace like a river' attending her way. Whatever her fate might turn out to be, she told herself, she would be able to bear it, because nothing could happen to her that was outside God's will. For all that, some of what she experienced brought her (the same was true of others) close to despair, in moments about which she preferred to remain largely silent.

One must have lived through it to understand that feeling of being trapped and surrounded by evil forces from all sides. That feeling of absolutely being suffocated, without any hope, without a way out, just drearily doing one's best every day, with the frantic effort to hold fast the faith that God must be somewhere although He let things happen. And in the darkest hours experiencing that He did care. Still, our spiritual life had suffered, standards had been lowered, faith in human beings was almost lost. Again, I say, this cannot be told, it must be experienced. But God never failed.[28]

Following her unexplained release, Becker leaves our story for the time being. Because she was an Estonian subject, money that had been taken from her was returned and she obtained permission and a ticket to join her father in that now separate country. She obtained also a small bowl of boiled peas to last through what should have been a 48 hour journey but in the event took a full three days.

Meanwhile, in Moscow...

There were arrests in Moscow also; three officers and two soldiers spent time in custody. (They had been forewarned by employees of the Cheka that Konstantinova and others were on the list of those marked for arrest.) The wrath of the Cheka had

---

28 Becker, *Scrapbook, Russia*, p. 11.

been aroused, it was thought, by the conversion, at a Salvation Army Meeting, of two of its agents. Konstantinova was summoned to Cheka no. 8, where she was examined by 'a red-haired Communist' who, she suspected, tried to hypnotize her. Close to losing her temper, she was strengthened by a voice telling her to 'Answer only with your testimony' and a white form (not seen by the interrogator) which stood with its hand on her shoulder. Was it God's will that the home at Vologda had been closed, she was asked. Would it be God's will if she were arrested? Was there, in fact a God? She stuck to her resolution.

> I witnessed to him about Christ. In that room it became clear to me that God in Christ is my personal helper and deliverer.[29]

Otherwise, the interview ended inconclusively. Shortly afterwards the hall was sealed off, although Salvationists continued to gather there, using the back door. One Sunday, they were visited by Tikhon, the Orthodox Patriarch. But at three o'clock in the morning of 4 March, 16 or 18 militiamen arrived. There was an exchange about a scrap of red flannel lying on a desk, which surprised the militiamen's leader by its colour.

> 'I know well that you don't like the red colour.'

> 'On the contrary', I answered, 'we love the red colour, the symbol of the blood of Christ that washes us white.'

She realized too late that she should not have mentioned white, because of its political implications. She and Lieutenant Kuznetsova were arrested. After a short, fervent prayer, during which the militiamen waited quietly, they were taken to a rat-infested basement in a Cheka post. This basement, they well knew, was where the firing squad operated. Someone had written with charcoal beside its terrible doors some words from the Koran: 'And even this shall pass.' When she was instructed to hand over her Bible, Konstantinova pretended not to hear. The demand was repeated. 'Over my dead body', she replied—and was allowed to keep it. They were marched to another prison, popularly known as 'The Ships', in company with, among others, Anna Sereyevna Sheremeteva of the Student Christian Movement. There they stayed a month, spied on by a Jewish comedienne who, however, became a convert. Sheremeteva and Lieutenant Kuznetsova were released at the end of that time but Konstantinova was marched across Moscow to a women's prison where she was kept for a further eight months. (No-one ever found out why: perhaps her use of the word 'white' counted against her and she was considered especially dangerous; perhaps she was simply forgotten.) She was treated as a 'political' at first, sharing a large cell with 50 doctors, students and teachers, many of them atheists and anarchists. Goodwill prevailed, although Konstantinova refused to join in their more blood-curdling revolutionary songs.

---

29 Konstantinova-Sundell, *The Smallness of Man—the Greatness of God*, p. 8.

After a month she was moved away from this cheerful company and as time passed, she became depressed and her faith was 'severely tested'. Her mind dwelt on her parents in Finland. They, who had been opposed to her becoming a Salvationist, must be suffering great anxiety. Then, quite unexpectedly, she had news of them. The woman dentist who periodically examined the prisoners' teeth took the opportunity to pass her a note: Commissioner Larsson had heard that her parents were anxious. Could she send them a note through the Finnish Legation. This, she says, was easier said than done. But the cell she was in had a window onto the street and when she realized that her comrades outside came there hoping to catch sight of her, visual contact was re-established.

Her spirits lifted until she heard that she and others were to be transferred to the criminal wing of the prison. The inmates there had a reputation for violence towards newcomers of whom they disapproved: a countess who had been moved in with them had been beaten up by a mob 18 strong. However, Konstantinova, 'the holy woman,' was actually welcomed; before she arrived the 18 cleaned out the cell and cut 'lace' doilies to prettify the windowsill and shelves. When, on 25 March, Good Friday, she arrived, they were sitting quietly on their beds. Later, when was she reading her Bible, they asked her to read aloud to them. She read one of the passion narratives, a story, she soon realized, which they had never heard. With 'great eagerness' she read on, interspersing expositions of the meaning of the story for her audience. In time they all knelt on the stone floor, praying for forgiveness. Konstantinova sang to them softly:

> Pass me not, O loving Saviour,
> Hear my humble cry;
> And while others Thou art calling,
> Do not pass me by![30]

The women asked Konstantinova to conduct morning and evening prayers with them and their increasing reliance on these sessions enabled her to exercise some calming influence on their behaviour. Soon they elected her as representative of criminal department number eight.

Then, as arbitrarily and abruptly as had been the case with Becker and the others in Petrograd, she was released. As she left, the 'politicals' and 'criminals' formed a guard of honour on the stairs and the 'politicals' sang the only one of their songs she had been willing to join in, a patriotic anthem, 'We Forge the Happiness of Our Land'. In the yard, the 'criminals' gathered round her and sang 'Praise, my tongue, Jesus Who Bought Me with His Blood'.[31]

---

30 Konstantinova was presumably unaware that the blind American writer of these words, Fanny Crosby, had derived her refrain from an exclamation by an inmate of a Manhattan prison where she was speaking at a service: 'Lord! Do not pass me by!'

31 Konstantinova's account of her imprisonment is in *The Smallness of Man—the Greatness of God*, pp. 9-12. Some additional details come from Olsoni's *Russian Pictures*.

Thus, after nine months in prison she returned to her Moscow corps in late November 1921. A little earlier, the English *War Cry* recorded the fact that Helmy Boije had recovered sufficiently to visit England, where she appealed for discarded Salvation Army uniforms to be sent to Russia, where such items were unobtainable and there was still a body of Salvationists eager to proclaim their faith by the way they dressed.[32]

Indian Summer

It might have seemed that this was a case of The Salvation Army hoping against hope, given that corps buildings were, at least officially, closed and the children's homes and other charitable institutions had all been taken from them. But, curiously, there was even yet to be a brief Indian Summer. This began with a request for registration, dated 3 April, 1922, sent by Olsoni to the Commissariat of the Interior (she was now General Booth's official representative in Russia, with power of attorney, and had moved from Petrograd to Moscow to conduct negotiations with the government). Referring to previous attempts to achieve registration, in Petrograd on 14 March, 1922 and Moscow on 16 May, 1918, she asked for The Salvation Army in Russia to be registered as 'the Russian Department of the International Salvation Army, the Headquarters of which is in London' (a point that a less scrupulous petitioner might have sought to disguise). She described The Salvation Army as 'a worldwide religious-philanthropic organization, which unites people of a truly religious outlook of life, for carrying out by different practical methods, certain efforts for the salvation of the lost', and that the use of military terms had 'proved to be very suitable in this spiritual warfare against evil'. Anyone determined to carry out the commandments of Christ in his own life could become a member, irrespective of any other Christian denomination he might belong to. Clearly not wishing to deceive the authorities in any way, she explained that the Army's administration was patriarchal and there were no elective offices within it. She described the two aspects of the organization's work. Its evangelical thrust, conveyed through public meetings, lectures, concerts, sales of work, processions, etc, was to invite people to live a truly Christian life. Its social-philanthropic work had a threefold character. It provided shelters, food depots, first aid, etc, at times of calamity or misfortune. It cared for the helpless: children, the sick and the aged in crèches, orphanages, hospitals, eventide homes etc. It worked with people who were striving to recover from some personal setback, providing cheap dining rooms, homes for inebriates, ex-prisoners, those in need of temporary shelter and protection in rescue homes, and others who needed a complete new start in life in what were generically called 'colonies'.

This detailed account, including as it does numerous activities that The Salvation Army had not been able to engage in Russia, indicates both that Olsoni was being entirely candid about the nature and purposes of the organization and that she still

---

32 *The War Cry*, 12 November, 1921.

hoped that it might expand until it was doing all of these things for the benefit of Russians.

Olsoni concluded with a note about Salvation Army finance (voluntary contributions from members, friends, collections at meetings, plus the income from the institutions already mentioned, which were expected to be self-supporting, as was the work in Russia as a whole) and a summary of the Army's activities in Russia from 1913 onward.

However powerful the Salvationists' faith in their Russian future may have been it must have come as a surprise when a certificate confirming registration by the People's Commissariat of the Interior was issued a mere five days later, on 8 April. Larsson wrote later that 'It is difficult to understand what the registration authorities were thinking about', but Salvationists in Russia had it in black and white that for the first time they were an unequivocally legal organization.

This happy situation lasted about seven months. The Children's homes and other social institutions were not recovered, of course, but much good work was done nevertheless. In a letter dated 10 January, 1923, Sjöblom reports that, working under the protection of the Finnish Consulate in Petrograd during this period, Captain Korhonen distributed 27,849 cooked meals to starving children, as well as 2,339 kg. of dry provisions to 455 families and 694 individuals.

Evangelical work also proceeded unhindered. The corps in Petrograd and Moscow both functioned busily, led by Russian officers who had been converted and trained there. They and the soldiers felt they had passed through their baptism of fire and were firmly established in the Salvationist way of life. The halls were soon too small for the numbers wanting to attend. Food supplies arrived from abroad, easing the situation of officers, soldiers and friends. *Vestnik Spaseniya* was revived, albeit only in typescript, with very limited circulation. Help and encouragement were given for some months by a German officer, delayed by passport difficulties on his way home from a Salvationist relief expedition to some distressed German colonists near Samara on the River Volga.[33]

Liquidation

This Indian Summer was terminated with the by now traditional abruptness. Captain Francis McCullagh, some-time member of the British Military Mission in Siberia, records that

> One dark night in the winter of 1922 I stumbled by chance on a meeting of Russian Salvationists in a remote quarter of Moscow, and was greatly impressed by their enthusiasm, by the martial note in the hymns which they sang, and by their great red banner whereon was embroidered, in huge, golden letters, the legend, 'Fire and Blood.' The agents of the G.P.U. had also been impressed, apparently, for a few

---

33 Larsson, *Tio År I Ryssland*, p. 226-27.

days afterwards all the Salvationist halls in Moscow and Petrograd were suddenly closed.[34]

On 22 December, the journalist F.A. Mackenzie cabled the *Chicago Daily News.*

The Salvation Army Halls have been closed. The Army has managed to keep up its work in the two centres, Moscow and Petrograd, and also a Child feeding centre in Petrograd up to now. The hall in Moscow was closed on Nov. 27th and in Petrograd the 8th of December. An appeal has been made to the Commissariat for the Interior to withdraw the ban but without result. The Army has struggled on amidst amazing difficulties since 1917, thanks be to the tenacity and heroism of the remarkable young woman, Ensign Olsoni. Last April the authorities granted the Army formal permission to recommence work and no reason is known for the present action. The movement here numbers ten Officers and thirty Soldiers.

In a letter he adds details:

Papers, documents and books were taken by the authorities in both cases and in Petrograd two typewriters were removed. Capt. Ihrberg and Polosova were taken to the Police Depot (Gorokova?) and held for a few hours only. They were told then that the closing of the hall there had been done under instructions from Moscow.

...In Petrograd they have been feeding 150 children daily.

In his book *The Russian Crucifixion* he adds anecdotal evidence.

I succeeded in reaching a high official with my plea. 'These Salvationists have been guilty of a very serious offence,' he said. 'They have been feeding day by day a number of children in Petrograd.'

'Yes,' I said innocently, 'Wasn't it splendid of them? There is an awful lot of hungry children there and I know these girls almost starve themselves to help.'

The high official looked at me...very amiably. 'Do you not know,' he demanded, bringing his hand down on the table to emphasize his words, 'that this is an offence against the state? Religious organizations are forbidden to try to bribe people to become religious.' So The Salvation Army had to go.[35]

On 6 and 21 December Olsoni sent appeals to the Commissariat for the Interior. On 29 January, they were rejected by the Extraordinary Committee, on the grounds that the aims of The Salvation Army were anti-constitutional.

---

34 Francis McCullagh, *The Bolshevik Persecution of Christianity,* London, John Murray, 1924, p. 301.

35 F.A. Mackenzie, *The Russian Crucifixion: The Full Story of the Persecution of Religion under Bolshevism*, London, Jarrolds, 1930, p. 34.

One last ditch possibility remained. Olsoni believed that there were still senior figures in the important commissariats, including Smidovich, 'an educated and humane personality' and a senior official of the Central Executive Committee, who were sympathetic towards The Salvation Army. She knew that other sects, including the Baptists, had appealed successfully to his sense of justice. His boss, Mikhail Ivanovich Kalinin, who had been chairman of the All Russian Central Executive Committee since 1919, she described as 'an insignificant, and, it is said, uneducated man'. She was right. With his goatee beard and continuous professional smile he looked and sounded like a village elder: indeed he was known, not kindly, as 'Stalin's pet peasant', a tool rather than an initiator of individual action.[36] Nevertheless, his committee could in exceptional circumstances change the decision of even the Commissariat of the Interior. Mackenzie wrote a letter for Olsoni to send to Rubenstein, Kalinin's secretary and legal adviser, who suggested asking the Norwegian explorer and philanthropist Fridtjof Nansen to supply a testimonial for The Salvation Army. His name (he had won the Nobel Peace Prize in 1922 for his organization of relief work amongst refugees and victims of the Russian famine and had intervened successfully in negotiations between the Soviets and western relief agencies, opposing some of Lenin's more vengeful policies)[37] would help to attract the attention of the committee. Olsoni went to Nansen's headquarters; in his absence his colleagues said he could not interfere in religious matters. Mackenzie advised Olsoni to telegraph International Headquarters asking it to bring direct pressure to bear on Nansen, and went himself to talk to Nansen's associates. When Nansen returned, he agreed to copy, sign and send to Kalinin a letter written by Mackenzie himself:

Moscow 2nd Feb. 1923.

Dear Mr Kalinin,

I have seen the work of The Salvation Army in many lands. It has done much good amongst the poorest and has never to my knowledge taken any part in politics.

Fridjuf Nansen.

Mackenzie hoped that this would win Olsoni an interview with Smidovich and that the matter would then be put before the Political Committee of the Communist Party. Meanwhile, he met the administrator for internal affairs, Commissar Zaitzev, who told him, as he cabled to the *Daily News,* that the separation of Church and State as legislated in 1918 required all religious organizations to confine themselves solely to religious matters. Despite the fact that The Salvation Army had been permitted by local authorities in Moscow and Petrograd to undertake relief work and

---

36 See McCauley, entry on Kalinin in *Who's Who in Russia since 1900*, London and New York, Routledge, 1997, pp. 106-07.
37 See Pipes, *Russia under the Bolshevik Regime*, p. 417.

the feeding of children, it had been in breach of the law: nobody was permitted to carry on both religious and charitable work simultaneously. In any case, it was a foreign organization, which, like the tsarist governments of old, used religion as an instrument of reaction. The present government wished to free religion from such reactionary control and restore to local churches the right of self-government. If The Salvation Army wished to continue work in Russia its Headquarters in London must open direct negotiations with the Soviet Government. It had to be said, however, that the changes that would be required in The Salvation Army's organization and methods would be such as to make it unlikely that the Army would accept them.

Whether because of Nansen's letter or not, Rubenstein secured for Olsoni a meeting with Smidovich, who proved to be well informed but had, of course already made up his mind. He told Olsoni that in aiming to bring religion into Russia The Salvation Army was necessarily opposing itself to the Russian Government.

> Your aim is the regeneration of man on the principle of the Gospel. We, the Soviet Government, stand on anti-religious foundations. You talk of the ennobling of the soul through faith—we do not believe in any gods, we believe in improvement through education and enlightenment.

Olsoni played her other card:

> But the Baptists and others work here. We thought liberty of conscience and speech existed in the R.S.F.S.R.

Smidovich was unmoved.

> Baptists and others of the kind are Russians, but The Salvation Army is an International Organization. You are strangers. I have followed the work of The Salvation Army in England; it is imperialistic, chauvinistic. Work there, work in Germany. Here you are not needed. There the need is far greater.

Olsoni's companion in arms, Sergeant-Major Nechyev put in a plea for those Salvationists who were Russians like himself and would remain behind.

> We do not ask for any great, extensive activities. We as Russian citizens only beg for the right to continue the little work we have begun. There is a little group of Russian Salvationists. We feel that The Salvation Army is our place, our calling. Our souls long for its spirit.

All to no avail: Smidovich minuted the petition Nechyev and Olsoni put before him—'Petition No 29, signed by our Soldiers and Friends in Moscow and Petrograd'—to the effect that the work of The Salvation Army was impossible in Russia.

This was finally confirmed a few days after Nansen's letter was written. Olsoni received written notification of the liquidation of The Salvation Army in Russia at large and Moscow in particular:

6 Febr. 1923 [No 316/4]

To the representative of The Salvation Army, E. Olsoni

The Commissariat of the Interior herewith informs you that the petition about the recognition of the Statutes of The Salvation Army and the granting to the same of the right to work in the R.S.F.S.R has been refused, in view of the anti-constitutional character of the aims of the organization. On these grounds the branches of the said organization have been closed in the general order of liquidation of unauthorized organizations.

Signed Ravish.

Saitzev

Alexandrov

And

On February 7th 1923, 1, Fortunatoff, Inspector of the Moscow Town Council, in accordance with a decree of Febr.6th under No 316/4 came, in company with a member of the 39th Militia Station, Kurotchkin, to the Quarters of the Society 'The Salvation Army', situated Pokrovka 9, lodg. 1, with the object of dissolving the organization. Decided the following: 'The organization "The Salvation Army" under the leadership of the representative Adjutant E.A. Olsoni, was under the investigation by the Chief Political Administration, which having sealed two cupboards with books and papers, had taken the papers away partly, to be examined by the C.P.A.' The seals are not yet removed from the cupboards for which reason there is no possibility to define the property of the Society. and according to the words of the representative Adjutant Olsoni, there does not exist any property belonging to the Society. The liquidation of the organization was communicated to citizen Olsoni, as the representative, and the stamps taken from her.

Representative of the M.T.C.	Fortunatoff	(Signed)
Ditto the 39th Militia Station	Kurotchlm	(Signed)
Ditto the S.A.	E. Olsoni	(Signed)

On 13 February, Mackenzie wrote to International Headquarters:

We have thus had the decisions of three great departments of the Government. First the G.P.U.—the political police—closed your halls. Then the Commissariat of the Interior—the equivalent of the Home Office—backed this with a formal order of suppression. Now the Central Executive Committee—the equivalent to the Cabinet—supports the suppression. There is nothing more to be done here.

I strove in every way possible to influence people whom I know at the head of the Communist Party in your favour, but in vain. Your people here, Ensign Olsoni and her helpers, did all that they possibly could.

Olsoni had now to disappoint those Russian Salvationists who—feeling that The Salvation Army was their place and their calling and that they yearned to embody its spirit—wanted to continue the work they had begun.

We had to submit... the S.A. was dissolved in Russia... We could not defy the decision, seeing the Army is a non-political organization, and we could not do harm to our good name and reputation. To defy the decision would have meant for our Russian comrades to accept great risks, as we now were, as never before, officially prohibited from continuing... Having recognized the decision of the Government we could not tell our comrades something else and continue in secret. Postponement might be fatal and would certainly be useless... The Army did not any longer exist and that we were now only private Christians.

I also told them that although we did not exist as an Army we still as individuals had the same responsibility before the Lord. The Officers should continue to care for the welfare of their Soldiers spiritually, and although meetings were stopped, visitations could continue. When the Lord opened the way I would let them know. I also told the Officers to look out for some outside occupation.

I destroyed all Statistical Reports as they were dangerous to keep.

I stated to the Officials that we had no property of The Salvation Army. Already earlier I had told our comrades that if it came to the point of confiscation, our Leaders would rather that the Officers should have the property than the State.

'This,' (she concluded her report to International Headquarters), 'is how things are here now.[38]

The end, bureaucratically speaking (and for the time being only) was posted as Protocol No. 15, on 27 February 1923:

Heard: 7. On the 'Salvation army' sect

Decreed: 7. Liquidate the sect as an anti-soviet organization.[39]

---

38 Copies of Mackenzie's letters and cables, the letter signed by Nansen and Olsoni's final report are held in the Russia files of The Salvation Army's International Heritage Centre.

39 Corley, *Felix, Religion in the Soviet Union: An Archival Reader*, London, Macmillan, 1996, pp. 52-53.

The Long Aftermath

Russian Salvationists in Paris

However uncompromisingly final it may have seemed, the proscription in 1923 did not mark the end of The Salvation Army among the Russians. As we shall see, some Russian Salvationists who remained in Russia itself held on to their faith for decades to come. Others emigrated to the west, in particular to Paris. Captain Zinovsky, a woman officer, was one such, and under her command a Russian post was established, attached to the central Paris corps. Interestingly, of the refugees drawn to it, most met The Salvation Army for the first time in Paris and were converted there. In 1925 *All the World* published a photograph of this group, 16 strong, and a few words introducing the members. Zinovsky had been for nine years an official stenographic reporter in the Russian parliament and her flock included naval and military officers, teachers and a chemist.

The adherent of longest standing, still an occasional visitor, was Matilda Ksheshinskaya, legendary ballerina and one-time alleged mistress to Tsar Nicholas the Second, who had 'embraced the spirit and faith of The Army when she was in Paris' at some time before 1908. When her profession took her to London she attended Army meetings there and was delighted by the 'streams of seekers for the blessings of pardon and purity. She would smile, clap her hands, and wave her handkerchief'. While she was still living in St Petersburg she circulated Army literature. After the revolution, when her house across the Neva from the British Embassy was commandeered and became Bolshevik headquarters, she lived in Paris. By now in her fifties, she had survived several further well-publicized liaisons, motherhood and marriage. Perhaps, too, she had outlived the days when a vituperatively indignant St Petersburg ballet critic described her as a 'morally impudent, cynical and brazen dancer, living simultaneously with two grand dukes and not only not hiding it but on the contrary, weaving this art as well into her stinking, cynical wreath of human offal and vice'. It may seem difficult to reconcile all this, her private life and her reputation for self-interested intrigues that ruined other dancers' careers, with approval of The Salvation Army. It is clear, however, from comments by another leading ballerina, Tamara Karsavina, that Ksheshinskaya had another side to her character. Karsavina's words, indeed, almost echo those of *The War Cry*. The two met in Monte Carlo in 1922, after Ksheshinskaya had fled Russia. Karsavina writes:

Although she had lost all her wealth, she was as cheerful as ever, without a single wrinkle or trace of worry... She told me with what mixed feelings of fear and hope she arrived at Cap d'Ail, uncertain as to whether her villa had been left her. Her joy at finding a home was immense. She told me of her wanderings. She made a joke of her many privations and viewed her present situation with philosophy and courage. She had continued to practise her dancing even without ballet shoes, and was as delighted as a child when I offered her a pair of mine.[1]

In any case, The Salvation Army has always enjoyed and made use of the support of people who would not have thought of signing the Articles of War or wearing the cap or bonnet. We need not suppose that the kings and queens and grand dukes and duchesses, the presidents, prime ministers, diplomats and leading industrialists who listened respectfully to Booth and his envoys and pulled strings and made donations on The Salvation Army's behalf ever contemplated signing the pledge or abiding by any of the organization's other disciplines—or embracing its beliefs. Nor need we imagine that Booth and his followers harboured any illusions to that effect. Booth was a pragmatist. If brewers gave him money he would wash it in the widow's tears. If he wanted to expropriate a music hall ditty he would ask 'Why should the devil have all the best tunes?'. And if the great ones of the earth wanted to ask him to tea and express approval of his work among the poor, the homeless, the drunken, the outcast and the smelly, he would make sure that the newspapers heard about it.

Ksheshinskaya, incidentally, seems to have made good use of Karsavina's spare ballet shoes and generally to have recovered her standing in the world she most comfortably inhabited: her final appearance as a ballerina was at Covent Garden when she was 64 and she lived to be 99, dying in 1971.

Alongside Captain Zinovsky, Major Maria Petrojitsky, another officer from Russia, also found plenty to do amongst Russian refugees in Paris. Born in St Petersburg of German-speaking parents, she trained as an officer in Finland. In September 1917 she was sent to Russia, returning to Finland in 1923. In 1926 she was transferred to Paris, where she was reunited with a Russian friend from earlier years, Lady Lieven, who was eventually enrolled as a Salvationist. Together they worked amongst the Russian emigrants, many of whom were impoverished. The ladies gave them practical and spiritual help. After Lady Lieven died Maria carried on alone. Her little flat was an open house for Russians, where they could meet and exchange reminiscences of the country they had lost. Quite frequently they were given financial help. Honest herself, but a little too trusting, Maria was occasionally swindled.

It was difficult to obtain financial support for her work, but she maintained herself by selling *En Avant*, the French *War Cry*, on the Champs-Elysées, where she used her fluent German and Russian, comprehensible if inaccurate French and a smattering of other tongues to good effect. At times her conversation was an idiosyncratic *mélange* of all of them.

---

1 Tamara Karsavina, *Theatre Street: The Reminiscences of Tamara Karsavina*, London, Columbus Books, 1988, pp. 260-61.

She retired, officially, in 1947, aged 62, but in fact continued to work as before. When Territorial Headquarters persuaded her to take a few days of rest outside Paris she was 'kidnapped' by a party of her Russians in a taxi and went back to work. She retired properly at the age of 85. Her last days were brightened by reconciliation with her son Vladimir who had previously denied all connection with her because of her opposition to Communism. She died in 1975.

Clara, Helmy, Elsa and Nadia

Clara Becker had also become reconciled, with her father, following her mother's death, when she left Russia for Estonia to look after him. When they talked about her time in Russia he realized the depth of her commitment to The Salvation Army and he made no objection when she returned to active officership and was appointed to the Literary Department at International Headquarters, where she was known as 'translator extraordinary'. Karl Larsson's *Ten Years in Russia* was just one of the vast number of documents that she translated for the Army, from and to a wide variety of languages. She liked functioning as a back-room girl—although, when engaged in 'lively and sometimes noisy discussion' with her literary colleagues she was, we are told, 'very outgoing'.[2] At public meetings she preferred to sit amongst the congregation rather than on the platform with other officers. Perhaps this is evidence that Boije was correct to think that she was not a plausible leader for The Salvation Army in Russia. Attending, as she did for many years, meetings at the Regent Hall Corps on Oxford Street in London ('The Rink', so styled because it had been a skating rink before becoming the home of The Salvation Army in the West End), she kept an eye open for young people from abroad, and her ability to address many of them in their own languages enabled her to befriend them and help them when they were in difficulty. (Can she have known that at 'The Rink' she was treading in the footsteps of a compatriot, the painter Vasily Vereshchagin, and probably also those of another, the ballerina Matilda Ksheshinskaya?) She was much missed, all over the world, when she died in 1968.

After Helmy Boije left Russia, she served in a number of senior positions, mainly in Scandinavia, although she spent nine months doing 'special work' in England in the mid-1920s (she and Becker were able to meet during this time). The typhus that almost killed her in Petrograd had, however, weakened her previously robust constitution and she was 'Promoted to Glory', as The Salvation Army expresses it, in 1945, two months short of her sixty-second birthday.

Elsa Olsoni, the first and the last officer to serve in Russia during The Salvation Army's ten years there, also returned to Finland to serve in The Salvation Army. Later, living in retirement in Helsingfors, she spoke, as already noted, only very seldom and with painful reluctance, of the hard, bitter years when she gave her youth

---

2 See Ronald Thomlinson, *A Very Private General: A Biography of Frederick Coutts CBE, Hon. DD (Aberdeen)*, London, Salvation Army International Headquarters, 1990, and John C. Izzard, with Henry Gariepy, *Pen of Flame: The Life and Poetry of Catherine Baird*, Alexandria, VA, Crest Books, 2002.

for the salvation of Russia. Nevertheless, she continued to read the Bible in Russian and the country and its people were always in her prayers.

By the time The Salvation Army in Russia was liquidated, Nadia Konstantinova-Sundell had gone home to Helsingfors. In 1924 she was sent, to her parents' displeasure, to Latvia, where, in Jelgava, south of Riga, she hired a former restaurant and opened a corps. In December she heard that her father had died. She returned to Helsingfors for his funeral and stayed on to care for her mother, who died in 1926. Nadia did not return to officership, but remained willing to help and serve. She was matron at a boys' home at Valamo monastery, worked in a home for invalids and, during the war, at a camp for Russian prisoners-of-war at Miehikkälä.

After the war she returned to Leningrad (as it then was) to visit a surviving Russian officer, Anna Polosova, who was still quietly pursuing Salvationist style work. They spent a couple of days together; it was their last meeting. When she was 76 she became matron of a Russian eventide home near Borgå and worked there for five years. Ill health forced her to retire and very shortly afterwards, in May 1970, she died aged 81.

Karl Larsson

Commissioner Karl Larsson continued to travel far and wide on behalf of The Salvation Army. After two and a third years in Czechoslovakia he was sent to take charge in South America, where the Army was working in Argentina, Uruguay, Paraguay, Chile, Bolivia and Peru. After that he spent 18 months at International Headquarters followed by periods in Finland, Norway and, finally, his native Sweden. During the war, at the age of 76, he undertook a year's tour of North and South America, acting as a kind of unofficial ambassador for war-torn Europe. He retired the following year but seldom interrupted his pattern of ceaseless work until he died seven years later.

In 1937 his book *Tio År I Ryssland* was published. It was reissued three times, putting a total of 11,000 copies into circulation. It is compiled, rather than written from scratch, much of it bringing together articles he, Boije and others had published in *All the World* from 1913 until the mid-1920s, with lengthy extracts from memoirs written by Olsoni, Konstantinova and others. This, indeed, is one of its many merits. It conveys Larsson's own personality very strongly but also allows his remarkable colleagues to speak in their own voices. He and they provide a passionate and engaging account of a decade's struggle against odds that, for the time being, proved overwhelming.

It brings home, too, a curious dichotomy in the Salvationist approach to life. On the one hand, they were working for an end that must strike most secularly minded people as impossibly idealist, abstract and misguided: they proposed, with the simplicity of the convinced, to win Russia for God. This overarching imperative, however, plunged them into practical details, great and small, of the most basic and crucial sort. Where could they meet? How could they attract the attention of those they sought to save? Who would finance them? Whence could they obtain food, for themselves and those still more poverty-stricken and needy? How could they avoid falling foul of the law, which, considered both as a code and as the practices based upon it, could be arbitrary and unpredictable? How could they resolve their relationship with the Christian churches already extant in Russia to the satisfaction of all parties? How could they be sure that they understood what was going on in the minds of the people they were dealing with? How could they best react when they were offered large buildings, for which they could certainly find a use, but were expensive to run and that they had too few officers to staff? How could they attract and train more officers? How could they make The Salvation Army in Russia convincingly Russian while retaining—something they saw as fundamental—its identity as part of a great international movement? What, meanwhile, could they say to the peasants, refugees, widows, drunks—some of them, from the Salvationists' relatively sheltered point of view, barely civilized beings—who visited their halls, sat in their cramped flats (with the police never far away) wanting and expecting them to be angels of mercy and bounty who would tell them something that would rescue them from their situation? Their answer to all of these questions was—could only be—that they were in God's hands.

Be that as it may, all of these people and their colleagues—what happened, I wonder, to Seligman and Tsuber, to name only two?—had abundantly earned their right to sing one of The Salvation Army's more gung-ho (and least elegantly written) songs:

> We'll be heroes, we'll be heroes,
> When the battle is fierce;
> When the raging storm louder grows
> Will our courage increase,
> By the cross, by the cross.

Russian Salvationists in Russia

Of those Russian Salvationists who remained at home there was, for the time being, little further news. Occasional reports suggested, at least initially, that they were continuing to meet in private. Eventually some linked up with the Baptists. There was one enigmatic piece of news in the 1950s. A Swedish visitor sitting on a bench in a Moscow park was approached by a woman of 73 who had recognized the badge of a Christian youth movement she was wearing. Identifying herself only as Vera—refusing, indeed, to give any other name—the woman was clearly glad to talk of matters that it was not safe to discuss amongst Russians. She recounted the conversions of her father and herself at The Salvation Army in St Petersburg before the First World War. She mentioned Karl Larsson and Helmy Boije, whom she obviously remembered well. She had left Petrograd in 1920 to live with relatives far away in the country, returning only in 1931. She had enjoyed Christian fellowship with Baptists until the group disintegrated as people went to live elsewhere or gave way to hostile pressure from the state. 'Since then, I go for prayer to the Orthodox Church, but I see before me the red flag of the Army.' She was working as housekeeper and nanny for relatives, but to her distress was not permitted to teach the children in her care the faith that was so important to her. The two women talked for two hours (the visitor had studied Russian) before Vera said good-bye and slipped away across the dusty park. The visitor asked if they could meet again, but Vera was non-committal. Back in Sweden, the visitor wrote an account of the conversation that was published in *Stridsropet*, the Swedish *War Cry*. It is surely reasonable to assume that the elderly woman was Vera Gorinovich, the first Russian to become a Salvation Army officer, whose father had been maimed by terrorists in 1876.

Perhaps the most remarkable survivor of all came to light when The Salvation Army returned to Russia in 1990. Vladimir Mikhailovich Fursenko had been converted as a 14 year old in Petrograd in 1918, but had moved to the Crimea, where he supported himself as a labourer, a little before the Army was proscribed in 1923. When he heard that The Salvation Army was re-established in Moscow, he telephoned the corps officer, Captain Sven-Erik Ljungholm, grandson of Otto Ljungholm, alongside whom he had worked seventy-odd years before. The Ljungholms, a little disconcerted by his story and by the fact that his followers called him 'General' Fursenko, went to Yalta to meet him. They found not merely Fursenko himself, but in effect a working corps, of almost 50 people, ready and eager to be enrolled as soldiers in the parent organization.

Fursenko had gathered a group of people who followed the Salvationist pattern of religious and charitable activities. This did not endear him to the Soviet government and in 1944 he was exiled to Siberia for 'actions against the state.' He served 20 years. After his release he started all over again, rebuilding the movement, with his house as its headquarters. With the cessation of religious persecution it emerged into the public gaze, strongly evangelistic and devoted to the service of the people. By 1993 it had become the official Yalta corps of The Salvation Army, and in that year, when the first intake of Russian cadets were commissioned as officers after an intensive six months of training, Fursenko was invited to the platform where, standing under the Yalta corps flag, he was presented with the Order of the Founder, The Salvation Army's highest honour, by the official General, Eva Burrows.

At the time of writing it is 15 years since The Salvation Army returned to Russia in July 1991. Events during the first ten of those years were narrated by Miriam Blackwell in her short book, *The Open Door*, published in 2001. She told a story of new beginnings and for the time being that is all that can sensibly be written as a history of this second attempt. Fifteen years of renewed heroic work have passed by but it is still too early to say what the outcome will be.

Bibliography

Salvation Army International Heritage Centre Archives

Files on

Clara Becker, Constantine and Helmy Boije, Catherine Booth, William Booth, Karl Larsson, Henry Mapp, George Scott Railton, Russia.

Typescripts

Becker, Clara, translated E.B., *Prisoner in Petrograd*, (translation 1965), typescript covering events from July 1917, n.d.

Russia, (notes from Becker's Scrapbook), n.d.

Konstantinova-Sundell, Nadja, dictated to Rakel Holm, trs. E.B.: *The Smallness of Man, the Greatness of God*, n.d.

Larsson, Karl, translated by Clara Becker, *Ten Years in Russia*, n.d.

—Another typescript covering some of the same material but with variations of detail, n.d.

Ljungholm, Otto M., *Diary, 8 September- 26 November 1918*.

Wahlström, Tor, *She Was a Pioneer in Russia*, n.d. (?1975).

Olsoni, Elsa, *Russian Pictures* (typescript of extracts).

English transcription of a Swedish television programme, *Frälsninsarmén I Ryssland*, 1992-3.

Salvation Army Periodicals and other Publications

All the World, 1904-1924 and 1942.

The Officers' Review, 1937,1938.

The Salvation Army Yearbook, 1906-24.

Vestnik Spaseniya, 1913-19.

The War Cry, 1904-24.

Salvation Army Songs, London, 1923.

The Official History of The Salvation Army

Wiggins, Arch R., *The History of The Salvation Army*, vol IV (London: Thomas Nelson & Sons, 1964).

—*The History of The Salvation Army*, vol.V (London: Thomas Nelson & Sons, 1968).

Coutts, Frederick, *The History of The Salvation Army*, vol. VI, *The Better Fight* (London: Hodder & Stoughton, 1973).

—*The History of The Salvation Army*, vol. VII, *The Weapons of Goodwill* (London: Hodder & Stoughton, 1986).

Gariepy, Henry, *Mobilized for God: The History of The Salvation Army*, vol. VIII, 1977-1994 (Grand Rapids, MI: William B. Eerdmans, 1999).

Non-Salvationist Newspapers and Magazines

Christian Standard, 26 April and 30 August, 1913.
Missionary Magazine, November, 1862, pp. 423-26.
The Missionary Review of the World, May 1904, pp. 326-31.
The Tablet, 29 March/5 April, 1997.
The Times, 3 August, 1908; 22 June, 1917; 5 September, 1917; September, 1917; 29 March, 1920; 4 March, 25 October, 1921; 29 May, 1923.

Articles in Learned Journals

Freeze, Gregory L., Subversive Piety: Religion and the Political Crisis in Late Imperial Russia, in *The Journal of Modern History*, June 1996.
Flenley, Paul, Rethinking the Russian Revolution, in *European History Quarterly*, vol. 19, 1989, pp. 105-13.
Heier, Edmund, A Note on the Pashkovites and L.N. Tolstoy, in *Canadian Slavonic Papers*, V, Edmonton, University of Alberta, 1962.
Jones, Malcolm, Dostoevsky, Zasetskaya, and Radstockism, in MacRobert, C.M., Smith, G.S. and Stone, G.C. (eds.) *Oxford Slavonic Papers*, New Series, vol. XXVII, Oxford: Oxford University Press), 1994, pp. 106-20.
Waldron, Peter, Religious Reform after 1905: Old Believers and the Orthodox Church, in MacRobert, C.M., Smith, G.S. and Stone, G.C. (eds.) *Oxford Slavonic Papers*, New Series vol. XX, Oxford: Oxford University Press), 1987, pp. 110-39.

Books

Acton, Edward, *Russia: The Tsarist and Soviet Legacy* (2nd edition) (London and New York: Longman, 1995).
Acton, Edward, Cherniaev, Vladimir Iu. and Rosenberg, William G. (eds), *Critical Companion to the Russian Revolution 1914-1921* (Bloomington & Indianapolis: Indiana University Press, 1997).
Alexandrov, Victor, *The End of the Romanovs*, trs. William Sutcliffe, (London: Hutchinson, 1966).
Allen, Charlotte, *The Human Christ: The Search for the Historical Jesus*, (Oxford: Lion Publishing, 1998).
Almedingen, E.M., *Tomorrow Will Come* (London: The Bodley Head, 1961).
Andrle, Vladimir, *A Social History of Twentieth-Century Russia*, (London: Hodder Education, 1994).
Ascher, Abraham, *P.A. Stolypin: The Search for Stability in Late Imperial Russia* (Stanford: Stanford University Press, 2001).

Babel, Isaac, *Collected Stories*, trs. David McDuff (London: Penguin Books, 1994).

Baedecker, K., *Russland,*(Leipzig: Karl Baedecker, 1904).

Barchatova, Y, and others, trs. Michael Robinson, *A Portrait of Tsarist Russia* (New York: Pantheon Books, 1989).

Barraclough, Geoffrey, and Parker, Geoffrey (eds.), *The Times Atlas of World History* (London: Times Books, 1992).

Batchelor, Mary, *Catherine Bramwell-Booth* (Tring: Lion Books), 1986.

Begbie, Harold, *The Life of William Booth, the Founder of The Salvation Army* (London: Macmillan, 1920).

Bely, Andrei, *Petersburg*, trs. Robert A. Maguire and John E. Malmstad (Bloomington: Indiana University Press, 1983).

Benn, Anna, and Bartlett, Rosamund, *Literary Russia: A Guide* (London: Papermac, 1997).

Berton, Kathleen, *Moscow: An Architectural History*, London: I.B. Tauris), 1990.

Billington, James H., *The Icon and the Axe* (London: Weidenfeld and Nicolson), 1966.

Blackwell, Miriam, *The Open Door* (London: The Salvation Army, 2001).

Boon, Brindley, *Play the Music, Play!*, (London: Salvationist Publishing and Supplies, 1978).

—*ISB: The Story of the International Staff Band*, Bristol, Record Greetings, 1985.

Booth, Catherine Bramwell, *Bramwell Booth* (London: Rich & Cowan, 1933).

Booth, William, *The General's Letters*, 1885 (London: Salvation Army International Headquarters, 1886).

—*A Talk with Mr Gladstone at His Own Fireside*, (London: Salvation Army International Headquarters, 1897).

Booth, William Bramwell, *Echoes and Memories* (London: Salvationist Publishing and Supplies, 1925).

—*These Fifty Years* (London: Cassell, 1929).

Booth-Tucker, Frederick de la Tour, *The Life of Catherine Booth, the Mother of The Salvation Army* (London: Salvation Army International Headquarters, 1892).

Bradley, Joseph, *Muzhik and Muscovite: Urbanization in Late Imperial Russia* (Berkeley: University of California Press, 1985).

Breshko-Breshkovskaya, Katerina, *Hidden Springs of the Russian Revolution: Personal Memoirs of Katerina Breshkovskaia* (Stanford: Stanford University Press, 1931).

Broido, Vera, *Daughter of Revolution* (London: Constable, 1998).

Brown, Archie, Kaser, Michael and Smith, Gerald S., (eds.), *The Cambridge Encyclopedia of Russia and the Former Soviet Union* (Cambridge: Cambridge University Press, 1994).

Brown, David, *Tchaikovsky: A Biographical and Critical Study*, (London: Victor Gollancz, 1992).

Buchanan, Meriel, *Petrograd, the City of Trouble, 1914-1918* (London: William Collins, 1918).

—*The Dissolution of an Empire* (London, John Murray, 1932).

Burke, Peter, *Popular Culture in Early Modern Europe* (Aldershot: Scolar Press, 1994).

Charques, Richard, *A Short History of Russia* (London: The English Universities Press, 1959).

Chekhov, Anton, trs. Ronald Wilks, *The Kiss and Other Stories* (London: Penguin Books, 1982).

Cohen, Selma Jeanne (Founding Editor), *International Encyclopedia of Dance*, vol. 4 (New York and Oxford: Oxford University Press, 1988).

Collier, Richard, *The General Next to God* (London: Collins, 1965).

Conquest, Robert (ed.), *Religion in the Soviet Union* (Soviet Studies Series) (London: The Bodley Head, 1968).

Conte, Francis (ed.), *Great Dates in Russian and Soviet History* (New York: Facts on File, 1994).

Corley, Felix, *Religion in the Soviet Union: An Archival Reader* (London: Macmillan, 1996).

Cragg, G.R., *The Church and the Age of Reason* (Harmondsworth: Penguin Books, 1960).

Crankshaw, Edward, *Russia and Britain* (London: Collins, n.d.—c. 1944).

–*The Shadow of the Winter Palace: the Drift to Revolution 1825-1917* (London: Macmillan, 1976).

Crisp, Olga, and Edmonson, Linda (eds.), *Civil Rights in Imperial Russia* (Oxford: Clarendon Press, 1989).

Cross, F.L., and Livingstone, E.A., (eds.), *The Oxford Dictionary of the Christian Church* (Third Edition) (Oxford: Oxford University Press, 1997).

Crummey, Robert O., *The Formation of Muscovy 1304-1613* (London: Longman, 1987).

Cunningham, James W., *A Vanquished Hope: The Movement for Church Renewal in Russia, 1906-1906* (New York: St Vladimir's Seminary Press, 1981).

Curtiss, John Shelton, *Church and State in Russia: The Last Years of the Empire, 1900-1917* (New York: Columbia University Press, 1940).

Custine, Marquis de: *Letters from Russia*, trs. and ed. Robin Buss (London: Penguin Books, 1991).

Dostoyevsky, Fyodor, *A Writer's Diary*, trs. Kenneth Lantz (London: Quartet Books, 1994).

Douglas, Eileen, and Duff, Mildred, *Commissioner Railton* (London: Salvationist Publishing and Supplies, 1920).

Dupuy, R. Ernest, and Trevor N., *The Collins Encyclopedia of Military History* (London: HarperCollins, 1993).

Engel, Barbara Alpern, and Rosenthal, Clifford N. (ed. & trs.), *Five Sisters: Women Against the Tsar* (New York and London: Routledge, 1992).

Ervine, St. John, *God's Soldier: General William Booth* (London: Heinemann, 1934).

Falkus, M.E., *The Industrialisation of Russia, 1700-1914* (Basingstoke and London: Macmillan, 1972).

Farmborough, Florence, *Russian Album, 1908-1918* (Salisbury: Michael Russell, 1979).

Farmer, David Hugh, *The Oxford Dictionary of Saints* (Oxford: Oxford University Press, 2004).

Fedotoff, G.P., *The Russian Church since the Revolution* (London: Society for Promoting Christian Knowledge, 1928).

Fennell, John, *The Crisis of Medieval Russia* (London: Longman, 1988).

Fernández-Armesto, Felipe, *Civilizations* (London: Macmillan, 2000).

Fernández-Armesto, Felipe, & Wilson, Derek, *Reformation: Christianity and the World, 1500-2000* (London: Bantam Press, 1996).

Figes, Orlando, *A People's Tragedy: the Russian Revolution 1891-1924* (London: Jonathan Cape, 1996).

—*Peasant Russia, Civil War: The Volga Countryside in Revolution 1917-1921* (London, Phoenix Press, 2001).

—*Natasha's Dance: A Cultural History of Russia* (London: Allen Lane, 2002).

Figes, Orlando, & Kolonitskii, Boris, *Interpreting the Russian Revolution* (New Haven and London: Yale University Press, 1999).

Finlayson, Geoffrey B.A.M., *The Seventh Earl of Shaftesbury 1801-1885* (London: Eyre Methuen, 1981).

Fitzlyon, Kyril, and Browning, Tatiana, *Before the Revolution* (Harmondsworth: Penguin Books, 1977).

Fountain, David, *Lord Radstock and the Russian Revival* (Southampton: Mayflower Christian Books, 1988).

Freeze, Gregory L., *From Supplication to Revolution: A Documentary Social History of Imperial Russia* (Oxford: Oxford University Press, 1988).

Freeze, Gregory L., (ed.), *Russia, a History* (Oxford: Oxford University Press, 1997).

Galitzine, Prince George, *Imperial Splendour: Palaces and Monasteries of Old Russia* (London: Viking, 1992).

Gariepy, Henry, *General of God's Army* (Wheaton: Victor Books, 1993).

Geifman, Anna, *Thou Shalt Kill: Revolutionary Terrorism in Russia, 1894-1917* (Princeton: Princeton University Press, 1993).

Gerhardie, William, *The Romanovs* (London: Rich & Cowan, 1940).

—*God's Fifth Column* (London: The Hogarth Press, 1990).

Gerhardt, Dietrich; Weintraub, Wiktor, and Winkel, Hans-Jürgen zum (eds.), *Orbis Scriptus: Festschrift für Dmitrij Tschizewskij zum 70, Geburtstag* (Munich: 1966).

Glennie, Misha, *The Balkans 1804-1999, Nationalism, War and the Great Powers* (London: Granta Books, 2000).

Gorky, Maxim (as told to), trs. and ed. Nina Froud and James Hanley, *Chaliapin, an Autobiography* (London, MacDonald, 1968).

Gosling, Nigel, *Leningrad* (London: Studio Vista, 1965).

Got'e, Iurii Vladimirovich, *Time of Troubles* (London: I.B. Tauris, 1988).

Graber, G.S., *Caravans to Oblivion: The Armenian Genocide, 1915* (New York and Chichester: John Wiley & Sons Inc., 1996).

Hamilton, Lord Frederick, *Vanished Pomps of Yesterday* (London: Hodder & Stoughton, 1937).

Hamilton, Gearge Heard: *The Art and Architecture of Russia* (Harmondsworth: Penguin Books, 1975).

Hardy, Deborah, Land and Freedom: *The Origins of Russian Terrorism, 1876-1879* (New York, Greenwood Press, 1987).

Hartley, Janet M., *A Social History of the Russian Empire 1650-1825* (London: Longman, 1999).

Hattersley, Roy, *Blood and Fire: William and Catherine Booth and Their Salvation Army* (London: Little, Brown, 1999).

Heier, Edmund, *Religious Schism in the Russian Aristocracy 1860-1900: Radstockism and Pashkovism* (The Hague: Martinus Nijhoff, 1970).

Herlihy, Patricia, *The Alcoholic Empire: Vodka and Politics in Late Imperial Russia* (Oxford & New York: Oxford University Press, 2002).

Herzen, Alexander, *Childhood, Youth and Exile* (Oxford: Oxford University Press, 1994).

Hingley, Ronald, *The Russian Mind* (London: The Bodley Head, 1977).

Hodder, Edwin, *The Life and Work of the Seventh Earl of Shaftesbury, K.G.* (London: Cassell & Co., 1886).

Honderich, Ted (ed.), *The Oxford Companion to Philosophy* (Oxford: Oxford University Press, 1995).

Horridge, Glenn K., *The Salvation Army: Origins and Early Days* (Godalming: Amonite Books, 1993).

Hosking, Geoffrey, *Russia: People and Empire 1552-1917* (London: HarperCollins, 1997).

—(ed.), *Church, Nation and State in Russia and Ukraine* (London and Basingstoke: Macmillan, 1991).

Hummel, Ruth & Thomas, *Patterns of the Sacred: English Protestant and Russian Orthodox Pilgrims of the Nineteenth Century* (London: Scorpion Cavendish, 1995).

Izzard, John C., with Gariepy, Henry, *Pen of Flame: The Life and Poetry of Catherine Baird* (Alexandria, Virginia: Crest Books, 2002).

Jacobs, Louis, *The Jewish Religion, A Companion* (Oxford: Oxford University Press, 1995).

James, William, *The Varieties of Religious Experience, (The Gifford Lectures,1901-02)* (London: Collins, 1960).

Jeffrey, David Lyle, *A Dictionary of Biblical Tradition in English Literature* (Grand Rapids, MI: William B. Eerdmans, 1992).

Jones, Malcolm V., and Miller, Robin Feuer (eds), *The Cambridge Companion to the Classic Russian Novel* (Cambridge: Cambridge University Press, 1998).

Karsavina, Tamara, *Theatre Street* (London: Columbus Books, 1988).

Keay, John (ed.), *The Royal Geographical Society History of World Exploration* (London: Guild Publishing, 1991).

Kent, John, The Study of Modern Ecclesiastical History since 1930 (in Daniélou, Couratin and Kent, *The Penguin Guide to Modern Theology, Volume Two* (Harmondsworth: Penguin Books, 1969).

Kirby, D.G, *Finland in the Twentieth Century* (London: Hurst, 1979).

Kitson Clark, G, *The Making of Victorian England* (London: Methuen, 1962).

Klein, Wilhelm, et al, *Insight Guide to St. Petersburg* (Singapore: APA, 1992).

Knightley, Phillip, *The First Casualty* (London: André Deutsch, 1975).

Kochan, Miriam, *The Last Days of Imperial Russia* (London: Weidenfeld & Nicolson, 1976).

Kolarz, Walter, *Religion in the Soviet Union* (London: Macmillan, 1961).

Larsson, Flora, *Viking Warrior* (London: Salvationist Publishing and Supplies, 1959).

—*My Best Men Are Women* (London: Hodder and Stoughton, 1974).

Larsson, Karl, *Tio År I Ryssland* (Stockholm: FA-Press Bokförlag, 1967).

Latimer, Robert Sloan, *Dr Baedecker and His Apostolic Work in Russia* (London: Morgan & Scott, 1907).

Leroy-Beaulieu, Anatole (trs. Zénaïde A. Ragozin), *The Empire of the Tsars and the Russians*, New York and London, G.P. Putnam, 1896-1903.

Leskov, Nikolai (trs. & ed. James Muckle), *Schism in High Society: Lord Radstock and His Followers* (Nottingham: Bramcote Press, 1995).

—(trs. David Magarshack), *Selected Tales* (Geneva: Heron Books, 1967).

—(trs. Isabel F. Hapgood), *The Cathedral Folk* (London, John Lane, The Bodley Head, 1924).

Lieven, Dominic, *Russia's Rulers under the Old Regime* (New Haven and London: Yale University Press, 1990).

—*Nicholas II, Emperor of All the Russias* (London: John Murray, 1993).

Lincoln, W. Bruce, *In War's Dark Shadow* (New York and Oxford: Oxford University Press,1994).

—*Passage Through Armageddon* (New York and Oxford: Oxford University Press, 1994).

—*Red Victory: A History of the Russian Civil War* (London: Sphere Books, 1991).

Lunn, Brian, *Salvation Dynasty* (London: William Hodge), 1936.

McCaig, A, *Wonders of Grace in Russia* (Riga: The Revival Press), 1926.

McCauley, Martin, *The Russian Revolution and the Soviet State 1917-1921: Documents* (London: Macmillan, 1975).

—*The Soviet Union Since 1917* (London: Longman, 1981).

—*Who's Who in Russia since 1900* (London and New York, Routledge, 1997).

McCullagh, Francis, *The Bolshevik Persecution of Christianity* (London: John Murray), 1924.

Mackenzie, F.A., *The Russian Crucifixion: Thhe Full Story of the Persecution of Religion under Bolshevism* (London: Jarrolds, 1930).

MacLean, Hugh, *Nikolai Leskov: The Man and His Art* (Cambridge, Mass. and London: Harvard University Press, 1977).

McManners, John (ed.), *The Oxford Illustrated History of Christianity* (Oxford: Oxford University Press, 1990).

Manson, John, *The Salvation Army and the Public: A Religious, Social, and Financial Study* (London & New York, 1906; Second edition Augmented, London & New York: Routledge, 1908).

Mawdsley, Evan and Margaret, *Blue Guide to Moscow and Leningrad* (London: A.C. Black, 1989).

Maylunas, Andrei, and Mironenko, Sergei, *A Lifelong Passion: Nicholas and Alexandra, Their Own Story* (London: Weidenfeld & Nicolson, 1996).

Milner-Goland, Robin, with Nikolai Dejevsky, *Atlas of Russia and the Soviet Union* (Oxford: Phaidon, 1989).

Moon, David, *The Russian Peasantry 1600-1930: The World the Peasants Made* (London: Longman, 1999).

Moorehead, Alan, *The Russian Revolution* (London: Collins & Hamish Hamilton, 1958).

Mossolov, A.A., *At the Court of the Last Tsar* (London: Methuen), 1935.

Moynahan, Brian, *Comrades* (London: Hutchinson, 1992).

—*The Russian Century* (London: Chatto & Windus, 1994).

—*Rasputin: The Saint Who Sinned* (London: Aurum Press, 1998).

Muckle, James Y., *Nikolai Leskov and the 'Spirit of Protestantism'* (Birmingham: Department of Russian Language and Literature, University of Birmingham, 1978).

Müller, Ludolf, *Russischer Geist und evangelisches Chrisentum* (Witten/Ruhr: Luther-Verlag, 1951).

Murdoch, Norman H., *Origins of The Salvation Army* (Knoxville: University of Tennessee Press, 1994).

Murray, Les, *The Paperbark Tree: Selected Prose* (London: Minerva, 1993).

Nichols, L., & Stavrou, Theofanis George (eds.), *Russian Orthodoxy under the Old Regime* (Minneapolis: University of Minnesota Press, 1978).

Nicholson, William, *The Romance of The War Cry* (London, Salvationist Publishing and Supplies, 1929).

Nicolson, Sir Harold, *Sir Arthur Nicolson, Bart, First Lord Carnock* (London: Constable, 1930).

Nowell-Smith, Geoffrey (ed.), *The Oxford History of World Cinema* (Oxford: Oxford University Press, 1996).

Obolensky, Chloe, *The Russian Empire: A Portrait in Photographs* (London: Jonathan Cape, 1980).

Oliphant, Laurence, *The Russian Shores of the Black Sea* (Köln: Könemann, 1998).

Ometev, Boris, and Stuart, John, *St Petersburg: Portrait of an Imperial City* (London: Cassell, 1990).

Orsborn, Albert, *The House of My Pilgrimage* (London: Salvationist Publishing and Supplies, 1958).

Osborne, Harold, *The Oxford Companion to Art* (Oxford: Oxford University Press, 1983).

Paléologue, Maurice, *An Ambassador's Memoirs 1914-17*, trs. Frederick A. Holt (London: Hutchinson, 1973).

Palmer, A.W., *A Dictionary of Modern History* (Harmondsworth: Penguin Books, 1962).

Pelikan, Jaroslav, *The Illustrated Jesus Through the Centuries* (New Haven and London: Yale University Press, 1997).

Pipes, Richard, *Russia under the Old Regime* (London: Weidenfeld & Nicolson, 1974).

—*The Russian Revolution 1899-1919* (London: Fontana Press, 1992).

—*Russia under the Bolshevik Regime* (London: Harvill, 1994).

Pitcher, Harvey, *Witnesses of the Russian Revolution* (London: John Murray, 1994).

Pobedonostsev, K.P., trs. Robert Crozier Long, *Reflections of a Russian Statesman* (London: Grant Richards & Co., 1898).

Pratt, Will, *A Funny Thing Happened on the Way!* (Mukilteo: Wine Press Publishing, 1996).

Price, Morgan Phillips (ed. Tania Rose), *Dispatches from the Revolution: Russia 1916-18* (London: Pluto Press, 1997).

Pushkin, Alexander (trs. John Fennell), *Selected Verse* (Harmondsworth: Penguin Books, 1964).

—(trs. Earl Sampson) *The History of Pugachev*, London, Phoenix Press, 2001.

Railton, George Scott, *General Booth* (London: Hodder & Stoughton, 1913).

Ransome, Arthur, *Six Weeks in Russia 1919* (London: Redwords, 1992).

—*The Crisis in Russia 1920* (London: Redwords, 1992).

Read, Christopher, *Religion, Revolution and the Russian Intelligentsia, 1900-1912* (London & Basingstoke: Macmillan, 1979).

Reed, John, *Ten Days that Shook the World* (Harmondsworth: Penguin Books, 1974).

Reid, Anna, *Borderland: A Journey Through the History of Ukraine* (London: Orion, 1997).

Richie, Alexandra, *Faust's Metropolis: A History of Berlin* (London: HarperCollins, 1999).

Rogger, Hans, *Russia in the Age of Modernisation and Revolution, 1881-1917* (London: Longman, 1983).

Roosevelt, Priscilla, *Life on the Russian Country Estate* (New Haven and London: Yale University Press, 1995).

Russell, Bertrand, *History of Western Philosophy* (London: George Allen and Unwin, 1957).

Russell, Dave, *Popular Music in England, 1840-1914* (Kingston and Montreal: McGill-Queen's University Press, 1987).

Ruud, Charles A. and Stepanov, Sergei A., *Fontanka 16: The Tsar's Secret Police* (Stroud: Sutton Publishing, 1999).

Saltykov-Schedrin, M.E., trs. I.P. Foote, *The History of a Town* (Oxford: Willem A. Meeuws, 1980).

Saunders, David, *Russia in the Age of Reaction and Reform, 1801-1881* (London: Longman, 1992).

Schmemann, Serge, *Echoes of a Native Land: Two Centuries of a Russian Village* (London: Little, Brown, 1997).

Schoolfield, George C., *Helsinki of the Czars: Finland's Capital, 1808-1918* (Columbia: Camden House, 1996).

Schultz, Raymond L., *Crusader in Babylon: W.T. Stead and the Pall Mall Gazette* (Lincoln NE, University of Nebraska Press, 1972).

Shaw, George Bernard, *The Complete Prefaces of Bernard Shaw* (London: Paul Hamlyn, 1965).

Shaw, Warren, and Pryce, David, *Encyclopedia of the USSR* (London: Cassell, 1990).

Shukman, Harold (ed.), *The Blackwell Encyclopedia of the Russian Revolution* (Oxford: Blackwell, 1994).

Solomon, Susan Gross & Hutchinson, John F. (eds.), *Health and Society in Revolutionary Russia*, Bloomington and Indianapolis: Indiana University Press, 1990).

Stites, Richard, *Revolutionary Dreams: Utopian Vision and Experimental Life in the Russian Revolution* (New York and Oxford: Oxford University Press, 1989).

—*The Women's Liberation Movement in Russia: Feminism, Nihilism, and Bolshevism, 1860-1930*, Princeton (Princeton University Press, 1991).

Sukhanov, N.N., ed., abr. and trs. Joel Carmichael, *The Russian Revolution 1917: A Personal Record* (Princeton: Princeton University Press, 1984).

Talbot Rice, Tamara, *Russian Art* (West Drayton: Penguin Books, 1949).

Taylor, A.J.P., *The Struggle for Mastery in Europe 1848-1918* (Oxford: Oxford University Press, 1954).

Taylor, Gladys M., *Translator Extraordinary* (London: Salvationist Publishing and Supplies, 1969).

Taylor, Gordon, *Companion to the Song Book of The Salvation Army* (London: International Headquarters of the Salvation Army, 1989).

Terras, Victor, *A History of Russian Literature*, New Haven and London: Yale University Press, 1991).

Thomlinson, Ronald, *A Very Private General: A Biography of Frederick Coutts CBE, Hon. DD (Aberdeen)* (London: International Headquarters of the Salvation Army, 1990).

Timberlake, Charles E., (ed.) *Religious and Secular Forces in Late Tsarist Russia: Essays in Honor of Donald W. Treadgold* (Seattle and London: University of Washington, 1992).

Todd, Albert C., and Hayward, Max (eds.), *Twentieth Century Russian Poetry*, Selected with an Introduction by Yevgeny Yevtushenko (London: Fourth Estate, 1993).

Tolstoy, Leo (trs. Rosemary Edmonds), *Anna Karenina* (Harmondsworth: Penguin Books, 1956).

—(trs. Vera Traill), *Resurrection* (Geneva: Heron Books, 1968).

—(trs. Louise & Aylmer Maude), *War and Peace* (London: Oxford University Press, 1958).

—(trs. Anon), *What Shall We Do?* London, Free Age Press n.d. (c. 1903)

Trotsky, Leon, *The History of the Russian Revolution* (London, Victor Gollancz, 1934).

Trotter, Mrs Edward, *Lord Radstock, an Interpretation and a Record* (London, Hodder & Stoughton, n.d.)

Troutt, Margaret, *The General Was a Lady: the Story of Evangeline Booth* (Nashville: A.J. Holman, 1980).

Troyat, Henri (trs. Malcolm Barnes), *Daily Life in Russia Under the Last Tsar* (London, Allen & Unwin, 1961).

—(trs. Nancy Amphoux) *Tolstoy* (London: W.H. Allen, 1968).

Tuchman, Barbara W., *The Guns of August* (London, The Folio Society 1995).

—*The Proud Tower* (London: The Folio Society, 1995).

—*The March of Folly* (London: The Folio Society, 1995).

van den Bercken, Wil, *Holy Russia and Christian Europe: East and West in the Religious Ideology of Russia* (London: SCM Press, 1999).

van der Kiste, John, *Princess Victoria Melita, Grand Duchess Cyril of Russia, 1876-1936* (Stroud & Wolfeboro Falls: Sutton Publishing, 1991).

Vernadsky, George, et al. (eds.), *A Source Book for Russian History, vol. III: Alexander II to the February Revolution* (New Haven and London: Yale University Press, 1972).

Vidler, Alec R., *The Church in an Age of Revolution* (Harmondsworth: Penguin Books, 1961.

Volkov, Solomon, *St Petersburg, A Cultural History* (London: Sinclair-Stevenson, 1996).

Walicki, Andrzej, trs. Hilda Andrews-Rusiecka, *A History of Russian Thought from the Enlightenment to Marxism* (Stanford: Stanford University Press, 1979).

Wardin, Albert W. Jr., *Evangelical Sectarianism in the Russian Empire and the USSR: A Bibliographic Guide* (Lanham, MD, & London: The American Theological Library Association and The Scarecrow Press, 1995).

Ware, Timothy, *The Orthodox Church* (Harmondsworth: Penguin Books, 1972).

Watson, Bernard, *Soldier Saint: George Scott Railton, William Booth's first Lieutenant* (London: Hodder & Stoughton, 1970).

Watts, Michael R., *The Dissenters, (vol. II), The Expansion of Evangelical Nonconformity* (Oxford: Clarendon Press, 1995).

West, James L., and Petrov, Iurii A. (eds.), *Merchant Moscow: Images of Russia's Vanished Bourgeoisie* (Princeton: Princeton University Press, 1998).

Williams, Harold Whitmore, *Russia of the Russians* (London, Pitman and Sons 1914).

Wilson, A.N., *Tolstoy* (London: Hamish Hamilton, 1988).

Wilson, P.W., *General Evangeline Booth of The Salvation Army* (New York: Charles Scribner's Sons, 1948).

Wisbey, Herbert A. Jr., *Soldiers Without Swords: A History of the Salvation Army in the United States* (New York: Macmillan, 1955).

Wolfe, Bertram D., *Three Who Made a Revolution* (Harmondsworth, Penguin Books, 1966).

Youssoupoff, Prince Felix, *Lost Splendour*, trs. Ann Green and Nikolas Katkoff (London, Foio Socciety, 1996).

Zbarsky, Ilya and Hutchinson, Samuel, *Lenin's Embalmers* (London: Harvill, 1998).

Zernov, Nicolas, *The Russian Religious Renaissance of the Twentieth Century* (London, Darton , Longman & Todd, 1963).

—*Eastern Christendom: A Study of the Origin and Development of the Eastern Orthodox Church*, New York: Putnam, 1961).

Zuckerman, Frederic S., *The Tsarist Secret Police in Russian Society, 1880-1917* (London: Macmillan, 1996).

General Index

BT Big Button 200
corded phone

- Extra large buttons for easy dialling
- Hearing aid compatible
- Handsfree speaker
- Amplified incoming / outgoing speech

RRP £27.99
Shareholder Offer **£19.99**
Quicklinx Order Code: 7SS3M100

Canon
PIXMA
MX395
All-In-One Printer

- Compact and stylish
- Print, scan, copy, fax
- FINE ink technology
- Efficient XL cartridges available

RRP £59.99
Shareholder Offer **£39.99**
Quicklinx Order Code: 8JDWM100

BT1000 Range
cordless phone

- Store 50 contacts
- Make internal calls
- 50 number call list
- 20 number redial list
- Clock and alarm

		RRP	Shareholder Offer
	Quicklinx Order Code: 8H2LM100	RRP £19.99	Shareholder Offer £15.99
	Quicklinx Order Code: 8H2QM100	RRP £34.99	Shareholder Offer £27.99

BT1000 without answer machine

Studies in Christian History and Thought

(All titles uniform with this volume)
Dates in bold are of projected publication

David Bebbington
Holiness in Nineteenth-Century England
David Bebbington stresses the relationship of movements of spirituality to changes in their cultural setting, especially the legacies of the Enlightenment and Romanticism. He shows that these broad shifts in ideological mood had a profound effect on the ways in which piety was conceptualized and practised. Holiness was intimately bound up with the spirit of the age.
2000 / 0-85364-981-2 / viii + 98pp

J. William Black
Reformation Pastors
Richard Baxter and the Ideal of the Reformed Pastor
This work examines Richard Baxter's *Gildas Salvianus, The Reformed Pastor* (1656) and explores each aspect of his pastoral strategy in light of his own concern for 'reformation' and in the broader context of Edwardian, Elizabethan and early Stuart pastoral ideals and practice.
2003 / 1-84227-190-3 / xxii + 308pp

James Bruce
Prophecy, Miracles, Angels, *and* Heavenly Light?
The Eschatology, Pneumatology and Missiology of Adomnán's Life of Columba
This book surveys approaches to the marvellous in hagiography, providing the first critique of Plummer's hypothesis of Irish saga origin. It then analyses the uniquely systematized phenomena in the *Life of Columba* from Adomnán's seventh-century theological perspective, identifying the coming of the eschatological Kingdom as the key to understanding.
2004 / 1-84227-227-6 / xviii + 286pp

Colin J. Bulley
The Priesthood of Some Believers
Developments from the General to the Special Priesthood in the Christian Literature of the First Three Centuries
The first in-depth treatment of early Christian texts on the priesthood of all believers shows that the developing priesthood of the ordained related closely to the division between laity and clergy and had deleterious effects on the practice of the general priesthood.
2000 / 1-84227-034-6 / xii + 336pp

Anthony R. Cross (ed.)
Ecumenism and History
Studies in Honour of John H.Y. Briggs
This collection of essays examines the inter-relationships between the two fields in which Professor Briggs has contributed so much: history—particularly Baptist and Nonconformist—and the ecumenical movement. With contributions from colleagues and former research students from Britain, Europe and North America, *Ecumenism and History* provides wide-ranging studies in important aspects of Christian history, theology and ecumenical studies.
2002 / 1-84227-135-0 / xx + 362pp

Maggi Dawn
Confessions of an Inquiring Spirit
Form as Constitutive of Meaning in S.T. Coleridge's Theological Writing
This study of Coleridge's *Confessions* focuses on its confessional, epistolary and fragmentary form, suggesting that attention to these features significantly affects its interpretation. Bringing a close study of these three literary forms, the author suggests ways in which they nuance the text with particular understandings of the Trinity, and of a kenotic christology. Some parallels are drawn between Romantic and postmodern dilemmas concerning the authority of the biblical text.
2006 / 1-84227-255-1 / approx. 224 pp

Ruth Gouldbourne
The Flesh and the Feminine
Gender and Theology in the Writings of Caspar Schwenckfeld
Caspar Schwenckfeld and his movement exemplify one of the radical communities of the sixteenth century. Challenging theological and liturgical norms, they also found themselves challenging social and particularly gender assumptions. In this book, the issues of the relationship between radical theology and the understanding of gender are considered.
2005 / 1-84227-048-6 / approx. 304pp

Crawford Gribben
Puritan Millennialism
Literature and Theology, 1550–1682
Puritan Millennialism surveys the growth, impact and eventual decline of puritan millennialism throughout England, Scotland and Ireland, arguing that it was much more diverse than has frequently been suggested. This Paternoster edition is revised and extended from the original 2000 text.
2007 / 1-84227-372-8 / approx. 320pp

Galen K. Johnson
Prisoner of Conscience
John Bunyan on Self, Community and Christian Faith
This is an interdisciplinary study of John Bunyan's understanding of conscience across his autobiographical, theological and fictional writings, investigating whether conscience always deserves fidelity, and how Bunyan's view of conscience affects his relationship both to modern Western individualism and historic Christianity.

2003 / 1-84227-223-3 / xvi + 236pp

R.T. Kendall
Calvin and English Calvinism to 1649
The author's thesis is that those who formed the Westminster Confession of Faith, which is regarded as Calvinism, in fact departed from John Calvin on two points: (1) the extent of the atonement and (2) the ground of assurance of salvation.

1997 / 0-85364-827-1 / xii + 264pp

Timothy Larsen
Friends of Religious Equality
Nonconformist Politics in Mid-Victorian England
During the middle decades of the nineteenth century the English Nonconformist community developed a coherent political philosophy of its own, of which a central tenet was the principle of religious equality (in contrast to the stereotype of Evangelical Dissenters). The Dissenting community fought for the civil rights of Roman Catholics, non-Christians and even atheists on an issue of principle which had its flowering in the enthusiastic and undivided support which Nonconformity gave to the campaign for Jewish emancipation. This reissued study examines the political efforts and ideas of English Nonconformists during the period, covering the whole range of national issues raised, from state education to the Crimean War. It offers a case study of a theologically conservative group defending religious pluralism in the civic sphere, showing that the concept of religious equality was a grand vision at the centre of the political philosophy of the Dissenters.

2007 / 1-84227-402-3 / x + 300pp

Byung-Ho Moon
Christ the Mediator of the Law
Calvin's Christological Understanding of the Law as the Rule of Living and Life-Giving
This book explores the coherence between Christology and soteriology in Calvin's theology of the law, examining its intellectual origins and his position on the concept and extent of Christ's mediation of the law. A comparative study between Calvin and contemporary Reformers—Luther, Bucer, Melancthon and Bullinger—and his opponent Michael Servetus is made for the purpose of pointing out the unique feature of Calvin's Christological understanding of the law.
2005 / 1-84227-318-3 / approx. 370pp

John Eifion Morgan-Wynne
Holy Spirit and Religious Experience in Christian Writings, c.AD 90–200
This study examines how far Christians in the third to fifth generations (c.AD 90–200) attributed their sense of encounter with the divine presence, their sense of illumination in the truth or guidance in decision-making, and their sense of ethical empowerment to the activity of the Holy Spirit in their lives.
2005 / 1-84227-319-1 / approx. 350pp

James I. Packer
The Redemption and Restoration of Man in the Thought of Richard Baxter
James I. Packer provides a full and sympathetic exposition of Richard Baxter's doctrine of humanity, created and fallen; its redemption by Christ Jesus; and its restoration in the image of God through the obedience of faith by the power of the Holy Spirit.
2002 / 1-84227-147-4 / 432pp

Andrew Partington,
Church and State
The Contribution of the Church of England Bishops to the House of Lords
during the Thatcher Years

In *Church and State*, Andrew Partington argues that the contribution of the Church of England bishops to the House of Lords during the Thatcher years was overwhelmingly critical of the government; failed to have a significant influence in the public realm; was inefficient, being undertaken by a minority of those eligible to sit on the Bench of Bishops; and was insufficiently moral and spiritual in its content to be distinctive. On the basis of this, and the likely reduction of the number of places available for Church of England bishops in a fully reformed Second Chamber, the author argues for an evolution in the Church of England's approach to the service of its bishops in the House of Lords. He proposes the Church of England works to overcome the genuine obstacles which hinder busy diocesan bishops from contributing to the debates of the House of Lords and to its life more informally.

2005 / 1-84227-334-5 / approx. 324pp

Michael Pasquarello III
God's Ploughman
Hugh Latimer: A 'Preaching Life' (1490–1555)

This construction of a 'preaching life' situates Hugh Latimer within the larger religious, political and intellectual world of late medieval England. Neither biography, intellectual history, nor analysis of discrete sermon texts, this book is a work of homiletic history which draws from the details of Latimer's milieu to construct an interpretive framework for the preaching performances that formed the core of his identity as a religious reformer. Its goal is to illumine the practical wisdom embodied in the content, form and style of Latimer's preaching, and to recapture a sense of its overarching purpose, movement, and transforming force during the reform of sixteenth-century England.

2006 / 1-84227-336-1 / approx. 250pp

Alan P.F. Sell
Enlightenment, Ecumenism, Evangel
Theological Themes and Thinkers 1550–2000

This book consists of papers in which such interlocking topics as the Enlightenment, the problem of authority, the development of doctrine, spirituality, ecumenism, theological method and the heart of the gospel are discussed. Issues of significance to the church at large are explored with special reference to writers from the Reformed and Dissenting traditions.

2005 / 1-84227-330-2 / xviii + 422pp

Alan P.F. Sell
Hinterland Theology
Some Reformed and Dissenting Adjustments

Many books have been written on theology's 'giants' and significant trends, but what of those lesser-known writers who adjusted to them? In this book some hinterland theologians of the British Reformed and Dissenting traditions, who followed in the wake of toleration, the Evangelical Revival, the rise of modern biblical criticism and Karl Barth, are allowed to have their say. They include Thomas Ridgley, Ralph Wardlaw, T.V. Tymms and N.H.G. Robinson.

2006 / 1-84227-331-0 / approx. 350pp

Alan P.F. Sell and Anthony R. Cross (eds)
Protestant Nonconformity in the Twentieth Century

In this collection of essays scholars representative of a number of Nonconformist traditions reflect thematically on Nonconformists' life and witness during the twentieth century. Among the subjects reviewed are biblical studies, theology, worship, evangelism and spirituality, and ecumenism. Over and above its immediate interest, this collection provides a marker to future scholars and others wishing to know how some of their forebears assessed Nonconformity's contribution to a variety of fields during the century leading up to Christianity's third millennium.

2003 / 1-84227-221-7 / x + 398pp

Mark Smith
Religion in Industrial Society
Oldham and Saddleworth 1740–1865

This book analyses the way British churches sought to meet the challenge of industrialization and urbanization during the period 1740–1865. Working from a case-study of Oldham and Saddleworth, Mark Smith challenges the received view that the Anglican Church in the eighteenth century was characterized by complacency and inertia, and reveals Anglicanism's vigorous and creative response to the new conditions. He reassesses the significance of the centrally directed church reforms of the mid-nineteenth century, and emphasizes the importance of local energy and enthusiasm. Charting the growth of denominational pluralism in Oldham and Saddleworth, Dr Smith compares the strengths and weaknesses of the various Anglican and Nonconformist approaches to promoting church growth. He also demonstrates the extent to which all the churches participated in a common culture shaped by the influence of evangelicalism, and shows that active co-operation between the churches rather than denominational conflict dominated. This revised and updated edition of Dr Smith's challenging and original study makes an important contribution both to the social history of religion and to urban studies.

2006 / 1-84227-335-3 / approx. 300pp

Martin Sutherland
Peace, Toleration and Decay
The Ecclesiology of Later Stuart Dissent
This fresh analysis brings to light the complexity and fragility of the later Stuart Nonconformist consensus. Recent findings on wider seventeenth-century thought are incorporated into a new picture of the dynamics of Dissent and the roots of evangelicalism.
2003 / 1-84227-152-0 / xxii + 216pp

G. Michael Thomas
The Extent of the Atonement
A Dilemma for Reformed Theology from Calvin to the Consensus
A study of the way Reformed theology addressed the question, 'Did Christ die for all, or for the elect only?', commencing with John Calvin, and including debates with Lutheranism, the Synod of Dort and the teaching of Moïse Amyraut.
1997 / 0-85364-828-X / x + 278pp

David M. Thompson
Baptism, Church and Society in Britain from the Evangelical Revival to
Baptism, Eucharist and Ministry
The theology and practice of baptism have not received the attention they deserve. How important is faith? What does baptismal regeneration mean? Is baptism a bond of unity between Christians? This book discusses the theology of baptism and popular belief and practice in England and Wales from the Evangelical Revival to the publication of the World Council of Churches' consensus statement on *Baptism, Eucharist and Ministry* (1982).
2005 / 1-84227-393-0 / approx. 224pp

Mark D. Thompson
A Sure Ground on Which to Stand
The Relation of Authority and Interpretive Method of Luther's Approach to Scripture
The best interpreter of Luther is Luther himself. Unfortunately many modern studies have superimposed contemporary agendas upon this sixteenth-century Reformer's writings. This fresh study examines Luther's own words to find an explanation for his robust confidence in the Scriptures, a confidence that generated the famous 'stand' at Worms in 1521.
2004 / 1-84227-145-8 / xvi + 322pp

Carl R. Trueman and R.S. Clark (eds)
Protestant Scholasticism
Essays in Reassessment
Traditionally Protestant theology, between Luther's early reforming career and
the dawn of the Enlightenment, has been seen in terms of decline and fall into
the wastelands of rationalism and scholastic speculation. In this volume a
number of scholars question such an interpretation. The editors argue that the
development of post-Reformation Protestantism can only be understood when a
proper historical model of doctrinal change is adopted. This historical concern
underlies the subsequent studies of theologians such as Calvin, Beza, Olevian,
Baxter, and the two Turrentini. The result is a significantly different reading of
the development of Protestant Orthodoxy, one which both challenges the older
scholarly interpretations and clichés about the relationship of Protestantism to,
among other things, scholasticism and rationalism, and which demonstrates the
fruitfulness of the new, historical approach.
1999 / 0-85364-853-0 / xx + 344pp

Shawn D. Wright
Our Sovereign Refuge
The Pastoral Theology of Theodore Beza
Our Sovereign Refuge is a study of the pastoral theology of the Protestant
reformer who inherited the mantle of leadership in the Reformed church from
John Calvin. Countering a common view of Beza as supremely a 'scholastic'
theologian who deviated from Calvin's biblical focus, Wright uncovers a new
portrait. He was not a cold and rigid academic theologian obsessed with probing
the eternal decrees of God. Rather, by placing him in his pastoral context and by
noting his concerns in his pastoral and biblical treatises, Wright shows that Beza
was fundamentally a committed Christian who was troubled by the vicissitudes
of life in the second half of the sixteenth century. He believed that the biblical
truth of the supreme sovereignty of God alone could support Christians on their
earthly pilgrimage to heaven. This pastoral and personal portrait forms the heart
of Wright's argument.
2004 / 1-84227-252-7 / xviii + 308pp

Paternoster:
thinking faith

Paternoster
9 Holdom Avenue,
Bletchley,
Milton Keynes MK1 1QR,
United Kingdom
Web: www.authenticmedia.co.uk/paternoster